ROUTLEDGE LIBRARY EDITIONS: THE VICTORIAN WORLD

Volume 7

SHOPKEEPERS AND MASTER ARTISANS IN NINETEENTH-CENTURY EUROPE

SHOPKEEPERS AND MASTER ARTISANS IN NINETEENTH-CENTURY EUROPE

Edited by
GEOFFREY CROSSICK AND
HEINZ-GERHARD HAUPT

Routledge
Taylor & Francis Group
LONDON AND NEW YORK

First published in 1984 by Methuen & Co. Ltd

This edition first published in 2016
by Routledge
2 Park Square, Milton Park, Abingdon, Oxon OX14 4RN

and by Routledge
711 Third Avenue, New York, NY 10017

Routledge is an imprint of the Taylor & Francis Group, an informa business

British Library Cataloguing in Publication Data
A catalogue record for this book is available from the British Library

ISBN: 978-1-138-66565-1 (Set)
ISBN: 978-1-315-61965-1 (Set) (ebk)
ISBN: 978-1-138-63924-9 (Volume 7) (hbk)
ISBN: 978-1-138-63928-7 (Volume 7) (pbk)
ISBN: 978-1-315-63730-3 (Volume 7) (ebk)

Shopkeepers and Master Artisans in Nineteenth-Century Europe

edited by
GEOFFREY CROSSICK

and

HEINZ-GERHARD HAUPT

METHUEN
London and New York

First published in 1984 by
Methuen & Co. Ltd
11 New Fetter Lane, London EC4P 4EE

Published in the USA by
Methuen & Co.
in association with Methuen, Inc.
733 Third Avenue, New York, NY 10017

Typeset by Scarborough Typesetting Services
and printed in Great Britain at
The University Printing House, Cambridge

British Library Cataloguing in Publication Data

Shopkeepers and master artisans in nineteenth-century Europe.
1. Middle classes—Europe—History—19th century
I. Crossick, Geoffrey. II. Haupt, Heinz-Gerhard
305.5'56 HT690.E855

ISBN 0–416–35660–5

Contents

List of tables		vii
Acknowledgements		ix

INTRODUCTION

1 Shopkeepers, master artisans and the historian: the petite bourgeoisie in comparative focus — 3
Geoffrey Crossick and Heinz-Gerhard Haupt

NATIONAL PERSPECTIVES

2 Between resignation and volatility: the German petite bourgeoisie in the nineteenth century — 35
David Blackbourn

3 The petite bourgeoisie in nineteenth-century Britain: the urban and liberal case — 62
Geoffrey Crossick

4 The petite bourgeoisie in France, 1850–1914: in search of the *juste milieu*? — 95
Heinz-Gerhard Haupt

5 A forgotten class: the petite bourgeoisie in Belgium, 1850–1914 — 120
Ginette Kurgan-van Hentenryk

THE RESEARCH FOCUS

6 Masters and manufacturers: social values and the smaller unit of production in Birmingham, 1800–50 — 137
Clive Behagg

7 The grocery trade in nineteenth-century Paris: a fragmented corporation 155
Alain Faure

8 The small shopkeepers' movement and politics in France, 1888–1914 175
Philip Nord

9 The artisan family in nineteenth-century Austria: *embourgeoisement* of the petite bourgeoisie? 195
Josef Ehmer

10 Rural artisans in the Beauce during the nineteenth century 219
Jean-Claude Farcy

11 Shopkeepers and the state in Britain, 1870–1914 239
Geoffrey Crossick

Index 270

List of tables

1	Estimated personal estates at time of death, Birmingham, 1820–40	140
2	Estimated personal estates in the Birmingham gun trade, 1820–40	147
3	Grocery shops in Paris	161
4	Paris grocery shops: analysis by *arrondissements*	162
5	Price of grocery businesses, 1880–95	165
6	Origins of bankrupt grocers, 1880–95	166
7	Sources of capital for Paris grocery businesses	168
8	Juvenile and adult sons in the households of master artisans	198
9	Transfer of trades amongst Austrian artisans	200
10	Sons in the households of master artisans, Vienna, 1857	207
11	Examples of household structure in nineteenth-century Vienna	213
12	Number of inhabitants subject to professional tax: cantons of Auneau, Janville and Voves	222
13	Distribution by sectors of activity and evolution of numbers subject to professional tax: cantons of Auneau, Chartres-Sud, Janville and Voves	223
14	Evolution of artisanal activity for the communes of Denonville, Louville-la-Chénard, Ouarville and Santeuil	225
15	Payers of the professional tax: cantons of Auneau, Chartres-Sud, Janville and Voves	227

16 Average rental values in francs, 1846–79: cantons of Auneau, Chartres-Sud, Janville and Voves 229
17 Average fortunes upon marriage between 1811 and 1820: Auneau, Janville and Voves 230

Acknowledgements

The subject of this book is one that has received all too little attention from historians of nineteenth-century Europe until recent years, and even now direct research and publications are not extensive. We have both drawn great strength and stimulus from our involvement with others working in this field over the last few years, and this has encouraged our belief in the rewards – personal as well as intellectual – of collective and co-operative research projects. We have a real debt of gratitude to acknowledge to the members of the round tables on the petite bourgeoisie in nineteenth-century Europe who have met together from time to time over the last five years to discuss this subject, not least to our fellow organizers of these gatherings, Ginette Kurgan-van Hentenryk of the Free University of Brussels and Philippe Vigier of the University of Paris X, Nanterre. We have learned a great deal from these round tables, and made good friends there.

The Volkswagen Foundation and the University of Bremen have generously given financial support for the round tables. Alain Faure's essay is a translation of one originally published in *le mouvement social* (number 108, 1979), while Philip Nord's essay and the first by Geoffrey Crossick are substantially revised versions of articles in the same journal (number 114, 1981 and number 108, 1979 respectively). We are very grateful to the editorial committee of *le mouvement social* for readily agreeing to the appearance of English versions of these pieces. Jean-Claude Farcy's essay will also appear in a French version in a collection of essays soon to be published in France under the editorial direction of Alain Faure and Philippe Vigier. The Centre d'Histoire de la France Contemporaine at the University of Paris X, Nanterre, has made a contribution to the cost of the translations for this book.

GEOFFREY CROSSICK
HEINZ-GERHARD HAUPT
Colchester and Bremen, June 1983

Introduction

1 Shopkeepers, master artisans and the historian: the petite bourgeoisie in comparative focus

GEOFFREY CROSSICK AND HEINZ-GERHARD HAUPT

THE SUBJECT[1]

The 'petit-bourgeois International', it must be admitted, never achieved very much. In the fifteen years that preceded the outbreak of war in 1914, however, representatives of shopkeepers, master artisans, peasant farmers and their organizations gathered in international congresses to debate and, if at all possible, to assure their future. Congresses of various kinds at Anvers, Namur, Munich and elsewhere[2] testified to a growing consciousness amongst small shopkeepers and small producers in much of Europe, but these congresses were even more emphatically proof of the discovery of this class as a potential political force by others – conservatives, social Catholics, and le Playists amongst them. The petite bourgeoisie[3] was in fashion, but the conjuncture of circumstances changed, politics changed, the petite bourgeoisie itself changed, and a collection of essays on this subject can now be presented as innovatory in a way that would have surprised those convinced of its importance eighty years ago. The angry agitations of the *petit patronat* in France at the very time that this introduction is being written, however, remind us that an understanding of that social group is of more than historical relevance.

The essays in this book testify to a renewed interest in the shopkeepers and master artisans of nineteenth-century Europe. This has partly derived from economic history's reluctant disenchantment with growth, which has stimulated a revisionist approach to the whole process of European industrialization, a concern to deflect attention from the dazzling but untypical manifestations of scale, factories and sophisticated technology and look instead at the industrialization process as one within which the less obvious transformations of small-scale production, urban services and commercial operations should be given greater prominence. The major consequence of this has been a new respect for French industrialization, but the ramifications have been far more widespread,[4] and in Britain at least have received their main stimulus from social historians who came to understand the impact of merchant capital on older and by no means displaced systems of production as central rather than peripheral to working-class formation.[5] The result has been to expose for attention the fate of these owners of small enterprises whose economic persistence was so striking and whose place in the world of popular politics and culture was so intriguing.

The attraction to the petite bourgeoisie felt by social theorists at the turn of the century is testimony to the ideological importance of this group within capitalist society.[6] The very language with which it was described emphasized its role in the middle, as mediator, as the embodiment of those qualities that were less commonly found as the social polarities were explored. Thus could the petite bourgeoisie appear not so much as the conciliator of class conflict but as its living denial. Its implied role in the process of social mobility was but one element in that conception of the petite bourgeoisie that was almost always expressed in metaphor – social bridge, *classe tampon*, and so on – as if the social reality was less capable of sustaining the ideological weight placed upon it. Yet the objective significance survives in a way that this book hopes to demonstrate.

In the most limited sense, it must be stressed that in any nineteenth-century society resting on private property, most owners of such property were small and thus arguably described as petit-bourgeois. As such, the defence of private property required attention to their interests – there is a real basis to their ideological importance in capitalist society. The implications for social relations are many. The most important is the most obvious: shopkeepers were that section of the propertied classes with whom working-class men and women came into the most regular and daily contact. They employed them, they sold bread and meat and clothing to them, they often rented housing accommodation to them. More than that, the commonplace necessities of family ties (not just marriage, but the occupations of brothers and sisters, of sons and daughters), personal mobility, and the flow of individuals between wage employment and independent enterprise, meant that the relationship between working class and petite bourgeoisie was a real and lived aspect of both daily and lifetime experience for much of the urban population of nineteenth-century Europe. Less attention has been given to the social relations between such small property owners and the larger bourgeoisie, even though these were fundamental to the question of social stability. The detachment of small shopkeepers and small producers from the world of popular radicalism by the middle decades of the nineteenth century, for example, may be central to the stabilization of British society in those years. This drawing of urban petits bourgeois into a larger bourgeois universe involved active construction that makes the study of voluntary associations so important.

Shopkeepers and master artisans have been most visible in politics. They have perhaps been too visible, for it has led to an excessively political focus that this book hopes to broaden. Their political importance is no illusion, not just in the later decades of the nineteenth century when they received most attention, but earlier too. They are there firstly in *events*, above all in the German and French revolutions of 1848. The place of these petits bourgeois in the events of that year emerges only as an incidental theme in the literature, which is sad because not only the movements, but also their social and ideological fragmentations, revolve in part around the social complexities of the popular tradition within which the petite bourgeoisie was embedded.[7] It was a position expressed repeatedly in the great *événements* of French history – from the *sans culottes* of the first revolution to the communes in Paris and Lyons. We find them secondly in *organizations*, for they formed a creative element in the popular radical movements of early nineteenth-century Britain, the equivalent popular republican organizations of France, and to a lesser degree the resistance to absolutism in Vormärz Germany. One might see the summer and autumn of 1848 as the moment when the petits bourgeois of Europe abandoned their popular democratic faith and their part in the forces of progress, and turned instead to the defence of property and fear of a dangerous working class. The evidence is there, but the real shift to the right was a longer process that required the problems and the conjunctures of the later nineteenth century to provide organizational expression. As the national studies in this book make clear, there was an upsurge of professional and trade organizations and pressure groups amongst shopkeepers and, to a lesser degree, master artisans. With it went a new political orientation whose exploration forms the partial concern of several of these essays. The organizational expression of interests and of politics was weakest in Britain, but striking elsewhere, whether we look at the mass of Belgian petit-bourgeois organizations, the Ligue Syndicale and the broader shopkeepers' movement in France, or the organizations of the *Mittelstand* in Germany.[8] To see these organizations simply as part of the pre-history of European fascism is to misunderstand the character of this shift to the right, but it also ignores a real petit-bourgeois involvement with the labour movement and socialism at the end of the century in France, Germany, Denmark and elsewhere.[9] As important as personal involvement is the fact that early socialist ideas throughout Europe were strongly influenced by those continuities from an older republican and popular radicalism that had been shaped and maintained by petit-bourgeois involvement.

The third area of political significance is as a *political factor* in the struggle between parties and in the construction of political ideologies. From the closing decades of the century, many politicians struggled to redefine the character of class society and to reshape the political system that it produced in such a way as to put at its centre a policy to incorporate the *Mittelstand* or *classes moyennes*. This development required parties that saw the petite bourgeoisie as an important part of their constituencies in a rapidly changing political situation (the Centre Party in Germany, the Catholic Party in Belgium, the Radical Party in France). Parties need supporters. More than that, parties that in one way or another represented the existing order came to discover in the petite bourgeoisie a basis for social stability. With the politics came those ideologies of class denial – social Catholicism and its conception of moral fusion in Belgium, which in France mixed uneasily with the increasingly conservative syntheses of a populist republicanism, and the idealization of the *Mittelstand* in Germany.[10]

Shopkeepers and master artisans may have failed in their attempts between the 1880s and the First World War to create a world more congenial to them, but their long-term historical significance remains in need of exploration. This book is constructed to further our understanding of such themes. The intention is to provide both discursive assessments of the petit-bourgeois experience in the four main European industrial societies of the period – the national perspectives essays – and analytical insights into specific areas of that petit-bourgeois experience. These essays reflect the state of research in a still young subject, but we have tried to balance the book away from what seems to us the most regrettable aspect of that state of research: that the main work is political, and all too often the economic and social situation of shopkeepers and master artisans has been simply deduced from their political behaviour. Political ideology and phenomena are of course examined – centrally in Nord's essay, as well as in the national studies – but we have tried to mark out new areas and new questions. In other ways the balance of the book reflects the state of research: for example, the petite bourgeoisie appears all too often here as a large city phenomenon, though it may well be true that they were most at home and most significant in small towns on which little work has been done.[11] Farcy's study of a rural milieu constitutes an important corrective. Overall, though, the research essays are intended to open up new analytical themes, rather than simply to add detail to the national essays.

How far do the master artisans and shopkeepers who are the subject of this book constitute a single social group, perhaps a class? The question is not an easy one, not least because of the way in which studies little concerned with the finer details of social reality happily throw together the owners of small retail and craft enterprises, as part of a general petite bourgeoisie. Such an allocation has its problems, though. If by social class we imply a social group which can be distinguished from others by its specific productive relations, close social contacts, distinctive social characteristics, and a sense of class identity,[12] then the economic heterogeneity, social instability, and lack of political unity of craftsmen and small shopkeepers all caution against the automatic use of the term in studies referring to these groups.

One might almost see the two groups involved in different modes of production. For if craft production is the dominant characteristic of the simple form of the production of goods, distribution, on the other hand, is on the small scale a reflection of a type of economy which did not appear until the capitalist relations of production were developed and self-sufficiency came to an end. Marxist theory distinguishes even more precisely between the two. Whereas master craftsmen are involved in producing surplus value, in so far as they employ labour, small shopkeepers can only convert surplus value which has been created elsewhere.[13] Alongside this fundamental point of distinction lies the not completely unconnected issue of the different extent to which the two elements were drawn into the capitalist process, for, as research in this book and elsewhere makes clear, the artisanat was caught up far earlier and more intensively within the capitalist system, whereas the small shopkeepers resisted for longer and with greater success.

We must add to difficulties such as these the profound social heterogeneity within the world of small enterprise. As many of the articles here show, there was an irreconcilable gap between men and women out of work, who sought to survive by opening a small shop or a workshop, and the well-established traders and master craftsmen of a town. Lack of training, lack of capital, and the rapidity with which most closed down, all mean that the former group were faced with a constant struggle to survive and to maintain what independence they had. The experience, income and ability to plan ahead that characterized the more substantial small businessmen, on the other hand, allowed them to seek a bourgeois life-style and opportunities for social advancement for their children. Between the two lay the myriad of positions that could pull small enterprises and their owners in either direction, according to their trade, their situation, their location, even the period in which they operated.

The high rate of social mobility – or at least instability – which research indicates for this group must also have served to hinder the development of anything comparable with common class relationships. It is clear that, in comparison with other classes, a greater proportion of the petite bourgeoisie was born in another class; a greater proportion spent only a period of their lives as master craftsmen or shopkeepers; and a greater proportion sent their children, willingly or not, into other trades and, more importantly, other classes.[14] This could not have encouraged the development of a sense of common experience, which we can see to have been equally limited by the distinctive position of the petite bourgeoisie within the overall structure of class relations. Structural definitions of the petite bourgeoisie are not symmetrical with those of the working class or the bourgeoisie, for whereas these last two take definition from their relation to each other, craftsmen and small shopkeepers, by reason of their relations to the means of production and the multi-directional character of their social relations, are orientated towards both bourgeois and proletarian positions and values. See, to take one precise example, the dual orientation that flowed from sources of finance and relationship with customers. While merchant and wholesaler credit drew them into contact with the bourgeoisie and its business imperatives,[15] and many of the essays in this book indicate that, workshops and small shops were also plunged into a daily contact with working-class customers. As a result of all these internal ambiguities, there was little expression of a consciousness of class identity of the kind which arises from common economic interests, socially reinforced, and defined in opposition to those of other classes. Here, in the petite bourgeoisie, we seem to find a social group that hints at a class character only at times of crisis, when its very existence seems under threat. The contrast with working class and bourgeoisie, which continue to exist for historical analysis even when not active in a class-conscious way, is fundamental. For reasons explored here and in the rest of this book, its existence as a class 'in itself' is very problematic. Massive barriers inevitably stood in the way, then, of its development as a class 'for itself'.

Nevertheless, the essays in this book and a wider historical literature suggest that there existed, within the nineteenth-century petite bourgeoisie of western European societies, a social phenomenon that was real, and, if not a class, something which seems at times to have behaved and acted as a class; and to be helpfully analysed in terms of class relations. Jürgen Kocka has developed a comparable argument in connection with the early nineteenth-century German working class and, in a way which has some relationship to E. P. Thompson's justification for the application of class analysis to eighteenth-century English society, we would suggest that the concept of class relationships has more to offer in the analysis of the petite bourgeoisie than does that of class identity.[16]

In many ways, the answer to the reservations outlined above lies in a reading of the essays in this book, but we would offer a number of points which weaken the power of these objections to the notion of a petite bourgeoisie. First of all, the question of heterogeneity. David Blackbourn, both in this book and elsewhere, has quite correctly presented the German *Mittelstand* as a congerie of often conflicting groups which could not simply be made one by the idealizing words of political social commentators.[17] This need to counter the mystifications of the *Mittelstand* ideal, however, may have led historians to over-emphasize the differences that separated master artisans from small shopkeepers. The boundary between the two groups was both indistinct and often crossed. It was not only the craftsmen-retailers (such as bakers and butchers) who occupied an intermediate position, but also those craftsmen who opened a retail enterprise in addition to their workshop, or went over entirely to trading. The last often included many displaced artisans seeking to maintain some economic independence. There were thus overlaps of functions and movements between the two, but even more important is the way in which historians have exaggerated the different relationships to industrialization of the craft and retail sectors of small enterprise. It is simply not true that capitalist industrialization threatened the existence of craftsmen while it encouraged that of small retailers.[18] The effect was far more selective, for while the consequence for some types of craft work and small shops was an improvement in business, prosperity and chances of survival, for others it was a far more precarious future.

Structural differences between master artisans and small shopkeepers thus need to be qualified, but the argument over social instability as an obstacle to petit-bourgeois identity remains an important one. No social group, of course, is ever homogeneous, least of all classes,[19] but this does not in itself resolve the problem of whether a group marked by a considerably fluctuating membership can be seen as a coherent social entity. This is a major area where more research is needed, and not research that merely measures movement rather than interpreting its consequences. The question of mobility – whether geographical or social – has been too little considered in the historical analysis of class relations and class formation, and the case of the petite bourgeoisie presents it particularly forcibly. Common characteristics surface above the social fluctuations, suggesting that much of the instability, both within and between generations, involved movement inside the world of small enterprise, of *l'atelier et la boutique*, and even more so inside the larger lower middle-class world that embraced white-collar employees. There is, for example, clear evidence of vigorous inter-generational movement between craft enterprise and shopkeeping in Bremen in the quarter century before the First World War;[20] much career instability among artisans took them into retailing, especially, but by no means exclusively, in old age; and, as some of the essays below indicate, it became increasingly common for shopkeepers and master artisans to seek white-collar careers for their children in order to keep them within an occupational group of comparable status. Indeed, anxiety about education, for which facilities and access were often inadequate, provided a common concern of the petite bourgeoisie in many countries.[21]

It is in turning to structural characteristics that the distinctiveness of the petite bourgeoisie, ambiguous in terms of productive and class relationships, becomes clearer. We find the unique feature of the petite bourgeoisie in the fact that its livelihood is derived from both its capital and its own labour. In the view of Bechhofer and Elliott it is the former that sets it apart from the proletariat, the latter from the bourgeoisie.[22] Its roots lie in a petty property that it works itself, with the consequence that any labour it hires is on a very limited scale. One cannot fix this quantitatively, but a unifying and typical feature of the petit-bourgeois business is its low level of capital and the limited – in some trades infrequent – use of labour from outside the family. From the consequences of this specific, and in definitional terms fundamental, mix of labour and capital flows a further source of identity between master artisans and retail traders. Theirs was a particular form of enterprise, and a particular form of running the enterprise, which placed the family at the centre of economic activity, even in cases where some wage labour was employed.

This particular form of enterprise – and not just its family aspect – structured petit-bourgeois consciousness in relation to the wider society within which they lived, and developed social and ideological forces of integration within the petite bourgeoisie that surface at times, with different results, in all the societies under focus here. For petits bourgeois everywhere – shopkeepers and craftsmen alike – independence together with a tenacious concern for small property were the most powerful values, and they were often defended more against the ravages of the rich and powerful than against the threat from the propertyless. In most cases the petit-bourgeois way of life was an introspective and family-centred one that concentrated on the limited and immediate world around them. From this came their characteristic suspicion of the outside world, of the assumed hostility of the unknown, that turned them against the state as much as against the forces of banking and high finance. In a particular way, to which we shall return in this essay, it kept them radical, but it also flowed into irrational reactions that drew some of them late in the century to anti-semitism.

These points of contact with regard to structure, relationships, and social values serve to focus our attention on some of the special features of the petite bourgeoisie. And they do at times – above all in crises such as that of the 1890s – seem to act as a class. It is certainly true that only the organized were active, and that they formed a small section of the petite bourgeoisie. But is that not true of all social classes? What is most striking for us is the increasingly joint action of craftsmen and shopkeepers on the continent. The more we learn of this action – and it is frequently discussed in this book – the more we see the need to revise the traditional Marxist view of the petite bourgeoisie as an irresolute social formation, swinging backwards and forwards under outside manipulation and in the service of whatever political forces required it.[23] Its political position may have been awkward, even ambivalent, but in its pattern of development and political trajectory we see, in spite of the real qualifications outlined above, more evidence of petit-bourgeois identity.

THEMATIC PROBLEMS

In this central section of the introduction, it is not our intention to discuss all of the problems which are important for an analysis of the petite bourgeoisie and its place in nineteenth-century European societies. The most significant themes will, in any case, emerge in the essays that follow. In these pages we shall isolate several themes which offer a particularly fruitful way into understanding the complexities of the petite bourgeoisie, and the potential for new ideas.

The *economic* history of the petite bourgeoisie and of small enterprise is the area about which we know least, and yet it is in many ways the most important. The numerical expansion of small enterprise that accompanied both industrialization and urbanization is well-established, but economic history's fixation on the larger aspects of capitalist development means that we know little about the inner workings of this expansion. Growth in numbers does not establish the importance of the petite bourgeoisie, it merely poses more questions about it, above all when we remember the remarkably high turnover rate amongst small enterprises, the growing specialization and interdependence within the urban economy, and so on. Nor do we know much at all about the profits made by craftsmen and small shopkeepers, the amount of capital they invested, the income they earned.[24] Indeed, how clear was the conception of profit anyway, and did it develop differently in differing sectors, leaving many small owners to conceive of their return more as income, almost as wages for effort, than as profits as such?[25] There is much to be explored in terms of economic variables, but a valuable way into what characterized the economic development of the petite bourgeoisie, and the differentiation within it, is through the two themes of dependency and crisis.

Independence has been seen both by contemporary and later observers as the hallmark of small shopkeepers and master artisans. Their self-identity and so many of their social values revolved around that notion, yet closer economic analysis reveals the mechanisms that set limits to the independence of the owners of small enterprises, and it is in the ambiguities of independence and dependence that the economic realities of petit-bourgeois business life can be valuably explored. All the national studies below have much to say on this, as does Behagg's essay on the small masters of Birmingham. Independence was undermined most of all by the forces of credit and contract. During the second half of the century – earlier in Britain, and in specific metropolitan trades like tailoring everywhere – independent producers became increasingly dependent on the merchant capitalists from whom they bought raw materials or to whom they sold their product, who might be the same person and who would all too often advance credit, even cash, for wage payments. In some areas of manufacturing the small craft business could resist, but in others it was reduced to little more than an outwork enterprise. Some trades (e.g. weaving, nail-making) suffered everywhere, but the size of town and the integration into a transportation and merchanting system that collapsed the effects of distance, seems particularly important within each trade. The rural artisanat might be relatively untouched by these problems, at least in those rural areas far from large manufacturing and urban centres, which explains the more rapid decline in Britain than France.[26] On the whole, though, it was hard to resist the competition that expressed itself through merchant controls and undermined independence. Small producers became increasingly dependent on supplying one or two merchants. From the 1850s onwards, more and more of Cologne's notionally independent masters were producing on contract for a single merchant (notably amongst tailors and eau-de-Cologne bottle case-makers), and in the eyes of Jeanne Gaillard the cabinet-makers of Paris came to look increasingly like *façonniers*.[27] Behagg's essay in this book shows a parallel process in the 'classic' small-producer town of Birmingham. Then, as large manufacturers grew, the small became suppliers to them, especially in boom periods.[28]

In by no means uniform ways, then, small producers became dependent first on commercial and then industrial capital, tied by the superior competitive, financial and distributive resources of the larger firms. Small shopkeepers, on the other hand, saw their freedom of action limited essentially by merchants and wholesalers alone, who advanced credit and loans, often on condition that the retailer bought goods only from them. This was especially true in the setting up of enterprises – as the essay on Britain shows – but it was more pervasive in the supply of continuing stock. Credit and dependency – those were the methods many a shopkeeper used to trap his proletarian clientele. They are illuminating forces through which to analyse petit-bourgeois economic experience. The essential conclusion is that their enmeshing in the structures of larger capitalist business through financial dependence produced drastic consequences for both sections of small enterprise.

If 'independence' means that members of the petite bourgeoisie were not constrained by unequal relationships with larger capitalists for either the purchase or sale of their goods, and in which no creditor held a monopoly position, then very few craftsmen and small shopkeepers were genuinely independent as the nineteenth century progressed – less than 5 per cent of master craftsmen in Paris during the second half of the century, according to Alain Cottereau's calculations.[29]

The result was great vulnerability in times of economic depression or crisis. Large manufacturers chose to transfer a portion of their orders to workshops in boom, precisely because they could pull back into their own factories in depression. So these small producers were the first to be affected by cuts in production. The high debts owed by (as well as to) shopkeepers is a primary reason for the fact that their finances lacked the flexibility to cope with business decline or even one miscalculated transaction. Fluctuations were high, as a result. Indeed, what do the notions of independence or dependence mean at a time of high mortality of enterprise? We clearly need to distinguish between layers of small enterprise, but 80 per cent of all businesses run by women failed in Bremen in the last decade of the century.[30] Many an enterprise could seek to escape the consequences of dependence – though in reality they might only intensify them – by turning increasingly in on family labour. This was true of a substantial section of the petite bourgeoisie, especially when shifting conditions in an industry led to increasing price competition and the need to control costs. The self-exploitation of the family is well-known in shopkeeping, but we shall see later in this introduction the way that it became an important strategy for survival in threatened artisanal trades.

As this suggests, for craftsmen the struggle to maintain their economic independence was under way in the first half of the century, but the essays here indicate a later date for small shopkeepers. The tailors' struggle against ready-made clothing and *confection* was well established by the 1830s,[31] while resistance by French bricklayers and joiners to *marchandage* (subcontracting) was victorious with its abolition by a law of the 1848 revolution. This remained a Pyrrhic victory, for it could not halt the advance of capitalist organization in the trade. Yet, in spite of the threats, it seems likely that before 1848 many craftsmen, at least in France and Germany, would maintain their independence. Once again, though, we ask what is this independence? When more secure, it was the centre of a radical social politics, an optimistic and even utopian insistence on independence. For the social vision of *sans-culottes*, or of Painite radicals, or of the French followers of Proudhon, was based on a general structure of small proprietorship and the guaranteed independence of producers.[32] Independence was a positive and assertive part of a radical vision. By the Great Depression it had changed – as had the reality of independence itself – and was now stridently shouted as part of an increasingly defensive and conservative vision that varied with national, regional and occupational conditions. Independence became a homogenizing value to which all sections of the petite bourgeoisie could subscribe in the face of the real or imagined advances of capitalism.

Independence and our second economic theme, crisis, tie closely together. During the *longue durée* of capitalist transformation, periodic crises accelerated the process of change or at least permanently affected the position of small producers and shopkeepers. The effects on the petite bourgeoisie of the crises of 1846 to 1849 and the 1880s and 1890s were particularly serious, and the differences between them revealing. Whereas the Great Depression was the result of simultaneous financial and structural crises, the middle years of the century might be seen on the continent as 'an Ancien Régime crisis'.[33] The general characteristics of the economic crises at the end of the century are sufficiently well known, and it remains the crisis of the longest-term economic significance for petit-bourgeois enterprise throughout Europe. Falling agricultural and industrial prices, credit restrictions, and increasing unemployment led to the bankruptcy of numerous small firms – but also to the modernization of a lesser number of others.[34] Firms able to produce more cheaply had a vital competitive advantage in this situation. While large firms sought to achieve this by intensifying the productivity of labour, such an option was seldom open to small workshops, let alone shops, and all that most of these could do was to resort to increasing self-exploitation. The differing reactions to the crisis can be seen in the at-first-glance paradoxical figures for Baden and Württemberg in the 1880s, where there was an increase in both the average number of people employed by each enterprise and in the number of independent proprietors with no hired labour.[35]

Concentration of the means of production, mechanization and rationalization of production, combined in the crisis to worsen the situation of most craftsmen. At the same time, however, small-scale production (as did trading) remained a refuge for unemployed workers, who sought a means of subsistence within this precarious 'independence'. Indeed, existing producers then found the competition from large enterprise augmented by growing numbers of marginal producers at the very time of crisis when they were least equipped to cope. We can detect in these diverse relationships – concentration alongside the proliferation of marginal independents – a classic impact of crisis on small enterprise. For the immediate effect of economic depression has often been to increase the numbers of small businesses, with the flight of unemployed workers into independent activity. The expansion of small-scale production and trading in Cologne between 1846 and 1849 rested on this tendency of unemployed journeymen to set up on their own, quite unlike the new, better-placed operations founded with ambition in the more prosperous years between 1835 and 1843.[36] Statistics can thus be misleading, for the effect of depression was generally (though not always) less good for the more viable small enterprises, those whose ambitions ran further than the mere provision of a short-term income. Much of this applied equally to retailing, which was jointly affected by economic and structural factors in the late nineteenth-century crisis. The realistic small retail enterprises (again, in contrast to the petty operations set up in despair) were now faced with an increase in large-scale competition, from department stores, chain stores, mail-order operations and consumer co-operation, especially from the 1890s, while wage reductions and unemployment often produced declining sales. Between 1880 and 1881 the number of bankruptcies in the Lyons food trades increased by 63 per cent.[37] Indeed, the effects of this crisis seem to have been more severe on the retail trades of Lyons than on its industry.

The Great Depression seems in so many ways to have been a decisive crisis for the petite bourgeoisie, confirming the notion that deflationary crises have the most severe impact on existing petit-bourgeois enterprises, and thus perhaps prompt the greatest agitational response. In contrast, the pre-revolutionary crisis of the 1840s on the continent was marked by rising food prices which led to a fall in purchasing power for manufactured goods, most notably textiles, and hence increasing unemployment and intensified poverty.[38] Sales by retailers and orders for master artisans both suffered. In Cologne the latter were forced on to poor relief, while in Paris they joined workingmen's associations, if only temporarily.[39] We know too little about the impact of this crisis to be sure – it has been too readily disposed of in generalized terms as the background to the events of 1848 – but the contrast with the later crisis seems illuminating, confirming the importance of the coincidence of two kinds of crisis, conjunctural and structural. The combination of the conjunctural crisis of the 1880s and a developing structural crisis in the industrial and retail economy was damaging, and, for French researchers at least, a critical turning point had occurred for the position of small enterprise.[40]

Beyond such general discussion of the impact of specific crises, a study of the petite bourgeoisie in economic crisis can take us into the precise inner workings of the world of small enterprise, yielding, for example, information about the chronology of change among craftsmen and small shopkeepers. We know too little about the order in which individual sectors were affected by a crisis, whether producer goods fell victim before the consumer goods sector, and whether in a 'modern' crisis falling agricultural prices and the need to maintain the working population led to the partial protection of businesses concerned with the production and distribution of food.[41] How far did size of enterprise affect ability to cope with difficulties? As some of the national studies below indicate, did small enterprises enjoy a flexibility of response in comparison with large? We are clearly talking here about different industries, and about different types and scale of small enterprise within each. What of geographical differences of the impact of crisis – did place within the urban hierarchy have differentiating effects? A precise study of the chronology of a crisis as it affected craft and retail trades would thus help uncover their internal structure; the degree of resistance offered by various sizes of business, types of activity and geographical location; and the social cost in terms of intensification of labour involved in mastering the crisis. In a variety of ways, then, economic crisis may prove a powerful light by which to illuminate both the structural position and the internal mechanisms of small-scale enterprise.

We know more about the *politics* of the petite bourgeoisie, it would seem, than anything else, and two themes in particular need probing. According to the first of these, the experience of 1848 proved a turning point in petit-bourgeois politics, as a result of which the petite bourgeoisie abandoned its radical past, and had shifted inexorably to the right by some point in the decades before the First World War.[42] The other theme is itself a revisionist one, explaining this political development less in terms of manipulation by political and social élites and more in the internal and partially autonomous evolution of the petite bourgeoisie itself, and this is an important theme in many of the essays in this book.

As the survey essay on Britain shows, the most significant period of petit-bourgeois political and social action in that country was the first half of the century, and it was precisely then that its presence was least exclusive (compared with continental movements later in the century) and most clearly rooted in a broader popular base. That can be said for most countries before 1848, where petit-bourgeois politics is often hard to separate from that of a wider populace that drew in journeymen and other wage-earners. Here was that *menu peuple* which shaped so much radical politics for the half century or more after 1789, above all in Britain and France. This co-operation often broke down and polarization ensued as the more proletarian, or at least plebeian, section of the populace radicalized in 1848. It is tempting to interpret this as the start of a process by which the petite bourgeoisie increasingly detached itself from democratic politics, but the break should not be exaggerated. There were still bridges that linked masters to journeymen, and, although they swiftly and in rather different ways became unstable in Germany and Britain (where they had been weakened before 1848), they were maintained in France by the radical movement and then party until the end of the century, as the survey essay on France makes clear. Indeed, in the grim years for the popular movement, between the June Days and Louis Napoleon's *coup*, the petit-bourgeois presence within – and frequently leadership of – the struggle for the social and democratic republic is striking.[43] From then on, the *petit patronat* defended a political vision that did not just place them on the French left through the nineteenth century, but was a central element in defining what the left actually was for much of that period.

Relics of this radical past – and not only in France – did not even disappear in the 1880s and 1890s when the petite bourgeoisie adopted new forms of economic and occupational organizations in response to economic crisis and political change. The shift to the right that accompanied this response was an ambivalent and distinctively petit-bourgeois one that retained vestiges, at least, of its old radicalism. As will be suggested later in this introduction, and it is confirmed by the essays on Germany and France, the corporatism, the anti-élitist and anti-state slogans, the rejection of the rich, the *gros*, and the retreat into local rights and self-administration, all survived to colour the now more fundamentally defensive and conservative politics. The *radicaux* in France continued to defend private property against the socialists, but their criticism of financial monopolies was maintained. Indeed, this over-simplifies the contrast, for that radical tradition of the republican people confronting the rich and powerful was one which fundamentally influenced French socialism, and linked it ideologically and iconographically to the petite bourgeoisie's own traditions.[44] Was this true only of France, or simply strongest there? Future research needs to give much more attention to the intervening years between 1848 and the 1890s, for explanation of the changing political attitudes, or at least allegiances, of the petite bourgeoisie in France, Belgium, Germany and even Britain requires that the missing links of those years be traced. We must, in any case, ask whether the tendency to drift to 'the right' is a subtle enough categorization. 'The right' meant very different things in different countries – orthodox liberalism in Britain, *Poincarism* and nationalism in France, social Catholicism in Belgium or the *Kartell der schaffenden Hände* in Germany.

A revisionist literature, above all on Germany, has refused to see this new level of petit-bourgeois right-wing mobilization on the continent as the result of manipulation from above,[45] and Blackbourn has much to say on this. The degree of ideological and organizational self-momentum of this awakening has rightly been stressed. While accepting this argument, we want to stress something different here, and that is the way that the petite bourgeoisie, easing itself from its radical past, became an object of official and bourgeois concern in all these countries from the mid-nineteenth century onwards. Indeed, the concern for detaching the petite bourgeoisie from its popular politics did not need the stimulus of 1848. Two years earlier, in the French woollen town of Lodève, an application for a *Société des arts* for shopkeepers and artisans was well received by the prefect, who hoped that it might help develop a social distance between them and the town's workers.[46] As the century progressed, both the state and the bourgeoisie sought partially to satisfy the demands of master artisans and small shopkeepers, while also integrating them in official or bourgeois structures, attaching them to the defence of the social order, or to support for its adaptation. The motives varied, but the countries that introduced a *weighted* universal male suffrage (Germany in 1848, Belgium in 1893) found the petite bourgeoisie to be the literally crucial element. The liberal bourgeoisie in Germany saw the integration of these groups as essential to their struggle against the old regime, at least until after unification, while in Second Empire France attempts were made to recruit them to the side of the industrial bourgeoisie in the struggle against the older Napoleonic élite. The process in Britain involved a more general social concern to attach them to the liberal social order.

These attempts to reshape and influence the petite bourgeoisie had a variety of tools available. Beyond the economic pressures that we shall read about in some of the essays,[47] there stood the institutions of sociability in all those countries – the choirs, the ex-servicemen's clubs, the charitable associations, the *cercles*, all of which drew in shopkeepers and masters.[48] Industrial and trade associations could be further means of integrating them, with chambers of commerce bearing on the continent a quasi-official status that helped the process, although tensions within them over representation of small-scale interests might create strains. Only on the continent was the extension of the right to vote in chambers of commerce to small masters and retailers seen to be a means of obtaining their acceptance for the decisions made, though it was significantly the 'healthy' sections of the petite bourgeoisie that were wooed in this way.[49] Finally, political parties might also be used, seeking to unite bourgeois and petit bourgeois under a common banner. This met with a degree of success in Germany, at least for as long as the liberal movement could restrain its economic policies and focus more closely on resistance to authoritarian politics, but the strategy achieved even more success in Britain, where petits bourgeois became the work-horses of local political parties. Such institutional efforts were in all probability a symptom of a much larger process of cultural and ideological diffusion than we know about at the moment, seeking to draw the petite bourgeoisie towards a more orthodox acceptance of a particular version of the social order. Education was an important element in this, and the article on Britain indicates a great deal of concern to use it for that purpose. The success of such efforts has been little explored – they were almost certainly more directly effective than simultaneous projects directed at the working class – but the increasing petit-bourgeois acceptance of the ideology of domesticity in Britain,[50] and Ehmer's argument about the artisan ideal of the family in his essay here, both constitute a beginning.

The state itself had to act in relation to such initiatives – over education, over chamber of commerce reform, and so on. More important was the increasing way in which the state, everywhere but in Britain, felt the necessity of responding to petit-bourgeois concerns and anxieties, or at least, as we shall argue below, of seeming to respond. In part this was a result of petit-bourgeois organizational reactions to states increasingly intervening over income and trading taxes, over worker protection, over social legislation, over compulsory weekly rest days. An exact analysis of the effects of fiscal, social and trade policies on petit-bourgeois orientation is still at an early stage – though the essay on shopkeepers and the state in Britain has a good deal to say on the theme – but we know that the state was rarely absent from the demands of Belgian, German and French organizations, whether as a force to be resisted or as a source of assistance: often both. The reasons for state responses are complex, and we shall have more to say at the end of our introduction about the comparative explanations for the way various states strove to appear, at least, to be helping small enterprise.

After all this, could it be that the unity and identity of the petite bourgeoisie was the result of external forces, as if it owed its existence to the solicitous attentions of a bourgeoisie and (perhaps 'or') a state concerned to find allies in the struggle against the working class? In this perspective, is the petite bourgeoisie what Bourdieu calls *une classe objet*, one that takes its identity and almost its very existence from the cultural and ideological definitions of them imposed by another, dominant class?[51] Bourdieu's conception is an interesting one, but that is not our intention. Our concern is to raise the theme of the tension between some supposedly autonomous process of petit-bourgeois social and ideological development on the one hand, and on the other, the manipulative efforts of bourgeois and at times aristocratic élites to draw the petite bourgeoisie into a greater conformity with the norms or aspirations of the social order that they sought to defend. It is to the interaction of the two, so little explored, to the generation but also the construction of the more socially and then politically conservative petite bourgeoisie, that our comments are directed, for it seems to us to be there that so many of the essays in this book are pointing.

The construction and social existence of the petite bourgeoisie do not, of course, derive exclusively from such political considerations. Nor do they flow simply (or even primarily, perhaps) from relations with a larger bourgeoisie. An exploration of the *social* dimensions of the petite bourgeoisie leads inexorably into its relationship with the working class of Europe's towns and cities: questions of mobility and origins, of stability and persistence, of *sociabilité* and the neighbourhood, of connections of power and a shared sense of powerlessness. Studies of mobility and origins reveal a proximity to the working class, an interpenetration in personal and family terms, that once again indicates how the petite bourgeoisie, above all at its lower levels, constituted an ambiguous social world. This leads to those essential questions of identity, of sociability, and of social relations with the working class. We shall isolate two social themes: the social world of the petite bourgeoisie and the petit-bourgeois family.

What were the relations between the working class and the shopkeepers and small masters around them? There were the inevitable ties of family and marriage – and perhaps these were the most important – but there were also the lived relations of work, community and sociability. The workplace relations between small employer and his workforce are losing their once rosy hue for historians. Assumptions about closeness are rooted in an eighteenth-century craft background that is itself being probed,[52] but whatever the character of its earlier existence the sense of common interest was being broken down by the pressures of economic change. For as long as masters rose by the traditional social methods of craft training, travel and the diffusion of craft culture, a sense of common identity could continue. But an increasing proportion of journeymen in most crafts could hold out little expectation of ascent to a viable mastership, and as concerns for wages, conditions and the rights of journeymen came to dominate relations, so the trade community progressively splintered. The economic difficulties of small masters, and the ways in which they responded to them, made a deterioration of that relationship almost inevitable. Behagg's study of Birmingham small producers in this book is a clear case study of this process, and more such investigations will help us construct a chronology of crises in master/journeyman relations. Lorcin's exploration of the strike of ribbon weavers in St Etienne at the end of the century shows how much can be revealed through a single explosion of conflict; studies of the crises in the Paris and London tailoring trades in the 1820s and 1830s emphasize the potential of such an approach, though they stress the changing worker rather than small-master consciousness.[53]

The patchy research on relations between shopkeepers and the working class concentrates not on employment – though we know work conditions for labour in retailing were far worse than in artisanal production[54] – but on the contacts between retailers and the wider community. The result is ambiguous, but then so too were the relationships. The working-class dependence on shopkeeper credit allowed adulteration and poor quality; it also produced legal action for debt recovery.[55] Yet shopkeepers were seen in France as 'the bankers of the poor', and the retailers' material interest in successful wage claims can not be the only explanation for their appearance on strike subscription lists. As with credit in economic crises or strikes, the motivation was complex. Of course there was the need to maintain custom. But there was also, confirmed by Robert Roberts's account of his mother's Salford grocery shop, what Madeleine Rebérioux has called 'these daily solidarities'.[56] The survey article on Britain suggests the fragility of the way dependence and support fitted together, and the social explosions that could result. The analysis thus points towards an increasingly important theme in research on the petite bourgeoisie – relations rooted in the neighbourhood or the *quartier*. The evidence is of conflict because that is what is noticed, yet they were there in the community, behind or above the shop or workshop, and the consequent community relationship needs exploring at the everyday level. The new interest, above all in France, in questions of sociability and of the *quartier*, provides some impetus for that exploration. There was real change – linked among other things to the reconstruction of urban space in the later decades of the nineteenth century – but the *quartier* was a fundamental unit tying together working class and local petits bourgeois within a social milieu that was essentially popular rather than proletarian. Accampo's work on Saint-Chamond, and that of Procacci and Jalla on Turin, confirm this, and Agulhon above all has shown that the world of working-class sociability in nineteenth-century France was very much one of a popular milieu that revolved around its bars and cafes.[57] In more specific ways the petits bourgeois provided informal social centres through their shops, their bars, even their furnaces and smithies.[58] A potter in the French Midi explained in 1852 that 'people came to warm themselves at my furnace, and they talked politics'.[59] A great deal about working-class culture, as well as politics, becomes more comprehensible when interpreted in this context. The democratic radicalism, the social egalitarianism, the attacks on the idle rich, the support for the useful against the useless, for the *menu peuple* against the *grand*, the culture of community leisure, of popular theatre with its passion for a burlesque and pantomime which ridiculed the pompous and the high-born: all of these are not simply the result of cultural lags, of some slow adaptation to proletarian values, but the expression of a lived social reality in everyday life, the power of community and populace that comprised more than the working class alone. The process of detachment from that milieu needs to be understood, and it needs to be given a chronology. Popular culture did yield, as the century progressed, to a more clearly proletarian one in the urban centres of most countries, reinforced by an emerging labour and socialist identity whose problems for the petits bourgeois of the towns were merely exacerbated by such specific offences as co-operative trading. Do we then find the growth of an internal sociability, an identifiable culture that might provide evidence of a petit-bourgeois distinctiveness? The evidence that we have merely allows the question to be posed.

The *quartier*, however, was not the whole social world of the petite bourgeoisie, and in some respects not the most important. These shopkeepers and master artisans were perhaps on the very frontier of the public and private worlds of the nineteenth-century city, protected as they were by the insulating force of the family. There is something irresistibly closed about the petit-bourgeois family, yet one must none the less resist. The introspection, the internal dependence, the turning away from a problematic outside into familial solutions – all of these are the archetypal picture of the small business family. One must be cautious in two very different ways. The first derives from the memories of childhood on which much of that atmospheric analysis rests:[60] childhood, and memories of it, will surely always exaggerate introspection through the child's limited vision. Secondly, the evidence of wider community and social activity, some of it referred to above, qualifies the simple notion of familial closeness.

Yet the family, as we have already suggested, is a critical force in the world of small enterprise, and its investigation will tell us much about the experience of the petite bourgeoisie. In the first place, there is the necessity for family labour. Most were family enterprises, conceived and run as such however oppressive that may have been for many of its members. Family labour was cheap, readily available, and could be coerced into action with pressures far beyond those to which wage labour was susceptible. This was most true of retailing, though the traditions of wife and children's involvement in small production warrants further investigation of the kind presented by Ehmer in his essay. The wife's involvement in the enterprise (leaving aside those shops that were run by the married woman alone) could pose problems, though, especially in those countries where the ideals of domesticity and separate spheres were, as we have noted, shaping bourgeois identity. Within the ideology of domesticity, the wife's place was to be resolutely detached from the corrupting world of business, and placed in the moral private sphere of home and family. That could pose real problems for small shops where the wife's labour was essential, but the extent to which the wife's role became hidden from view in Britain, keeping the books or making goods for sale while withdrawn from the public gaze, is an indication of the desire of some petits bourgeois at least to identify themselves with wider bourgeois values. At that level change seems to be under way. But we must set against it, certainly for the artisanal trades, the way family labour intensifies as the economic position of the enterprise or the industry deteriorates. A good example is that of the silk weavers of Lyons, where from the 1830s many workshop owners eked out a marginal existence by shedding hired labour and retreating into family production. The next thirty years saw the trend strengthen, producing self-exploitation as the price of nominal independence.[61] The intensification of family labour appears in this light not so much as a norm of artisanal production, but as a response to its decline. Nor was it limited to Lyons, for the same process has been shown amongst Parisian tailors in the 1830s and 1840s, and master artisans in general during the Great Depression in Germany.[62]

In various ways, then, the introspection of petit-bourgeois family life is no mere cultural eccentricity, but the outcome of close ties between families and their very demanding enterprises. Such demands would carry them out into a dependence on wider family and kin, for financial support in launching the enterprise, in supporting it at times of difficulty, and in warding off the threat of bankruptcy. Inheritance and marriage appear to have been important sources of finance for the setting up of new small enterprises, as Faure shows in his essay on the Paris grocery trade. Marriage was the more important in July Monarchy Paris – the wife's dowry, training and family contacts could all prove vital, and Daumard argues that male *boutiquiers* generally married above themselves socially.[63] The family role went beyond that, however, for its primary concerns had to be initially the survival of its members – we have seen how in crisis it could close in on the enterprise as a work unit – and then the maintenance and, where possible, improvement of their life chances. The problem was that low resources to be passed on to the next generation – only one at best could inherit the business – were matched by high expectations of stability at least. The extent to which the eldest son inherited a parental enterprise inevitably varied, partly with size or success of enterprise, partly with the ambitions of those involved, and to an unexpected degree with the familial supports and securities available. If Jean Le Yaouanq is correct, then the number of children in the family itself was of great importance.[64] Alternatives had to be found, above all as problems of petit-bourgeois enterprise grew in the later nineteenth century, and doubts mounted as to the desirability, let alone the possibility, of the inherited small business. So, as the national survey essays show, parents began to educate their sons for the rapidly expanding world of white-collar work (with increasing marriage of daughters into that milieu). Here perhaps some continuity of status could be achieved. Education seems especially important to these groups, representing perhaps an alternative investment of limited financial resources in the quest for social stability if not advance.[65]

The structure of the petit-bourgeois family thus needs exploring, as does the relationship of that changing structure to the place of the family within petit-bourgeois ideologies. It is within that context that work on fertility and family size within the petite bourgeoisie – Spree's work on Germany is the most important here[66] – could prove particularly interesting. We can see in both France and Germany a politics and a culture of sections at least of the petite bourgeoisie rooted in images of an ordered society and the forces that gave it structure – workshop, patriarchal work groups, the moral primacy of honesty and effort, and above all the family.[67] Yet to what did this ideology refer – a real or a mythical past? If the petit-bourgeois family became the repository of so much hope for social order, we must surely follow Ehmer and ask exactly what the traditional artisanal (and then retailing) family might have been.

COMPARATIVE DIMENSIONS

Historians' interest in these shopkeepers and master artisans has been predominantly political. That is a point that we have already emphasized. That political focus has made much of the contrasting political roles and ideologies of the petite bourgeoisie in different countries. The generalizations have at times been too easy, the contrasts made to seem too obvious, and our own writings can certainly not be excused from that criticism.[68] Yet the drawing out of a comparative dimension to research on this subject has been valuable, for it is within comparative analysis that an understanding of the petite bourgeoisie and the forces that shape its development may best emerge. The problem is to control the comparisons, to specify the issues, and not simply to read off from too evident differences of political behaviour equivalent variations on other social and economic matters. Indeed, one could argue that political similarities were as important as the contrasts; that the neat typology that equates the German petite bourgeoisie with right-wing movements, the French with republicanism, and the British with liberalism is too neat, especially if we refuse to read into the period before 1914 our knowledge of what happened in the thirty years that followed it. The political historian might then find real similarities, in a localism that links to the theme of the *quartier* that we have already indicated, in a politics that flowed from it and feared a certain kind of interventionist state, and in a more or less articulated belief in the economic and social assumptions of autarky. The challenge to the structures of local community had real repercussions in later nineteenth-century Europe, above all as the large cities came to be reconstructed by the forces of substantial capital. Research on Paris, almost the ideal type of such reconstruction of urban space, suggests that the disruption had important consequences for petit-bourgeois politics and social ideology.[69] Liberalism in Britain, republican autarky in France, corporatism in Germany might all share a rejection of outside intrusion, a search for a political framework to support an older and more comfortably local petit-bourgeois world.

The political contrasts remain important, of course, but do they imply economic and social differences? Our sense is that at the level of national comparisons similarities might be more striking than differences, especially in daily existence and experiences. The interesting contrasts might be less those amongst countries, and more the distinctions between types of town. The real similarities might thus be those amongst the petits bourgeois of the great metropolitan cities of Europe, and amongst those of the iron and steel towns, or the factory textile towns, or the small metal goods regions centred on Birmingham, St Etienne or Solingen, or the small regional centres such as Niort, Esslingen or Colchester. Comparative analysis of the petite bourgeoisie remains potentially fruitful and important, and in the closing pages of this introduction we shall indicate, drawing in part upon issues already touched upon, four of the possible areas for such attention: patterns of industrialization, the relationship between petits bourgeois and the countryside, corporatism, and the state and party politics.

Patterns of industrialization and their implications for small enterprise are a recurrent theme of this book, and the arguments about the expansion of the retail sector and the complexities of pressure and revitalization in small-scale production need not be rehearsed here. A revisionist economic history has enabled us to see the similarities of artisanal experience in Britain and France; attention in Germany has been on the capital goods character of its industrialization, though the German experience might look less unique if we knew more about the consumer goods industries there. The danger, though, is that the fashionable tendency to emphasize continuities of experience over time and between places, might lead us to ignore the mpact of more precise national or regional differences. Jeanne Gaillard has stressed the persistence of *l'atelier et la boutique* alongside the economic and structural modernization of Second Empire Paris, delineating the renewal of artisan methods rooted in new techniques and a new division of trade.[70] If we replace the notion of linear evolution with that of adaptation, we need to explore those processes in different urban and economic settings as the nineteenth century progressed, to see how far increasingly integrated markets smoothed over the differences between trades, between national economies. Transportation and the development of larger markets are vital here. For as long as the size of markets was severely restricted by limited transport and commercial development, so small-scale enterprise could be both viable and realistically independent.[71] As market constraints were broken down, so small enterprise was not so much destroyed as rendered increasingly vulnerable, even within expanding sectors. The protection of localism had been lost. One can understand why later petit-bourgeois movements sought to retreat into an ideal of economic autarky. How did such new pressures work their way through the spatial economy? If London, Berlin and Paris all saw the fracturing of the artisan community before mid-century, notwithstanding the differential development of their respective national economies, how did it spread from there? Even the English wheelwrights and smiths serving a small agricultural area seem to have lost their place in the face of larger urban competition by 1850, while their resilience in rural France was predictably far greater, and especially so where the rural world was opened up by travel routes and a market agriculture.[72] That might not have been predicted.

The relationship between *the petite bourgeoisie and the countryside* is about far more than this, however, and it centres on the question of peasant agriculture. If Farcy's article tells us much about the complex world of the rural petits bourgeois, we need comparative investigations of the transfer of capital, people and ideology between the countryside and the urban world of small enterprise. Rural origins seem prominent amongst the intensively studied Parisian *boutiquiers*. Daumard shows this for the first half of the century, while Faure indicates below how the Parisian grocery trade depended on a flow of rural savings from the Paris basin. The food trades may not be typical. Le Yaouanq's study of migrants to Paris from le Loire Moyenne shows the prominence of food shops, cafés and bars amongst the enterprises they opened – ease of entry together with low capital and skill requirements encouraged them in a way probably less common for other retail trades.[73] Artisanal enterprise was even more difficult to initiate. Retailers in other European cities seem to have been disproportionately drawn from rural migrants, and if we knew more on this matter for Britain we would be able to assess the importance of peasant accumulation within the overall picture.[74] A strong peasant economy also generated a distinctive form of urban network, with the small scattered marketing centres which we have already suggested as the most comfortable setting for the petite bourgeoisie. There were real political implications. Corbin has shown their radical role in the Limousin countryside, while for Margadant these small town marketing structures underlay their role within Montagnard support for the French Second Republic.[75] Peasant agriculture itself, and the small artisanal and trading enterprises of the minor marketing centres which it supported, have real ideological implications. Traditions of peasant agriculture provided the basis for those ideologies of small proprietorship in France and south-west Germany that were so absent from Britain. Can we understand French republicanism and its persistent appeal without that? Could it not help explain the relative weakness of the politics of small proprietorship in Britain – the ease with which it was dismantled in the 1840s and 1850s? A clear perspective on the importance of the peasantry in the economic, social and ideological development of the French petite bourgeoisie can thus be related to the range of experiences offered by other countries and regions.

If the significance of the countryside has been neglected in discussion of the petite bourgeoisie, the contrasting effects of *corporate institutions and ideologies* have not, for their strength in late nineteenth-century Germany shaped the distinctive experience of Europe's most politically visible petite bourgeoisie.[76] The faith in corporate solutions spread fast in Europe in the decades before the First World War, encouraged by the Austrian guild reforms of 1883, and nowhere with more vigour than in Germany. Britain lies at the other extreme, with no corporatist elements discernible in petit-bourgeois demands. The essay on British shopkeepers shows their lack of an independent framework within which to interpret their experience and generate demands. France is the most awkward case, for while formal corporate controls were firmly rejected by artisans and shopkeepers rooted in a liberal republican tradition, so many of their demands and the social ideals that surrounded them partook of the corporate spirit. See the social conceptions of Léopold Christophe, leader of the shopkeepers' Ligue Syndicale in the 1890s, as examined by Nord. They expressed notions of specialization, of the right of each to live by his trade, of the right to control entry, of the economic self-sufficiency of the *quartier*, that stood, as did other European movements with the same sense of grievance, against the organized economy and the modern bureaucratic state. The guild, the *quartier*, the trade – such ideals, fuelled by this corporatist social vision, leads us back to the recurrent radicalism of small men and small communities against the distant state. Corporate legal structures had disappeared by the end of the eighteenth century in Britain, Belgium and France, whereas their effective dismantling in Germany had to wait until the 1860s, only to be resurrected in a weaker form in later years. Yet the fate of corporate structures must not obscure the continuities of corporate ideas. Indeed, the ideology of the craft as a closed and self-regulating moral body was even more pervasive, with significant effects on working-class development. The explanations cannot be explored here, but the question of who rejects the 'corporate' tradition first, masters or journeymen, is an important one. The differences are of emphasis, but in Britain the masters in artisan production rejected the craft traditions before their journeymen, who sought to preserve it, while the balance lay the other way in Germany with masters clinging to their trade and corporate traditions while their journeymen increasingly sought defences outside them, at first in 1848 and then later. The strategy of journeymen workshop resistance which characterized working-class formation in Britain was made possible because a substantial section of small masters detached themselves from the craft milieu in the way that Behagg shows for Birmingham. The French pattern approximates to this. Was conflict over corporate and craft ideas less central to the formation of the German working class precisely because it was the German masters, rather than their journeymen, who were the carriers of the craft tradition? The exploration of corporatism can thus illuminate much more than the petite bourgeoisie alone. The ideological influence of the ideas remains the issue, rather than the precise survival of corporate structures or even formal corporate demands.

Such corporatist demands were frequently directed at the *state and political parties*, which is the final comparative theme for which we have space here. The extent to which organizations of shopkeepers and master artisans demanded from the state protection against outside threats varied between countries in ways explored by the national essays that follow. They varied in response to the strength of corporate ideas as an alternative to economic liberalism; to the character of the different state systems and the ideologies that sustained them; and to small enterprise's own sense of identity in relation to larger capital. Such a small business identity was least evident in late nineteenth and early twentieth-century Britain, where small property lacked ideological or cultural cohesiveness. The petite bourgeoisie in Britain was more uncritically linked to laissez-faire liberalism than elsewhere. A small business identity emerged on the continent from the 1880s, and lost focus only as labour and socialist pressure after the turn of the century sent the bulk of the petite bourgeoisie scurrying for the shelter of larger capital. For a period, demands for legislative protection against 'unfair competition' formed the dominant concern of organizations of small enterprise in many countries. The state's own structures, or its recognition of quasi-state institutions, could help forge that identity and at the same time generate state-oriented demands. The struggles of the small for a place in the French tribunaux de commerce, or in the German chambers of commerce, show the ways both institutional and ideological structures could shape distinctive petit-bourgeois identities.[77]

Actual intervention by the state on behalf of small enterprise amounted to little in all of these countries, but many governments, most of all in Germany, made a great deal of what they were doing. As Kurgan shows, governments in Belgium did even less, in spite of setting up special departments for the petite bourgeoisie. These patterns can be explained in terms of the differing characteristics of the states, and of the political party systems. The structural evolution of party politics and the suffrage on the one hand, combined with the specific conjuncture of the years between 1890 and 1914 on the other, created the context in which political parties in all of these countries except Britain sought to win the support of the petite bourgeoisie. The essays below emphasize further the concerns of *Mittelstandspolitik* in Germany, of the Radical Party in France, of the Catholic Party in Belgium. All could thrive in a dual situation absent from Britain: increasingly mobilized small entrepreneurs alongside a party system in transition or crisis, in which conflict created the space that could be occupied by petit-bourgeois demands and mobilization (though never sufficiently, it must be said, to allow the formation of a successful autonomous petit-bourgeois party). In a conjuncture of economic instability, the party systems were in many ways in flux, certainly where they lacked the evolutionary roots of the once aristocratic parties that ruled Britain. In Rosenberg's words, 'exposed to the pressure of an electorate in a state of uproar, all political parties have, in order to maintain or fortify their position, to become mass parties, to put into motion and get hold of the indifferent non-voter, and to overhaul their leadership, platforms and propaganda techniques'.[78] In Britain, the organized petite bourgeoisie posed no threat to the existing order, nor was it needed as a third force. It had already been won to the ideals of a liberal social order. Elsewhere, a section at least of shopkeepers and small masters was mobilized behind various kinds of nationalist, conservative or right radical movements. If petit-bourgeois problems, and their expression in relation to the state and politics, are a fundamental comparative issue, then the complex relationship with liberalism must form an early part of that analysis.

After all our protests, we have ended with the political issues. Of course. It is not our intention to argue that the petite bourgeoisie can be understood apart from its political activities and significance. Nevertheless, we do insist that this political focus must be integrated into a comprehensive economic and social analysis that revolves around the kinds of issues with which this book is concerned. The failure to do that has deformed the historical analysis of a fundamental part of the nineteenth-century social structure, and an important element for the understanding of the development of European society during that period.

NOTES

1 We have chosen not to burden this essentially argumentative introduction with too large a body of references. The notes to the essays in this book, especially those in the national perspectives section, provide a very full bibliography of work in the field, upon a reading of which this introduction is based.

2 For the most important of these conferences, see *Premier Congrès international de la petite bourgeoisie, compte-rendu sténographique, tenu à Anvers les 17 et 18 septembre 1899*, Brussels, 1900; *Deuxième Congrès international de la petite bourgeoisie, compte-rendu sténographique, tenu à Namur les 15 et 16 septembre 1901*, Namur, 1902; *Troisième Congrès international des classes moyennes, compte-rendu sténographique*, Munich, 1911; and the French *Association de Défense des Classes Moyennes* which attracted wide international representation at its congresses – see the report of proceedings at its 3rd Annual Congress, in *Les Etudes fiscales et sociales, troisième congrès annuel (Novembre 1910)*, Limoges, 1911.

3 We have decided to write of a 'petite bourgeoisie' and 'petits bourgeois' because of a wish to shift attention from the pejorative and, more importantly, narrowing implications of the older term 'petty bourgeoisie'. In this we are following the pattern set in the recent

historical and sociological literature. See F. Bechhofer and B. Elliott (eds), *The Petite Bourgeoisie: Studies in an Uneasy Stratum*, London, 1981; R. J. Morris, 'Samuel Smiles and the genesis of *Self-Help*: the retreat to a petit bourgeois utopia', *Historical Journal*, 24, 1981, 89–109.

4 P. O'Brien and C. Keyder, *Economic Growth in Britain and France 1780–1914: Two Paths to the Twentieth Century*, London, 1978; R. Roehl, 'French industrialization. A reconsideration', *Explorations in Economic History*, 13, 1976, 233–81.

5 E. P. Thompson, *The Making of the English Working Class*, London, 1963; I. Prothero, *Artisans and Politics in Early Nineteenth-Century London: John Gast and His Times*, Folkestone, 1979.

6 Examples are V. Brants, *La Petite Industrie contemporaine*, Paris, 1901; G. Duplat, *La Classe moyenne. Son rôle social, son action politique, sa situation économique, les réformes urgentes*, Brussels, 1914; F. Funck-Brentano, *Grandeur et décadence des classes moyennes*, Paris, 1903; O. Pyfferoen, *La Petite Bourgeoisie aux Pays-Bas*, Brussels, 1902; E. Martin Saint-Léon, *Le Petit Commerce français. Sa lutte pour la vie*, Paris, 1911; and numerous articles in *La Science sociale* and *La Réforme sociale* for this period. In Germany, the *Verein für Sozialpolitik*, a group of university professors concerned with social issues, was especially interested in the Mittelstand. See 'Untersuchungen über die Lage des Handwerks in Deutschland mit besonderer Rücksicht auf seine Konkurrenzfähigkeit gegenüber der Großindustrie', *Schriften des Vereins für Sozialpolitik*, 62–70, Leipzig 1895–7, and 76, Leipzig, 1899.

7 There is little research that tackles this issue directly, but see P. H. Noyes, *Organization and Revolution. Working-Class Associations in the German Revolutions of 1848–1849*, Princeton, 1969; R. Aminzade, 'The transformation of social solidarities in nineteenth-century Toulouse', in J. Merriman (ed.), *Consciousness and Class Experience in Nineteenth-Century Europe*, New York, 1979, 91; A. Corbin, *Archaïsme et modernité en Limousin au XIXe siècle, 1845–1880*, 2 vols, Paris, 1975, 790–4; G. Dupeux, *Aspects de l'Histoire Sociale et Politique du Loir-et-Cher 1848–1914*, Paris, 1962, e.g. 325–31, 376–80.

8 This is the area of most substantial research on the petite bourgeoisie. The most important publications include Philip Nord's essay on France in this book, and also H. A. Winkler, *Mittelstand, Demokratie und Nationalsozialismus. Die politische Entwicklung von Handwerk und Kleinhandel in der Weimarer Republik*, Köln/Berlin, 1972; R. Gellately, *The Politics of Economic Despair: Shopkeepers and German Politics 1890–1914*, London, 1974; S. Volkov, *The Rise of Antimodernism in Germany. The Urban Master Artisans, 1873–1897*, Princeton, 1978; H. Fode, 'Denmark. Industrialism and the small-scale businessman. The self-employed craftsman and retailer', in Commission internationale d'histoire des mouvements sociaux et des structures sociales, *Petite entreprise et croissance industrielle dans le monde aux XIXe et XXe siècles*, Paris, 1981, 314ff; B. S. Chlepner, *Cent ans d'histoire sociale en Belgique*, Brussels, 1972, 141–5.

9 See David Blackbourn's essay in this book; D. F. Crew, *Town in the Ruhr. A Social History of Bochum, 1860–1914*, New York, 1979, 135; Fode, op. cit., 324–7; M. Rebérioux, 'Les socialistes français et le petit commerce au tournant du siècle', *Le Mouvement social*, 114, 1981, 61.

10 On social Catholicism see P. Delfosse, 'La petite bourgeoisie en crise et l'état: le cas belge (1890–1914)', *Le Mouvement social*, 114, 1981, 85–103; R. Rezsohazy, *Origines et formation du Catholicisme social en Belgique, 1842–1909*, Louvain, 1958; M. H. Elbow, *French Corporate Theory, 1789–1948. A Chapter in the History of Ideas*, New York, 1953. In Germany the Protestant church also turned towards the middle classes – see *Die Verhandlungen des achten Evangelisch-sozialen Kongresses, abgehalten zu Leipzig am 10 und 11 Juni 1897*, Göttingen, 1897.

11 But see Mack Walker, *German Home Towns. Community, State and General Estate 1648–1871*, Ithaca, 1971; D. Blackbourn, *Class, Religion and Local Politics in Wilhelmine*

Germany. The Centre Party in Württemberg before 1914, New Haven, 1980; J.-C. Martin, 'Commerce et commerçants à Niort au XIXe siècle. Les faillites', *Bulletin de la Société historique et scientifique des Deux-Sèvres*, 13, 1980, 337–500.

12 See for example Max Weber, *Wirtschaft und Gesellschaft*, Köln/Berlin, 1964, vol. 1, 223–7; vol. 2, 679–82; A. Giddens, *The Class Structure of the Advanced Societies*, London, 1975; P. Bourdieu, 'Klassenstellung und Klassenlage', in his *Zur Soziologie der symbolischen Formen*, Frankfurt, 1974; N. Poulantzas, *Classes in Contemporary Capitalism*, London, 1975, 13–35.

13 C. Baudelot, R. Establet and J. Malemort, *La Petite Bourgeoisie en France*, Paris, 1974, 18–28.

14 J. Le Yaouanq, 'La mobilité sociale dans le milieu boutiquier parisien au XIXe siècle', *Le Mouvement social*, 108, 1979, 89–112; H.-G. Haupt, 'La petite bourgeoisie, une classe inconnue', ibid., 13–14. See also the discussion of social mobility in G. Crossick, 'The petite bourgeoisie in nineteenth-century Europe: problems and research', in K. Tenfelde (ed.), *Internationale Forschungen zur Geschichte der Arbeiterschaft und Arbeiterbewegung*, Munich, 1984.

15 Examples of different kinds are Behagg's essay in this book, and J.-C. Martin, 'Hiérarchie et structure de la société commerçante: les listes d'électeurs au tribunal de commerce de Niort en 1864 et 1874', *Le Mouvement social*, 112, 1980, 57–77.

16 J. Kocka, *Lohnarbeit und Klassenbildung. Arbeiter und Arbeiterbewegung in Deutschland 1800–1875*, Berlin/Bonn, 1983, 9–31; E. P. Thompson, 'Eighteenth-century English society: class struggle without class?', *Social History*, 3, 1978, 149ff.

17 D. Blackbourn, 'The *Mittelstand* in German society and politics, 1871–1914', *Social History*, 4, 1977, 409–33.

18 An explicit statement of the view we are criticizing is to be found in Gellately, op. cit., 12–27.

19 T. Geiger, *Die soziale Schichtung des deutschen Volkes. Soziographischer Versuch auf statistischer Grundlage*, Darmstadt, 1967, 106–38.

20 Forschungsgruppe Bremen, 'Binnenstruktur des Bremer Kleinhandels zwischen 1890 und 1914', unpublished paper delivered at the 2nd Round Table on the European Petite Bourgeoisie in the Nineteenth Century at the University of Bremen 1980.

21 A recent collection of essays on Britain is interesting in this connection: P. Searby (ed.), *Educating the Victorian Middle Class*, Leicester, 1982.

22 F. Bechhofer and B. Elliott, 'Persistence and change: the petite bourgeoisie in industrial society', *Archives européenes de sociologies*, 17, 1976, 78. See also A. Cottereau's introduction to D. Poulot, *Le Sublime*, Paris, 1980, 63ff. The most notable recent sociological studies of the petite bourgeoisie are the works already cited by Bechhofer and Elliott (eds), Baudelot *et al.*, and Poulantzas.

23 Cf. A. Leppert-Fögen, *Die deklassierte Klasse. Studien zur Geschichte und Ideologie des Kleinbürgertums*, Frankfurt, 1974, 39–70.

24 An attempt is made by A. Noll, *Sozio-ökonomischer Strukturwandel des Handwerks in der zweiten Phase der Industrialisierung unter besonderer Berücksichtigung der Regierungsbezirke Arnsberg und Münster*, Göttingen, 1975.

25 S. Bruchey in Commission internationale, op. cit., 45.

26 J. A. Chartres and G. L. Turnbull, 'Country craftsmen', in G. E. Mingay (ed.), *The Victorian Countryside*, London, 1981, 317–20; on France, Corbin, op. cit.

27 P. Ayçoberry, *Histoire sociale de la Ville de Cologne (1815–1875)*, 2 vols, Lille, 1980, 626–7. (A shorter version has been published as *Cologne entre Napoléon et Bismarck. La croissance d'une ville rhênane*, Paris, 1982). J. Gaillard, *Paris, la Ville (1852–1870)*, Lille, 1976, 448.

28 M. Lévy-Leboyer, 'Le patronat français a-t-il été malthusien?', *Le Mouvement social*, 88, 1974, 9–18.

29 Cottereau, op. cit., 70.
30 Haupt, op. cit., 14.
31 Joan Scott, 'Men and women in the Parisian garment trades: discussions of family and work in the 1830s and 1840s', in P. Thane, G. Crossick and R. Floud (eds), *The Power of the Past. Essays for Eric Hobsbawm*, Cambridge, 1984; C. H. Johnson, 'Patterns of proletarianization: Parisian tailors and Lodève woollen workers', in J. Merriman (ed.), op. cit., 65–84; C. H. Johnson, 'Economic change and artisan discontent. The tailors' history, 1800–1848', in R. Price (ed.), *Revolution and Reaction. 1848 and the Second French Republic*, London, 1975, 87–114; T. M. Parsinnen and I. J. Prothero, 'The London tailors' strike of 1834 and the collapse of the Grand National Consolidated Trades' Union: a police spy's report', *International Review of Social History*, 22, 1977, 65–107.
32 W. H. Sewell, jr, *Work and Revolution in France. The Language of Labor from the Old Regime to 1848*, Cambridge, 1980.
33 The term is used by E. Labrousse, 'Un livre ouvert sur les élans et les vicissitudes des croissances', in F. Braudel and E. Labrousse (eds), *Histoire économique et sociale de la France*, vol. 3/2, Paris, 1976, 987–1008.
34 H. Rosenberg, 'Political and social consequences of the depression of 1873–1896 in Central Europe', *Economic History Review*, First Series, 13, 1943, 58–73.
35 H. Sedatis, *Liberalismus und Handwerk in Südwestdeutschland. Wirtschafts-und Gesellschaftskonzetionen des Liberalismus und die Krise des Handwerks im 19. Jahrhundert*, Stuttgart, 1979.
36 Ayçoberry, op. cit., 304–5. There is confirmation in J. Gaillard, 'La petite entreprise en France au XIXe et au XXe siècles', in Commission internationale, op. cit., 137–8; T. Hanisch and E. Lange, 'The importance of small industrial establishments in Norway over the last hundred years', ibid., 364.
37 J. Bouvier, 'Les crises économiques', in J. Le Goff and P. Nora (eds), *Faire de l'histoire*, vol. 2, 44–6.
38 See Labrousse, op. cit.
39 P. Ayçoberry, *Cologne entre Napoléon et Bismarck*, 227–56; J. Rançière, *La Nuit des prolétaires. Archives du rêve ouvrier*, Paris, 1981, 337.
40 Gaillard, 'La petite entreprise', 144–5; Volkov, op. cit., 13; K. Brooker, 'The changing position of the small owner in the English shoemaking industry, 1860–1914', unpublished paper delivered to the 2nd Round Table on the European Petite Bourgeoisie in the Nineteenth Century, at the University of Bremen, 1980; S. Pollard, *A History of Labour in Sheffield*, Liverpool, 1959, 202ff. See also Fode, op. cit., 304–9.
41 This is the argument of R. Hilferding, *Das Finanzkapital. Eine Studie über die jüngste Entwicklung des Kapitalismus* (1910), East Berlin, 1947, 388–407.
42 One of the best-known studies is Winkler, op. cit., but many of the articles in this book refer to studies on this theme.
43 On this see the works already cited by Johnson, Aminzade, Corbin and Dupeux.
44 Rebérioux, op. cit. See also T. Judt, *Socialism in Provence 1871–1914. A Study in the Origins of the Modern French Left*, Cambridge, 1979. Evidence for other countries confirms the need for a closer exploration of the way socialism and the labour movement penetrated the world of the petite bourgeoisie. See Fode, op. cit., 327; Blackbourn 'The *Mittelstand*', 431–2; Volkov, op. cit., 229–30.
45 See the essays by Blackbourn, Kurgan and Nord in this book, and also Blackbourn, *Class, Religion and Local Politics*, and G. Eley, *Reshaping the German Right: Radical Nationalism and Political Change after Bismarck*, New Haven, 1980.
46 Johnson, op. cit., 80.
47 See especially the essay here by Behagg. For the use of bankruptcy to this end, see J.-C. Martin, 'Le commerçant, la faillite et l'historien', *Annales ESC*, 35, 1980, 1251–68.

48 See for example R. Huard, 'La genèse des partis démocratiques modernes en France. L'expérience du XIXe siècle', *La Pensée*, 201, 1978, 96–119.
49 A. Saur, 'Die Organisationen der Bremer Kleinhändler vor 1914 und ihre soziale Basis', *Beiträge zur Sozialgeschichte Bremens*, 4, 1982, 41–84.
50 L. Davidoff and C. Hall, 'The petite bourgeoisie and the sexual division of labour in England, 1780–1850: countryside and town', unpublished paper delivered to the 3rd Round Table on the European Petite Bourgeoisie in the Nineteenth Century, at the University of Paris X, Nanterre, 1981; I. Joseph and P. Fritsch, 'Disciplines à domiciles', *Recherches*, 28, 1977.
51 P. Bourdieu, 'Une classe objet', *Actes de la recherche en sciences sociales*, 17/18, 1977, 2–5.
52 S. Kaplan, 'Refléxions sur la police du monde du travail, 1700–1815', *Revue historique*, 261, 1979, 17–77; Sewell, op. cit., 16–61; *Journal de ma vie. Jacques-Louis Ménétra. Compagnon vitrier au 18e siècle*, presented by Daniel Roche, Paris, 1982 – see especially ch. 3 of Roche's excellent commentary, pp. 333–54; C. R. Dobson, *Masters and Journeymen*, London, 1980.
53 J. Lorcin, 'Un essai de stratigraphie sociale: chefs d'ateliers et compagnons dans la grève des passementiers de Saint-Etienne en 1900', *Cahiers d'histoire*, 13, 1968, 179–92; Parsinnen and Prothero, op. cit.; Johnson, op. cit.
54 See for example C. Niermann, A. Saur, P. Schottler and E. Sinner, 'Petit commerce et apprentissage à Breme au début du XXe siècle', *Le Mouvement social*, 108, 131–8; W. B. Whitaker, *Victorian and Edwardian Shopworkers*, Newton Abbot, 1973.
55 G. Jacquemet, 'Belleville ouvrier à la Belle Epoque', *Le Mouvement social*, 118, 1982, 66–8; D. Englander, 'Wage arrestment in Victorian Scotland', *Scottish Historical Review*, 60, 1981, 68–75.
56 R. Roberts, *The Classic Slum. Salford Life in the First Quarter of the Century*, Harmondsworth, 1973; Rebérioux, op. cit., 61.
57 E. Accampo, 'Entre la classe sociale et la cité: identité et intégration chez les ouvriers de Saint-Chamond, 1815–1880', *Le Mouvement social*, 118, 1982, 39–59; D. Jalla, 'Le quartier comme territoire et comme représentation: les "barrières" ouvrières de Turin au début du XXe siècle', ibid., 79–97; M. Agulhon, 'Working class and sociability in France before 1848', in Thane, Crossick and Floud, op. cit.
58 Johnson, op. cit., 80; Ayçoberry, *Histoire sociale de la ville de Cologne*, 330; E. J. Hobsbawm and J. Scott, 'Political shoemakers', *Past and Present*, 89, 1980, 86–114.
59 T. W. Margadant, *French Peasants in Revolt. The Insurrection of 1851*, Princeton, 1979, 174.
60 Examples are H. Corke, *In Our Infancy. An Autobiography, Part I: 1882–1912*, Cambridge, 1975; H. G. Wells, *Experiment in Autobiography*, London, 1934.
61 L. Strumingher, 'The artisan family: traditions and transition in nineteenth-century Lyon', *Journal of Family History*, 2, 1977, 211–22; G. J. Sheridan, jr, 'Household and craft in an industrializing economy. The case of the silk weavers of Lyon', in Merriman, op. cit., 111–12.
62 Scott, op. cit.; Volkov, op. cit., 74.
63 A. Daumard, *Les Bourgeois de Paris au XIXe siècle*, Paris, 1970, 129–33; Martin, 'Le commerçant'.
64 Le Yaouanq, op. cit., 89–112.
65 P. J. Harrigan, *Mobility, Elites, and Education in French Society of the Second Empire*, Ontario, 1980; R. Gildea, 'Education and the *classes moyennes* in the nineteenth century', in D. N. Baker and P. J. Harrigan (eds), *The Making of Frenchmen. Current Directions in the History of Education in France, 1679–1979*, Waterloo, Ontario, 1980; Ayçoberry, *Histoire sociale de la ville de Cologne*, 600; G. Crossick, 'Angestellte: Uberlegungen am englischen Beispiel', in J. Kocka (ed.), *Angestellte im europaischen Vergleich*, Göttingen, 1981, 103–5.

66 R. Spree, 'The German petite bourgeoisie and the decline of fertility: some statistical evidence from the late 19th and early 20th centuries', unpublished paper delivered to the 3rd Round Table on the European Petite Bourgeoisie in the Nineteenth Century, at the University of Paris X, Nanterre, 1981.

67 For example, P. Dumont, *La Petite Bourgeoisie vue à travers les contes quotidiens du Journal (1894–95)*, Paris, 1973.

68 G. Crossick, 'The emergence of the lower middle class in Britain: a discussion', in G. Crossick (ed.), *The Lower Middle Class in Britain 1870–1914*, London, 1976, 11–60; H.-G. Haupt, 'La petite entreprise et la politique en Europe au XIXe siècle', *Le Mouvement social*, 114, 1981, 3–9. See also A. Mayer, 'The lower middle class as a historical problem', *Journal of Modern History*, 47, 1975, 409–36.

69 P. Nord, 'Commerce and culture in *fin de siècle* Paris', University of Columbia PhD dissertation, 1982; Gaillard, *Paris*.

70 Gaillard, *Paris*, 401–2, 430–54.

71 G. Kurgan-van Hentenryk, 'Belgique. La petite entreprise depuis la fin de l'Ancien Régime jusqu'à nos jours', in Commission internationale, op. cit., 192–4. See Volkov's stress on the impact of the Zollverein in Germany: Volkov, op. cit., 44.

72 See the references in note 26, and also Dupeux, op. cit., esp. 120–1.

73 Daumard, op. cit., 126; J. Le Yaouanq, 'Aspects de l'immigration départementale à Paris au XIXe siècle. Les commerçants et artisans ligériens', *Cahiers de l'Institut d'histoire de la presse et de l'opinion*, 3, 1974–5, 7–39.

74 In Copenhagen in 1880 67 per cent of all retailers were immigrants to the city, compared with 46 per cent for the population as a whole: Fode, op. cit., 309; for Germany, see Gellately, op. cit., 34.

75 Corbin, op. cit., 790ff; Margadant, op. cit., 91ff, 138–9, 154–60, 169.

76 Examples abound – English-speaking readers may turn to the works already cited by Blackbourn, Volkov, Eley and Gellately.

77 Martin, 'Hiérarchie et structure'; Gellately, op. cit., 96–111; F. Peiter, 'Institutions and attitudes: the consolidation of the business community in bourgeois France, 1880–1914', *Journal of Social History*, 9, 1975–6, 510–26; K. van Eyll, *Die Geschichte einer Handelskammer, dargestellt am Beispiel der Handelskammer Essen 1840–1910*, Köln, 1964.

78 Rosenberg, op. cit., 165.

National perspectives

2 Between resignation and volatility: the German petite bourgeoisie in the nineteenth century

DAVID BLACKBOURN

The petite bourgeoisie is less of an 'unknown class'[1] in some countries than in others. There is certainly no absence of work on German craftsmen and shopkeepers in the nineteenth century. In the case of craftsmen this is partly explained by a long tradition of writing on the guilds. The nineteenth-century public debate over the abolition of the guilds, and then over the partial reintroduction of corporate organizations, ensured a high degree of visibility for craftsmen, as well as ready-made sources for the historian. Argument about corporate organizations for shopkeepers at the end of the century, although less important, had something of the same effect. Both groups have therefore come down to us with a collective identity more pronounced than that of their counterparts in countries where organizations of this kind were weaker or non-existent. German economic historians in recent years have cut across the grain of these corporate identities by writing about the contribution of 'small businesses' to economic growth. But this has still served to keep our attention on the place of craftsmen and shopkeepers. The growing volume of work on pressure groups in the later nineteenth century has worked in the same direction. The petite bourgeoisie has taken its place alongside heavy industry and commerce, estate owners and peasants, as one among many noisy interest groups.

There is another and more obvious reason why the German petite bourgeoisie has attracted attention. In the twentieth century craftsmen and shopkeepers were prominent both as members and as electoral supporters of the Nazi Party. Their importance for the advent of German fascism is generally acknowledged. There has been predictable interest in tracing back the pattern of craftsman and shopkeeper politics into the last century. This concern with continuity has spawned work dealing, among other things, with the impact of economic change, status anxiety and the crystallization of an 'anti-modern' petit-bourgeois politics. Perhaps the most striking thing about this literature is the language in which so much of it has been couched. Argument on the petite bourgeoisie has frequently been submerged in argument about the *Mittelstand*. As a category, the *Mittelstand* – literally 'middle estate' – is both elastic and imprecise.[2] The peasantry has sometimes been counted as part of it, others have wanted to include the so-called 'new *Mittelstand*' of lesser officials and white-collar workers. But this imprecision is not the central difficulty for our present purposes, for craftsmen and shopkeepers are normally regarded as the essential core of the *Mittelstand*. The debate about the *Mittelstand* has often therefore been a debate about the petite bourgeoisie with a different label. The real problem is the label itself and its connotations. The term *Mittelstand* carries a powerful ideological charge. It would be difficult and even impoverishing to try to discuss the petite bourgeoisie in nineteenth-century Germany without recognizing the frequency with which contemporaries clothed their arguments in these terms. But there was a gap between rhetoric and reality, and this essay will partly be concerned with this gap.

The term *Mittelstand* has strong corporatist overtones. It implies that the collectivity in question should be regarded as a unity – indeed, as a traditional unity, as a *Stand* or estate, not a class. It is no accident that many contemporaries preferred the term *Mittelstand* to the term *Kleinbürgertum* (the direct equivalent of petite bourgeoisie). The latter, with its Marxist provenance and associations, suggested a divided class doomed to polarization in a two-class society. Indeed Social Democrats generally thought and wrote about the petite bourgeoisie in just this way. The term *Mittelstand*, by contrast, was used by conservatives to suggest that the petite bourgeoisie was a buffer against the polarization of society. Situated in the middle, it supposedly cut across the lines of class conflict, captured neither by the recklessness of *laissez-faire* capitalism nor by the 'class hatred' of the worker. The political corollary was the presumed conservatism of the *Mittelstand*. This view, it should be said, did not have currency throughout the century. In the first half of the century craftsmen and shopkeepers were often suspected of radicalism, and their role in 1848 was difficult to ignore. Yet thoughtful conservatives began to argue as early as the 1850s that these groups, like the peasantry, had ultimately come round to loyalty. And in the second half of the century a picture of traditional craftsmen and shopkeepers came increasingly to reassure them. They were 'the best and strongest bulwark against the red flood, and whoever fights for the *Mittelstand* fights at the same time against revolution'.[3]

Such a view is not surprising. What is interesting is the way many historians have, from a rather different perspective, taken these claims at face value. They have sought reasons for the persistence of the old regime in Prussia-Germany through a period of rapid industrialization and social upheaval. And they have found one explanation in the capacity of the ruling élite to shore up its position against liberal reformers and the socialist challenge by turning to the petite bourgeoisie for support. The Great Depression of 1873 to 1896 has been particularly noted as a period when petit-bourgeois resentments and uncertainty were exploited by conservative forces. This is held to have worked partly through a policy of 'social protectionism', which enlisted the petite bourgeoisie behind the *status quo* by reintroducing neo-corporate chambers and guilds, and by a broadly protectionist policy of *Mittelstandspolitik*. This 'reinsurance of the *Mittelstand*' has been presented as a trade-off between petite bourgeoisie and state, from which each gained by agreeing to support the other. More generally it has been argued that a conservative ruling élite harnessed petit-bourgeois anxieties in winning them over to an aggressive foreign policy and a 'throne and altar' policy at home.[4]

This is a re-statement of an old case with all the moral signs reversed: the conservative dream as liberal nightmare. Arguments of this kind have been directly or indirectly challenged by recent writing, but this broad interpretation continues to have a hold in the secondary literature. In the essay which follows I hope to present a rather different picture, of a petite bourgeoisie whose place in nineteenth-century Germany was more ambiguous. It is particularly important to try to break down the categories of 'craftsmen' and 'shopkeeper', for only by doing so can we recover the truly Janus-faced qualities of the petite bourgeoisie. The second section accordingly deals with the material fortunes of small producers and retailers, emphasizing the important divisions within the ranks of each. The third section takes this point further, considering the ambiguous social relations of a petite bourgeoisie which stretched across the class lines between bourgeoisie and working class. I try finally to probe the way in which these ambiguities found political expression.

Craftsmen and shopkeepers are often bracketed together as the common victims of economic giantism. This is misleading in several ways, not least in suggesting an absolute identity between the two. I shall deal with each in turn, bringing out dissimilarities as well as the obvious similarities. The fate of nineteenth-century craftsmen can usefully be considered in terms of the debate between 'optimists' and 'pessimists'. The pessimist case traditionally stressed the parallel decline of the guild system and artisanal fortunes. The role of the guilds was progressively sliced away in the German states, starting before the nineteenth century but quickening in tempo then, culminating for most in the 1860s with the passage of liberal commercial codes. This stage-by-stage dismantling of guild controls over prices, craft entry, production levels and labour force was confirmed by the North German Confederation and carried over into the new Reich.[5] There is now general agreement, however, that this approach lays too much stress on formal government regulations.[6] It is now more common to emphasize the direct impact of market forces, especially the effects of factory competition and industrial concentration. Craftsmen, argue the pessimists, were at a disadvantage in competing for labour and capital, while suffering from rapid changes in taste and demand prompted by the new industrial civilization. Whole groups like potters, farriers and basket-makers were laid waste, and others (like metal-workers) made insecure through specialization and vulnerability to market changes.[7]

This seemingly plausible case has been subjected to some telling counter-arguments. Optimists have, in the first place, questioned the thesis of decline by blackening the picture of what preceded it. They have little time for the golden age (*Goldener Boden*) of German craftsmen. In the nineteenth century things were not what they were; but they never had been, at least since 1600. The guilds had been steadily declining, tarnished within by abuses, threatened without by non-guild competition and the aspirations of the absolutist state, which sought to clip the wings of all autonomous corporate institutions.[8] It is difficult to resist the basic truth of this. It is also true that the real economy of craftsmen around 1800 was often as parlous as the state of many guilds. If the number of assistants is taken as an index of prosperity, it is a telling fact that no German state could boast a ratio of men to masters which exceeded 1 : 1. In many trades, and in the south more generally, this was very much lower.[9] Optimists generally stress the plight of craftsmen in pre-industrial Germany, noting the decline of real incomes in the decades before mid-century, as growing population led to overcrowded crafts. Many studies have pointed to the hand-to-mouth existence and poverty of masters, concentrated in overstocked branches of immediate consumption (food, clothing, furniture) in the pre-1850 era of agricultural subsistence, periodic slump and sluggish demand. Thus it is lack of industrialization which is held to explain straitened circumstances in the pre-railway age.[10] Optimists stress the improvement following industrialization, which increased purchasing power, stimulated growth branches and widened the possibilities for auxiliary and service roles.[11] Moreover – so the argument runs – new forms of co-operative and savings bank credit became available, stimulating capital investment in the small workshop. The growing use of the electric motor at the end of the century is the conventional symbol of this.[12] Typical of such arguments is Adolf Noll's study of two contrasting Westphalian regions, where he argues that craftsmen in the more industrialized Arnsberg markedly outstripped their fellows in less-developed Münster between 1875 and 1907. Not only were Arnsberg concerns larger and more capitalized as a result of 'pruning'; they also weathered the depression better, suffering less in the downturn and recovering more quickly with the upturn.[13] In short, craftsmen benefited overall from industrialization: the Great Depression cleaned out the weakest one-man concerns, while still removing far fewer independent producers from the economy than industrial growth had added since 1850.

This is a bold reversal of the pessimist case. Instead of the degraded craftsman we are offered the embryonic small businessman, bristling with Schumpeterian initiative. In place of the languishing traditional craftsman, we are asked to look at the plumber and hairdresser, and at the building or metal-working entrepreneur who successfully modernized his concern.[14] This is helpful in giving a measure – almost a metaphor – of the distance between 1800 and 1900. But the roseate picture of resourceful adaptation (a favourite word) also has its omissions. Optimists are generally not very forthcoming on the way that a developing capitalism generated old problems in new form, replacing the old agriculture-based boom and slump with cycles of a new kind, as well as accelerating concentration. It is certainly true that industrialization leavened the crowding of craftsmen in the simplest branches of consumer goods, widening the market for (say) ceramics; yet later concentration in turn posed a serious threat to craftsmen in this branch. There were others like soap-makers, dyers and tanners for whom the market worked unevenly, both giving and taking away.[15]

There is, in addition, the problem of what exactly is being investigated. Is it craftsmen or small businessmen employing up to five people, and is it all of these or only the more successful? Aggregate statistics on small businesses can disguise what was happening to craftsmen proper. Nor is this the only difficulty with macro-economic data: there has been a tendency to iron out regional and sectoral differences as well as cyclical fluctuations. Ironically, optimists run the risk of presenting a mirror-image of generalized pessimist accounts. The latter saw industrialization as a juggernaut destroying the old craft world; the former see it as a vehicle for advancement. What can easily fall through the net in both cases is the continuity, in different forms, of differentiation and competition among craftsmen, and the importance of their *de facto* dependence on distributors of various kinds.[16]

It is clear that mature capitalism often reinforced long-standing disparities of wealth and income between different crafts. At the end of the century, as at the beginning, butchers, bakers and glaziers were amongst the highest-earners and most stable, while tailors, shoemakers and carpenters were amongst the poorest and most precarious.[17] This leads to a further point. In 1895 more than a third of all master craftsmen were tailors, shoemakers or carpenters, and they were commonly one-man businesses – there were only seven assistants to every ten shoemakers at that time, nine to every ten tailors.[18] Moreover, half of all masters were rural, at the end of the century as at the beginning. They also had a smaller average number of assistants than their urban counterparts. These were clearly not the budding entrepreneurs of optimist accounts; yet they seem to have survived the 'healthy' shake-out of the Great Depression, signalled by the rising average number of employees in small concerns. How do we explain these contradictory tendencies? It seems likely that the aggregate statistics of growing small businesses mask a more complex double process, of concentration on the one hand and semi-proletarianization on the other. A prominent revisionist, Wolfram Fischer, himself suggests that the growing size of concerns in construction may be explained by concentration among a narrow group of masons and locksmiths who were effectively small contractors.[19] In other crafts, too, a minority of craftsmen turned themselves into genuine entrepreneurs. These were the masters who so often decided the fate of craftsmens' producer co-operatives by refusing to join them.[20] Below them were masters working with family labour and maybe one assistant. They lived a 'proletaroid'[21] existence, threatened on the occasion of a downturn in business with the prospect of joining the truly proletarianized *Alleinmeister*. The latter owned little capital, rented back rooms and cellars at a time of rising rents, competed chronically with each other, were usually backward technically. They were hardly independent. This internal differentiation at the close of the nineteenth century was structurally as well as conjuncturally similar to the pattern of shake-out and crisis, concentration coupled with proletarianization, which can be observed in the 1830s and 1840s.

The small number of entrepreneurial success stories,[22] and the larger number of precariously independent middling craftsmen, therefore have to be set against the marginal craftsmen, above all those working alone. A local survey of 1890 showed that up to 87 per cent of craftsmen in the clothing branches worked alone. In 1895 the figure was over 50 per cent for all trades; in Berlin it was almost 60 per cent.[23] These were the shoemakers who sewed on the soles of factory shoes, the tailors who worked in the sweated out-trade, the masons who hired themselves out to the newly-risen contractor, the carpenters like the one in Heilbronn described by Theodor Heuss who made cupboards for a furniture store.[24] The successes emphasized by the optimists exacted a price. It was paid not only by the craftsmen who were squeezed out of production altogether, but by many of those who remained nominally independent.

De facto dependence of this kind had, of course, existed in the early nineteenth century and before, in tailoring and furniture-making for example. But its extent increased as the relative importance and autonomy of craft production within the capitalist economy as a whole diminished. In 1800 small commodity production still employed ten times as much of the labour force as industry and mining together.[25] In 1875 almost two-thirds of all those engaged in manufacturing production were employed in concerns with fewer than five employees. By 1907 this figure stood at one-third.[26] Figures for craft production specifically suggest a slightly lower figure still. Evidence on small workshops' share of the total capital stock tell broadly the same story, although one study suggests a stabilization around the 10 per cent mark after the middle of the 1890s.[27] Overall, craftsmen were *relatively* dwarfed by larger concerns, and increasingly so. They were correspondingly locked into processes of production and distribution over which their own control was slight. This was not only true of the pauperized tailors and shoemakers, who constituted a genuine reserve army of labour which could be employed or laid off as cycle or season dictated. Other craftsmen were effectively built into larger concerns: coopers tied to large breweries, painters to shipbuilders, smiths and wheelwrights to coach-builders.[28] Sometimes these independent workshops were directly integrated into a larger production process, although Reich statistics (which measured technical units, not plant or geographical units) would give no indication of this.[29] Similarly, artisans who turned to repairs, and those *Kunsthandwerker* who specialized in the limited production of high-quality goods, testified in their different ways to the fact that petty commodity production had, by the end of the nineteenth century, become a marginal activity.

The position of shopkeepers was different in some respects. In the early decades of the century they were, simply, an inconsiderable group by comparison with craftsmen. There were only 33 small retailers to every 10,000 inhabitants of the old Prussian provinces in 1837 (there were perhaps ten times as many craftsmen).[30] The density was naturally higher in the market towns and cities, but the overall numbers remained low, except in major trading cities like Hamburg and Cologne. Non-subsistence consumer needs, still very limited, were largely met by pedlars or by markets and fairs. For items of regular use, direct trade between artisan and customer was the norm. In fact, as the roles of craftsman and shopkeeper started to become distinct, a conflict of interest emerged. In the great mid-century debates over 'freedom of trade', shopkeepers often sided with liberal reformers, hoping to benefit from the final demise of the guilds.[31] Sources of friction remained after that time. At the end of the century, bakers complained that milk sellers, greengrocers and even schnapps sellers were encroaching on their preserves;[32] while conflicts arose when craftsmen competed with shopkeepers in the repairs sector.

Above all, industrialization provided an overall stimulus to the expansion of small retail outlets which outweighed its effects on craftsmen. As a contemporary noted, the factory was 'the ally of the retail trade'.[33] At the same time, declining self-sufficiency, urbanization, new forms of transportation and increased purchasing power reinforced the growing retail market. The number of shopkeeping outlets per head of population grew at an accelerating rate. Between the 1860s and the 1890s the ratio of customers to retailers halved. Between 1895 and 1907 the number of shops increased again by 42 per cent while the population rose by less than 8 per cent. By 1907 there were almost 800,000 retail outlets employing fewer than five people.[34] Shopkeepers have nevertheless been seen as the victims – like craftsmen, but at a later date – of large-scale competition. On the one hand they faced the rise of chain and department stores. The latter were slower to develop than in France, but by the 1890s they were 'springing up like mushrooms'[35] and by the next decade numbered over 200 in Germany. There was also competition from mail-order outlets, which made wide use of advertising in the expanding local and popular press. The extension of railway branch lines not only speeded the movement of goods from large firms into the countryside and small towns; it also brought automatic vending machines, sited on station platforms. On the other side stood the competition of the working-class consumer co-operatives. These also developed more slowly than in other countries, notably Britain. But by the First World War they could point to a membership of 2 million and an annual turnover of 750 million marks.[36] Finally, shopkeepers continued to compete with the activities of hawkers and pedlars, even if their importance was gradually eclipsed by the growing army of travelling salesmen – the 'itinerants in patent-leather shoes'[37] as one critic called them.

The impact of department stores, chain stores and co-operatives in the large towns, and of mail-order business in the countryside, was considerable for some retail branches. But they accounted for only a small percentage of total retail turnover before 1914. The central problems of small shopkeepers were rather different. In small-scale distribution, as in petty commodity production, the statistical appearance of large numbers of independents disguised enormous discrepancies of wealth, income and security. A minority of concerns in central city areas and the wealthier suburbs, like solidly established businesses in the market towns, enjoyed a material standard which bordered on the bourgeois. Those with high-priced stock like jewellers clearly fell into this category, as did shops selling many kinds of factory-made goods like leatherware and furniture. Drapery businesses were also commonly located towards the upper end of small retailing. Haberdashers, ironmongers and colonial goods traders tended to occupy a middling position.[38] There was undoubtedly a good deal of movement within and between branches as shopkeepers sought to better themselves. The overall expansion of the market allowed considerable scope for those like the ambitious grocer described by Karl Scheffler, who expanded an old family concern, rented out the floors above the shop to raise capital, undercut, advertised and installed plate-glass windows, until he had turned his corner shop into a substantial store.[39]

The majority of shops, however, fell into a different category. Even in the first half of the century insecure, under-capitalized small concerns had existed in branches like second-hand clothes, perishables and 'mixed goods', merging into stallholding and itinerant selling.[40] Greengroceries, mixed goods and – later – tobacco remained the commercially precarious branches. They were the overcrowded, semi-proletarian equivalents of the impoverished tailor or shoemaker. Overall, more than half of all retail outlets were one-man concerns at the end of the century. In many cases they were actually one-woman concerns, run by a widow or by the wife of a craftsman or factory worker as an extra source of income. In Bremen a third of all shops were part-time in 1907, a proportion which had risen steeply from the previous decade. A third were run by women. Other full-time but single-handed concerns were run by craftsmen squeezed out of production into distribution, by black-listed or unemployed factory workers, even by former miners, denied advancement within the manual hierarchy, who sank their savings into a business which relied on the custom of former colleagues.[41] Small publicans often shared a similar background. Declining levels of commercial expertise, along with low incomes and high rates of bankruptcy and business turnover, testify to the insecure and insubstantial character of such concerns. In Bremen a third of all retailing concerns listed in trade directories did not survive longer than six years.[42]

All shopkeepers, moreover, shared problems which threatened to compromise their notional independence. Shortage of capital was perhaps the key. Overheads like insurance rose through the century, even for those who owned their own premises and were free from rising rents. The need to extend credit to customers, universal in poorer areas, compounded the problem; so did the slower turnover of stock compared with large concerns. Banks geared to the *Mittelstand* certainly increased their activity in the last decades of the century, but against that shopkeepers' purchasing co-operatives signally failed to alleviate credit problems. In the grocery branch, where co-operatives of this sort made particularly good sense, only three had been set up in Bavaria by 1906. No more than one in twenty shopkeepers belonged to a co-operative organization, compared with perhaps one in four peasants involved at least in a credit co-operative.[43] The reasons for this failure, like the comparable failure of craftsmen, lay in individualism and trade jealousy, but also in the great internal differentiation within shopkeeping. Even the relatively homogeneous retail chemists were described by their historian as 'in so many ways and so frequently disunited'.[44] A common result was dependence on wholesalers and deliverers for credit, a relationship which could effectively turn the independent small shopkeeper into an agent of large-scale commercial capital. By the beginning of the twentieth century it was not so much the competition of department store and consumer co-operative which threatened German shopkeepers, but the tendencies towards incorporation by capital on the one hand, and towards proletarianization on the other. In that respect the problems of shopkeepers and craftsmen converged as the pace of capitalist development quickened.

In its social relations, as in its economic location, the petite bourgeoisie was a hybrid. Craftsmen and shopkeepers had the use of their own labour in common with the working class; they had the ownership of their own means of production, however meagre, in common with the bourgeoisie. They also shared some of the values of each. The petite bourgeoisie as a whole therefore occupied a no-man's-land between the class lines.[45] This awkward location is open to different interpretations. Many petits bourgeois undoubtedly singled out this 'neither/nor' status as a special virtue. Guild masters had seen themselves neither as *fainéant* patricians, nor as feckless paupers. Within the moral economy of the guild world they claimed to stand for a *juste milieu*: owners of small property (neither too much, nor none at all); honourably independent (neither dominating, nor dominated); exemplars of 'fair' competition (neither exploiting, nor exploited). The idea of a fair clientele for every master (the *Nahrungsprinzip*) embodied these claims. The intensely moral and wide-ranging values of the guild system left a powerful imprint on many craftsmen, which survived the demise of the guilds.[46] Indeed elements of a similar outlook were taken over by shopkeepers in the nineteenth century, with their condemnation of 'unfair' competition.

This is a reminder that such a view of the world was not just a 'traditional' survival; it continued to be generated by economic developments. These confirmed the propensity of some petits bourgeois to define themselves against those both above and below, stressing the unique value of their own contribution to a society which was being torn in two directions. It was precisely this which was seized upon by the conservative apostles of the *Mittelstand*, who cast the petite bourgeoisie as a buffer against the polarization of society. But it is in the nature of buffers to absorb shock, and it is worth exploring the price which members of the petite bourgeoisie paid for acting in this capacity. When the problem is posed in this way it is also easier to take into account the divided nature of the class. For we have seen how the material basis of many craftsmen and shopkeepers undermined the conservative rhetoric of 'independence'. Not only were craftsmen and shopkeepers stretched out socially between bourgeoisie and working class. Many, as a result of economic cycle or changing family circumstances, moved in a single lifetime between the fronts. This complex pattern will be explored in the present section.

Occupational and social mobility offer one means of addressing the issue. The upward gaze of craftsmen and shopkeepers has often been commented on: the petite bourgeoisie has been seen as a ladder opening up access to the bourgeois world proper.[47] How far is this true in the German case? The opportunities for artisan masters or shopkeepers to turn their businesses into large-scale concerns were decidedly limited, especially after the middle of the century. Yet Germany's relatively well-developed educational system provided potential opportunities at least for inter-generational upward mobility. From the early nineteenth century onwards we can note the aspirations of craftsmen to send at least one son to the classical Gymnasium, of the shopkeeper's desire that his son be trained to enter commerce or the professions.[48] The available work on social mobility provides no clear answers on the plausibility of these aspirations. Lack of capital to sustain secondary and – even more – higher education was an obvious barrier. Reinforcing this was the rudimentary educational level of most petit-bourgeois parents, together with the normal absence of books, maps, educational picture-books from the home, or the visit to cultural events, which had become a feature of the upbringing of bourgeois children.[49] These questions have been explored by a recent study of Schleswig-Holstein, which suggests that the self-recruiting of a narrow educated bourgeois élite set in as early as the 1840s.[50] But there is other evidence of the same period, from Cologne and Minden for example, which suggests greater use of a Gymnasium education by petit-bourgeois children. Certainly children from this background seem to have made considerable use of non-classical secondary schools (*Realgymnasien, Realschulen, Oberrealschulen*).[51] As far as post-secondary education is concerned, indications from the first half of the nineteenth century hardly suggest an invasion of petit-bourgeois progeny – but this, of course, was a period when the bourgeoisie itself was still carving out a social place. Only one master artisan's son and one shopkeeper's son were counted among the 110 students from Cologne at Heidelberg between 1840 and 1860.[52] Figures from Berlin University from the 1830s to the 1870s also suggest a growth in the share of students from commercial and landowning backgrounds at the expense of the petite bourgeoisie. Only at the end of our period, in the decades before the First World War, does there seem to have been a significant increase in the number of students from petit-bourgeois families.[53]

Further detailed studies will be necessary before these statistics can be reliably interpreted. What the evidence does suggest is that upward mobility out of the petite bourgeoisie commonly proceeded crab-wise, by means of sideways movement of children into the new lower middle class. Craftsmens' and shopkeepers' sons entered the rapidly expanding ranks of the lesser public and private bureaucracies. They became petty officials in transport utilities, welfare institutions, schools and libraries and various policing agencies; or they took one of a wide range of posts spawned by an increasingly organized capitalism.[54] Daughters also found jobs of this kind, with some expectation of marrying into the world of clean collar and cuffs, regular salary and pension.[55] Mobility of this kind, however, was double-edged.

'Placing' one's children might also entail a recognition that the petit-bourgeois milieu itself offered fewer opportunities for independence and respectability. By the end of the century it was commonplace for craft chambers to report on the reluctance of male children to apprentice themselves to a master.[56] An example brings home the emotional charge that this could carry. Walter Hofmann rejected pressure to follow his father's engraving trade, entering the lower reaches of public bureaucracy instead: he would not stay within the 'narrowness, darkness and Cinderella social life' of the craftsman.[57] The father, for his part, was eventually reconciled to a similar move in the case of his daughter:

> He decided on a step which even half a decade before would have been regarded as monstrous in the old artisan and *Mittelstand* circles: he sent his daughter to a language and commercial course, to prepare her for an office career! Just a few years on and the father, once so ardently bent on handing over his 'fine little business' to his son, would see occupational salvation for his children and grandchildren in an official's post – not because it was 'the best', but because it was the 'most secure'.[58]

For all the contrived autobiographical pathos, the account illuminates the mood of resignation in petit-bourgeois circles in the second half of the nineteenth century. The reports of official and semi-official bodies confirm a sense of declining social status and narrowing horizons. The scope for children to rise in society was not inconsistent with a feeling among craftsmen (an ageing group) and shopkeepers themselves that they were becoming more marginal members of society.

One recent work actually talks of a 'de-classed class'.[59] Certainly there is some support for this. Take for example the changing meaning of the term *Mittelstand*. Up to 1850 it had still frequently referred to the embryonic bourgeoisie as well as the petite bourgeoisie: both could consider themselves the healthy and productive middle of society.[60] Needless to say, there were always very significant income differentials separating even the house-owning and wealthy master dyer, goldsmith or butcher from the average merchant or manufacturer; and these differences were growing in the years before mid-century.[61] The more self-conscious bourgeois were very aware of this. The steamship and insurance magnate Peter Merkens was disdainful that voters to the Cologne Chamber of Commerce should include craftsmen, fruit sellers and small restaurateurs. He complained to the Prussian authorities that under French occupation the membership of the chamber had been determined only by 'the most *excellent* merchants and wholesalers'.[62] But there were few like Merkens in the early nineteenth-century bourgeoisie; and in a town like Bochum, substantial craftsmen and shopkeepers still enjoyed a prominent social position well into the 1850s.[63] The broader meaning of the word *Mittelstand* until that time implied the potential social closeness of at least the better-off petite bourgeoisie to merchants and factory owners. The localist cast of mind in much of the bourgeoisie itself reinforced this, by giving both groups 'outside' enemies in common.

After mid-century, however, *Mittelstand* came significantly to be applied only to the petite bourgeoisie. As the economic and professional bourgeoisie drew socially closer to landowners and officials, so on the other side the line between greater and lesser bourgeoisie became sharper. One measure of this divide was the declining number of *Mittelstand* families which employed a domestic servant, at a time when this was standard in bourgeois households.[64] There are also signs that the petite bourgeoisie began to play a less active role in voluntary associations. It is certainly revealing to find a staunchly status-conscious master book-binder, on giving up honorary posts in the Giessen veterans' association, fire brigade, historical association and trade association, arguing that these 'cost money and bring nothing in'.[65] Active membership in bodies of this kind had customarily been a hallmark of petit-bourgeois civic pride. Butchers illustrate this marginalized social position. Theirs was and remained one of the richest trades; they were, along with bakers, notably effective in sustaining co-operative self-help organizations;[66] and they also seem to have been more than averagely successful dynasts. In the 1840s the 'sausage brigade' was a recognizable element in the 'brigade' of Cologne property speculators;[67] in Mainz the 'silver sausages' had been equally prominent socially, jealously guarding their reputation for dispensing money freely during carnival.[68] Yet even butchers appear to have sensed a decline in social worth in the course of the century, perhaps connected with them ceasing, on the one hand, to buy their meat direct from the peasant, and their surrender on the other hand of self-regulatory slaughtering powers to public authorities.[69]

This picture should not be overdrawn. Wealthier craftsmen and shopkeepers did retain a place in municipal affairs. And in villages and small towns they would often enjoy considerable social prestige, acting as a kind of surrogate bourgeoisie and taking key roles in local religious, philanthropic, recreational and political life.[70] Some of the many expressions of resentment emanating from the petite bourgeoisie were perhaps examples of what the liberal politician Eugen Richter called 'Klagen ohne Leiden' – social hypochondria. But the resentment was often well-founded, and the expression of it was significant in itself. It also reveals the contours of a petit-bourgeois hostility towards the bourgeoisie. This rather defensive set of sentiments stressed local rootedness against bourgeois 'outsiders', with their growing regional, national and even international links; it juxtaposed petit-bourgeois frugality with bourgeois conspicuous consumption on servants, villas and philanthropy; and it contrasted the solid virtues of the petite bourgeoisie with the speculative propensities of the capitalist and the over-educated nonsense of the professional.[71] Extravagant construction schemes and artistic licence were likely to arouse particular fury, for the petite bourgeoisie shared the early moralism of the bourgeoisie with little of the latter's insouciance.

No doubt many of these attitudes betrayed thwarted aspirations; but they were no less real. As a result, when craftsmen or shopkeepers did bridge the gap with this more expansive bourgeois world, directly or through their children, they necessarily had to deny some of their own values. Joining the 'movers and doers', as Mack Walker has called them,[72] meant deserting the ideal of rootedness. Engaging in financial speculation – as the petite bourgeoisie very conspicuously did in 1846–7 and 1873[73] – contravened the dictates of prudence and rectitude. Seeking credit or social advancement from a bourgeois patron meant repudiating one's own sturdy independence. Sending a son into pharmacy or librarianship entailed questioning the worth of one's own 'fine little business'. In these circumstances the finely struck balance of envy and resentment not only separated some petits bourgeois from others; it could co-exist within one individual. It is evidence of this kind which has led some to talk of the self-hate of the petite bourgeoisie.

This contradictory and burdensome pattern of attraction and repulsion also manifested itself in petit-bourgeois relations downwards, with the working class. Here it has usually been the line of division between the classes which has attracted attention. There are good reasons for this, for the second half of the nineteenth century saw an increase in areas of potential conflict. There was, first, a sharpening of class relations at the place of work. These had never taken the idyllic form sometimes claimed. Yet the period from the 1840s to the 1870s was characterized by important changes. In the craft workshop the decline of the living-in system for apprentices and (especially) journeymen, the advent of larger concerns and the development of journeymen's organizations into trade unions signalled a 'break between masters and men'.[74] Trade unions were often notably strong in craft-based trades, partly because smaller masters were particularly vulnerable to disputes. The formation of masters' counter-organizations only underlines the sharpening of class conflict in the workshop.[75] In retailing there was also a growth of employees' organizations, and the setting up of courts of arbitration to deal with disputes over hours, wages and conditions testified to growing awareness of distinct class roles in the shop.[76]

Craftsmen and shopkeepers complained that patriarchal authority had been eroded. There was similar opposition to government technical education and work-release schemes which were alleged to rob the small employer of crucial labour.[77] Measures of this kind were also seen, like social insurance and welfare provision, as an unwarranted addition to the small man's overheads and a subsidy to the undeserving. Such reactions continued, in a re-worked idiom, the arguments of 1848, when the petite bourgeoisie attacked public relief for pauperized workers. As one petition had put it: 'The humanity shown to the workers exceeds common sense, only the artisan, the productive *Mittelstand*, has been deserted.'[78] In 1848 these expressions of petit-bourgeois rancour were accompanied by fears of the mob and the dangerous classes; by the 1890s they were associated with fears about the tyranny of the trade unions and consumer co-operatives. In rapidly growing areas like the Ruhr, where the petite bourgeoisie already resented the municipal tax burden which financed new roads and schools, this antagonism could be bitter. It was shown in the pressure shopkeepers brought to bear on customers who used the co-operatives, on householders who rented them shop-space and on newspapers which accepted their advertisements.[79] Here the class line between petite bourgeoisie and working class was clear enough.

But this is not the whole story. In the first place, the material circumstances of substantial numbers of the petite bourgeoisie raises the question of how representative these sentiments were. How widespread were complaints about taxes among the 91 per cent of master craftsmen in Bochum who were not assessed for the business tax in 1884?[80] What relevance did worsening relations between masters and men have for the majority of artisans and shopkeepers who worked alone, or with family labour? How does it modify our view of *Mittelstand* hostility to consumer co-operatives when we learn that the Lübeck co-operative drew 21 per cent of its members from this group at the turn of the century, the Breslau co-operative 27 per cent?[81] There were many areas of life which the petite bourgeoisie, and not only the most indigent, shared with workers. The use of their own labour is an obvious example: master craftsmen often worked longer hours than factory workers, while shopkeepers frequently worked as long as or longer than their assistants, commonly over twelve hours a day, sometimes more than fifteen.[82] Here, as in the working class, a sudden change in family circumstances could have a major impact on the margin of subsistence. There were also many social links between the classes – occupational mobility upwards and downwards, as well as intermarriage.[83] This is not surprising when we consider the degree of residential proximity (except in the mushrooming industrial conurbations), and the fact that so many smaller tradesmen and tradeswomen sold from the front of their homes or from stalls. Their children, serving proletarian customers, running errands and playing with workers' children, were likely to grow up more familiar with working-class street life than with a more genteel domestic regime based on a bourgeois model.[84] The sizeable number of shopkeepers who rented out rooms to workers,[85] and those who extended credit during strikes,[86] also demonstrate the closeness of part, at least, of the petite bourgeoisie to the working class. The relationship of shopkeeper to working-class customer or tenant might have been one of social superiority; but (like that of rural craftsman or shopkeeper to the peasant) it was also one on which his livelihood depended.

None of these social ties between petite bourgeoisie and working class imply a necessarily close and positive relationship. The gap between objective class position and perceived class consciousness is a commonplace in writing on the petite bourgeoisie. It is likely that fears of proletarianization led many craftsmen and shopkeepers to exaggerate the remaining 'small differences' – home-owning, the absence of unemployment (although not under-employment), or outward badges of respectability. The presence of a tenant who was a skilled worker earning more than his landlord for shorter hours would not automatically prompt a sense of kinship. Nor, perhaps, would the mutual dependence of landlord–tenant relations generally. And those tradesmen who lifted themselves out of street selling might be correspondingly keen to deny the world they had left behind. It may even be possible to hypothesize about the origins, at this end of the petit-bourgeois spectrum, of a further form of self-hate induced by proximity to, but resentment of, the working class – a mirror-image of feelings towards the bourgeoisie.

It is necessary to exercise great caution, however, in making such judgements, for it is very difficult to penetrate such structures of feeling. Statistical evidence on occupational and family mobility does not disclose intentions and reactions. What seems clear is the range of divisions within the petite bourgeoisie, and even the divided self of the individual craftsman or shopkeeper. The double-edged and ambiguous social relations of the class were a product of its role as a buffer. Just as, in economic terms, it functioned partly as a reserve army of labour within the capitalist system, so its social existence took some of the edge off the class divisions of a burgeoning bourgeois society. It took urban workers and rural refugees into its ranks, while offering some of its members the prospect of direct or vicarious advancement into the bourgeoisie. As a transitional zone, its members' values were made up of contradictory elements. And as the petite bourgeoisie shaded off into the classes above and below, so the mix of these elements produced differing compounds which nevertheless retained traces of the common elements.

Craftsmen and shopkeepers often paid a heavy price for membership of this contradictory class. The family was a particular arena of conflict. Self-exploitation of family labour was the basis of all concerns which employed no outside help and of many which did. This raised problems, too, when the requirements of the family business conflicted with social aspirations for the children. It was also through the family that respectability was expressed – without servants, and on a tight budget.[87] Finally, the values of fairness, thrift and self-reliance were sufficiently at odds with prevailing conditions of production and distribution that they probably account for some of that commonly noted 'overcompensation' in the domestic sphere, which took the form of moral rigidity and patriarchal authoritarianism.[88]

It is, of course, a commonplace that the petite bourgeoisie looked inwards, to the private sphere, rather than outwards towards public and political life. As we shall see, this is not quite accurate. It might be more helpful to suggest that the habitual petit-bourgeois view of public affairs was one of private affairs writ large – a moralistic approach, in which the state was pictured as a stern but fair paterfamilias. This raises a broader question: to what extent was the *Mittelstand* movement, the political mouthpiece of the German petite bourgeoisie, a pawn in the hands of the ruling élite? It is to this question I want to turn now, and to the related issue of how representative the *Mittelstand* movement was of the petite bourgeoisie as a whole.

The evidence of craftsman and shopkeeper conservatism seems impressive. In 1848, it is true, they played an important part in the revolution, forming a link between the parliamentary notables and the popular revolt. This role, above all locally, is beyond dispute.[89] Yet even here the 'restorationist' demands of craftsmen in particular have often been emphasized. Petitions to the Frankfurt parliament and debates in the parallel craft congress displayed a massive nostalgia, coupled with arguments that craftsmen formed a peculiarly state-preserving stratum.[90] Similar claims were made by artisan spokesmen during the debates over freedom of trade in mid-century, and with notable sharpness in the Great Depression which followed.

In the last quarter of the century this case was increasingly put by autonomous petit-bourgeois organizations. To some extent at least, the petite bourgeoisie became a class 'for itself' as well as 'in itself'. The social marginalization of the class had, as a political corollary, a retreat above all from bourgeois liberalism, tainted by harmfully *laissez-faire* policies.[91] Craftsmen from the 1870s and shopkeepers from the 1890s created their own special-interest organizations and defence leagues, separate from the old trade associations. Some of these organizations were trade- or craft-specific; others were more general, and local, regional or even national in scope. Characteristic of their message was the argument of the *Westfälischer Handwerkerfreund* that 'a strong broad middle stratum is indispensable for the social structure'.[92] Retailers' organizations made similar points. One petition to the Prussian government claimed that the state had a duty to protect the 'loyal classes', while the founding conference of a national organization of defence leagues argued that preserving shopkeepers would 'protect the fatherland' from 'revolutionaries'.[93] These were the stock claims of the *Mittelstand* umbrella movement. Accompanying these arguments were familiar calls for protection: for tax reforms to favour the small man, changes in the tender system to help the artisanal producer, department store taxes.[94] The demands were often highly detailed. One south German government was asked to alter the beer tax in favour of small brewers, not to sell land on which it was rumoured a department store was to be built, and to remove vending machines from station platforms because they constituted unfair competition.[95] At the same time craftsmen called for the reintroduction of a guild system which would return control over apprentices to those with a formal master's qualification.

These aspirations were undoubtedly taken up and flattered by the parties of the right and centre-right. In the 1890s the Conservatives explicitly referred in their revised Tivoli programme to the 'state-preserving' qualities of the *Mittelstand*. Similar policies and sentiments were prominent in the Agrarian League, the Conservatives' mass organization, while the policies of the National Liberal and Centre parties underwent a comparable change of emphasis in the crucial decade of the 1890s.[96] At a time when the newly-legalized SPD was making electoral headway, and the last downturn of the recession had caused exceptionally bitter industrial disputes, the parties of the right were receptive to arguments about the loyalty of the petite bourgeoisie. The government also showed its interest. Measures to support small producers and retailers were part of a broader governmental retreat from the economically liberal policies of the 1860s and 70s. Voluntary guilds were established as legal corporations in 1881 and their powers extended by subsequent amendments. Reich legislation of 1897 then allowed for the setting up of compulsory guilds, while establishing craft chambers as semi-public bodies. In 1908 masters were given tighter control over the supervision of apprentices.[97] Boetticher expressed the official mind when he hoped that 'the handicraft estate will continue to be, as it has been until now, a protection for the crown and fatherland'.[98] Legislation was also enacted at various levels to meet shopkeepers' complaints. The Hesse government justified extra taxation of consumer co-operatives on the grounds of 'the present difficult situation of small shopkeepers and the interest of the state in preserving the greatest possible number of independent *Mittelstand* existences'.[99]

All of this suggests that there was – as historians have argued – a trade-off between state and petite bourgeoisie in this period, whereby each pledged itself to support the other. The broader illiberal context of government policy underlines the point; and it is reinforced by the statements of *Mittelstand* organizations on morality, the family, religion and (above all) the threat of Social Democracy. Here, apparently, was a class intoxicated with 'statolatry' and wedded to the conservative order.[100]

Even if we take the *Mittelstand* organizations as representative, however, ambiguities appear when we look at the nature of their arguments. These were intensely moralistic and their central concept was fairness ('*unfair* competition'). Hence the appeal to the state to intervene and restore (as it was imagined) conditions in which public life would resemble an idealized version of private family life. But this same moralism and attachment to fairness provided a basis for questioning established authority. At the very least the outward conduct of the state and its patterns of public spending and display were judged in these terms. That is what links the petit-bourgeois attacks on civil lists and the tyranny of officials in 1848, with similar condemnations of public authority in later years – the attacks on postal services which favoured big business, on state slaughterhouses where 'young gentlemen' wasted the time of the honest butcher.[101] The social conservatism within the petite bourgeoisie was coupled with a resentful and vengeful political radicalism whose precise form was unpredictable. Hostility was likely to come to a head over issues where 'scandal' was involved;[102] but a sense of grievance towards the arrogant or olympian official was ubiquitous.

Resentment of this kind was not mere paranoia. Craftsmen and retailers were right to sense that, for all the lip-service paid to preserving the *Mittelstand*, this was actually a more marginal concern of governments at the end of the century than it had been at the beginning. The shrill representations of petit-bourgeois organizations were often received with a sense of weariness,[103] and there was certainly less to the imposing edifice of *Mittelstandspolitik* than meets the eye. Taxes on department stores, for example, were largely ineffectual.[104] Even right-wing politicians admitted their scepticism privately.[105] Measures against consumer co-operatives also had a much smaller effect than shopkeepers hoped for, and the same was true of changes in the tender system supposedly beneficial to craftsmen. The Prussian War Minister argued that they produced poor-quality work and missed their delivery dates. Tenders were often invited in publications which no craftsman read.[106] Above all, the new guilds of 1897 lacked muscle, and even the legislation of 1908 fell short of establishing the masters' desired control over apprentices.[107] As disgruntled craft spokesmen pointed out, the fact that the Reich government did not include a category of 'Handwerk' in its occupational censuses was in itself indicative. In fact the needs of Germany's increasingly sophisticated economy, coupled with the state's own labour and revenue requirements, gave governments as great an interest in pruning the petite bourgeoisie as in preserving it. Much of *Mittelstandspolitik* remained cosmetic.

Only within certain limits was the state prepared to 'preserve the *Mittelstand*'. Perhaps we should therefore question the tidy symmetry whereby the *Mittelstand* was prepared to preserve the state. It would certainly be misleading to think in terms of an automatic petit-bourgeois deference to established authority. Their organizations were angry and frustrated at the end of our period: they felt their worth went unrecognized, and their functionaries were suspicious of being patronized by authority. Petitions betrayed alternate wariness and truculence.[108] There were even expressions of anti-militarism and doubts expressed about imperialism, which was thought to be a distraction of money and energy from domestic concerns.[109] It is true that the height of the direct action they took was probably the setting free of mice in 'Jewish' department stores.[110] Shopkeepers were generally unwilling even to use the boycott weapon because of its associations with the SPD.[111] Yet the rhetoric and style of the petit-bourgeois organizations were not conventionally conservative and deferential. In some ways they were less legalistic than the SPD, and it is worth noting how demagogic *Mittelstand* leaders brandished their libel actions and brushes with authority as badges of honour. We are reminded of the German peasant and anti-semitic organizations of the same period, and also of the affinities with the earlier revolutionary volatility of the petite bourgeoisie itself. These groups were not, as one historian has it, simply 'waiting to be organised'.[112]

Similar points apply to relations with the right-wing parties. This was partly a matter of hard policies. Some of the measures demanded by large industrialists on different parts of the right, or by large agrarians in the Conservative Party, were clearly inimical to the interests even of the more substantial petite bourgeoisie.[113] Tariffs provide an example.[114] The most obvious breach of this kind came in 1909 when a section of the *Mittelstand* movement deserted the right over financial reform and sided with the liberal Hansabund.[115] But there was perennial *Mittelstand* suspicion that it was the pawn of the right. This was, indeed, a major cause of disunity and splintering within the movement. The re-grouping of many of these organizations in 1911 under the aegis of the Conservatives, and their entry into the Cartel of Productive Estates, by no means signalled the unproblematic co-optation of the *Mittelstand* by the old right.[116] Policy differences and petit-bourgeois suspicion remained; and political appetites fed on the eating. The right had become adept at addressing petit-bourgeois grievances, but they had not invented them, nor could they completely control them.[117]

The prickliness of *Mittelstand* organizations needs to be stressed. It is nevertheless true that the very moralism of their politics implied that a fair solution to their grievances could ultimately be found within the existing order. Hence their identification of real enemies on the left and symbolic enemies on the right like 'mobile' or 'Jewish' capital. Similarly, attacks on particular laws were not attacks on lawful authority as such, nor attacks on particular officials attacks on official authority as such. Hostility to the government did not mean hostility to the idea of the state. The *Mittelstand* movement could often be *plus royaliste que le roi*, attacking authority in its own name for 'leniency'. This was clearly the case when it came to softness with the SPD, but also manifested itself over many moral and cultural issues.[118]

If this is true of the *Mittelstand* movement, the question remains: how representative was it of the petite bourgeoisie as a whole? We have seen that many craftsmen and shopkeepers eked out a living in ways which belied the idea of sturdy independence; they personified the process of proletarianization rather than forming a bulwark against it. And it is certainly true that official *Mittelstand* politics largely spoke for the more substantial petite bourgeoisie. The revived guild system was predictably supported by those masters for whom control over apprentices and journeymen still meant something. In 1887 all but one of the 156 members of the Hamburg bakers' guild employed non-family labour in their businesses. This pattern was general.[119] Among shopkeepers the picture was more confused. Some retailing organizations were dominated by substantial shopkeepers, like the Rhineland-Westphalia group centred on *Der Detaillist*, which also had major Bavarian supporters. Wealthy drapers were prominent here, while the *Bund der Kaufleute* was founded by the more secure owners of specialty shops.[120] The local defence leagues, on the other hand, had roots in the small shopkeeping world. But it was grocers, not the sellers of mixed and perishable goods, who were decisive.[121] It is significant that the Bremen discount savings union *Brema* specifically excluded small stallholders. And it is clear from the attention paid to department stores rather than, say, the problem of hawkers, that they viewed the question of unfair competition through the eyes of the substantial shopkeeper. The hostility of organizations like this to the granting of credit to customers betrays a similar provenance.[122] Corporate bodies set up under the aegis of the state similarly discriminated against marginal retailers through property qualifications which denied most shopkeepers the right to vote for their own corporate representatives.[123]

The lack of identity between formal *Mittelstand* movement and petite bourgeoisie makes it difficult to generalize about political attitudes. We should not be tempted, of course, to reduce political sentiments simply to the size and health of a concern. Marginal craftsmen and shopkeepers did not necessarily reject the views of the craft chamber or *Der Detaillist*. Struggling masters might have looked back to the mythical golden age, insecure retailers might have believed that Jewish department stores and socialist co-operatives were destroying their fragile independence. But it is more likely that their feelings, like their position, diverged from the *Mittelstand* model lauded by the right. Shopkeepers in working-class areas often lived within the subculture of the labour movement; so did many of the small publicans who played such an important part in the SPD.[124] This was still more true of craftsmen, who were prominent in the SPD from its earliest years.[125] Rapid changes in the capitalist economy did not dislodge all craftsmen from political liberalism; and it certainly did not dislodge them all to the right. The Kassel craft chamber noted how 'indifference and despondency' led to 'open support for the revolutionary movement'.[126] Governments and the political right argued, of course, that the small producer had to be saved from socialism. Given the failures of *Mittelstandspolitik*, however, it might be more useful to see the craftsman as a potential proletarian, not the proletarian as a prodigal craftsman. While producer co-operatives languished,[127] trade unions, consumer co-operatives and the SPD made headway among small masters in the clothing, footwear, construction and other trades.[128] The SPD could also offer an attractive political home for more established masters, even those within the ambience of the 'traditional' guilds. In 1912 the master joiners of Schramberg formed a voluntary guild and elected the local SPD parliamentary candidate as *Obermeister*.[129] Perhaps it is not surprising that many formally independent craftsmen should have looked to the labour movement, given its growth and élan when set against their own *de facto* dependence on capital and the uneven development of the *Mittelstand* movement. The number of small men who were members and leaders of the SPD[130] has often been seen as evidence for the embourgeoisement of the labour movement. It might also be regarded as evidence for the radicalization of the petite bourgeoisie.

There is a familiar picture of German craftsmen and shopkeepers as traditional groups, traumatized in the nineteenth century by modern industrialization. 'Pessimist' writers helped to establish this picture; more subtle brush-strokes have been added by historians concerned with the development of an anti-modernist outlook, and with the reactionary political potential of the petite bourgeoisie. The *Mittelstand* has become fixed in much writing as a dangerously backward entity, one of the reasons why German history went wrong. This is the inverted image of what contemporary conservatives said – or hoped. I have tried to show that it is misleading, at least in the way it is usually presented.

The real petite bourgeoisie, as distinct from that construct called the *Mittelstand*, was not a cohesive group threatened by industrialization. Some craftsmen and rather more shopkeepers benefited from an unfolding capitalism; some were victims; some had both experiences in turn. This element of fluidity is important. For material transformation continued to generate and to renew a hybrid class awkwardly situated between bourgeoisie and proletariat. The petite bourgeoisie had ambiguous material ties and social relations both upwards and downwards. These were manifested in patterns of social mobility, values and personal contacts as well as in the market place. Some craftsmen and shopkeepers were closer to the bourgeoisie, others to the working class. Many were torn between attraction and repulsion towards both. Class divisions ran through the petite bourgeoisie, and often through the individual petit-bourgeois family or individual. I have suggested that we might look here for the roots of that often-cited but seldom investigated self-hate of the class.

What, then, of politics? I have tried to show how that part of the petite bourgeoisie which was closest to the working class did not always, necessarily, turn its back on the labour movement. Indeed, if we are to take SPD reformism seriously, we must take account of the petit-bourgeois presence in the party. This is not a story which ended in 1914. Parts of the petite bourgeoisie continued to be attracted to the SPD, while struggling 'proletaroid' groups may even, in the crisis of the late 1920s, have turned in desperation to communism. It should perhaps be added that the left also harboured an ingrained (and not entirely unjustified) suspicion of the petite bourgeoisie, which certainly contributed to the Nazis' success in mopping up so many oscillating and distracted petit-bourgeois voters. This should remind us of the convulsiveness of petit-bourgeois politics. It remained the unstable 'swing group' it had been in 1848. Even if we look at the (unrepresentative) *Mittelstand* organizations, we can see how their politics were prickly and unpredictable. They did not automatically defer to authority and the right-wing parties. Their very moralism – which this essay has tried to examine – made them, at best, awkward partners for conservatism. This story did not end in 1914 either. Indeed, the demagogy by which the right sought to harness the petite bourgeoisie to its own purposes had dangerous long-term implications. It raised expectations rather than satisfying them, like the superficially imposing structure of *Mittelstandspolitik*. The effects of war, inflation, the Weimar 'system', and economic rationalization followed by crisis in the 1920s served only to heighten petit-bourgeois uncertainty and unpredictability. After 1928 the old parties of the right and centre-right felt the furious revenge of a class which they had for too long taken for granted. This helped temporarily to swell the regional and special interest parties. But petit-bourgeois rancour and moralism were largely subsumed in the end by the Nazis, appealing deftly to an awkward class which had rejected the old politics of the right, yet found no secure anchorage on the left.

NOTES

The following abbreviations have been used:

AfS	*Archiv für Sozialgeschichte*
GG	*Geschichte und Gesellschaft*
HStA	Hauptstaatsarchiv
HZ	*Historische Zeitschrift*
JMH	*Journal of Modern History*
JSH	*Journal of Social History*
MS	*Le Mouvement social*
SH	*Social History*

1 H.-G. Haupt, 'La petite bourgeoisie, une classe inconnue', *MS*, 108, 1979, 11–20.

2 On attempts to define the Mittelstand, see G. Schmoller, *Was verstehen wir unter dem Mittelstande?*, Göttingen, 1897, and J. Wernicke, *Kapitalismus und Mittelstandspolitik*, Jena, 1907, 320ff.

3 The National Liberal Schröder-Kassel, cited in H. A. Winkler, 'Der rückversicherte Mittelstand. Die Interessenverbände von Handwerk und Kleinhandel im deutschen Kaiserreich', in W. Rüegg and O. Neuloh (eds), *Zur soziologischen Theorie und Analyse des 19. Jahrhunderts*, Göttingen, 1971, 173.

4 See esp. H. Rosenberg, *Große Depression und Bismarckzeit*, Berlin, 1967; Winkler, 'Rückversicherte Mittelstand'; H. A. Winkler, *Pluralismus oder Protektionismus*, Wiesbaden, 1972; H.-U. Wehler, *Bismarck und der Imperialismus*, Cologne and Berlin, 1969, 473, 480–1; H.-U. Wehler, *Das deutsche Kaiserreich*, Göttingen, 1973, 102.

5 See the articles by Koselleck, Wolfram Fischer and Zorn, which summarize their own and others' work, in W. Conze (ed.), *Staat und Gesellschaft im deutschen Vormärz*, Stuttgart, 1970. Local studies: A. Popp, *Die Einführung der Gewerbefreiheit in Bayern*, Leipzig, 1928; U. Branding, *Die Einführung der Gewerbefreiheit in Bremen und ihre Folgen*, Bremen, 1951.

6 F.-W. Henning, 'Die Einführung der Gewerbefreiheit und ihre Auswirkungen auf das Handwerk in Deutschland', in W. Abel (ed.), *Handwerksgeschichte in neuer Sicht*, Göttingen, 1978, 147–77.

7 This position underlay most of the studies commissioned by the *Verein für Sozialpolitik* in the 1890s and published in its *Schriften* 62–70, Leipzig, 1895–7.

8 J. Bergmann, 'Das "Alte Handwerk" im Übergang. Zum Wandel von Struktur und Funktion des Handwerks im Berliner Wirtschaftsraum in vor- und frühindustrieller Zeit', in O. Büsch, *Untersuchungen zur Geschichte der Frühen Industrialisierung vornehmlich im Wirtschaftsraum Berlin-Brandenburg*, Berlin, 1971, 224–69.

9 K. H. Kaufhold, 'Umfang und Gliederung des deutschen Handwerks um 1800', in Abel, op. cit., 57–60. Kaufhold has calculated the average number of assistants per master throughout Germany as 0.54:1.

10 This is true of many of the essays in Abel, op. cit., and of K. Aßmann and G. Stavenhagen, *Handwerkereinkommen am Vorabend der industriellen Revolution*, Göttingen, 1969.

11 K.-H. Schmidt, 'Bestimmungsgründe und Formen des Unternehmenswachstums im Handwerk seit der Mitte des 19. Jahrhunderts', in Abel, op. cit., 241–84. Wilhelm Abel has stimulated much of this work, but Wolfram Fischer has also played an important role. See his collected articles in *Wirtschaft und Gesellschaft im Zeitalter der Industrialisierung*, Göttingen, 1972, esp. 285–357.

12 W. Fischer, 'Die Rolle des Kleingewerbes im wirtschaftlichen Wachstumsprozess in Deutschland 1850–1914', in F. Lütge (ed.), *Wirtschaftliche und soziale Probleme der Gewerblichen Entwicklung im 15.–16. und 19. Jahrhundert*, Stuttgart, 1968, 131–42 (reprinted in *Wirtschaft und Gesellschaft*, 338–48).

13 A. Noll, *Sozio-ökonomischer Strukturwandel in der zweiten Phase der Industrialisierung*, Göttingen, 1975.

14 Fischer, 'Die Rolle des Kleingewerbes', 132–3, 137–9.

15 For a differentiated discussion, see S. Volkov, *The Rise of Popular Antimodernism in Germany. The Urban Master Artisans, 1873–1896*, Princeton, 1978, 32–60.

16 There are some penetrating remarks about the problem of distribution rather than production in P. Ayçoberry, 'Probleme der Sozialschichtung in Köln im Zeitalter der Frühindustrialisierung', in W. Fischer (ed.), *Wirtschafts- und Sozialgeschichtliche Probleme der frühen Industrialisierung*, Berlin, 1968, esp. 519–24.

17 On the early part of the century: Kaufhold, op. cit., 41–3; D. Saalfeld, 'Handwerkseinkommen in Deutschland vom ausgehenden 18. bis zur Mitte des 19. Jahrhunderts', in Abel, op. cit., 81–2. On the later nineteenth century: Noll, op. cit., 68–9; Volkov, op. cit., 84–94.

18 Wernicke, op. cit., calculated from table, 138.

19 Fischer, 'Die Rolle des Kleingewerbes', 138.

20 See D. Blackbourn, 'The *Mittelstand* in German society and politics, 1871–1914', *SH*, 4, 1977, 417–18.

21 On 'proletaroid' masters: Ayçoberry, op. cit., 522–4. The concept was used in the important work of Theodor Geiger on the late Weimar Republic: *Die soziale Schichtung des deutschen Volkes*, Stuttgart, 1932.

22 For a concise and differentiated summary of the evidence on this: J. Kocka, *Unternehmer in der deutschen Industrialisierung*, Göttingen, 1975, 47–50.
23 Volkov, op. cit., 92.
24 T. Heuss, *Preludes to Life: Early Memoirs*, London, 1955, 87.
25 Kaufhold, op. cit., 37–40.
26 Fischer, 'Die Rolle des Kleingewerbes', 136.
27 Noll, op. cit., 118–20; K.-H. Schmidt, 'Die Rolle des Kleingewerbes in regionalen Wachstumsprozessen in der zweiten Hälfte des 19. Jahrhunderts', in I. Bog *et al.* (eds), *Wirtschaftliche und soziale Strukturen im säkularen Wandel: Festschrift für Wilhelm Abel*, Hanover, 1974, III, 720ff.
28 Schmidt, op. cit., 726, 738; Wernicke, op. cit., 143.
29 Fischer, 'Die Rolle des Kleingewerbes', 134.
30 R. Gellately, *The Politics of Economic Despair. Shopkeepers and German Politics 1890–1914*, London and Beverly Hills, 1974, 30.
31 Branding, op. cit., 31–2.
32 P. Arnold, *Das Münchener Bäckergewerbe*, Stuttgart, 1895, 50.
33 Wilhelm Roscher, cited in Gellately, op. cit., 13.
34 ibid., 29–33.
35 H. Crüger, *Vortrag über gewerbliches Genossenschaftswesen, Warenbazare und Grosswarenhäuser . . .*, Stuttgart, 1899, 13.
36 Gellately, op. cit., 37–50.
37 The Württemberg Centre deputy Karl Walter, cited in Blackbourn, op. cit., 424. On travelling salesmen (there were over 70,000 by the end of the century) see F. Weyer, *Der reisende Kaufmann*, Cologne, 1948.
38 H.-G. Haupt, 'Der Bremer Kleinhandel zwischen 1890 und 1914. Binnenstruktur, Einfluss und Politik', in W. U. Drechsel *et al.* (eds), *Geschäfte. Teil I: Der Bremer Kleinhandel um 1900*, Bremen, 1982, esp. 12–21. The articles by Achim Saur and Charlotte Niermann in the same volume also contain valuable material.
39 K. Scheffler, *Der junge Tobias. Eine Jugend und ihre Umwelt*, Leipzig, 1927, 112–13.
40 P. Ayçoberry, 'Der Strukturwandel im Kölner Mittelstand 1820–1850', *GG*, 1, 1975, 87–8.
41 Blackbourn, op. cit., 416, 421–2; contributions by Haupt, Saur, Niermann to Drechsel, op. cit.; Gellately, op. cit., 34–6; D. Crew, 'Definitions of modernity: social mobility in a German town, 1880–1901', *JSH*, VII, 1973, 56–7.
42 H.-G. Haupt, 'Kleinhändler und Arbeiter in Bremen zwischen 1890 und 1914', *AfS*, XXII, 1982, 108–10.
43 J. Wein, *Die Verbandsbildung im Einzelhandel*, Berlin, 1968, 62–3, 164; Gellately, op. cit., 64–5.
44 J. Thiessen, *Die deutschen Drogisten*, Berlin, 1929, 133.
45 See the introduction by H.-G. Haupt to Haupt (ed.), *'Bourgeois und Volk zugleich'? Zur Geschichte des Kleinbürgertums im 19. und 20. Jahrhundert*, Frankfurt/M, 1978, 9–32.
46 Bergmann, op. cit., 225–61; Mack Walker, *German Home Towns, Community, State, and General Estate 1648–1871*, Ithaca, 1971, esp. 73–107. R. Stadelmann and W. Fischer, *Die Bildungswelt des deutschen Handwerkers um 1800. Studien zur Soziologie des Kleinbürgers im Zeitalter Goethes*, Berlin, 1955. For a contemporary account of the guild system as a 'moral partition' against outside forces and sentiments, see W. Jung, *Der Gewerbsmann und die gewerblichen Verhältnisse Württembergs*, Ulm, 1845, 30.
47 See, for example, Arno J. Mayer, 'The lower middle class as historical problem', *JMH*, 1975, esp. 424, 432.
48 Ayçoberry, 'Probleme der Sozialschichtung', 524–7.
49 Stadelmann and Fischer, op. cit.; J. Schlumbohm, '"Traditional" collectivity and

"modern" individuality: some questions and suggestions for the historical study of socialisation. The example of the German lower and upper bourgeoisies around 1800', *SH*, 5, 1980, 71–103. On the low levels of formal education among masters in the nineteenth century, Volkov, op. cit., 25.

50 R. S. Elkar, *Junges Deutschland in polemischem Zeitalter. Das schleswig-holsteinische Bildungsbürgertum in der ersten Hälfte des 19. Jahrhunderts*, Düsseldorf, 1979, esp. 81–151.

51 J. Kocka, *Die Angestellten in der deutschen Geschichte 1850–1980*, Göttingen, 1981, 108, and the further literature cited in note 30.

52 Ayçoberry, 'Probleme der Sozialschichtung', 523.

53 C. E. McClelland, *State, Society, and University in Germany 1700–1914*, Cambridge, 1980, 199, 244.

54 R. Engelsing, *Sozial- und Wirtschaftsgeschichte Deutschlands*, Göttingen, 1976, 146. Further details in the same author's *Zur Sozialgeschichte deutscher Mittel- und Unterschichten*, Göttingen, 1973, and in Kocka, *Die Angestellten*, chs 1–4.

55 U. Nienhaus, 'Von Töchtern und Schwestern. Zur vergessenen Geschichte der weiblichen Angestellten im deutschen Kaiserreich', in J. Kocka (ed.), *Angestellte im europäischen Vergleich*, Göttingen, 1981, 309–33. See also Blackbourn, op. cit., 423–4; and Haupt, 'Kleinhändler und Arbeiter', 118–19.

56 See the report of the Frankfurt/Oder Craft Chamber for 1900–4, cited Wernicke, op. cit., 175–84.

57 W. Hofmann, *Mit Grabstichel und Feder. Geschichte einer Jugend*, Stuttgart and Tübingen, 1948, 206.

58 ibid., 400.

59 A. Leppert-Fögen, *Die deklassierte Klasse. Studien zur Geschichte und Ideologie des Kleinbürgertums*, Frankfurt/M, 1974.

60 On the evolution of the term's meaning, H. A. Winkler, *Mittelstand, Demokratie und Nationalsozialismus*, Cologne, 1972, ch. 1.

61 Aßmann and Stavenhagen, op. cit., 4–72.

62 J. M. Diefendorf, *Businessmen and Politics in the Rhineland, 1789–1834*, Princeton, 1980, 299.

63 D. Crew, *Town in the Ruhr. A Social History of Bochum 1860–1914*, New York, 1979, 112ff.

64 Engelsing, *Zur Sozialgeschichte*, 240, 253.

65 P. Adam, *Lebenserinnerungen eines alten Kunstbuchbinders*, Stuttgart, 1951, 95.

66 Blackbourn, op. cit., 417.

67 Ayçoberry, 'Probleme der Sozialschichtung', 517–18.

68 B. Gottron, *Erlebtes und Erlauschtes aus dem Mainzer Metzgergewerbe im 19. Jahrhundert*, Mainz, 1928, 3–9.

69 ibid., esp. 52ff.

70 Examples in D. Blackbourn, *Class, Religion and Local Politics in Wilhelmine Germany*, London and New Haven, 1980.

71 Walker, op. cit., and Volkov, op. cit., both contain much material illustrating these attitudes.

72 Walker, op. cit., 119–33.

73 On the 1840s, see J. Bergmann, 'Ökonomische Voraussetzungen der Revolution von 1848', in H.-U. Wehler (ed.), *200 Jahre amerikanische Revolution und moderne Revolutionsforschung: Geschichte und Gesellschaft, Sonderheft 2*, Göttingen, 1976, 277–8. On the boom prior to the 1873 crash, Rosenberg, op. cit., 63ff; M. Kitchen, *The Political Economy of Germany 1815–1914*, London, 1978, 133–8.

74 Volkov, op. cit., 95–122.

75 K. Saul, *Staat, Industrie, Arbeiterbewegung im Kaiserreich*, Düsseldorf, 1974, 61, 84, 99.

On counter-organizations, see *25 Jahre Deutscher Handwerks- und Gewerbekammertag 1900–1925*, Hanover, 1925, 156–8; Branding, op. cit., 92–4.

76 Gellately, op. cit., 50–7.

77 See the complaints aired at the AGM of the Rottenburg *Gewerbeverein*, reported in the *Neckarbote*, 1 March 1904. Generally, Noll, op. cit., 124–66, 381–6.

78 Cited in W. Buzengeiger, *Die Zusammenhänge zwischen den wirtschaftlichen Verhältnissen und der politischen Entwicklung in Württemberg um die Mitte des 19. Jahrhunderts*, Munich, 1949, 49. See also Blackbourn, *Class, Religion and Local Politics*, 64–73.

79 See G. Huck, 'Arbeiterkonsumverein und Verbraucherorganisation', in J. Reulecke and W. Weber (eds), *Fabrik, Familie, Feierabend*, Wuppertal, 1978, esp. 239–40; and, in the same volume, Reulecke, 'Von der Dorfschule zum Schulsystem', esp. 256–7.

80 Crew, *Town in the Ruhr*, 114.

81 F. Naumann, *Demokratie und Kaisertum*, Berlin, 1904, 79–80. The figure in Stuttgart was about 15 per cent by 1914: E. Hasselmann, *Und trug hundertfältige Frucht*, Stuttgart, 1964, 66.

82 Haupt, 'Kleinhändler und Arbeiter', 101–4.

83 ibid., 111–19; J. Kocka, 'The study of social mobility and the formation of the working class in the 19th century', *MS*, 111, 1980, 97–117. As Kocka notes, however, the East German historian Hartmut Zwahr, in a detailed investigation of Leipzig, has suggested a sharpening class division between petite bourgeoisie and working class in the years 1830–70: Zwahr, *Zur Konstituierung des Proletariats als Klasse*, Berlin, 1978.

84 For an imaginative attempt to reconstruct street-life as part of the pattern of socialization at the end of the eighteenth century, see Schlumbohm, op. cit.

85 Haupt, 'Kleinhändler und Arbeiter', 128–9.

86 Crew, *Town in the Ruhr*, 131–45, esp. 135, 142–3.

87 There is interesting evidence on the tensions within petit-bourgeois families in K. Schlegel, 'Domestic servants in Hamburg before 1914', MA dissertation, University of East Anglia, 1980. An article based on this work is to appear in *History Workshop Journal*.

88 Leppert-Fögen, op. cit., ch. III: 'Zur Sozialpsychologie des Kleinbürgertums'.

89 There are references to many local studies in D. Langewiesche, 'Republik, Konstitutionelle Monarchie und "Soziale Frage". Grundprobleme der deutschen Revolution von 1848/49', *HZ*, 230, 1980, 529–48. Langewiesche's own monograph on Württemberg is extremely valuable: *Liberalismus und Demokratie zwischen Revolution und Reichsgründung*, Düsseldorf, 1974.

90 Walker, op. cit., 362–5, 390ff; Langewiesche, *Liberalismus*, op. cit., 41–55, 141ff, 212–19; T. S. Hamerow, *Restoration, Revolution, Reaction*, Princeton, 1958, 140–55.

91 Rosenberg, op. cit., 62–78, 118ff; Volkov, op. cit., 172–91; H. Sedatis, *Liberalismus und Handwerk in Süddeutschland. Wirtschafts- und Gesellschaftskonzeptionen des Liberalismus und die Krise des Handwerks im 19. Jahrhundert*, Stuttgart, 1979; Leppert-Fögen, op. cit., 161–83.

92 Cited in Winkler, 'Rückversicherte Mittelstand', op. cit., 207.

93 Gellately, op. cit., 90–1, 129.

94 The full range of demands for state intervention is suggested by Wernicke's rather indigestible compendium, *Kapitalismus und Mittelstandspolitik*, Jena, 1907.

95 Blackbourn, *Class, Religion and Local Politics*, esp. 149–51.

96 On the Conservatives and *Bund der Landwirte*, H.-J. Puhle, *Agrarische Interessenpolitik und preussischer Konservatismus im wilhelminischen Reich 1893–1914*, Hanover, 1966; on the Centre, Blackbourn, *Class, Religion and Local Politics*, 53–7, 92–9, 141–64. On programmes: F. Salomon, *Die deutschen Parteiprogramme*, Leipzig and Berlin, 1907, vol. 3, 73, 83–4.

97 Winkler, 'Rückversicherte Mittelstand', for details.
98 Volkov, op. cit., 277.
99 B. Adelung, *Der 34. hessische Landtag 1908–11*, n.p., 1911, 93.
100 On 'statolatry' and the petite bourgeoisie, see N. Poulantzas, *Fascism and Dictatorship*, London, 1974, 241; and *Classes in Contemporary Capitalism*, London, 1975, 291ff.
101 Blackbourn, *Class, Religion and Local Politics*, esp. 158–64; Gottron, op. cit., 51.
102 The role of 'scandal' deserves greater attention: it had a central place in petit-bourgeois politics, providing suitable symbols of 'injustice' and 'unfairness'. Construction scandals, especially, were to the petite bourgeoisie what commodity and stock-exchange scandals were to the peasantry – particularly when they could be tied to 'Jewish' capital. For some pointers, see Blackbourn, *Class, Religion and Local Politics*, 158–60; and G. Zang (ed.), *Provinzialisierung einer Region: Zur Entstehung der bürgerlichen Gesellschaft in der Provinz*, Stuttgart, 1978, esp. the articles by Bellmann and Zang.
103 Cf. the response of the Württemberg government to a petition from the *Centralvereinigung deutscher Vereine für Handel und Gewerbe*, concerning state officials' consumer co-operatives and the damage they allegedly did to the shopkeeper. The analysis of the *Centralvereinigung* was dismissed as 'superficial' and its recommendations not acted on. (HStA Stuttgart, E 130 II, Bü 486, Nr. 84.) The south German and Hanseatic governments were also opposed to a strong pro-guild line in 1897. See, for example, *25 Jahre Deutscher Handwerks- und Gewerbekammertag*, 24–5.
104 Crüger, op. cit., 14; J. Wernicke, *Der Mittelstand und seine wirtschaftliche Lage*, Leipzig, 1909, 44.
105 G. Tietz, *Hermann Tietz*, Stuttgart, 1955, 46, cites a good example.
106 *25 Jahre Deutscher Handwerks- und Gewerbekammertag*, 121–5.
107 On the cynicism with which craftsmen reacted to the 1897 legislation, see Blackbourn, '*Mittelstand*', 418–19 and note 62.
108 Volkov, op. cit., 241, 278, 332–3, shows how craftsmen's aspirations were first raised, then dashed, by government actions. This pattern of appetites which fed on the eating is an important component of the history of the petite bourgeoisie in Imperial Germany. The dialectic of raised and shattered hopes would repay further attention.
109 See Gellately, op. cit., 92, 96; E. Böhm, *Überseehandel und Flottenbau*, Düsseldorf, 1972, 183–263; G. Eley, 'Defining social imperialism: use and abuse of an idea', *SH*, 3, 1976, 278.
110 On violence against the Tietz stores: Tietz, op. cit., 45.
111 Gellately, op. cit., 67–8.
112 V. R. Berghahn, *Germany and the Approach of War in 1914*, London, 1973, 151: 'Here was a potential group of voters which responded to the emotional propaganda of the conservative élites and was waiting to be organised. And organised they became.'
113 Winkler, 'Rückversicherte Mittelstand', 175; Gellately, op. cit., 158–61, 165ff.
114 For the negative effect of tariffs on butchers, millers and bakers, see Wernicke, *Kapitalismus*, 162 and Blackbourn, '*Mittelstand*', 414.
115 On the desertion of the Conservatives by the *Deutsche Mittelstandsvereinigung*, Winkler, 'Rückversicherte Mittelstand', 169; S. Mielke, *Der Hansa-Bund für Gewerbe, Handel und Industrie*, Göttingen, 1976, 30ff, 45–51. Support for the Conservative-backed successor varied from region to region, but was strongest (like the new guilds) in the east: D. Stegmann, *Die Erben Bismarcks. Parteien und Verbände in der Spätphase des wilhelminischen Imperialismus*, Cologne, 1970, 254.
116 Details of the Cartel in Stegmann, op. cit., 342ff.
117 I have tried to show in *Class, Religion and Local Politics* how this pattern of *incomplete* absorption of demands by the right helped to generate an unstable form of demagogic politics.
118 Wilhelm Keil noted in his memoirs how there was an alliance on such issues in the

Stuttgart city council between SPD and progressive governmental figures like von Gauss, against the 'wine-growers and petite bourgeoisie': W. Keil, *Erlebnisse eines Sozialdemokraten*, Stuttgart, 1947–8, I, 158. See also R. J. V. Lenman, 'Politics and culture: the state and the avant-garde in Munich 1886–1914', in R. J. Evans (ed.), *Society and Politics in Wilhelmine Germany*, London, 1978, 90–111.

119 Volkov, op. cit., 257–9.

120 Gellately, op. cit., 119–20, 144–5.

121 ibid., 121ff.

122 See the articles by Haupt and Saur in Drechsel, op. cit. A Centre Party functionary expressed the view of the more established shopkeepers when he referred to the fringe of small retailers as 'an evil', and as 'unhealthy parasitism'. See Blackbourn, '*Mittelstand*', 422.

123 Gellately, op. cit., 106–7.

124 The Munich SPD in 1906 had 369 members (5.5 per cent) who were publicans or drink retailers: R. Michels, *Political Parties*, New York, 1968, 269.

125 Some examples, from the Palatinate, Nuremberg and Brunswick, in W. Guttsman, *The German Social Democratic Party 1875–1933*, London, 1981, 35, 56, 255.

126 Wernicke, *Kapitalismus*, 159.

127 Blackbourn, '*Mittelstand*', 416–18.

128 Volkov, op. cit., 229–37. Eugen Sinner ('La politique de la social-démocratie allemande vis-à-vis de l'artisanat à la fin du XIXe siècle', *MS*, 114, 105–23) suggests that the SPD lacked sympathy with the 'backward-looking' demands of the craftsmen. While there is considerable evidence for this, it should also be noted that – in parts of Germany, at least – the party made explicit attempts to woo the small masters for the socialist cause. Examples in Blackbourn, *Class, Religion and Local Politics*, 171–5, 185–6.

129 *Deutsches Volksblatt*, 26 October 1912. Carl Severing also reported in his memoirs how the customs and emblems of former guild organizations were taken over by carpenters and masons into the trade union movement: *Mein Lebensweg*, Cologne, 1951, I, 29.

130 Many of the foremost SPD leaders had this background: Wilhelm Liebknecht, August Bebel, Philipp Scheidemann, Friedrich Ebert, Carl Severing, Wilhelm Keil, Paul Löbe. Nearly a quarter of SPD Reichstag deputies between 1893 and 1914 had a petit-bourgeois occupation. Of these forty-one, nearly a half were practising craftsmen – shoemakers, printers, cabinet-makers, carpenters, cigar-makers, P. Molt, *Der Reichstag vor der improvisierten Revolution*, Cologne/Opladen, 1963, 212.

3 The petite bourgeoisie in nineteenth-century Britain: the urban and liberal case

GEOFFREY CROSSICK

The existence of a 'rural bourgeoisie' may be a matter for historical dispute,[1] but that does not apply to the rural petite bourgeoisie. In all the other societies covered in this book there existed a substantial group of small property owners in the countryside: most importantly a small-scale, landowning peasantry, but also the craftsmen and traders sustained by the village and small town economy that went with it. Any regional qualifications that one might feel obliged to make to this generalization shrink to secondary importance when compared with the British case, for there are two commonplaces about nineteenth-century Britain without which we cannot understand its petite bourgeoisie. The first is that Britain became an urban country very rapidly, and extremely early in international terms; the second is that it lacked a peasantry, a rural petite bourgeoisie. It is as an urban formation that the British petits bourgeois developed, and the significance of that fact will run as a thread through this essay.

This essentially urban force was not evenly distributed around the country. There were those ubiquitous petits bourgeois, the shopkeepers and, to a lesser extent, producers serving humdrum local consumption, and these would be distributed in rough proportion to the urban population. But there were also two kinds of concentration. The first is represented by those towns whose industrial structures gave particular emphasis to small enterprise – Birmingham and Sheffield are the most obvious examples. The second is towns with a substantial commercial and service function, where tertiary activities and small consumer industries proliferated to give a distinctive character to the local social structure. Such towns ranged from the national capitals of London and Edinburgh, through regional centres such as Bristol, Newcastle and Leeds, to more locally oriented county and market towns such as Northampton and Newcastle-under-Lyme.[2] Indeed, those last-mentioned centres might be seen as the most satisfactory home for the petite bourgeoisie where, least threatened socially or even economically, they could occupy a significant place in local society.

This was not just an urban location, but an urban orientation as well. The universe of the British petits bourgeois tended to remain enclosed within their own towns and localities, marking out their social and cultural localism in a way quite different from the trend within the more substantial middle class. Their politics, their organizations, one might almost say their concerns, failed to take on a significant national character during this period. Urban orientation involved more than all this, however, for the economic functions of the petite bourgeoisie inserted it into a local economic structure and gave it a key function in the development of the nineteenth-century urban economy.[3] In part this derived from the place of small enterprise in providing the infrastructure of this economy – retailing, services, secondary manufactures – but it also grew out of the way petits bourgeois helped shape the structure and the fabric of the nineteenth-century town, most obviously in the finance and ownership of working-class housing.

From such arguments stem the need to re-assess the importance of the petite bourgeoisie within the expanding urban industrial economy of nineteenth-century Britain, yet neither its economic nor its social history have received substantial attention from historians. As a result, much of the research upon which such a re-assessment must rest remains to be done. In this general overview, I shall concentrate on certain themes: the changing economic position of shopkeepers and small producers; politics, organization and ideology; and some of the wider relationships of the petite bourgeoisie within urban society.

SHOPKEEPERS

Shopkeeping has a far longer history than it has been given credit for. Fixed shop retailing, traditionally portrayed as a product of the mid-nineteenth century and the subsequent decades,[4] was in fact widespread from the early years of the century, even in small towns and villages, but especially so in rapidly expanding commercial and manufacturing centres.[5] Indeed, shop provision in six northern towns rose faster than population in the first half of the century, only achieving a greater stability between 1851 and 1881,[6] as if conserving its strength for the new forms of competition that were to hit the traditional shopkeeper from the closing decades of the century. Two trends of the first half of the century need emphasizing. The first is the decline of the craftsman/retailer, a necessary unit for a poor transportation economy, and the emergence of specialist retailing. The other trend grew out of that, and that was the proliferation of small-scale retailers on the basis of highly local and individual initiatives. Fast urban and suburban growth made such activity particularly attractive, and it seems that only from the 1860s did a high and increasing association between shop location and population distribution introduce more intense competition.[7] In other words, although there was the inevitable and endemic instability of small retail businesses, competition remained limited in the first half of the century.

The general problems of small retailers began to emerge from the 1860s. It is difficult to be specific about the structural changes that occurred in British retailing during these years, for they have been little investigated.[8] One certainty, however, is the clear shopkeeper feeling that new and worrying forms of competition were developing, and that their novelty lay in both scale and capitalization. A shift towards more capital-intensive distribution methods can be traced back to the closing decades of the last century. Its origins have received but limited attention, though they must include the expansion of effective consumer demand that accompanied rising real incomes; the changing occupational structure, above all the emergence of a white-collar lower middle class; the increasing opportunities for standardized goods, with greater urban concentration and new outlets for advertising; and the availability of investment capital.

Department stores were a later development in Britain than in France, but by the 1870s were well-established in London, and penetrating provincial towns. Selfridges in London, Lewis's in Liverpool, and the so-called 'civil service co-operatives' such as the Army and Navy Stores, and their many counterparts, all built their markets well beyond their immediate vicinity, with extensive use of delivery vans and mail-order selling. This last method was judged by one French observer to be more extensive in Britain than anywhere else in Europe.[9] Multiple retail chains appeared first in the food trades, but by the 1880s were spreading rapidly throughout retailing, and it was not just the size of these chains that was striking, but the range of trades affected. Both stood out in contrast to other European countries.[10] In the formation of new multiple companies and the deepening of capitalization, the years between 1895 and 1903 seem a watershed.[11] Finally, there were the increasingly professional and expansive consumer co-operative stores, growing from the 1860s, but entering a new period of explosive growth in the 1890s. During that decade they seemed in many towns to be bidding for dominance, with the shift to main shopping street locations marking greater visibility, and a new level of product diversity hurting a widening range of retail trades. Membership rose from 100,000 to 3 million between 1863 and 1913, turnover from £2½ million to £88 million.[12] The quantitative impact of all these changes has not been satisfactorily measured, but they represented a major challenge to traditional retailing methods, in their level of capital, vertical integration, ubiquity and identifiability, and in their new style of selling. Their self-advertisement was distressingly public. How can the smaller retailers have felt when faced with the excitement of David Lewis's Liverpool store, with its model of Strasbourg Cathedral clock? Each hour it played melodies from Mozart, Rossini or Haydn, while the cathedral doors opened and twelve apostles marched into view.[13] Thomas Lipton's capacity for publicity and extravagance they could read of in their *Daily Mail* each morning, before eyeing anxiously his shop in the High Street. The psychological impact on petit-bourgeois shopkeepers is of importance in a way that simple calculations of market share cannot indicate.

Alongside such explicit pressures went a longer-term trend degrading the traditional skills of the shopkeeper and the premium placed upon them. These skills had required a knowledge of a wide range of goods, the ability to judge, to divide, process and prepare them. Price competition, proprietary goods, pre-packaging all undermined the pride and the craft-consciousness of the traditional retailer. So it was that apprenticeship had died out in the London grocery trade by the late nineteenth century. 'It is not wanted,' said one assistant, 'there is little or nothing to learn,'[14] though a grocers' leader felt that such a view was a dangerous one. 'Many of these men set up for themselves and are ruined by their ignorance.'[15] Overall, though, W. B. Robertson observed in 1911 that 'knowledge of a shopkeeping trade is not nowadays considered nearly so necessary as purely commercial ability.'[16]

Yet however much we might talk of a retailing revolution that created a new degree of scale in a previously Lilliputian world, however much we might indicate the new types of shop and be drawn to investigate the venomous shopkeeper responses to them, it remains none the less true that shopkeeping was the home of the small man and woman throughout the century. Contemporary retailers almost certainly overstated the new challenges, for a significant proportion of their problems were in fact due to the intensification of older patterns of retailing. Most of all, it was due to the increasing internal competition amongst individual retailers, as ease of entry and wholesaler support for new and increasingly dependent retail ventures produced a level of prices and hours competition amongst ordinary shopkeepers that was a major reason for their late nineteenth-century unease. We really need to know a great deal more about such competition, and the structures of dependency within the 'traditional' sector. Many a large grocer in Manchester with a wholesale trade (and presumably not just there) would set up a couple as small grocers in an outer part of the town.[17] Such dependency could appear in other ways. It had become common by the 1890s for failing retailers with relatively expensive stocks (above all small drapers) to get assistance from the wholesaler to whom the bulk of the debts was owed. The wholesale firm effectively took over the control of the business, sometimes even using the debt as a means of acquiring a smaller shop (Josiah Chater did this in Cambridge[18]). Taken together, then, the various forces discussed here made the quarter century that preceded the First World War a peak period of price competition in the retail trades as a whole. The small independent retailers were not declining, but they now faced new and intensifying difficulties. There were threats to their skill and pride, to their economic viability, most of all perhaps to their ambitions. The real extent of these problems may be unclear, but a sense of being embattled against the forces of size and competition prevailed amongst independent shopkeepers. The responses – organizational, political and ideological – were, as we shall see, marked by their paucity and ineffectiveness.

SMALL PRODUCERS

Industrialization in Britain produced no withering away of small-scale production. Economic necessity pointed to large-scale concentrated production in no more than a handful of specific sectors (mostly certain textiles and producers' goods), and the slow spread of powered machinery in Britain is merely generalized confirmation of that.[19] It is now clear that the industrial revolution generated a whole new set of possibilities for small producers, even if by the middle of the nineteenth century the context in which they operated was often very different and more constrained. They persisted most of all in a mass of consumer trades: clothing, leather, boots and shoes, food and drink, building, printing, cutlery, domestic hardware, hosiery, knitwear, lace, and much more.[20] Their position was certainly eroded by 1914, but in such a heterogeneous fashion as to confirm the remarkable diversity of these small producers.

Diversity of size must be recognized at the outset, for small producers were of varying degrees of substance, shading almost imperceptibly into an under-employed working class. We must try to distinguish the petite bourgeoisie from that layer of marginal producers hurled into existence by depression, under-employment or simple poverty, as unemployed journeymen and others sought to create or augment an income. This is a world of 'penny capitalism' whose aspirations seem to have been more desperate and fairly distinct.[21] Such marginal enterprises, seeking to survive in crisis or to add a little income to a wage, were even more common in shop-keeping.[22] Another form of very marginal producer appeared in many trades where intense subdivision and sweating generated a plethora of minuscule work units: amongst the 'little masters' of Sheffield, in building, in the late nineteenth-century London shoe trade, in cabinet-making, and in other depressed trades where outwork and the garret-master system flourished, if that is the word.[23] A distinction, however blurred in the sources and indeed on the ground, must be drawn between potentially viable petit-bourgeois producers and those workers exploiting one of the many methods other than wage employment by which nineteenth-century working people might obtain an income.

There was also a diversity of geographical distribution that was important for social and political relations. If all towns contained small producers, they were not necessarily a prominent element within the local economy. At one extreme stood such towns as Middlesbrough and Merthyr Tydfil, to which we should add Patrick Joyce's smaller factory towns,[24] where large employers dominated social as much as economic affairs. At the other were those industrial towns with a more broadly based employing class, towns based on some species of workshop production. The best-known examples are Birmingham, Sheffield and the traditional areas of production in London, but, as Behagg argues in his essay later in this book, it is a mistake to see the prominence of small producers as a sign of their continuing and unchanging independence.[25] To these must be added the larger commercial and manufacturing centres themselves: the rapid economic growth of early nineteenth-century Leeds saw not just large-scale factory production in textiles, but the exploding force of an increasingly specialized labour-intensive craft workshop sector.[26]

Finally, of course, there was a diversity of relationships to industrial and economic change. An essential starting point, in that it relates so pointedly to the social and political character of British small employers, is the absence from mid-century of a small master artisan class committed to its traditional place both in its craft and in local society, a group of small masters resisting change out of normative objections to the economic, social and political system as they saw it being transformed.[27] The older craft framework did allow a response, as Behagg's work suggests, but it was one that was rapidly defeated in Britain, leaving to the bulk of masters a developing petit-bourgeois identity. Long-established, even multi-generational, small firms embedded in a framework of values based upon a master artisan culture and its place in society seem increasingly rare in Britain. The absence of a corporate structure denied small producers even the myths of an idealized guild age to inform responses to change. Overall, the relations of small producers to industrial change were both more complex and more creative than the notion of a declining traditional sector would allow. We need to know a great deal more about the economic history of small-scale production in Britain, and its analysis will require close attention to such issues as capital concentration, the geographical organization of production, the technical division of labour, and the relation of that to mechanization. It is the variety of relationships of small producers to industrial change that stands out but, at the risk of being over-schematic, we can isolate three types of small producer in nineteenth-century Britain. Adding a chronological dimension to this framework means that any single industry might experience all three of these situations.

The first category saw the continuation of a small producer sector without substantial change in either technology or unit size. Such apparent continuities, however, often hid fundamental changes in the organization of the industry which threatened the viability of individual small producers however much it supported small production as a general structure. The early reorganization of the tailoring trade of London, and the subsequent experience of the light metal industries of Birmingham and the Black Country, are the most obvious examples. By the 1860s these midlands industries were characterized by a subdivision of trades and the advent of small hand-powered machines. Where steam power was advantageous, systems for power-sharing allowed a small master structure to accompany powered machinery. Alternatively, factory space and a concomitant access to a power supply could be hired from larger manufacturers, as in the cutlery and related trades of Sheffield by the 1860s, which were characterized by a high level of market integration, the division of operations, and a very low-level mechanization. The archetypal unit could thus remain the small firm.[28]

These Sheffield and Birmingham trades shared a more pervasive characteristic with light industrial towns elsewhere, and with other small, unrevolutionized manufactures: the integration of the producer into a larger structure of factoring on the one hand and subcontracting on the other. Most petit-bourgeois producers operated in sectors being transformed by the power of merchant capital, the new link between producer and expanding market. These became the basic method of organizing this category of small-scale manufacturing – or of reorganizing it. In trade after trade of this kind, the differential impact of the market, and its expression through merchant and wholesaler interventions, forced a divide between a viable small master class that sought to behave in a 'business-like' fashion (see Behagg's essay) and accept merchant domination, detaching itself from the culture and custom of the craft community, and on the other hand a depressed body of marginal small masters whose independence became no more than notional, even where they survived. The industrial revolution was characterized more by commercial change than by factories, and nowhere more so than in the way in which it affected small producers. Commercial organization, factoring, and national merchant operations turned these small firms into new types of producer bound into increasingly dependent relationships long before mechanization put different pressures upon them.[29]

The level of technology might have discouraged concentration in any case, but the factoring system perpetuated the very fragmentation upon which it depended.[30] With the merchant or factor organizing production and not merely distribution, often supplying raw materials and weekly financial advances, he not only bound the workshop owner into his operations, but threw the whole burden of fluctuations onto him. The factor's bargaining position was strong, knowing as he did the liquidity problems of the small masters, and their needs to sell goods to pay their wage and other costs. The dependence on credit was thus a critical force undermining master independence. Thus, as commercial advances took place – classically in the trades of Sheffield, Birmingham and the Black Country – the general economic logic behind small production was precisely the force determining the vulnerability of individual petit-bourgeois producers.

Those industries where small producers as a major element in production were actually created by the process of industrial and technological change form my second category. In a number of industries once characterized by domestic workers organized by merchant capitalists, the mid-century combination of market expansion and minor advances in a still essentially labour-intensive technology led to an upsurge of small firms. The shoemaking industry, where small enterprise was first created and then threatened by industrial growth, is the clearest example.[31] The early nineteenth-century shoe trade, above all in Northampton, was controlled by large-scale wholesalers organizing outworkers, supplemented throughout the country by traditional craftsmen/retailers working alone to supply local needs. The 1860s saw an expansion of demand, and the introduction of simple machines, notably the sewing machine. The combination stimulated the growth of mainly small firms, acting as both manufacturers and wholesalers, often combining small workshops with putting out. The 1880s brought depression, home-based competition, and price cutting. This was the classic situation in which the small producer would be squeezed in many industries, and the larger shoe manufacturers responded with a higher level of mechanization and factory rationalization, as well as by opening retail outlets of their own. The competitive advantages of the large manufacturers now accumulated, and by 1900 struggling small firms survived only by subcontracting or becoming highly specialized producers.

Here is a good example of a small and simple machine element leading to the proliferation of small-scale workshop producers in a hitherto unmechanized industry. These are not traditional masters being squeezed, but largely new firms, in new activities, and substantially created by industrial change. We may find in this area further clues to the absence of a strong, craft-based small-master ideology in nineteenth-century Britain: too few producers would have fitted that traditional characterization. There are other examples. In Sheffield, the application of small machines to the cutlery trades led to some shift from domestic production to larger workshop operations. Early powered mechanization in the hosiery industry similarly encouraged a proliferation of small firms as factory production spread in Nottingham from the 1850s. Space and access to power could be rented, and small firms could readily buy second-hand machinery in an industry prone to bankruptcy.[32] The availability of lighter sources of power encouraged this process – at first the gas engine, but more significantly electricity towards the end of the century. Indeed, market conditions and technical subdivision of processes provided the context for electrical power to act as a stimulus to the emergence of small firms at a time when the trend towards concentration seemed to be set the other way.

The third and final category covers those industries which experienced marked concentration in the scale of production, but where small producers survived and were at times even stimulated by their relationship to the new and larger firms. As Kropotkin commented on Britain in 1912, 'each new factory calls into existence a number of small workshops'.[33] Small firms became an integral if dependent part of industries shifting towards more highly capitalized operations, and they often found the reason for their growth in that changing cost structure of their industry, with the commitment of large firms to continuing and high fixed costs finding relief in subcontracting to small firms to meet periods of high demand, or to provide auxiliary services. Ready-made tailoring is one example, where the 1880s saw a massive increase in the number of large clothing factories in Leeds (from seven in 1881 to fifty-four in 1891), but that growth was accompanied by a boom in 'client' workshops taking on contracts from the great establishments.[34] There were other reasons for large and small firms to co-exist. There could grow up a more complex subcontracting and buying in system amongst enterprises operating at a more marginal level, as in the midlands brass industry, where large integrated units co-existed with small workshops, or in jewellery where 'the small businesses are in some sort the satellites of the larger ones, and move in their orbit'.[35] This was the more exploitative relationship, but the connections could have greater subtlety. Different sizes of firm could produce distinct types of product within a range, as with the edge-tool trades; chain-making, where a factory would contract out to small workshops the lighter part of an order;[36] or van-building, where lighter vans for which there was a less regular demand were left to small employers.[37] This leads into the indistinct world where subcontracting could merge into sweating and garret-masters, but if the line between these categories can never be rigid (indeed, the depressed garret-masters might be declined workshop owners) my concern is to stress that genuine small businesses often survived – and to a degree flourished – in this changing environment. Yet it carried with it a decline in independence, as petit-bourgeois producers, in this category as in the first, found themselves bound into increasingly dependent business relationships.

In these three ways amongst others small production units survived, and were often encouraged by, industrialization and economic change. As I have stressed, however, small business in all three forms of persistence was under increasing strain towards the end of the century. The need to increase investment in order to reduce costs at a time of depression and competition meant that the same business pressures that were stimulating the growth of larger firms provided for petit-bourgeois producers challenges with which they were ill-equipped to deal. Examples are the wood-screw industry in the midlands, where expensive equipment had by the 1860s forced most small businesses out of existence; and the more dramatic decline of the small victualling brewer between the 1860s and the 1880s.[38] In times of declining trade, it was the small firms who more readily disappeared, and the more gradual trend towards a larger scale of enterprise is particularly noticeable during the Great Depression in many of the small metal goods industries. In this connection, it is important to distinguish the proliferation of tiny enterprises in economic crisis, as workers sought an income, from the role of depression during structural crises in eliminating once viable small firms. The 1890s seem to mark a critical moment in this respect, with the advance of capital equipment lifting onto a new level in many industries.[39]

All of this would be experienced as actual competition from larger and more efficient firms, which often themselves took over the role of factors. The advancing scale of retail organization intensified this by making small producers disadvantageously dependent on wholesalers who dealt with increasingly distant and cost-conscious markets. Under these combined pressures many small masters felt obliged to move into the factories within a no more than notional system of subcontracting. G. H. Shaw of Sheffield observed in 1908 that 'a great many of these large firms are buying up the little masters, and instead of having these little masters, who perhaps employ a dozen or a score of men, and who supply some of these large houses, they buy a firm up, and appoint the little master as manager over a department, as a rule, to make that class of knife, or other article which he has been used to manufacture for the firm.'[40]

More diffuse social pressures encouraging a lack of confidence among small producers must be added to concrete difficulties such as these. The very towns in which they operated were coming to be dominated by large employers, especially the metal towns as new industries appeared (steel in Sheffield, engineering in Birmingham). This changing social context became generalized, as small producers sensed a national process of business concentration that fuelled a feeling of embattlement. As Joseph Brown commented about his small Birmingham tool-making firm, 'evidently we are destined to disappear before long'.[41] This must have been experienced through the declining opportunities open to small business, not so much to enter as to grow from small beginnings. Capital and technological requirements shut down the horizons for growth at this time in many sectors, perhaps well before small producers as such were generally endangered.

If we are to understand the paucity of organized small producer resistance to these changes, then the ideological issues that will be analysed below must be linked to the complex picture of small-scale production outlined here. Three points must be emphasized in particular. Firstly, these firms were not generally traditional master artisans adhering to an older set of craft values. They became businesses, expanding or declining with the opportunities to do so. See de Rousier's judgement of Joseph Brown in the 1890s. 'The trade which seems on the eve of slipping from him has not been in his case a time-honoured refuge, in whose shelter he grew to manhood, but merely an opportunity of which he availed himself, as he would have done of any other.' The consequences were a reluctant resignation in the face of change. 'He is accustomed to rely upon himself and not on the fortunes of his trade, on his personal rather than on his technical aptitudes.'[42] The second point leads on from that. These were not generally long-established firms. On the contrary, the limited evidence available suggests that small producers were characterized by a very high rate of turnover.[43] Thirdly, I have emphasized the responsiveness of the small production sector to changing circumstances. The decline of opportunities in one area was matched by their expansion in another; the fate of individual producers was distinct from the persistence of small-scale production. Indeed, changing economic opportunities could provide the stimulus to which small producers, with their low capitalization and small adaptable technology, were often well-placed to respond. Thus the faltering small firms in the light metal trades of the midlands found new life in the 1890s when the bicycle industry sought parts for assembly.[44]

This is the starting point for an analysis of small producers in nineteenth-century Britain. We know all too little about them, and discussion is still over-dependent, as my own references will have suggested, upon the important economic histories produced in the early decades of this century. Only when we recognize the vitality and the complexity of small producers in Britain, and their diverse relation to capitalist industrialization, and stop viewing them as a declining pre-industrial sector, shall we be able to interpret their social and political role.

POLITICS, ORGANIZATION AND IDEOLOGY

In literary and even historical portrayal, the petite bourgeoisie in Britain has too often been the object of patronizing rejection, above all as culturally imitative, and that caricatured treatment comes frequently from writers such as H. G. Wells who were themselves from that background. Yet the caricature relates to the reality, for it seems that from the middle of the nineteenth century there was little distinctive or coherent about the voice of the petite bourgeoisie in British political life. The politics and values came to seem fundamentally derivative. The characteristic rejection of both state and élites that had shaped the ideology that grew with dissenting religion survived wherever petit-bourgeois politics found expression, but it became subsumed within a blander liberalism that allowed many to move further towards social conservatism when faced with an increasingly organized working class.

The chronological emphasis there is important, for in the period from the late eighteenth century through to the 1840s, a vigorous petit-bourgeois radicalism had been more present in movements of militant opposition to the existing political system than historians' concentration on working-class politics has allowed. E. P. Thompson recognized this, and portrayed vividly a rationalist, individualist and democratic strand of radicalism that he identified with an artisanal and petit-bourgeois milieu.[45] In many towns through to the Chartist period, a section of the petite bourgeoisie (we can be no more precise than that) was a major radical voice confronting the older local élite, and limiting its ability to carry out its policies. It may be correct to see the reform of municipal government that stemmed from the 1835 Municipal Corporations Act as an attempt to shut down popular access to local politics and, with a weighted and often narrowed franchise, to incorporate the small propertied interests of the town within what was often a more restricted form of local government.[46]

This radical tradition is best understood through the notion of the *menu peuple*, the ordinary useful people, a radical conception that held at its centre a cultural and political rejection of opulence and oppression.[47] These notions structure so many early nineteenth-century movements of popular protest and struggle, to the extent that the language of 'capitalist oppression' that they talk is unwisely seen as a proletarian rejection of the new industrial capitalist order. We are beginning to understand how rooted that was in a *menu peuple*'s denunciation of privilege, oppression and parasitic wealth of a financial and speculative kind, rather than in a proletarian conception of capitalist exploitation. Theirs was an ideology of modest means, hard work and independence as a solution to injustice and as an alternative to subordination. Therein lay the appeal of Cobbett and also, in a different way, of Paine and Thelwall to British radicals. Finance and speculation were the economic ogres, and for good reason. Credit and small-scale finance were continuing petit-bourgeois concerns – interest rates were too high, access to finance too poor in local personalized capital markets, and the process seemed at the mercy of outside speculation. Condemnations of financial speculators in eighteenth-century Britain by those small borrowers who suffered most in panics, were thus rooted in practical experience and not just moral predilections. Credit certainly does not alone explain the radical analysis, far from it, but it shows the specific attractions of that analysis to those with small enterprises, and why they developed it as they did.[48]

Independence and the dismantling of economic and political monopoly were the aims of this radicalism, as political democracy and a particular economic morality intertwined in a way that gave priority to the former. We can observe the vitality of a shopkeeper and master artisan politics, often rooted in Painite democratic ideas, in the local politics of many towns between 1815 and the challenging Chartist experience of the early 1840s. Neale has characterized it as the 'rational anarchism of a community of small producers', concerned with democratic suffrage and the secret ballot, opposition to monopoly and the corn laws, civil and religious liberty, and national education. It was an expectant, optimistic radicalism, and its characteristics are becoming clarified by local studies. In Salford, an amorphous group of shopkeepers, teachers, and small manufacturers used a proliferation of local institutions to penetrate urban affairs;[49] the vestry radicals of London in the 1820s and 1830s had a very similar social base;[50] a radical petite bourgeoisie in Leeds used minor political institutions to gain a foothold in local politics from which to oppose narrowly based and wealthy élites, whether old or new.[51] Their rejection of dependency, of the client economy and politics, can be traced back to the eighteenth-century construction of an economic and organizational basis for independence among the 'middling sort' of the provincial towns. It was their mutual clubs and subscription societies which flocked to the support of Wilkes, and they read radical papers such as the *Middlesex Journal* which were directed specifically at them.[52] Their independence was to be important. A school proprietor in Birmingham who supported the Hampden Clubs during 1816 could not join for fear of offending gentlemen on whose custom he depended. But he noted in his journal that 'my brother Edwin who is a saw-maker and, of course, unfettered, is a member of the Hampden Club'.[53]

The ability of this petit-bourgeois radical milieu to cohere with a developing working-class politics, to create a world of popular politics that came under real internal pressure only from the 1830s, was made possible by the character of the traditional, older analysis of political oppression which held sway through to Chartism and in many ways within it.[54] That concentration on 'old corruption', taxation, representative government, and the conflict between productive and unproductive, formed the basis of a wider radical co-operation that broke down but slowly after the middle of the 1830s, as the older Painite radical formation splintered, though it was to leave a lasting imprint on the character of working-class politics. Prothero has persuasively demonstrated the interweaving of shopkeeper and master artisan radicalism with working-class politics in the radical movements of London between 1815 and the rise of Chartism, and his argument about the ideological and social roots of artisan politics is an implicit explanation of why such an alliance could have been possible. It was determined primarily by political not economic roles and analyses.[55] The substantial petit-bourgeois involvement in Chartist localities has been neglected by a historical emphasis which until recently has struggled to identify Chartism too exclusively as a proletarian movement. It was, in many ways, also the final *campaigning* commitment of the radical petite bourgeoisie to a democratic, liberal, anti-privilege and anti-monopoly ideology. Evidence for the Black Country, Wales, Bath, Nottingham and Halifax – where 'their values of independence and self-determination were the backbone of Halifax Chartism' – provides examples of this.[56]

Where they were prominent in Chartist organization, strategy was at its most constitutional, though still radical and aggressive. In Leeds, the local government strategy of Chartists derived from the issue-based democratizing ideals of an essentially petit-bourgeois section of the local Chartist leadership. Its success depended upon its integration into long-established local radical traditions that were by no means exclusively petit-bourgeois.[57] Its bite derived not from policy, but from its belief in democratic control. That could readily draw upon the historically radical concerns of dissenters, and it often did.[58]

The substantial enrolment of petit-bourgeois special constables to handle the feared Chartist disturbances in London in 1848[59] does no more than symbolize the detachment of the small propertied from the radical movement, but the 1840s did see the decreasing viability of the older radical tradition. The rationalist belief in a consensual popular social order once corruption and privilege were eliminated was undermined for the petite bourgeoisie by social fear, conflict, and the intense experience of depression. It was an optimistic vision with declining prospects and, in a valuable case study, Morris has shown its hold on Samuel Smiles during the Leeds politics of that decade. Indeed, for Morris, the genesis of 'self-help' lay in the retreat into a purely individualistic struggle for self-development, and he labels it a 'petit-bourgeois utopia'.[60] That process, over the period since the early 1830s, denied 1848 its role as a turning point in the composition of the popular movement that it had in other countries. The change was more gradual in Britain. The subsequent years saw the development of a political liberalism that was to be critical to the relative stabilization of mid-Victorian society, and at its centre lay the fragile urban liberal community of local bourgeois, shopkeepers and small employers, and radical artisans; a community built around the often tense but viable assertion of notions of equality based on ideals that were narrowly individualistic and specifically political. The petite bourgeoisie was not simply drawn into it – it helped shape those ideals. It was embedded in local organizations. More strikingly, it led the struggle to oust Whig élites in places like the north-east where the struggle continued into the mid-Victorian period. It is this success of mid-Victorian liberalism that is vital to understanding the political limits within which the British petite bourgeoisie operated. The conflict between expanding bourgeoisie and a threatened petit-bourgeois sector elsewhere in Europe could weaken liberal co-operation of the British kind, and the low incidence of such tensions in Britain is important to an understanding of the political, and perhaps also social, development of the petite bourgeoisie from mid-century. Furthermore, if it was their experience and ideology as dissenters that helped shape earlier petit-bourgeois conceptions of the state, then the weakening of sectarian conflict within the state helped further this overall process.

Mid-Victorian liberalism as a local phenomenon created a circumscribed area within which political conflict and even social dispute could operate. At its least settled level it drew in sections of the radical working class; at its most successful it drew the petite bourgeoisie into the political nation in a lasting and ultimately quiescent way. Joyce has shown that in northern industrial boroughs, as they became embedded in Liberal electoral organization, so the radical dimensions of their liberalism became weaker.[61] The success was in some ways the result of an effort by urban bourgeois élites to detach the petite bourgeoisie from its radical alliances. There are grounds for seeing many voluntary and benevolent institutions established by local élites in this period as directed as much at involving small propertied interests in formal associations as in shaping working-class behaviour. Success with shopkeepers was the most emphatic. The incorporation of small employers is less clear, because of the need to distinguish between that declining group enmeshed in an artisanal milieu that had helped give shape to their earlier radicalism, and those of different orientation who joined other small business interests at the heart of the liberal movement. The economic changes in small-scale production, the breaking of artisanal culture at the master level, the increasingly business-like atmosphere and imperatives, and the activities of large-scale producers and merchants in encouraging these trends, were all central elements reconstructing the character of masters in small-scale production, and this helped lay the basis for the political and cultural changes that we can detect.

This ultimately became a drift towards a social – and eventually political – conservatism that emerged fully only after 1918. The move of the lower middle class as a whole – white-collar as well as small business elements – towards Toryism was slow but discernible, one facet of the declining viability of mid-Victorian community liberalism towards the end of the century. The petite bourgeoisie had helped bind together the liberal urban ideals, at times injecting them with a radicalizing attack on privilege and protection. As that declined in the changing social climate of the late nineteenth century, so the business élite's drift towards 'Villa Toryism' seems to have carried much of the white-collar and small business lower middle class with it.[62] The Tory organization in London, the London Municipal Society, was by 1905 reserving places on its local committees for representatives of property owners' and ratepayers' associations, though not all wanted that full identification.[63] The petite bourgeoisie was pressed increasingly into a small business commitment to private property, *laissez-faire*, and the market that defined itself more in relation to labour than to big capital. It is significant that early socialist strategies from the 1880s sought to penetrate the administration of local government and the poor law – the very areas where the local interests of small property were most decisively represented. Local small businessmen like Frank Bullen were appalled: 'The doctrines I heard preached by the socialists in the open air simply filled me with dismay. For it was nothing else but the unfit and incurably idle, the morally degenerate, at the expense of the fit, the hard-working, and the striving classes.'[64]

The politics of the petite bourgeoisie did not disappear after the 1840s, but it lost its distinctive presence as its focus and its concerns narrowed. The older positions did not vanish. We can see this in the way that the ratepayers of Bath and Great Yarmouth, and what has been called the 'cranky radicalism' of the west midlands small master belt, gave local organized support to the Administrative Reform Association in the middle of the 1850s.[65] We would probably find it in the Tichborne movement of the 1870s. And it was an independent and individualistic small business radicalism that led the struggle against the enclosure of a section of beech by the Pier Company at Southsea in the 1870s.[66] Hardly heroic causes, though still rooted in many of the old ideals and drawing upon their vocabulary. The petit-bourgeois political presence survived essentially as a ratepayer cause and became locally introverted, in significant contrast to developments within both the bourgeoisie and the organized working class. The national political framework is important here, for there were no attempts to mobilize the petite bourgeoisie against any subversive threats to the existing order. As a political force, they were not needed in Britain. No one tried to win, to bribe, or to appease them.

The very nature of petit-bourgeois problems outlined earlier in this essay encouraged this withdrawal into local and highly specific affairs. The distinctive interventions after mid-century were largely limited to pressure group activities in support of precise interests, as the British petite bourgeoisie no longer sought any broader re-orientation of political or social practice. The unity of the German *Mittelstand* may have been illusory, but the ideal of the *Mittelstand* was not. No such formulation appeared as historical ideal or policy argument within British politics, where a petit-bourgeois presence became limited to the defence of sectional interests.

Such interest groups most commonly involved the petite bourgeoisie as shopkeepers, ratepayers or house owners. This is not the place to explore the shopkeeper associations that grew from the 1850s, mostly at the town level but with the formation of national trade associations from the last decade of the century, for the organizations and their ideology and activities are the subject of my essay later in this book. What must be emphasized are the limited demands of these associations, and the absence of either a political perspective or demands for government help. The principal efforts were to maintain 'free' competition, and to do that involved little in the way of national political organization. Services to members and local responses to issues provoked by municipal government prevailed. The way in which all these associations, and even the brief agitational movements such as those over co-operatives, eschewed any autonomous politics – in contrast to many petty commercial defence associations on the continent at this time – is striking evidence of the assumption that a distinctive political voice was not needed.

It was as cost-conscious ratepayers that a once radical petite bourgeoisie, fighting monopoly and privilege, now expressed its anxieties. Municipal investment in new sanitary schemes put pressure on the rates in the 1850s, and that decade saw the appearance of ratepayers' associations all over the country. The attack on the rich élite was there, as local shopkeepers and small masters organized to resist its profligate ways in the town's affairs. The evidence we have from Salford, Newcastle-under-Lyme, and most explicitly the Economy party in Birmingham reflects a more widespread phenomenon.[67] They were a continuing force in local affairs by late in the century and, if Offer's analysis of the unequal rate burden afflicting the small businessmen of London[68] is of wider validity, then their concern is explicable, however narrow its political perspective. Ratepayer concerns also characterized the house owners' associations which, with their concern for local government rate demands and their anxieties over building and housing regulations, became widespread as the century progressed. Stable associations grew from the 1860s with a national federation established in 1888. Most associations seem to have been small, and could have organized no more than a minority of the myriads of small property owners.[69] Englander finds in these property owners' associations a sense of embattlement during the late-Victorian and Edwardian years, a feeling that economic and political developments were leaving them isolated.[70] A better comprehension of that atmosphere might come from an exploration of the social bases of landlordism, and its wider anxieties.

In none of these organizations do we see any weakening of the commitment to economic liberal assumptions on the part of British shopkeepers and small producers. They continued to visualize their future alongside, rather than dominated by, the larger bourgeoisie. The corollary of this commitment to economic liberalism is the absence of right-extremist political organizations growing out of or mobilizing small business interests. In Britain, the lower middle class as a whole remained committed to mainstream party politics. Organizations of a militantly right-wing complexion, such as the Liberty and Property Defence League and the Anti-Socialist Union,[71] were large-business backed groups concerned with opposing socialism and the threat of state intervention, and they never sought to appeal to the forces of the small man, to mobilize him with an alternative politics. Nor is there any evidence of a petit-bourgeois social base for nationalist organizations like the Navy League.[72] The unusual and virulently anti-socialist Cardiff Ratepayers' and Property Owners' Association set up in 1900 won little support.[73] Most interesting of all, perhaps, was the Middle Class Defence Organization founded in 1906 as an anti-socialist and pro-economy force directed at municipal affairs, for its propagandists talked a language familiar to students of movements of the *classes moyennes* on the continent. 'We are the buffer interest', noted one correspondent,[74] and there was much talk of those ground between capital and labour. Yet the sins of capital, when listed, were no more than its willingness to buy off labour by increasing taxes on the 'middle classes'.[75] There was no real infusion of the movement with petit-bourgeois concerns,[76] no distinctive identity in relation to capital.

In other words, petit-bourgeois politics in Britain stayed resolutely within the existing party structure, and there was no real pressure from the petite bourgeoisie or from outside political interests to break that. In part we are seeing the consequences of the absence of a distinctive petit-bourgeois ideology of a traditional kind. There had developed no body of economic or political ideas that distinguished small proprietorial aspirations and ideals from the dominant ideology of *laissez-faire* liberalism to which the British petite bourgeoisie remained resolutely wedded. The closer examination of shopkeeper ideas in my essay below shows this clearly. An understanding of why there never developed in Britain, in the way that there did, especially in Germany, but also in France and Belgium, a conception of the petite bourgeoisie as a stabilizing force in modern society would take us beyond those petits bourgeois and into larger questions of ideological and structural comparison. It is clear, though, that the lower middle class as a whole (small business and white-collar groups) was given no wider political and social tradition to which to attach themselves and through which to develop a distinctive consciousness in relation to larger capital. The absence of a small proprietorial peasantry might well be a central element in explaining that, but there was also the deeper hold in Britain of those competitive free trade ideas to which the petite bourgeoisie clung more persistently at the very time at the turn of the century when political and business leaders were relaxing the rigidities of non-intervention. The Birmingham tool-maker, Joseph Brown, for example, told de Rousiers of his deeply individualistic philosophy of life. Unhappy experiences had taught him that 'the best capital a man can have is himself', and that 'each man's life is a problem of which he must find the solution; . . . that each man must seek it for himself.'[77] The petit-bourgeois voice had none of the bite of the *Mittelstand* critique, and was characterized by an ideological diffuseness. That is why it was amongst such petits bourgeois in late nineteenth-century London that eccentric individualist concerns best flourished: anti-state fanatics, no popery extremists, political anti-clerics.[78] The combined effect of economic position and work situation, aspirations and anxieties, was to reinforce that faith in rational competitive individualism, and with it a view of the economic order that ascribed symbolic moral importance to the free enterprise system.

This narrow moral individualism might be viewed as the natural consequence of the work situation, vulnerability, and restricted capital resources of the petite bourgeoisie – though similar characteristics elsewhere in Europe were accompanied by a higher degree of mobilization and social association. The differences are perhaps only of degree. Theirs was an introspective way of life, and shopkeepers and small masters in Britain were reluctant to experience their problems except as individuals. Small enterprise was too fragile in its resources and its vulnerability to the pressures of credit, not to mention ill-health or family crisis, ever to feel secure. But the problems were individualized, as were the options for improvement. This must be a factor in the reluctance to organize. It must also explain the characteristic investment of any savings in secure and visible local forms, above all housing for rental. This helps us to see one of the most important features that distinguished these people from the more substantial bourgeoisie, and that is the specificity of petit-bourgeois property. Their belief in the rights of property became bound up, morally as much as economically, in a particular piece of property. Petit-bourgeois capital and property remained essentially immobile in practice – something well recognized by Cardiff councillors protesting against the threat that the shipping élite could simply shift to docks elsewhere.[79]

The anxieties that could flow from this were intensified by the problems of maintaining family status. How to ensure that those sons who could not hope to inherit the business entered suitable alternative occupations? What little evidence we have suggests a lower than average continuity between father and son in retailing.[80] The problem of suitable marriages for daughters could prove even more awkward for those with sufficient property to fear the threat to its security that was implied by a bad marriage,[81] but for much of the petite bourgeoisie such choices were probably not available and a family flow across the divide from the working class was inevitable. Provision for daughters who did not marry and for widows leads us back to investment in small property, and produced a very evident female rentier class in Victorian Britain.[82]

There were therefore many forces committing the British petite bourgeoisie in the second half of the nineteenth century to a life-style that focused on the family with an intensity that may have been less strong earlier in the century when a larger proportion of shopkeepers and small producers would have been involved in the popular world of the street and the *quartier*. The autobiographies of those born into shopkeeping families testify to the introverted world of their childhood, and oral history evidence supports that picture.[83] This was not a purely cultural introspection that grew out of fears of the rough world outside, but far more strongly one imposed by the economic and social necessities of a small enterprise that dictated its own life-style, its own sense of being tied to a demanding business. Yet a family-centred existence did indeed offer a means of separating such people from the working class that often lived around them, of preserving values and status. Helen Corke was born into a shopkeeping family of the 1880s, and had reached the age of eight before being allowed to associate with a neighbour's child or enter a neighbour's house. The Vincent family, with their shop and lodging house in Cardiff, likewise coped with the poverty around them by turning in on the home. Yet they were at the same time an element in the community. More precisely, the father was, for 'when anyone died they'd come for him to head the funeral'.[84]

The resources with which to maintain that family-centred and respectable status for the next generation were very limited. As the problem of small enterprise grew in the late nineteenth century, and fuelled doubts as to the possibility and even the desirability of passing on such businesses, so we find petit-bourgeois parents all over Europe using education to obtain white-collar and minor professional careers for their sons. Status could thus be maintained, or so it was hoped. Education as a result came to assume great importance, for with limited financial resources to pass on, this offered a useful way to invest in their children's future.[85] In Britain, expanding white-collar employment (paradoxically based on that growth of state, commercial and financial institutions which so many petits bourgeois feared) thus proved an attractive solution to these perpetual petit-bourgeois problems, and evidence suggests that they were indeed taking it up.[86] Did such opportunities attenuate petit-bourgeois social frustration? And what was the consequence of the relatively limited availability in Britain of the state employment that carried so much more prestige to continental white-collar occupations? Whatever the answers, the prior problems of education itself remained real, for in contrast to France, where a hierarchy of educational institutions gave peasant and small business families potential access to professional and government service,[87] the counterparts of such people in Britain remained fairly well detached from the educational system of the upper middle class. Indeed, the provision of education for petit-bourgeois families was to become a real problem in the closing decades of the century. An increasing section of the wealthier élite saw reform of education as a means by which to embed these people into an existing or reformed social and political order. Hence T. H. Green's scheme for Birmingham schooling, which concerned itself with the need to impregnate the petite bourgeoisie with a general culture from above, while simultaneously giving children of that group some real prospects for advance. He achieved little real success, and the difficulty continued. At the end of the century it was higher grade schools and the scholarship system, rooted in many ways in a petit-bourgeois quest for good and respectable education for their children, that made the problems even more explicit, for here was an attachment of such children to an educational system unconnected with that of the élite and not under the clear control of bourgeois culture and ideas. The setting up of a 'ladder of opportunity' with the 1902 Education Act was in part about the cultural co-option of these shopkeepers, small employers and traders, and clerks.[88]

The petit-bourgeois concern for advance or at least stability through education was the consequence of a status that lacked economic security or a more than limited potential for growth. The capital was usually too restricted and trapped. H. G. Wells's parents saw the poor prospects of their Bromley shop in the mid-Victorian period, 'but they had now no means of getting out of it and going anywhere'.[89] East Anglian trawling unexpectedly reveals exactly the same problem, the classic petit-bourgeois dilemma, as the fisherman owner could neither realize his existing capital effectively nor find any alternative use for it. So he continued trawling.[90] In his *Confessions of a Tradesman* Frank Bullen articulates this sense of having to keep going, for even when the venture was going poorly he was trapped with it. For one reason, there was too much tied up in it. He went on not in hope, but because 'as far as my limited intelligence went I couldn't do anything else'.[91] All of these factors shaped the social localism and the moral individualism of the petite bourgeoisie.

While the established bourgeoisie would be marked out by its regional and even national contacts, there was something irreducibly local about much of the petite bourgeoisie. Further, if they were most publicly important in those small towns where a wealthier social élite was barely apparent, and where introspective communities in much of Europe might reinforce a small propertied identity,[92] then the British shopkeepers and small producers were in an especially difficult position in a society that urbanized both rapidly and early. Compared with a great deal of the continent, Britain was just not a small town society. The localism would thus become less assertive. The parochial character of its culture must have severely impaired the ability of the British petits bourgeois to cope with change, and must have been responsible for much of the rigidity of values that only hardened as the period progressed.

A strict and conventional concern for respectability was one way to assuage these tensions. Helen Corke's father may have been stirred by the new bicycle craze, but he spent the money instead on a piano.[93] A symbol of the petit-bourgeois dilemma? An attachment to the values of a more prosperous bourgeoisie certainly characterizes these small business people in the social as much as in the political sphere. See the growing separation of workplace from home in shopkeeping during the second half of the century, which not only dramatically altered the female involvement in the enterprise but signalled a purposeful identification with middle-class evangelical ideas about the separation of spheres.[94] Status aspirations and social identity were essential, and they rested on a deep sense of economic independence, reinforced by the social ideals of religious nonconformity and the narrow dissenting historical culture that went with them. Did the passion for reading and for literature that some retailers seem to have passed on to their sons challenge that?[95] No culture can be purely imitative, but we know too little about that of the petite bourgeoisie. It does seem that personal effort, personal struggle and personal propriety were seen as the bases of success,[96] and in an economic milieu characterized by instability that must have been a disturbing ideology with which to interpret one's fate. The inability to imagine change or to organize for it derived not just from structural position but also from the specific ideology and values of the British petite bourgeoisie in the closing decades of the century. It was a view of the world that must have condemned many of them to a great deal of personal pain. Yet the ideology seems barely to have shifted to cope with a world which was, towards the end of the century, less and less favourable to them. There were, in any case, always new recruits for whom their position represented hope rather than despair. Instability of enterprises, instability between generations[97] must be one reason why they failed to develop what we might call a class experience, a cultural transmission of history and understanding.

SOCIAL RELATIONSHIPS AND THE COMMUNITY

The precise areas of integration of petits bourgeois into the economic and social structure and into networks of power and dependence might well prove to be the most illuminating way into an understanding of this group. Its economic significance has already been urged, but some of the other spheres of importance will at least be indicated – space permits little more – in the pages that remain: local government, the material fabric of the Victorian town, and relationships with the working class, notably over work, residence and retailing.

Local government in Victorian Britain enjoyed a degree of autonomy unusual in contemporary Europe, and the strong petit-bourgeois role in local administration is thus especially important. Each town had its own history in this respect. In some towns municipal reform led to liberal town councillors who were overwhelmingly traders, shopkeepers, minor professionals and small manufacturers from as early as the end of the 1830s: Stockport is one example.[98] Sometimes larger bourgeois involvement withered away early – by 1844 in Newcastle-under-Lyme – but often petit-bourgeois domination was the outcome of the eviction of larger business interests, as in Hull and Salford. According to the Salford local newspaper in 1868, the town's large businessmen were 'gradually compelled to give up all hopes or claims to posts of distinction in the town' by those from whom the inhabitants 'bought their beef and beer.'[99] The most striking case is that of Birmingham, with a continuing conflict from the 1860s between a municipally-minded dissenting élite and economy-minded small businessmen which produced a fluctuating balance of control.[100] None of this should be any surprise. Local government finance in Britain was derived exclusively from a tax on real property which gave those whose livelihood rested on the use of small property (shops or houses or workshops) a strong incentive to keep tight control on expenditure and therefore rates.[101] Petit-bourgeois strength in local government, resting as much on the willingness of a larger bourgeoisie to withdraw to a greater regional or national stage as on their actual displacement, was therefore a recurrent feature of town affairs. The fact that they could be permitted to occupy that position leads us back to the victory of liberalism amongst them: petit-bourgeois local government did not threaten liberal economic and social policy, certainly not until that changed with the rise of municipalism at the end of the century.

Self-interest could also drive small businessmen into local government. It was unlikely to have been a pure concern for public service that took three innkeepers and a pawnbroker onto Bridgwater watch committee in 1859,[102] and the drink trade was generally well-represented, as were builders concerned about both building bye-laws and contracts, and house owners seeking control over public health officials and rate assessment. Retailers might have been anxious about excessive freedom for market traders, especially where the council controlled the town's market. Such a list could continue, but to attribute petit-bourgeois strength on local government to precise self-interest would be as mistaken as to present the professional and business élite as 'natural leaders'.[103] Indeed, it was the small businessmen who stayed on Salford council far longer than average.[104] If local commitment and identity, sharpened by the dissenting values of the liberal community, characterized the petite bourgeoisie; and if immobility of capital and the nature of the local taxation base engendered special anxieties; then the natural leaders of many communities might plausibly be seen as not the plutocrat or the lawyer in the villa beyond the fields, for whom the prestige of local office seemed increasingly insignificant, but the grocer, the draper and the small engineer whose local community was as much the centre of their lives as they were of its. Hennock has shown the cost-conscious yet inefficient character of petit-bourgeois local government, and when the Plymouth medical officer of health complained in 1900 that 'the small shop element was what he disliked. Down with everything was their motto,'[105] he was indicating their detrimental effect on municipal services.

It was not just through council inaction that the urban petite bourgeoisie could determine the character of local housing, for the small businessman stood at the centre of the provision and ownership of housing for the working class in most British cities. They could help finance house construction by making short-term credit available to speculative builders,[106] but they were more frequently the actual proprietors of houses that they let to working-class tenants. They might purchase new houses on completion, or purchase existing housing stock, and the shifting balance between the two investments is fundamental to the character of the housing problem. Even without that relative transfer, their specific investment needs could distort the local housing market. One contemporary attributed speculative over-production of houses in early-Victorian Sheffield to 'the petty capitalist . . . desirous of realizing a handsome percentage'.[107] The attractions of owning houses have already been stressed, and to that security was increasingly added the desire to invest capital for subsequent retirement, a pattern that seems to have been growing stronger by the 1880s.[108] The motives were complex, but their interaction with local capital and building markets left the men and women of small capital as the overwhelming force in working-class housing.[109]

House ownership leads us into the ambiguous question of the relationship between the petite bourgeoisie and the working class, an ambiguity only partly attributable to the heterogeneity of the small business men and women and their social milieux. If, as Bechhofer and Elliott have suggested, the two social groups progressively separated as the century advanced,[110] then the control of housing constituted an important arena within which the divide opened up. The petit-bourgeois freemen's interest in the unenclosed burgess lands of Nottingham in the first half of the century, and their involvement in the house-building that followed enclosure, were two distinct mallets driving a wedge between the town's working people and its small business class.[111] Housing was an area of particular vulnerability and insecurity, for tenants inevitably, but also for landlords, given their limited stature. It was the small house proprietors who were identified time and again as the worst of the landlords, least able to afford repairs or improvements, and least willing to afford them.[112] This behaviour was rooted in insecurity, and from that stemmed much of the tension of the housing relationship. The small landlord was dependent on his tenants for the return on his capital, and felt vulnerable to their non-payment and moonlighting. The working-class tenants – or a good proportion of them – depended on landlord credit as part of a strategy for survival, with arrears that accumulated in the winter being paid off as work prospects improved. It was for the property owners to decide who might be allowed to defer their rent. In Englander's words, 'a bond of debt united landlord and tenant'.[113] Not all could be allowed that, at least not willingly, and the extraction of rents from reluctant and impecunious tenants, rents often high to allow for the inevitable defaulters, was a continuing source of irritation. Landlords sought greater legal support, and the Small Tenements' Recovery Act of 1838 made eviction a great deal simpler. Riot and disturbance over evictions became common in the early-Victorian period, and continuing tensions were engendered by the use of bailiffs and debt collectors to distrain for rent.[114] None of this was made any easier by the close supervision that many a small landlord sought to exercise over his tenants. In the 1830s, the small shopkeeper and small proprietor of Derby 'invest their money in running up rows of little tenements, the rents of which they rigidly collect every Monday', while tradesmen in one Middlesex parish were pleased to possess such property, 'having the opportunity of personally looking after the occupiers'.[115] Not a great deal had changed in this respect a half-century on, for one Bristol observer confirmed that these small men who invest their savings in houses to let 'look very sharply after their tenants'; and that they liked to be able to collect their rents personally.[116] Concern for proper tenant behaviour, as much as pecuniary anxiety, inspired this closeness of inspection. Maybe the two motives cannot be separated in that way. 'Small capitalists' might even seek to use this control to influence their tenants' voting choices in local elections – that was certainly the claim of many witnesses to an 1859 parliamentary committee.[117]

These house owners were often the local shopkeepers. Often enough, perhaps, to influence popular images of the petite bourgeoisie, whatever the reality. In this way could other sources of tension find reinforcement? Adulteration of produce was notorious amongst those retailers selling to the working class, and the credit system was the lynchpin of their success. Irregular income meant that many working-class families needed a reliable structure of credit in order to survive. That usually entailed dependence on one shop where credit was available to the family. The shopkeeper secured a trapped clientèle in return. A South Wales grocer in favour of cash only trading at the end of the period knew full well that 'the tradesman favours the credit system because it has a tendency to keep his customers under an obligation to deal with him'.[118] For many traders operating to tight and uncertain profit margins, the dependence allowed poor quality and short-weighting. 'All the small traders give credit,' noted Frank Bullen. 'Of course, in this way much very inferior stuff is got rid of.'[119] It is unfortunate that we know so little beyond such generalizations about the daily relationship between shopkeepers and their customers. The self-evident abuses of this kind have to be counterbalanced by the power of the customers to shop elsewhere – and that generally rested on not needing credit. The practice of 'exclusive dealing' by popular radicals in the 1830s and 1840s was its most politicized expression, though there is disagreement as to the extent of its success.[120]

Against such tensions must be set the closeness and sense of identity that existed between small employers and shopkeepers[121] on the one hand, and sections of the working class on the other. The supposedly close relationship between masters and men in small workshop industries has provided the basis for a whole interpretation of the politics of Birmingham,[122] and that cohesion model has been extrapolated to other towns.[123] Little evidence is generally presented as to the content of this social cohesiveness, which tends to be assumed from political co-operation. It is an analysis of workplace relations that is too readily applied, irrespective of time and place. We know that later in the century the new kinds of petit-bourgeois employer, who had lifted himself from a proletarian background, all too often regarded his workers with a critical superiority. Joseph Brown, the Birmingham tool-maker, had a 'poor opinion of men who find it hard to make a living for themselves and their families in a trade where he has been able to raise himself and his family to a good position'. A small employer's craft pride ('he still flatters himself that no smith in Birmingham can turn out better or quicker work') implied no necessary identification with his journeymen.[124] It is that fracturing of craft identity and cohesion[125] that is the key to the changing relationship, and it is a process that Clive Behagg has examined persuasively for the case of Birmingham.[126] That same capitalist restructuring of productive relations in the London artisan trades radically altered social relationships within small-scale production there too.[127] The economic difficulties of small masters, and the way that so many responded by intensifying work methods and behaving less and less according to the artisanal expectations of their trade, made increasing conflict between masters and journeymen unavoidable.

Small employers became notorious for paying low wages and maintaining poor work conditions. Even when workshop regulation grew in the 1860s, few localities had the staff of inspectors to enforce the law.[128] All of which should come as no surprise, for small enterprises were the most vulnerable to changing economic conditions, with their low capitalization, and tight credit and liquidity problems. Depression saw them suffer rapidly,[129] while in better times they found it hard to hold onto their best workmen. The Master and Servant Acts, compelling employers to fulfil contracts, were most frequently used by small manufacturers seeking to keep workers in order to complete orders. Staffordshire, the Black Country, Birmingham and Sheffield – the classic small master districts – regularly saw more prosecutions than any other area.[130] Anyone who has worked through Victorian local newspapers will have seen the countless cases brought by building firms against recalcitrant craftsmen. So, even where social and workplace proximity might imply cohesiveness, the realities of small-scale production and its uneven transformation made for often tense relationships. It also made for those strike waves in such industries, movements about which we know too little. We find an early and ferocious example in the London tailoring trades of the 1820s and 1830s, as journeymen, together with some masters, sought to retain traditional modes of workshop production.[131]

The cohesion argument might prove to be an illusion that rests, as Behagg argues below, on a conflation of older master artisans rooted in the culture and assumptions of the craft, and newer small businessmen tied ever more closely not into the craft but into the world of business. There was, nevertheless, a degree of ambiguity to the workplace relationship quite absent from situations where shopkeepers and other small businessmen acted as middlemen in outwork and subcontracting. It was a classically petit-bourgeois activity to organize at a secondary level the putting-out system that abounded in British industry. During the first half of the century they increasingly owned the hosiery frames in Nottingham, and rented them out to knitters – an investment not unlike that in houses, and a good way for men of small capital to obtain a steady return without being involved in production itself. 'Foggers' was the Black Country name for those shopkeepers and publicans who acted as middlemen, notably in nail-making, and often gave part payment in kind through their pubs and 'tommy shops'.[132] Publicans would often organize an industry. Many of the High Wycombe chair makers in the 1870s were publicans, controlling the manufacturing in the surrounding districts; while the 'lumpers' on the London docks were similarly organized by publicans and chandlers acting as subcontractors of dock labour gangs.[133] Systems such as these proliferated in structures of production and employment geared to irregular or small-scale tasks. The organizational problems of industrialization were frequently overcome by such fragmentary means, and shopkeepers and small tradesmen rushed to play the middleman's part.

However, to press the tensions between working people and those small men who owned their houses, organized their work, gave them employment and sold them their food is to swim against a still resilient orthodoxy which has tended to stress the areas of propinquity and community that bound many small businessmen in Britain to the working class around them. The orthodoxy is not wholly wrong. Many a small master retained his trade union membership. John Watson, a pearl button maker with his own workshop, was actually secretary of the trade society.[134] They did so not just as an insurance against a return to wage employment, but as a sign of identification with the artisanal culture, the trade union and friendly society, and the public house.[135] In the context of nineteenth-century British society, the transition from wage-earner to small master was not *necessarily* experienced as upward mobility. It gave some freedom from wage labour, to be sure, but implied no automatic change of social identity or milieu. The power of popular sociability, of craft culture, of personal values, could all fundamentally shape the way that people experienced such change.[136] As the means to success or survival changed in small-scale production, as the traditional methods of production and distribution which partially insulated small masters against the competitive world of commercialized production declined, so the craft community was being fractured by economic change in more and more industries.

Those problems of differentiation within the world of small enterprise, and the implications for relationships with the working class, are just as great when we turn to shopkeepers. It is relatively easy to place the retailers whose custom was drawn from the middle class of the town, for their contact with the working class would become increasingly patrician as more substantial retailers inserted themselves into that structure of urban charity and voluntary associations that the wealthy were abandoning. The position of those who dealt with the working class in increasingly segregated cities, where the retail petite bourgeoisie might be the only non-proletarian element left in inner districts, is more ambiguous. Many clearly felt at least sympathy and understanding for their customers, especially in depression or strikes. Robert Roberts's recollections of his mother's small grocery shop in a Salford slum before the First World War confirm the complex but close relationship with that neighbourhood of which she saw herself a part. She identified with local working-class struggles, and in times of crisis the granting of credit could prove a difficult decision, as her generosity and sense of identity fought with her instincts for self-preservation.[137] An oral history investigation of shopkeepers in East Brighton has shown the fragile and delicate operation that was the allowance of credit by small shopkeepers. 'There was a fine line between being too free with credit and taking on too many bad debts, and not being free enough and losing custom as a result.'[138] Giving credit in times of individual or community need was partly a business operation, partly a form of support or charity, and partly a source of what Melanie Tebbutt has called in relation to pawnbrokers 'an important source of authority and control'. She sees the result as 'a peculiar interdependence which impinged most directly upon the lives of women who were the retailers' main customers'.[139] It all tied at the daily level into the female world of the working-class community, struggling to make ends meet in ways often hidden from their husbands. Credit – and the ability to get it at short notice – was essential to that. It is hardly surprising that shopkeepers, ambivalently tied into the popular world around them, were so frequently the closest targets for outbursts of fury. When political protest turned to riot, it was shops that were all too often the focus of attack, usually over issues apparently unconcerned with retail trade. Chartist protest in London was one example, but much more striking were the Tonypandy riots in South Wales over sixty years later.[140] The complex web of dependence, positive support and consumer aspiration, was woven with fragile threads, and the social explosion that crises could produce gives us only a partial insight into relationships almost ignored by historians.

We return to the recurrent theme of the changing relationship between the shopkeepers, the small masters, and the working-class community around them, that has surfaced so regularly in this essay. R. J. Morris has suggested of the publican James Kitson in early-Victorian Leeds that he identified with the 'labouring classes', although as an innkeeper he was owning and managing capital in a bourgeois manner. 'Like many small shopkeepers and tradesmen he took his class identity from his customers rather than from his relationship with capital and property.'[141] If we distinguish the Roberts's sympathy from Kitson's class identity, we might merely be drawing attention to the changing definitions of class within the British social structure over the intervening three-quarters of a century. It is more likely that we are uncovering the relationship of petit-bourgeois identity to personal origins and family history, to political culture and social community, which introduced a myriad of distinctions within the social group itself. Against Kitson, against Roberts, stands the Corke family who feared and despised their inevitable contact with the working class. The very character of the British petite bourgeoisie means that so many of our unanswered questions are the most important: the precise questions of its relationship to the working class and to the larger bourgeoisie. If the shift in balance towards an identification with the latter is a general conclusion of this essay, that identification was never total and, more importantly, a dissection of the petit-bourgeois world would open up its own internal stratification. These were people whose changing economic and political character seems to have been shaped by forces, movements, transformations outside their own control, even influence.

Yet the too ready conclusion has been to see them as no more than the objects of history. This essay has sought to indicate their real historical and analytical importance for the study of British society in this period. Closer examination of the way in which different types of small producers and shopkeepers operated in relation to their communities, workforces and customers will enable us not only to differentiate more precisely within the small propertied groups, but also to understand their various relationships to the changing political and social structure of nineteenth-century Britain.

NOTES

1 P. M. Jones, 'The rural bourgeoisie of the southern Massif-Central: a contribution to the study of the social structure of *ancien régime* France', *Social History*, 4, 1979, esp. 65–6.

2 Bédarida has calculated that small employers and shopkeepers formed nearly 10 per cent of the occupied population of London in 1851: F. Bédarida, 'Londres au milieu du XIXe siècle: une analyse de structure sociale', *Annales ESC*, 1968, 292. For other towns see R. Gray, *The Labour Aristocracy in Victorian Edinburgh*, Oxford, 1976, 28; W. G. Rimmer, 'The industrial profile of Leeds, 1780–1840', Thoresby Society Publications 113, *Miscellany*, 14, Leeds, 1967, 130–57; F. Bealey, 'Municipal politics in Newcastle-under-Lyme, 1835–1872', *North Staffordshire Journal of Field Studies*, 3, 1963, 75; J. Foster, *Class Struggle and the Industrial Revolution. Early Industrial Capitalism in Three English Towns*, London, 1974, 76.

3 F. Bechhofer and B. Elliott, 'Persistence and change: the petite bourgeoisie in industrial society', *Archives européenes de sociologie*, 17, 1976, 81.

4 Cf. J. B. Jefferys, *Retail Trading in Britain 1850–1950*, Cambridge, 1954. The best surveys of the development of retail trading are D. Alexander, *Retailing in England during the Industrial Revolution*, London, 1970, and D. Davis, *A History of Shopping*, London, 1966.

5 R. Scola, 'Food markets and shops in Manchester, 1770–1870', *Journal of Historical Geography*, 1, 1975, 153–68; R. Scola, 'Retailing in the nineteenth-century town: some problems and possibilities', in J. H. Johnson and C. G. Pooley (eds), *The Structure of Nineteenth-Century Cities*, London, 1982, 153–69.

6 G. Shaw and M. T. Wild, 'Retail patterns in the Victorian city', Institute of British Geographers, *Transactions*, 4, 1979, 280.

7 M. T. Wild and G. Shaw, 'Population distribution and retail provision: the case of the Halifax-Calder Valley area of West Yorkshire during the second half of the nineteenth century', *Journal of Historical Geography*, 1, 1975, 193–210.

8 The literature on increasing competition in the retail trades is dominated by the now rather dated, and in places speculative, study by Jefferys, op. cit. The only recent work is P. Mathias, *Retailing Revolution. A History of Multiple Retailing in the Food Trades Based upon the Allied Suppliers Group of Companies*, London, 1967. See also the brief but valuable studies by F. G. Pennance and B. S. Yamey, 'Competition in the retail grocery trade 1850–1939', *Economica*, 22, 1955, 303–17, and B. S. Yamey, *The Economics of Retail Price Maintenance*, London, 1954, chs 7 and 8. Contemporary work in Britain was very limited, but see H. W. Macrosty, *The Trust Movement in British Industry. A Study of Business Organisation*, London, 1907; and J. A. Rees, *The Grocery Trade. Its History and Romance*, London, 1910, vol. 2, 220–57. French social scientists were predictably far more interested in these questions. See Pierre Moride, *Les Maisons*

à succursales multiples en France et à l'étranger, Paris, 1913, who has much to say on Britain, and L. Sénéchal, *La Concentration industrielle et commerciale en Angleterre*, Paris, 1909, chs 8 and 9. For a close study of a single trade, there is only P. J. Atkins, 'The retail milk trade in London, *c.* 1790–1914', *Economic History Review*, second series, 33, 1980, 522–37.

9 Moride, op. cit., 66–9.

10 'In England, the rate of concentration by multiples has reached a quite remarkable degree of intensity,' according to Moride, op. cit., 78. Shoes, grocery, pharmacy, bakers, booksellers, coal, dyers and cleaners, tailors, restaurants, milk, wine, tobacco all had major national chains. The most striking was amongst butchers, with no major chains elsewhere in Europe, while in Britain the three largest companies boasted 2300 shops between them (ibid., 78–9). For the way that the multiples swept into one suburb in the 1890s, see H. J. Dyos, *Victorian Suburb. A Study of the Growth of Camberwell*, Leicester, 1966, 149–52.

11 H. W. Macrosty, *Trusts and the State. A Sketch of Competition*, London, 1901, 193.

12 Jefferys, op. cit., 16.

13 A. Briggs, *Friends of the People. The Centenary History of Lewis's*, London, 1956, 38.

14 Booth Collection (at the British Library of Political and Economic Science), B 133 f. 19.

15 ibid., f. 34.

16 Cited in Jefferys, op. cit., 36.

17 Select Committee on the Shop Hours Regulation Bill, *Parliamentary Papers*, 1886, XII, Q. 274–82.

18 Booth Collection, B 134, f. 3; E. Porter, *Victorian Cambridge. Josiah Chater's Diaries 1844–1884*, Chichester, 1975, 63.

19 R. Samuel, 'The workshop of the world: steam power and hand technology in mid-Victorian Britain', *History Workshop*, 3, 1977, 6–72.

20 There are no systematic published data on size of firm in nineteenth-century Britain. In their absence, see J. H. Clapham, *An Economic History of Britain. vol. 2: The Early Railway Age, 1820–1850*, Cambridge, 1964 edn, 33–5; P. Kropotkin, 'The small industries of Britain', *The Nineteenth Century*, 48, 1900, 256–71.

21 J. Benson, *The Penny Capitalists. A Study of Nineteenth-Century Working-Class Entrepreneurs*, Dublin, 1983.

22 An example of how tiny these operations could be is in J. Blackman, 'The development of the retail grocery trade in the nineteenth century', *Business History*, 9, 1967, 115–16; T. Vigne and A. Howkins, 'The small shopkeeper in industrial and market towns', in G. Crossick (ed.), *The Lower Middle Class in Britain 1870–1914*, London, 1976, 187–8.

23 G. I. H. Lloyd, *The Cutlery Trades. An Historical Essay in the Economics of Small-Scale Production*, London, 1913, 193; S. Pollard, *A History of Labour in Sheffield*, Liverpool, 1959, 157–8; H. Mayhew, *London Labour and the London Poor*, London, 1861 (Dover edn 1968), vol. 3, 228–9; E. P. Thompson and E. Yeo (eds), *The Unknown Mayhew. Selections from the* Morning Chronicle *1849–1850*, London, 1971, 390, 448–9; K. Brooker, 'The changing position of the small owner in the English shoemaking industry, 1860–1914', unpublished paper delivered to the 2nd Round Table on the European Petite Bourgeoisie in the Nineteenth Century at the University of Bremen, 1980, 4–5.

24 P. Joyce, *Work, Society and Politics: the Culture of the Factory in Later Victorian England*, Brighton, 1980.

25 G. C. Allen, *The Industrial Development of Birmingham and the Black Country 1860–1927*, London, 1929 (1966 edn), 113. On London see G. Stedman Jones, *Outcast London. A Study in the Relationship Between Classes in Victorian Society*, Oxford, 1971, 19–32, and Bédarida, op. cit.

26 Rimmer, op. cit.
27 Compare the German master artisans discussed by S. Volkov, *The Rise of Popular Anti-modernism in Germany. The Urban Master Artisans, 1873–1896*, Princeton, 1978.
28 On the London tailors see T. M. Parsinnen and I. J. Prothero, 'The London tailors' strike of 1834 and the collapse of the Grand National Consolidated Trades' Union: a police spy's report', *International Review of Social History*, 22, 1977, 65–107; on Birmingham and the Black Country, Allen, op. cit., and C. Behagg, 'Radical politics and conflict at the point of production: Birmingham 1815–1845. A study in the relationship between the classes', University of Birmingham PhD thesis, 1982; on Sheffield, Lloyd, op. cit.
29 Saddlers' and coachbuilders' ironmongers were one of the most nationally oriented of such factors. See Allen, op. cit., 130–1. For a helpful typology of the declining economic independence of craftsmen producers drawn into mercantile dependence, see H. D. Fong, *Triumph of the Factory System in England*, Tientsin, 1930, 9–11.
30 On London tailoring and furniture-making in the last quarter of the century in this connection, see Clapham, op. cit., vol. 2, 126.
31 For this discussion, see the paper by K. Brooker referred to already. I am very grateful to Keith Brooker for helpful discussions on this subject based on his doctoral research on the Northampton shoemaking industry.
32 Pollard, op. cit., 54; C. Erickson, *British Industrialists. Steel and Hosiery 1850–1950*, Cambridge, 1959, 94–102, 124. For workshop growth with small-scale machinery in the late nineteenth-century London clothing trades, see J. A. Schmiechen, 'State reform and the local economy: an aspect of industrialization in late-Victorian and Edwardian London', *Economic History Review*, second series, 28, 1975, 413–28.
33 P. Kropotkin, *Fields, Factories and Workshops*, London, 1912 edn, 281.
34 Clapham, op. cit., vol. 3, 183. In cutlery working grinders and cutlers with a handful of employees took work from larger factories with excessive demand, Lloyd, op. cit., 196–7.
35 For brass see Allen, op. cit., 123–4. The words quoted are those of P. de Rousiers, *The Labour Question in Britain*, London, 1896, 95.
36 Allen, op. cit., 127, 136.
37 C. Booth, *Life and Labour of the People in London*, London, 1902 edn, second series, vol. 1, 234.
38 Allen, op. cit., 127, 140; Booth, op. cit., second series, vol. 3, 117–26; Clapham, op. cit., vol. 2, 122–3.
39 Pollard, op. cit., 202ff; Brooker, op. cit.
40 Evidence to the Fair Wages Committee, cited by Pollard, op. cit., 206.
41 De Rousiers, op. cit., 10. On business concentration see P. L. Payne, 'The emergence of the large-scale company in Great Britain, 1870–1914', *Economic History Review*, second series, 20, 1967, 519–42; L. Hannah, 'Mergers in British manufacturing industry, 1880–1918', *Oxford Economic Papers*, 26, 1964, 1–20.
42 De Rousiers, op. cit., 31.
43 For an example, see Geoffrey Crossick, *An Artisan Elite in Victorian Society. Kentish London 1840–1880*, London, 1978, 47–8. Of Northampton footwear firms failing in the years 1885–1912, 38 per cent had been in existence for less than two years, 60 per cent for less than five: Brooker, op. cit., 11.
44 Allen, op. cit., 294–5.
45 E. P. Thompson, *The Making of the English Working Class*, Harmondsworth, 1968 edn, 781–915. Compare the abrupt dismissal by John Foster, who presents petit-bourgeois radicalism as little more than a response to working-class pressure on vulnerable shopkeepers: Foster, op. cit., 131–3, 150.
46 J. Garrard, *Leaders and Politics in Nineteenth-Century Salford: a Historical Analysis of Urban Political Power*, Salford, n.d., 20; T. J. Nossiter, 'Shopkeeper radicalism in the

nineteenth century', in T. J. Nossiter (ed.), *Imagination and Precision in the Social Sciences*, London, 1972, 425.

47 This discussion of petit-bourgeois radicalism develops an argument presented in a comparative European framework in Geoffrey Crossick, 'The petite bourgeoisie in nineteenth-century Europe: problems and research', in K. Tenfelde (ed.), *Internationale Forschungen zur Geschichte der Arbeiterschaft und Arbeiterbewegung*, Munich, 1984.

48 J. Brewer, 'Commercialization and politics', in N. McKendrick, J. Brewer and J. H. Plumb, *The Birth of a Consumer Society: the Commercialization of 18th-century England*, London, 1982, 197–262.

49 Garrard, op. cit., 55–7.

50 J. Epstein, *The Lion of Freedom. Feargus O'Connor and the Chartist Movement, 1832–1842*, London, 1982, 24ff.

51 D. Fraser, *Urban Politics in Victorian England. The Structure of Politics in Victorian Cities*, Leicester, 1976, 107.

52 Brewer, op. cit.

53 Behagg, op. cit., 337.

54 P. Hollis, *The Pauper Press. A Study in Working-Class Radicalism of the 1830s*, Oxford, 1970, 203–19; G. Stedman Jones, 'The language of Chartism', in J. Epstein and D. Thompson (eds), *The Chartist Experience. Studies in Working-Class Radicalism and Culture, 1830–1860*, London, 1982, 3–58.

55 I. Prothero, *Artisans and Politics in Early Nineteenth-Century London: John Gast and His Times*, Folkestone, 1979.

56 D. Jones, *Chartism and the Chartists*, London, 1975, 25; J. T. Ward, *Chartism*, London, 1973, 96; R. S. Neale, *Class and Ideology in the Nineteenth Century*, London, 1972, 54–8; J. Epstein, 'Some organizational and cultural aspects of the Chartist movement in Nottingham', in Epstein and Thompson, op. cit., 227–32; K. Tiller, 'Late Chartism: Halifax 1847–58', in ibid., 335–6.

57 J. F. C. Harrison, 'Chartism in Leeds', in A. Briggs (ed.), *Chartist Studies*, London, 1959, 65–98.

58 P. T. Phillips, *The Sectarian Spirit: Sectarianism, Society, and Politics in Victorian Cotton Towns*, Toronto, 1982, 24; R. J. Morris, 'Samuel Smiles and the genesis of *Self-Help*: the retreat to a petit bourgeois utopia', *Historical Journal*, 24, 1981, 97. For a valuable discussion of changing petit-bourgeois political ideology from these early nineteenth-century roots, see Bechhofer and Elliott, op. cit.

59 D. Goodway, *London Chartism*, Cambridge, 1982, 74–8.

60 Morris, op. cit.

61 Joyce, op. cit., 317.

62 J. Cornford, 'The transformation of conservatism in the late nineteenth century', *Victorian Studies*, 7, 1963, 65.

63 K. Young, *London Politics and the Rise of Party*, Leicester, 1975, 90.

64 F. Bullen, *Confessions of a Tradesman*, London, 1908, 158.

65 O. Anderson, 'The Administrative Reform Association 1855–1857', in P. Hollis (ed.), *Pressure from Without in Early Victorian England*, London, 1974, 275.

66 J. Field, '"When the Riot Act was Read": a pub mural of the Battle of Southsea, 1874', *History Workshop*, 10, 1980, 152–63.

67 E. P. Hennock, 'Finance and politics in urban local government in England, 1835–1900', *Historical Journal*, 6, 1963, 217; Bealey, op. cit., 74–5; Garrard, op. cit., 64–5; E. P. Hennock, *Fit and Proper Persons. Ideal and Reality in Nineteenth-Century Urban Local Government*, London, 1973, 31–3.

68 A. Offer, *Property and Politics 1870–1914. Landownership, Law, Ideology and Urban Development in England*, Cambridge, 1981, 121–2, 288–9.

69 D. Englander, *Landlord and Tenant in Urban Britain 1838–1918*, Oxford, 1983, 55–7.

For associations of this type, see T. C. Barker and J. R. Harris, *A Merseyside Town in the Industrial Revolution. St Helens 1750–1900*, London, 1959, 291; Garrard, op. cit., 66. See also the organizations of Blackpool lodging-house owners discussed in J. Walton, *The Blackpool Landlady: a Social History*, Manchester, 1978, ch. 8.

70 Englander, op. cit., 69–70.

71 E. Bristow, 'The Liberty and Property Defence League and individualism', *Historical Journal*, 18, 1975, 761–89; N. Soldon, 'Laissez-faire as dogma: the Liberty and Property Defence League, 1882–1914', in K. Brown (ed.), *Essays in Anti-Labour History*, London, 1974, 208–33; K. Brown, 'The Anti-Socialist Union', ibid., 234–61.

72 On these see Anne Summers, 'The character of Edwardian nationalism: three popular Leagues', in P. Kennedy and A. Nicholls (eds), *Nationalist and Racialist Movements in Britain and Germany Before 1914*, London, 1981, 68–87.

73 M. J. Daunton, *Coal Metropolis. Cardiff 1870–1914*, Leicester, 1977, 165–6.

74 *The Referee*, 11 February 1906.

75 ibid., February to April 1906.

76 See the general nature of the suggested programme in *The Elector*, March 1909.

77 De Rousiers, op. cit., 33–4.

78 H. McLeod, *Class and Religion in the Late Victorian City*, London, 1974, 61–2.

79 Daunton, op. cit., 155–8.

80 B. Preston, *Occupation of Father and Son in Mid-Victorian England*, Reading Geographical Papers, 1977, 31. For the struggle of H. G. Wells's parents to find an occupation for him of acceptable status, see his *Experiment in Autobiography*, London, 1934, 103–52.

81 The church or chapel community was one means of protecting the choice of marriage partner. See Foster, op. cit., 164–9.

82 B. Elliott and D. McCrone, 'Landlords in Edinburgh: some preliminary findings', *Sociological Review*, 23, 1975, 548–9, 559.

83 See especially H. Corke, *In Our Infancy. An Autobiography, Part I: 1882–1912*, Cambridge, 1975; Norman Nicholson, *Wednesday Early Closing*, London, 1975; N. Griffiths, *Shops Book. Brighton 1900–1930*, Queenspark Book, Brighton, n.d.

84 Corke, op. cit., 38, 44–5; P. Thompson, *The Edwardians*, London, 1977 edn, 125–8.

85 Case studies remain few, but see P. J. Dixon, 'The lower middle class child in the grammar school: a Lancashire industrial town 1850–1875', in P. Searby (ed.), *Educating the Victorian Middle Class*, Leicester, 1982, 57–70.

86 Preston, op. cit., 17–28; Crossick, *An Artisan Elite*, 115–16.

87 R. Anderson, 'Secondary education in mid-nineteenth-century France. Some social aspects', *Past and Present*, 53, 1971, 121–46; P. J. Harrigan, 'Secondary education and the professions in France during the Second Empire', *Comparative Studies in Society and History*, 17, 1975, esp. 358–9.

88 On Birmingham, see D. Smith, *Conflict and Compromise. Class Formation in English Society, 1830–1914*, London, 1982, 180. Also see W. E. Marsden, 'Schools for the urban lower middle class: third grade or higher grade?', in Searby, op. cit., 45–56.

89 Wells, op. cit., 60.

90 T. Lummis, 'The East Anglian fishermen: 1880–1914', University of Essex PhD thesis, 1981.

91 Bullen, op. cit., 120, 172.

92 Cf. D. Blackbourn, *Class, Religion and Local Politics in Wilhelmine Germany. The Centre Party in Württemberg Before 1914*, New Haven, 1980, 108ff; A. Corbin, *Archaïsme et modernité en Limousin au XIXe siècle, 1845–1880*, Paris, 1975, 305.

93 Corke, op. cit., 56–7.

94 C. Hall, 'The butcher, the baker, the candlestickmaker: the shop and the family in the

Industrial Revolution', in E. Whitelegg *et al.* (eds), *The Changing Experience of Women*, London, 1982, 2–16.

95 P. Searby, 'The schooling of Kipps. The education of lower middle class boys in England, 1860–1918', in Searby, op. cit., 123–4.

96 For this ideology in Edinburgh, see R. Q. Gray, 'Religion, culture and social class in late nineteenth and early twentieth century Edinburgh', in Crossick, *Lower Middle Class*, 149–50.

97 Some comments on the instability of small enterprise are in Bechhofer and Elliott, op. cit., 91.

98 Phillips, op. cit., 95.

99 Bealey, op. cit., and also his 'Municipal politics in Newcastle-under-Lyme, 1872–1914', *North Staffordshire Journal of Field Studies*, 5, 1965, 64–73; Hennock, *Fit and Proper Persons*, op. cit., 315; Garrard, op. cit., 91.

100 Hennock, *Fit and Proper Persons*, 17–176.

101 In 1875 some 80 per cent of Edinburgh councillors were landlords: B. Elliott, D. McCrone and V. Skelton, 'Property and political power: Edinburgh 1875–1975', in J. Garrard *et al.* (eds), *The Middle Class in Politics*, Farnborough, 1978, 103.

102 Select Committee on the Small Tenements Act, *Parliamentary Papers*, 1859, 2, vii, Q. 138–9.

103 On house owners, Englander, op. cit., 60.

104 Garrard, op. cit., 16.

105 Hennock, *Fit and Proper Persons*, 316.

106 H. J. Dyos, 'The speculative builders and developers of Victorian London', *Victorian Studies*, 11, 1967–8, 641–90.

107 D. J. Olsen, 'House upon House', in H. J. Dyos and M. Wolff (eds), *The Victorian City. Images and Reality*, London, 1973, vol. 1, 335.

108 Select Committee on Town Holdings, *Parliamentary Papers*, 1886, xii, Q. 7875–6.

109 For evidence of this see J. Burnett, *A Social History of Housing*, Newton Abbot, 1978, 69; J. Treble, 'Liverpool working-class housing 1801–1851', in S. D. Chapman (ed.), *The History of Working-Class Housing. A Symposium*, Newton Abbot, 1971, 191–2, 213; J. Butt, 'Working-class housing in Glasgow, 1851–1914', in ibid., 79; Elliott and McCrone, op. cit., 542; Pollard, op. cit., 21, 101; Daunton, op. cit., 114–21; R. S. Holmes, 'Ownership and migration from a study of rate books', *Area*, 5, 1973, 245–6. Evidence from all over the country for the early part of the century appears in Appendix B2 to the Royal Commission on the Poor Laws, *Parliamentary Papers*, 1834, xxxvi.

110 Bechhofer and Elliott, op. cit., 86.

111 S. Taylor, 'The political implications of urbanisation, with specific reference to the working-class housing market in Nottingham, 1830–1850', University of Essex MA thesis, 1977, 60–91.

112 Royal Commission on the Housing of the Working Classes, *Parliamentary Papers*, 1884–5, xxx, Q. 6813–16; Pollard, op. cit., 101; S. Meacham, *A Life Apart. The English Working Class 1890–1914*, London, 1977, 34.

113 Englander, op. cit., 11.

114 ibid., 15–16, 22–32.

115 Royal Commission on the Poor Laws, 31, 171.

116 Royal Commission on the Housing of the Working Classes, Q. 6801–4.

117 Select Committee on the Small Tenements Act, *passim*.

118 *The Grocer*, 6 March 1909, 696.

119 Bullen, op. cit., 160. On the practice of adulteration in the mid-Victorian period, see the evidence to the Select Committee on the Adulteration of Food, *Parliamentary Papers*, 1856, viii; Select Committee on the Adulteration of Food Act (1872), *Parliamentary Papers*, 1874, vi.

120 Foster, op. cit., 131–4; J. Vincent, *The Formation of the British Liberal Party*, London, 1966, 101–3; Nossiter, op. cit., 428.
121 On the diversity of small shopkeepers and their social situations, see Vigne and Howkins, op. cit., 184–209.
122 A. Briggs, 'Social structure and politics in Birmingham and Lyons (1825–1848)', *British Journal of Sociology*, 1, 1950, 67–80; T. R. Tholfsen, 'The artisan and the culture of early Victorian Birmingham', *University of Birmingham Historical Journal*, 4, 1954, 144–66.
123 C. O. Reid, 'Middle-class values and working-class culture in nineteenth-century Sheffield', University of Sheffield PhD thesis, 1976; D. J. Rowe, 'The failure of London Chartism', *Historical Journal*, 11, 1968, 472–87.
124 De Rousiers, op. cit., 5–7.
125 I recognize of course that there is good eighteenth-century evidence of growing conflict within artisanal production – see C. R. Dobson, *Masters and Journeymen*, London, 1980. It is a matter of degree.
126 In addition to his essay in this book, see Behagg's thesis, and his 'Custom, class and change: the trade societies of Birmingham', *Social History*, 4, 1979, 455–80.
127 See Parsinnen and Prothero, op. cit.; Prothero, op. cit.; Goodway, op. cit., 9.
128 Lloyd, op. cit., 195, 203; Booth, op. cit., vol. 5, 117; on inspection see Schmiechen, op. cit., 417–22.
129 P. E. Razzell and R. W. Wainwright (eds), *The Victorian Working Class. Selections from the* Morning Chronicle, London, 1973, 183.
130 Select Committee on Master and Servant, *Parliamentary Papers*, 1866, XIII, Q. 1372–80.
131 Parsinnen and Prothero, op. cit.
132 Report of the Truck Commissioners, *Parliamentary Papers*, 1871, XXIII, p. xxviii. On foggers, see Allen, op. cit., 128.
133 J. R. Oliver, *The Development and Structure of the Furniture Industry*, Oxford, 1966, 70. For shopkeeper middlemen in cabinet-making, see Mayhew, op. cit., 223, and as lumpers, ibid., 290–2.
134 Children's Employment Commission, *Parliamentary Papers*, 1864, XXII, 102–3; Crossick, *An Artisan Elite*, 114; E. J. Hobsbawm, *Labouring Men. Studies in the History of Labour*, London, 1964, 296.
135 For the way that many small masters stayed within an artisanal social world, see Gray, *Labour Aristocracy*, 134–5.
136 For a broader discussion of the problems posed by the petite bourgeoisie for the study of social mobility, see Crossick, 'The petite bourgeoisie'.
137 R. Roberts, *The Classic Slum. Salford Life in the First Quarter of the Century*, Harmondsworth, 1973, 81–2.
138 Griffiths, op. cit., 53–60.
139 M. Tebbutt, *Making Ends Meet. Pawnbroking and Working-Class Credit*, Leicester, 1983, 35.
140 Goodway, op. cit., 114–16; D. Smith, 'Tonypandy 1910: definitions of community', *Past and Present*, 87, 1980, 158–84.
141 R. J. Morris, 'The rise of James Kitson: trades union and mechanics institution, Leeds, 1826–1851', Publications of the Thoresby Society, *Miscellany*, 15, 187.

4 The petite bourgeoisie in France, 1850–1914: in search of the *juste milieu*?

HEINZ-GERHARD HAUPT

'All of us here belong to those *classes moyennes* [middle classes] who are the backbone of the nation, those reasonable people who demand no more than what is just and possible.' Without the middle classes, the ladder of social mobility would lose those middle rungs that lay 'within the reach of ordinary people, and by which they can, through courage, perserverance and good management, raise themselves from the employee and the worker of yesterday to become the shopkeeper and the employer of tomorrow.'[1]

In the speech from which this is an extract, Thierry, president of an association for trade and industry, assigned small shopkeepers and craftsmen to a single group for which he used the term *classes moyennes*, the name normally associated with the French bourgeoisie in its struggle against the nobility. The term implied that they were a positive force. The *classes moyennes* were not only the incarnation of the most important bourgeois values such as common sense, hard work and assiduity, but they also remained open to the upwardly mobile members of the lower classes. Parallel to this recognition of the class nature of society stands the prospect of overcoming such class divisions, a form of expression commonly found in France at the beginning of the twentieth century. Since the time of Léon Gambetta, who in the 1880s had seen the republic as simply the triumph of the *couches nouvelles*,[2] class concepts had come into general use: the small shopkeeper joined together with the craftsmen to form an *Association de défense des classes moyennes* in 1907. *La Reforme sociale*, an organization inspired by Le Play, held a conference on the fate of the *classes moyennes* in 1910 and the relevant international congresses were known in France as *Congrès internationaux des classes moyennes*.[3] The use of these words involves three premises which will serve as a basis for the following discussion. Firstly, the petite bourgeoisie did not derive its name for itself from the terminology of the feudal estates of the past, but from that associated with the process of emancipation of the bourgeoisie. Secondly, it implied that there were not such great differences between the interests and the living conditions of craftsmen and small shopkeepers as to prevent them from being considered as one class. Finally, it departed from a two-pole view of society which distinguished between the nobility and the third estate or between the bourgeoisie and the people and introduced a third pole, the 'middle classes'. This left open the question of whether the new division occurred at the expense of the bourgeoisie or as a breakaway from the *peuple*, the people.[4]

If we compare the group's perception of itself with a discussion based on class analysis, we must immediately ask how far the term *classes moyennes* can be taken as referring to a social class formed by a similarity of economic conditions, united by close social relationships, and held together by political ideas, one which solidified even further through social conflicts, and came to see itself as the 'middle classes'. Such an opinion would be shared by those studies which interpret a group's view of itself as an adequate description of reality and which proceed to use this as an analytical category.[5] Should it prove, however, that from both the economic and the social points of view the degree of heterogeneity between craftsmen and small shopkeepers was greater than that of homogeneity, and that there were profound differences within the group, this would give a different meaning to political consciousness, which could then perhaps be interpreted as compensating for a lack of common interests.[6] In terms of class situation, class relationships and class position this means asking whether master craftsmen and small shopkeepers had more points in common with each other than divided them, and whether they joined together to speak with one voice or to defend themselves against other classes or the state. Faced with this problem, the discussion about whether the class should be known as 'the middle class' or the 'petite bourgeoisie' is of secondary importance.

Although in numerical terms small firms dominated trade and industry in France until after 1945, and their owners were courted by several political parties,[7] there have been no studies on this subject until recent years. Apart from the theses, mostly by law students, written before 1914, such work was restricted until the last decade to a small number of sociological studies of the period between the wars, and the analysis of Poujadism.[8] In addition to this, craftsmen were always mentioned in regional studies that aimed at a 'total' history of an area, and they also appeared in histories of the working-class movement. The most important impetus to recent studies of the social history of the petite bourgeoisie, however, seems to have been given by the changing social structure of France in the last fifteen years, a change in which the disappearance of small firms and shops is especially evident. This regrettable research situation means that this essay is, of necessity, more of a broad outline of developments than a detailed picture.

I shall examine the class situation of craftsmen and small shopkeepers in relation to specific questions. Were they subject to similar long-term socio-economic changes? Did living and working conditions vary as widely in both groups? Which centrifugal and centripetal forces affected the group?

In the course of the *longue durée* of the second half of the nineteenth century, and in spite of all the pessimistic forecasts, craftsmen and traders enjoyed a remarkable period of expansion. The tax yield from those small craft and trading businesses which came under Table A of the *patente* (professional tax) rose by more than a half between 1845 and 1910, the number of taxpayers by a quarter, and the average amount of tax from 21.95 francs to 35.50 francs.[9] As a series of reforms had excluded very small firms from paying any tax at all, this means that the growth was even greater than the tax files show.[10] Before the First World War small firms have been shown to have been typical in the department of Nièvre and they were widespread in Bordeaux. Even in those trades such as the textile and shoe industries in which production was mechanized at an early date, small firms remained common. Hence shoe factories existed side by side with family enterprises in Fougères before 1914, hosiery was organized as a domestic industry in parts of Picardy, and small workshops checked the concentration of the means of production in Roubaix. Large numbers of workers were also employed by small firms in the Parisian metal trades.[11] There is little evidence of this dominant position to be found in the occupational and business censuses of the period, which were only given a new and sounder basis after 1896. The reason for this is that the census authorities capitulated when faced with the problem of disentangling the complicated relationships of small producers, and distinguishing between piece-workers, independent masters, family businesses and firms employing labour from outside the family. Alain Faure has attempted such a historical analysis for the year 1901. According to his findings, three-quarters of all French manufacturing enterprises were either domestic producers, independent masters or family enterprises. Amongst the quarter of firms which employed any non-family labour at all, 80 per cent had between one and five wage labourers.[12] The French industrial landscape was thus dominated by very small and family businesses, and the country remained an Eldorado for small employers before 1914.

For a long time scholars interpreted this situation as an expression of economic backwardness rather than as a specifically French road to industrial capitalism. Only when it was pointed out that the country had growth rates which compared favourably with those of other western European countries did historians come to see the dynamic effect of small and medium-sized businesses in a country where there was hardly any population growth during the nineteenth century. Under these conditions small firms producing and exporting high-quality goods on a craft basis could survive for a long time. The advance of capitalism in France did not occur as a result of the spread of large-scale industry, but through the subjugation of small and medium-sized businesses to the interests of merchant and industrial capitalists. Their principle was that of functionalization, rather than the exclusion of small firms from the market.[13] This long-term pattern of growth did, however, conceal a number of disparities. Craft work and trading expanded more than small industrial firms, country areas were especially affected by changes, and commercial and industrial activities came increasingly to be separated.

In contrast with the spread of trading and craft firms there was a decline in the number of small industrial firms. Until the end of the century the number of industrial firms listed in Table C of the *patente* fell, but at the same time the value of installations liable to tax rose. Although there are still no detailed studies available, this points to a defeat for small firms in the face of competition from medium-sized and large mechanized firms.[14] A clear example of this trend was the ruin of the old-fashioned, small-scale Catalan forges which gave way to modern ironworks in the 1860s, or the introduction of machinery into cotton spinning mills, which deprived the hand spinners of their livelihood.[15] It was clear that the future of small firms lay in the trading and craft sectors rather than in production. The nineteenth century was above all the golden age of the small shopkeeper. As a result of improvements in transport and the decline of self-sufficiency there was an explosive increase in the number of businesses liable to the *patente*: six-fold in the case of café owners, four-fold in the case of grocers, three-fold in the case of butchers and a doubling of the number of innkeepers and bakers.[16]

Even though industrial work had not yet disappeared in rural areas at the turn of the century, and a third of the businesses paying the *patente* were still to be found in parishes with fewer than 2000 inhabitants,[17] the importance of craft work in the countryside began to decline in 1880. It was threatened by a fall in agricultural incomes and an inability to compete. The mechanization of industry and the unification of the national market worsened the situation of rural craftsmen still further. They often gave up their workshops, and by 1880 were for the most part leaving the country for the towns. Hence the number of hat makers in the department of the Loire decreased, many workers in the textile industry of Beaujolais gave up working at home, and the Great Depression put an end to linen-making as a domestic industry in northern France. These changes had a more drastic effect on industries in the textile and metal-working fields than on those of food and agriculture. In spite of this, rural domestic industries had not died out before 1914, craft workshops continued to exist in rural areas and small shops were flourishing. In Vron, a fairly large agriculturally based parish in the department of the Somme, 15 per cent of the working population in 1911 were still either craftsmen in the building trade or blacksmiths, wheelwrights and saddlers working for the farming community. Even after 1880 the merchant capitalists continued to move a part of their production into rural areas and out of the towns. Dupeux underlines the continuity of this process in the department of Loir-et-Cher: 'there had been no great upheavals affecting the category of heads of enterprises'.[18] Before 1914 the great majority of the French population still lived in the country and, in spite of all the changes which had taken place, industrial activities continued there. It took the slump and its aftermath to bring about a permanent change in the relationship between the numbers of agricultural and industrial workers.[19]

In the second half of the nineteenth century a separation of trading and craft activities took place. In 1848 there were still a large number of small shopkeepers in Paris involved in production: they produced 17 per cent of the jam they sold, 23 per cent of the chocolate and roasted as much as 77 per cent of their coffee. Alongside that stood those craftsmen who combined a shop with their workshops, and sold the goods which they produced. Statisticians of the middle of the century still had difficulty in distinguishing between trading and industrial functions.[20] Hence, in 1848, bakers in Paris were listed as manufacturers, but butchers as traders. In the course of the century a separation of the two functions then occurred, except in these craft trades of baker and butcher, although some small shopkeepers were still packing and processing goods up to the First World War. For a century this separation of the two functions seems to have clarified the boundaries between the two sectors until the present-day struggle for survival has once again led to a combination of the two aspects of small enterprise. It would be interesting to know whether the figures for Paris in about 1860, which show that craftsmen were pouring into the trading sector faster than shopkeepers were engaging in industry, represented a general trend.[21] If that were the case, it would mean that there was a clear hierarchy within the petite bourgeoisie.

Finally the trade and craft sectors went through phases of development at different times from each other. It was not simply that retail trade continued to expand at a time when craft work had already passed its peak, but also that the capitalist transformation of the two sectors began at different times. The advance of the merchant capitalists under the July Monarchy forced tailors, shoemakers and building craftsmen to give up their independence and work for them, a development which continued and even accelerated during the Second Empire, especially in the towns.[22] Small shopkeepers, on the other hand, first found themselves in a similarly precarious situation in the large towns after 1880, and in smaller places at the end of the century. Although the first department stores had been founded during the Second Empire, it was not until the end of the century that chain-stores and mail-order businesses began to spread from the urban centres into the provinces and to provide serious competition for smaller shops.[23] In the decades during which masters and journeymen were fighting to prevent a capitalist reorganization of production, the distribution network had not yet been fully developed and small trading businesses were still taking over markets for themselves. When the trading sector was itself confronted with the threat from large-scale business organizations, it had just enjoyed a relatively long period of numerical expansion and it was in a position not only to follow the example of the craft sector, which shared similar problems, but also to seek support from the state. As these developments did not occur simultaneously, it was no accident that the retail trade played a more active role in the organization of the *classes moyennes*. It also explains why that term only began to be used more widely when the situations of small shopkeepers and craftsmen became more alike.

Greater than these differences however was the deep division *within* the trading and craft sectors. Although both rested on a combination of capital and labour, this division resulted from the differing amounts of capital and labour involved. Hence, in Paris, the amount of starting capital required in around 1848 varied from 19,260 francs for a baker's shop to 2040 francs for a shop selling fabric, whereas a grocer often needed as little as 700 francs to set up in business. A grocery shop could thus be paid for out of a worker's or a journeyman's savings, but a bakery required extra capital.[24] It was not just the amount of capital invested that varied but also the extent to which the owners were personally involved in the work; from the small master in the Lyons silk industry, who by 1870 had subjugated himself and his family to the demands of production, to the craftsman employing several wage-earners, who spent most of his time supervising them and only occasionally took any part in the actual work process.[25] Although craft and trading firms without capital and dependent on intensive labour were highly vulnerable to crises, frequently only existed for a short time and often did not even provide the minimum required to live on, yet they time and again managed to find niches within which to exist. Hence tiny shops were set up to provide working-class families with extra income – the husband went out to work and the wife looked after the shop. Such businesses were especially common in the suburbs of larger towns and cities, but also in rural areas. Domestic textile production by craftsmen paid on a piece-work basis not only survived but even increased in the second half of the nineteenth century. These proletarianized groups of traders and craftsmen were subject to the inexorable pressures of long working days and weeks, low incomes and high insecurity, and very intensive labour.[26] They constituted a very large proportion of the people employed in both sectors. Only about 30 per cent of all small shops, and even fewer workshops, employed labour from outside the family. Even if masters working on their own and family businesses had different levels of profit, their economic problems suggest that they still belonged to that proletarianized petite bourgeoisie whose existence and size is confirmed by the frequency with which they left little or nothing to be inherited.[27] They were especially numerous in the grocery and fruit trades, less so in selling textiles, household goods, and wines and spirits. In contrast to the retail trade, it is more difficult to determine the hierarchies within the craft sector. Whereas in the towns it is obvious that butchers and bakers and, to some extent craftsmen and members of the building trade, were the richest and had the highest incomes, in country areas food manufacturing and textile businesses formed an additional element in this aristocracy of the crafts.[28]

In comparison with these myriads of small traders and craftsmen, the average businessman and the craftsman who had capital and even employed journeymen must have seemed positively wealthy. This description given by the chamber of commerce of Sens (Yonne) in 1913 would apply to such a person: 'An intelligent, hard-working and economical young man, having served an apprenticeship in a large retail establishment, supported by a wife with the same qualities, worth 20,000 francs and with an enterprise in a good village close to Sens, in the combined trades of grocery, haberdashery, hosiery, lingerie, ready-made clothing and various fabrics.' With such favourable conditions at the outset, he could achieve a turnover of 30,000 francs per year.[29] Members of this group would find it much easier to cope with a crisis, occupational training was taken seriously and long-term planning for the future took place. A lot of the evidence indicates that this *bourgeoisie populaire* (to use Daumard's term) was to be found more frequently in the retailing than in the craft sector.[30]

There was thus no broad movement of expropriation changing the small industrial and trading sectors in France, but their independence was none the less undermined in various subtle ways. They became dependent on merchant and financial capitalists as a result of the latters' control over credit, supplies of raw materials and sales of goods. When he opened a shop, above all, a retailer was forced to seek credit from members of his family, colleagues or even notaries or financiers.[31] Throughout the nineteenth century – an example is Niort after 1870 – wholesalers increasingly took on an intermediary role between manufacturers and retailers and acted as sources of credit.[32] Frequently a wholesaler would only advance money on condition that the retailer agreed to buy all his goods from him. Retailers were primarily subject to two forms of dependence.[33] If the turnover of goods was slow and the firm held large stocks, income remained low, as did profits, which could be used to pay back a loan. In addition to this, the freedom of action of retailers was drastically restricted by the practice of giving credit to customers, especially common in small shops. In a situation of falling sales and unpaid debts, with creditors insisting on the regular repayment of instalments of their loans, shopkeepers were frequently forced into closure. Small shops were also dependent in more direct ways. Many multiple chains were organized on the principle that goods were delivered to tenants or owners of shops, and they were obliged to accept all of these goods. For branch managers of the *Docks Rémois*, which in around 1900 more or less controlled the whole grocery trade in the area around Rheims, as for their colleagues in the 330 branches of the *Casino* chain in central and southern France, the role of the independent shopkeeper had been reduced to a mere formality.[34]

The freedom of action of craftsmen was not much greater. Putters out and industrialists, who delivered raw materials and half-finished products and then bought back the finished goods, kept a suspicious eye on the quality of the products manufactured, returned some items and could easily lower the price of labour, for the craftsmen doing the work had little means of resistance. Although the term 'craftsman' suggests an occupation involving autonomy and skilled training, it often concealed the situation of a producer dependent on suppliers, large firms, even department stores. He might well still own his means of production, but he no longer had control over a significant part of the production and distribution process. Cottereau has estimated that in 1847 5.1 per cent of craftsmen in Paris were independent in the true sense of the word; in 1901 only 1.9 per cent.[35] The majority of urban craftsmen were subject to the constraints not only of industrial capitalists who contracted work out to them yet dispensed with their services when orders declined, but also to those of the department stores. They gave much of their manufacturing and repair work to small and domestic producers – in 1900 there were 85,000 such producers working in the Paris ready-made clothing industry.[36] The existence of such conditions was revealed in the findings of the *Commission Mesureur*, set up to consider a reform of the *patente* laws in 1891. In their evidence brush, textile and glove-makers defended the department stores with arguments similar to those used by Tréfousse, a glove-maker from Troyes: 'All limits set to the expansion of department stores would spell ruin for working glove-makers. Of 100,000 pairs of gloves made annually by the Tréfousse house, some 40,000 were sold to Au Bon Marché.'[37]

Although there is little mention of these forms of financial dependence in the publications of retail and craft organizations, they obviously had as great an effect as competition. The subject of unfair competition was a frequent topic for independent shopkeepers and craftsmen complaining about capitalist forms of business and production. Small shopkeepers complained particularly vociferously when the spread of department stores, mail-order businesses, co-operatives, and above all, chain-stores, began to limit their own expansion.[38] It would, however, be wrong to overestimate the consequences of this competition in the retail trade, complaints of which became especially fierce after 1890. The number of bankruptcies in retailing since the middle of the century proves that vigorous competition was nothing new.[39] At the end of the nineteenth century, however, it was now affecting those medium-sized and larger specialist shops which drew their custom from the same social groups as did large-scale capitalist retailers and which, like the latter, insisted on cash payment. It is no accident that these better-established specialist shopkeepers were especially prominent amongst those who spoke out in defence of shopkeeper interests. But the expansion of the 'giants', which is difficult to assess quantitatively, also had a serious effect on the development of very small businesses. Not only was their share of business reduced, but they had to make do with those customers who could afford little and who often could not pay at all.[40]

In general, one can conclude that the retail trade developed more quickly in the ninteenth century than the craft and small industrial sectors. This different rate of development made it difficult for the two groups to join in protest against capitalist development before the end of the nineteenth century, in spite of the fact that the advance of capitalism in both the retail and craft sectors had undermined their independence on a large scale, and had reduced large numbers to almost proletarian working and living conditions. If this general trend encourages us to emphasize the common interests of small shopkeepers and craftsmen, at least after the 1880s, the great heterogeneity of the two groups should caution against too readily assigning them to a single class. The structural similarities, and the combination of labour and capital common to both, found such different forms of expression that quite different forms of work and ways of life set the class situation of the proletarianized layers of craftsmen and retailers firmly apart from that of the better-off.

This section will examine the living and working conditions of craftsmen and small shopkeepers, to see the extent to which social relationships helped the two groups to unite within a single class and to determine how far the petite bourgeoisie occupied a significant and central position within French society. Marriage contacts, and relationships both at work and at home, can help us to determine the closeness of social relationships. In de Tocqueville's words 'If you want to know whether castes, ideas, customs, barriers which have been created amongst a people have been really obliterated, then take a look at marriage. There you will find that decisive, missing clue'.[41] Although recent research has shown that the choice of a wife from the same class was not quite so important for the petite bourgeoisie in Paris as Alexis de Tocqueville claimed it generally to be,[42] a man's marriage did involve an important decision that affected his future career. A study of Paris under the July Monarchy by Adeline Daumard has revealed that the wives of shopkeepers often came from a higher social class than their husbands, and that it was especially common for butchers and bakers to marry women from the 'middling bourgeoisie'. A third of all wives of *boutiquiers*, however, came from the world of the shop itself.[43] It is true that at the beginning of the nineteenth century there were grocers and drapers in Rouen who married into the upper ranks of the bourgeoisie (*bonne bourgeoisie*); at the same time it was more common for them to take the daughters of workers and white-collar employees as wives than was the case in Paris. They continued to seek their wives among the employed classes during the Second Empire and broke off their connections with the more substantial bourgeoisie completely.[44] Le Yaouanq, who has established what he calls 'a large zone of contact' between the petite bourgeoisie and the working class, also shows that bourgeois circles in Paris were increasingly isolating themselves from the lower classes in the middle of the nineteenth century.[45] Although at the beginning of the twentieth century the petits bourgeois of Orléans were also isolating themselves from groups below them,[46] research in general suggests that craftsmen and shopkeepers remained open to contacts with both labouring and non-manual groups, and that the class had not become distinct and separate. The emphasis with which Maurice Colrat in 1910 exclaimed 'we are also, and everyone must know it, the hope of the proletariat',[47] was to a certain extent justified.

Whereas an analysis of marriage links seems to emphasize an openness of the petite bourgeoisie in terms of social contacts, relationships at work may give some indication of the social distance between manual and white-collar workers on the one hand and small businessmen on the other. For employees from outside the family were made to feel the full force of the pressure which competition exerted on the craftsmen or shopkeepers. Very long working hours and bad conditions, low pay and constant supervision made these workers into what the unions, without exaggeration, called the 'pariahs' of the labouring classes.[48] The freedom of action of these workers was even more restricted in the second half of the nineteenth century by the widespread practice of living in.[49] Hence the miserable working conditions in craft occupations, such as in bakeries, were a frequent cause of industrial action, although this rarely affected the purely retail shops.[50] The frequency of strikes in small craft businesses, together with the number of cases heard by the *Conseils des Prud'hommes*,[51] indicate that neither in the middle nor at the end of the nineteenth century were the relations between masters and journeymen, or between shopkeepers and assistants characterized by that trust attributed to them by writers in search of social harmony and consensus. This social barrier between certain members of the petite bourgeoisie and workers was none the less restricted to a minority of the class. It could not develop in firms with no wage labour or in which the conditions of work were the same as those of the non-manual employees. The vast majority of retailers and craftsmen found that their social status was not greatly different from that of employees.[52]

One area of social experience which was common to a substantial number of craftsmen and small shopkeepers in medium-sized and large towns was the district in which they lived, the *quartier*.[53] Close contacts were established there between the inhabitants and the petite bourgeoisie which went beyond mere business relations. In 1913 the Chamber of Commerce in Le Havre wrote of the 'way of life of a small shopkeeper who, more in contact with his clientèle, often living a similar life-style to it, facing the same difficulties and hardships, sympathized with the needs of his customers and often gave them not inconsiderable help'. A police report from Paris on the strikes of 19 May 1906 shows that help could take a practical form, 'The help of the shopkeeper can be very effective . . . collections, for goods as much as for money, yield a great deal.'[54] The same was probably true of the craftsmen.

Before 1914 districts of this kind outside town centres were still the bastions of the small shops and workshops in which, as Alain Faure shows in his article in this book, goods were sold in small quantities and on credit to customers from humble backgrounds. Social life in these areas was based on a close network of choral societies and cafés, political circles and social events where shopkeepers, craftsmen and their customers were always meeting each other. It is no accident that the *journées populaires* which the people of the towns used to express their disapproval of high prices and taxes or inadequate supplies of goods originated in such *quartiers*.[55] The common political past joined with contemporary forms of sociability and economic interdependence to forge close links between shopkeepers, craftsmen and their customers.

Nevertheless, Yves Lequin is correct to warn against the tendency to idealize life in the *quartiers* and to point out the violence with which conflicts between workers and small shopkeepers were often resolved.[56] With customers as dependent on credit as were retailers on their customers, the two parties had always to settle these differences, but this did not preclude violent quarrels over the price or quality of goods. Nor were shopkeepers and craftsmen in full agreement. Quarrels broke out over the question of whether itinerant traders should be allowed to operate, or whether and when shops and workshops should be shut.[57] For all these reasons one should not present a monolithic view of the *quartier*.

Whilst there is no doubt that social experiences such as these within a specific area of a town might help to lessen differences within the petite bourgeoisie, it might also have contributed to a localized fragmentation of the class. Their parochial orientations and basis, together with their resistance to national and other less obvious outside influences, combined to strengthen their *esprit du clocher* (parochial mentality).[58] There were, however, considerable differences within the petite bourgeoisie, especially as regards whom they married and their relations with their employees. In contrast to the bourgeoisie, who had been progressively isolating themselves from those below since the middle of the nineteenth century, craftsmen and small shopkeepers remained open to contacts with the working classes. Even though the conflicts between small businessmen and their employees were becoming fiercer, and the line between the classes was becoming clearer, the proletarian conditions under which large numbers of shopkeepers and craftsmen continued to live helped to form a bridge linking them to the working class. The emergence of the French petite bourgeoisie as a separate class was certainly not complete before 1914.

The term *classes moyennes* also carried the implied sense of a central position in society. In this view they lived between the opulence of the bourgeoisie and the poverty of the proletariat, between a stable situation in life and one that was precarious, and between accumulation of property and lack of it. In addition to this they were to form a rung on the ladder of social mobility. If the role played by these petits bourgeois is to be examined, their share in property ownership and the security of their existence, then we must carefully distinguish between the various forms of consciousness of the *classes moyennes*. Studies of social mobility give rise to a number of problems unless it is made clear how socially significant each occupation was in the process of upward or downward mobility. These general problems common to all studies of mobility are especially serious in the case of the petite bourgeoisie, owing to the fact that the designation 'employee' can cover someone without independence as well as the son of the owner of a business waiting to take it over. At the same time, a permanent job as an employee in the right business might well provide a superior social position to that attached to the ownership of a shop that lacked any real prospects.

In spite of reservations such as these mobility studies do offer some preliminary conclusions. On the whole there was more openness towards the classes below than towards those above. The retail trade and craft workshops of Paris in the middle of the century were a common ambition for small farmers and rural craftsmen leaving home for the big city. In some towns, it was craftsmen from the textile industry who most benefited from this migration, but not so in Paris, where migrants from the Auvergne would establish shops while those from Limousin opened businesses in the building trade.[59] Members of the urban working class would also enter craft and commercial occupations. Before the 1848 revolution a fifth of the shopkeepers in Paris had once been employed as skilled craftsmen, while in answer to the question of a parliamentary commission of 1913 about the previous occupations of some 240 small shopkeepers, 95 stated that they had been workers, 92 had been non-manual employees and 53 domestic servants.[60] Domestic industry and *travail à façon* were also open to workers, who set up on their own during periods of expansion but would become employees again during a crisis.[61]

At the same time, however, significant developments were producing differences within the world of retail and craft enterprise. Opening a shop or setting up a craft business which required minimal capital still remained within the reach of newcomers and formed an area of constant interchange between workers and petits bourgeois in the large towns, but a layer of better situated and more stable shops and workshops began to separate themselves off from the rest. That is why Le Yaouanq speaks of a 'permanent tendency . . . to internal recruitment and to introspection'[62] in such Parisian enterprises around the middle of the century. There was evidence of a similar tendency in Rouen, where social mobility almost came to an end after 1850, as well as in Orléans around 1900, where upward mobility was no longer really evident.[63] In the rural areas, on the other hand, retail traders and craftsmen continued to operate as an upwardly mobile group.[64]

It was very unusual for someone from a petit-bourgeois occupation to advance into the bourgeoisie during the second half of the nineteenth century. Some members of the Nancy bourgeoisie came from craft and retail trading circles, it is true, as did some high-ranking civil servants and teachers. And Léon Blum was of course the son of a draper in central Paris.[65] That regal progress up through society by means of an education at a good school, which the radical socialists claimed to be the lot of the petite bourgeoisie, proved in reality to be no more than a narrow gate through which very few members of the class were allowed to pass.[66] It was easier to obtain a post as a low-ranking civil servant or work as a non-manual employee than it was to enter the higher echelons of the administration or to have a successful career as a businessman. Information about the social origins of elementary school teachers in Saint Lô suggests that aspiring petits bourgeois were by the end of the nineteenth century faced with increasing competition in schools from working-class children, whose numbers grew at their expense.[67] If these findings were confirmed from other areas, and if it could be proved that the bourgeoisie in other towns increasingly cut themselves off from below, as they did in Rouen and Orléans, then dashed hopes for upward mobility might help explain the so frequently mentioned 'crisis of the middle classes' around 1900. But these must remain tentative conclusions.

Craftsmen and small shopkeepers formally belonged to that large class of property owners who formed the backbone of the existing social order, both in the countryside and the towns of nineteenth-century France. In the course of that century, however, their importance in the overall structure of property ownership declined, most notably in the large towns, although they seem to have maintained their position in rural areas. Under the Second Empire almost half of all craftsmen who died in Lille had nothing to pass on to their heirs, and the petite bourgeoisie as a whole in that town had to watch its financial basis being eroded. Paris was no different. They still owned 17 per cent of all inherited property there in 1820, but by 1911 this figure had sunk to 3 per cent.[68] One can detect a similar decline in importance in smaller places such as Honfleur and Bayonne, although small industrialists and shopkeepers in Lyons seem to have been able to maintain their admittedly mediocre situation.[69] Although some branches of craft production and retail trade were more successful than this in keeping step with the general concentration of property, both these groups as a whole must be counted among the losers in the nineteenth-century process of redistribution. They simply possessed too little capital in relation to their numbers.

In their own eyes, the middle classes ought to have been in a situation which, while not without risk, should at least have been stable. The reality was very different for it is striking just how insecure large numbers of shopkeepers and craftsmen seem to have been. This is especially apparent in periods of financial crisis when credit was expensive, turnover low, and customers had difficulties in paying their debts. Although the 1830 crisis in Paris hurt larger and medium-sized businesses more than small ones, this situation was reversed from 1848 onwards.[70] In the course of the second half of the nineteenth century crises did more damage to small businesses and – if the findings for Lyons in the 1880s can be generalized – were more likely to ruin shops than workshops.[71] Yet outside such periods of crisis the instability in the world of craft work and trading was very considerable. There were relatively few cases of bankruptcy it is true, for this carried with it a loss of civil rights. In spite of this 26 per cent of all bankruptcies between 1903 and 1905 occurred in the manufacturing and sale of food and 16 per cent in the manufacturing and sale of drinks. Yet these striking figures represented only seven out of every thousand firms in these lines of business.[72] Much more serious was the number of businesses which ceased trading before formal bankruptcy proceedings could be opened. Developments in this field can be traced for Paris.[73] After 1900 they rose in number, only to fall back again from 1909 until the First World War, and it was grocers and very small shopkeepers who were especially hard hit. No fewer than a third of all grocers' shops in Paris changed hands in 1910 and the turnover in other branches of the food trade was little smaller. The average price of these shops was less than the 10,000 francs which specialist books quoted as the minimum amount of investment required for a flourishing business. Two-thirds of all businesses sold before 1914 belonged to this low price category. The smaller the shops and the lower their capital, the greater was their instability.

Parisian greengrocers, on the other hand, did not conform to this pattern; between 1902 and 1912 their rate of fluctuation fell from 17.5 per cent to 10.1 per cent. The explanation for this relative stability in a line of business characterized by low capital requirements lies in the social structure of the people involved. For the prefecture of police gave licences for itinerant trade in fruit and vegetables to men over fifty years of age or women over forty-two, who would otherwise have had to live on poor relief. As this was their last chance of a more or less secure existence, most greengrocers clung to their businesses more doggedly than did other retailers.[74] Even though the shops and workshops in the small towns and villages, and the specialized shops of the larger towns, can be regarded as oases of stability, around them stood a world of business in which insecurity was more the rule than the exception. This aspect of their lives brought craftsmen and small shopkeepers closer to the working class, with which they were already closely connected by their lack of effective property and the way in which their ownership of the means of production had often been reduced to a mere formality. The social world of craftsmen and small shopkeepers was deeply divided amongst those petits bourgeois, especially in rural areas and in small towns, but they were there too in larger cities, whose traditions and stability enabled them to amass a considerable fortune; those independent craftsmen and businessmen who, whether temporarily or permanently, abandoned their position as skilled workers for the sake of an often-threatened independence; and, finally, those itinerant traders and *façonniers* of sub-proletarian origin, for whom trade and craft production were associated not with the dream of independence, but with one way of staying alive. Neither upward mobility, whether in expectation or reality, nor social orientation, could unite these very different elements. The shared existence of the *quartier* served to establish closer links between the last two groups rather than to create some *union sacrée* of all shopkeepers and master craftsmen. It cannot be said that the petite bourgeoisie, with all its internal differentiation, occupied a position in the middle of the French social structure; the majority lay firmly below the centre. What is more, French society in the nineteenth century was characterized by an increasingly rapid decline in social mobility. As a result, to use the words of Chaline, the petite bourgeoisie remained 'an extremely narrow bridge between the people and the more substantial bourgeoisie'.[75]

With these substantial economic and social differences in mind, it is particularly important to consider the extent to which a political unity of the petite bourgeoisie might have served to conceal the divisions.[76] The broad middle-class movement which developed after the turn of the century did in fact suggest a high degree of cohesion in the class. In contrast to the nineteenth century, when small shopkeepers and craftsmen defended their interests in a fragmented way, on the basis of occupation and locality, the beginning of the new century saw an increase in the number of associations directed at national and class organization of the petits bourgeois. These included not only the *Confédération des Groupes commerciaux et industriels de France*, which in 1913 was represented in 190 French towns, but also the short-lived *Parti commercial et industriel de France*, as well as the *Association de défense des classes moyennes* from 1907 onwards.[77] All were typified by their organization on a national basis and by their efforts to attract both craftsmen and small shopkeepers. Retail trade tended to be emphasized, while employees were long excluded until in the popular front crisis of 1936 conservative forces began to court them.[78] By joining together at a national level the middle classes showed that they had learned the lessons of the failure of their earlier attempts to achieve their demands through occupational organizations or interest groups that had been either inside the Republican Party or closely allied to it. The crises of the 1880s and 1890s had violently shaken the petite bourgeoisie's traditional allegiance to republicanism and set them off in search of a new political home. Philip Nord has shown convincingly how their travels took them via Boulangism and social Catholicism to such extremes as nationalism and Poincarism. At the same time xenophobia, already evident in the 1880s, but still of secondary importance then, and the rejection of socialism and of all ideas connected with it, came to the forefront of the movement. This movement now saw itself as a real political force and united behind an ideology that centred on opposition to social legislation by the state and a vigorous defence of private property. From 1910 it allied with large-scale industrialists in a powerful new front fully capable of looking after its own interests.[79] Whilst the term *classes moyennes* might in the mid-nineteenth century have carried resonances of bourgeois emancipation, it was to take on a more conservative meaning in the years leading up to the First World War. The president of the *Fédération nationale des Batîments et des Travaux publics* made it clear in a speech in 1910 that it had become synonymous with the unity of conservatives in their opposition to revolution. It was easy to associate with the idea of *classes moyennes* the praise of manual workers for intellectual workers, the beneficial effects of family life, and the harmonious principle of 'a place for everything and everything in its place'.[80] The movement acted as if it represented something it saw as the *Mittelstand*. When small businessmen introduced corporatist ideas in their answers to the Landry enquiry, we can see how the movement was claiming a real *Mittelstand* identity.

Their demand that the triumphant advance of the department stores be brought to a halt by limiting the range of goods they could sell, the number of *specialités*, derived from their belief that they constituted a corporate *stand* or estate.[81] We can see these ideas just as clearly in the defence of craft guilds. 'Today's commercial organisation', wrote the *Union Commerciale de Laon* in 1913, 'is, in effect, directing and orienting itself towards a return to the corporations of the past.'[82] The Bayonne Chamber of Commerce, for example, supported the corporatist idea of some kind of qualifying examination for small shopkeepers.[83] Nevertheless, in responses to the Landry enquiry, views such as these were as much a minority as were the scapegoat theories, which saw the problems of small shopkeepers explained by the effects of German and Jewish competition.[84] More common were attacks on the inadequacy of state policies, and the government was regularly accused of failing to maintain conditions in which retailing might prosper, and of passing laws which only caused problems and made the situation worse.[85]

These organizations intervened in French politics on a large scale and they were courted by both republican and conservative deputies, to the extent that it is hard to detect any difference between the election promises of republicans and nationalists in Paris after 1900, as both sides sought to win over the decisive votes of small shopkeepers.[86] A precise analysis of social legislation passed at the beginning of the twentieth century shows that a variety of governments all took the interests of craftsmen and retailers into consideration when formulating new legislation or when issuing the decrees that put it into practice. In case of conflict they generally took the employer's side rather than that of the workers.[87] What this all amounts to is that in the years before 1914 the *classes moyennes* had intervened in an increasingly national politics and had succeeded in making themselves heard. They had achieved this by organizing on a national basis, although it must be admitted that clear tendencies remained which favoured work at a local level.

But were all members of the petite bourgeoisie involved, and did they all turn to Poincarism? The high level of instability which we have seen among craftsmen and small shopkeepers points to the real difficulties of organizing this class, since a relative stability must be an important pre-condition for resistance. According to Alain Corbin it was the length of their presence in a locality that enabled the craftsmen of Limousin to play an important role in shaping political opinions there.[88] According to figures given by shopkeepers themselves, which should therefore be interpreted with caution, only a minority were organized. About 10 per cent of all tax-paying retailers were claiming to be members of the *Ligue syndicale* in the 1880s, and in 1912 there were some 28,000 small shopkeepers, about 10 per cent of the total, in the 96 *chambres syndicales*.[89] This implies a degree of retailer organization greater than that of workers in trade unions. This is improbable and suggests a tendency for the middle-class movement to inflate the size of its membership.[90] Many of their organizations were short-lived, a feature which the petite bourgeoisie shared with the working class. In 1912 only 27 out of these 96 organizations were more than ten years old. In contrast to the working class, however, more of whose members could be mobilized to take part in strikes and demonstrations than were actually organized, those petits bourgeois who opposed public action successfully kept their protests within the confines of their organizations, drawing in few who were not members. Here is an additional reason why we must take care in equating the aims of these organizations with those of the petite bourgeoisie as a whole.

Contemporaries complained not only about the difficulties of organizing small shopkeepers and craftsmen but also about the fact that the wealthier among them were disproportionately active in the organizations. When asked whether there were organizations for retailers, a wholesaler from Chateauroux answered 'they don't exist for the little grocer who is linked to a wholesale house, and who remains outside the unions, for these only really organize grocers with a good trade, whose defence needs are quite different from those of the little trader'.[91] This verdict is confirmed by low levels of organization among women – in 1900 only 787 out of 165,574 female retailers were organized – and among *épiciers regrattiers* (itinerant grocers), who in 1912 were represented in only two *chambres syndicales*.[92] We can sense the relatively secure situation of shopkeepers who were members. A good indication is the repeated complaints about the low level of skill and the absence of qualifications among small businessmen, which can be seen as a search for some degree of professionalism, and for a separation of qualified shopkeepers from the unqualified by means of specific criteria established for that purpose. The better-off shopkeepers were particularly interested in creating such distinctions.[93] Petit-bourgeois organizations also gave more attention in their public pronouncements to the interests of those employing wage labour than to those of family businesses. Although they tried to achieve as wide an alliance as possible, when conflict arose they opted for the aims of the property owning sections of the class.[94]

Nevertheless, this tendency to turn to the right should not be exaggerated. Jeanne Gaillard has indicated the way that petit-bourgeois republicanism continued to flourish in the provinces more strongly than it did in Paris. Yet even in Paris the cause of the small shopkeepers was successfully advocated in 1909 by Senator Mascuraud, chairman of the *Comité républicain du commerce, de l'industrie et de l'agriculture*, and a section of the organized grocers remained loyal to the *Comité de l'alimentation* led by the radical socialist Seigneurie.[95] Nor was there any decisive split between petits bourgeois and socialism after 1900. Socialist workers, retailers and craftsmen not only continued to form coalitions of interest in the case of strikes,[96] but many petits bourgeois continued to work within the Socialist Party. In the department of Isère one finds a master tailor, a small manufacturer, and a wine merchant among the leaders of the socialists in that part of eastern France. Dupeux goes so far as to conclude from the large number of craftsmen and small shopkeepers among the cadres of the SFIO in Loir-et-Cher that 'socialism was established in the department of Loir-et-Cher by the petite bourgeoisie'.[97] Finally, there were a number of points of contact between the ideas expressed by the retailers' organizations and those of the socialists, and these allowed some co-operation. In 1913 Jacobin language was added to the loud chorus of anti-semitic, nationalistic and corporatist voices, providing echoes of the involvement of craftsmen and small shopkeepers in the revolutions of the preceding century. These ideas combined anti-aristocratic sentiment, egalitarianism and liberalism. One organization compared the advance of the department stores with the victory of a new aristocracy, 'a new and all powerful aristocracy: the capitalist aristocracy that is enserfing the whole nation'.[98] In the terminology of the *sans-culottes*, the large-scale business organizations become *monopoles* and *accapareurs* (monopolists), to be opposed at all costs.[99] The *Syndicat des épiciers au détail* in Nancy called for laws enabling everyone to become a small property owner. It was as if it were 1793 all over again.

> Indeed it is in the general interest that the state should favour the acquisition of property by the greatest possible number of people. That is the guarantee of progress of civilization, of liberty. The revolution of 1789 was carried out with a cry of *Vive la Liberté*. Are we really going to be so spineless and degenerate as to let ourselves be robbed of that liberty?[100]

Although the socialists argued that the decline of small property ownership was inevitable, and that it should be replaced by co-operative ownership, they were not averse to glorifying the French revolution with a Jacobinism like that to be found in some at least of the retailers' organizations.[101] Moreover their interpretation of the situation of the petite bourgeoisie, of whose 'precarious and poverty stricken condition' Jaurès had complained, gave them the opportunity to depict them as victims of large-scale capitalist exploitation.[102] The Parliamentary Socialist Party's call for an enquiry into the retail trade in France must be interpreted in this light. The dogmatic wing of the SFIO led by Jules Guesde was opposed to working with the middle classes, it is true, but before 1914 tactical considerations made the centre of the party frequently seek co-operation with the radical-socialists, the party whose base lay in the petite bourgeoisie.[103] Although conflicts between workers and small capitalists became more violent at the end of the nineteenth century, many petits bourgeois who employed no outside labour found no problem in supporting the SFIO.

The noisy and in some ways successful agitations of petit-bourgeois organizations cannot conceal the fact that, just as the class consisted of a wide variety of economic and social elements, so were its politics equally disparate. This disparity derives in part from the generally low level of organization which must be set against the disproportionately high level of activity by the more prosperous of the craftsmen and small shopkeepers; in part from the co-existence of reactionary, conservative, republican and even socialist tendencies. This is of course no answer to the often-repeated argument that it is when the material living conditions of classes became similar that the political or ideological distinctions within them become most evident.[104] Whether the French petite bourgeoisie did draw a line between themselves and the workers, whose situation was often so much like their own, can only be revealed by analysing forms of cultural expression, ways of life, tastes and so on. Pierre Bourdieu has carried out such an analysis for the present day, but for the period before 1914 the work remains to be done.[105]

An attempt to analyse the situation and the behaviour of small shopkeepers and craftsmen in France before 1914 that uses the concept of the *classes moyennes* has the advantage that it takes into consideration people's own sense of themselves. Behaviour cannot be adequately deduced from a rigid socio-economic framework of analysis, for it is within the words and the discourse of people themselves that ideological complexities and contradictions are revealed. Nevertheless, class analysis provides an essential correcting factor, to improve the value and the persuasiveness of such more broadly cultural and ideological approaches. These emphasize the fact that the published views of French middle-class organizations before 1914 are by no means representative of those of the whole of the petite bourgeoisie. Indeed, the very concept of the *classes moyennes* can be shown to have little analytical force, whatever its contemporary ideological resonances. Its ideological connotations place craftsmen and retailers in a central position in society, in the *juste milieu*, a position which they came to support and defend. It was a concept which carried unbroken and unquestioned traditions and ideas which came together to underpin social values and prescriptions. It is significant that studies which use the concept all begin with the political issues, and in this way make into an absolute determinant what is no more than one aspect of class reality. A further problem posed by this concept of the middle classes is that it defines the boundaries within which craftsmen and small shopkeepers are to be found purely in terms of two other classes, the working class and the bourgeoisie. However necessary it is to have recourse to the two 'main' classes in order to make such a distinction, we must remember that they are based on the principle of subordinating reality to the concept and not vice versa. Just as distinctions have to be made within the petite bourgeoisie, a precise analysis would reveal differences within the working class and within the bourgeoisie. One particularly relevant example of the differences which existed within the working class is the fact that the achievement of some kind of independence from wage employment was possible not only for skilled workers, but also for the lower sections of the working class and those employed on piece-work.

In contrast to this class definition there is another one which is often, but not always entirely, Marxist in origin. Common relationship to the means of production is its economic basis, and its ideological consequence is the development of class consciousness. Whatever degree of refinement this model has now reached, and it certainly enables us to discover how far the concept of class is from the historical reality of the petite bourgeoisie, it has an essential weakness in its implication that there is one general concept of class valid for all time which should be used to analyse historical structures and processes no matter where, no matter when. It is precisely in cases such as that of the petite bourgeoisie that we can see the importance of not trying to force empirical studies into the framework of a general class theory but to formulate a theory that fits each case. In terms of the petite bourgeoisie, this must take into consideration a number of points made in this article; that ownership of the means of production was less important in the formation of class attitudes than was financial dependence; that social instability made a greater impact than an individual's overall position in society; that sociability was a greater force for unity than were formal organizations; and that experience at a local level was often just as important as that at the national level. Such an approach will not only assist the formulation of appropriate theoretical approaches – it will also help us to penetrate and understand the historical reality.

NOTES

1 AN (Archives Nationales) C 7468, Union des commerçants-industriels de Tours et de l'arrondissement, 14 January 1912; *La Réforme sociale* 9, 1910, 170: 'There is nothing so important for the maintenance of order and of social peace than the prosperity of families which are involved in small-scale industry broadly understood, for, as Le Play correctly observed, they are distinguished from all others by their morality, by their sober spirit of independence, by their unflagging application to work.'

2 Léon Gambetta's words in 1874: 'and in this way there have come into being those new social strata whose advent I predicted. Gentlemen, I say new strata not classes. That is a bad word which I never use.' P. Barral (ed.), *Les Fondateurs de la troisième république*, Paris, 1968, 232; S. Elwitt, *The Making of the Third Republic. Class and Politics in France, 1868–1884*, Baton Rouge, 1975, 53–102.

3 See the article by Nord in this collection; Martin Saint-Léon in *Musée social*, 1911, 372; J. Dubois, *Le Vocabulaire politique et social en France de 1868 à 1872*, Paris, 1962, 14–16; M. Fischer, *Mittelklasse als politischer Begriff in Frankreich seit der Revolution*, Göttingen, 1974.

4 This is the argument of A. Daumard, 'L'évolution de l'industrialisation, 1815–1914', in P. Léon, F. Crouzet, R. Gascon (eds), *L'industrialisation en Europe au XIXe siècle. Cartographie et typologie*, Paris, 1972, 315–34.

5 Association Française de Science Politique, 'Les classes moyennes et la politique; enjeu, stratégies et mobilisations', Round Table, November 1980. These papers will shortly be published.

6 For a discussion of this problem in relation to the French working class in the nineteenth century, see H.-G. Haupt, 'Frankreich: Langsame Industrialisierung und republikanische Tradition', in J. Kocka (ed.), *Europäische Arbeiterbewegungen im 19. Jahrhundert*, Göttingen, 1983.

7 S. Hoffman, *Le Mouvement Poujade*, Paris, 1956; M. Roy, *Les Commerçants entre la révolte et la modernisation*, Paris, 1971; D. Borne, *Petits bourgeois en revolte? Le mouvement Poujade*, Paris, 1977.

8 H.-G. Haupt, 'Einleitung', in H.-G. Haupt (ed.) *'Bourgeois und Volk zugleich?' Zur Geschichte des Kleinbürgertums im 19. und 20. Jahrhundert*, Frankfurt and New York, 1978, 9–40.

9 A. Landry, *Rapport fait au nom de la commission du commerce et de l'industrie chargée de proceder à une enquête sur la situation du commerce en France et notamment, sur la condition actuelle du petit commerce*, Chambre des Deputés, 10ème Législature 1914, 85, impression 3432, 20–5.

10 P. Sorlin, *La Société française*, Paris, 1969, vol. 1, 128; A. Faure, 'Note sur la petite entreprise en France au XIXe siècle. Répresentation d'etat et réalité', paper delivered at the Congrès annuel des historiens économistes français, Paris, 1980 (forthcoming).

11 P. Guillaume, *La Population de Bordeaux au XIXe siècle*, Paris, 1972, 36–9; G. Thuillier, *Georges Dufaud et les débuts du grand capitalisme dans la métallurgie en Nivernais au XIXe siècle*, Paris, 1954, 115; P. Pinchemel, *Structures sociales et dépopulation rurale dans les campagnes picardes de 1836 à 1936*, Paris, 1957, 116–17; B. Legendre, 'La vie d'un prolétariat. Les ouvriers de Fougères au début du XXe siècle', *Le Mouvement social*, 98, 1977, 10; W. H. Reddy, 'Family and factory: French linen weavers in the Belle Epoque', *Journal of Social History*, 8, 1975, 102–12; AN F[22]574, Inspecteur du travail divisionnaire de la 1ère circonscription, 23 August 1910: Enquête sur l'industrie des métaux ordinaires à Paris; see also P. du Maroussem, *La Question ouvrière*, Paris, 1891–1896: vol. 1, 'Charpentiers de Paris: compagnons et indépendants' (1891); vol. 2, 'Ebénistes du faubourg Saint-Antoine' (1892).

12 Faure, op. cit., 15–17; D. Poulot, *Le Sublime ou le travailleur comme il est en 1870 et ce qu'il peut être*, Paris, 1980; Introduction by A. Cottereau, 63–80.

13 P. O'Brien and C. Keyder, *Economic Growth in Britain and France, 1780–1914: Two Paths to the Twentieth Century*, London, 1978; R. Roehl, 'French industrialization. A reconsideration', *Explorations in Economic History*, 13, 1976, 233–81.

14 Faure, op. cit.

15 A. Armengaud, *Les Populations de l'est-acquitain au début de l'époque contemporaine. Recherches sur une région moins developpée (vers 1845–vers 1871)*, Paris, 1961; C. Fohlen, *L'Industrie textile au Second Empire*, Paris, 1956.

16 Faure, op. cit.; H. Bourgin, *L'Industrie de la boucherie dans le département de l'Oise au XIXe siècle*, Paris, 1907.

17 Faure, op. cit.

18 J. Merlin, *L'Industrie en Haute Loire de la fin de la monarchie de juillet aux débuts de la 3ème république*, Lyon, 1972, 274–6; G. Garrier, *Les Campagnes de l'ouest lyonnais et du Beaujolais, 1800–1970*, Grenoble, 1973, vol. 1, 451–8; Y. Lequin, *Les Ouvriers de la région Lyonnaise, 1848–1914*, Lyons, 1977, vol. 1, 142–256; Reddy, op. cit., 104; Archives de la Chambre de Commerce de Mende, Session of the *Chambre consultative des arts et manufactures de Mende*, 21 March 1895; 'The chamber regrets to have to make it known that the industrial establishments which in the past were here in good number, such as spinning, handloom weaving, and the manufacture of Escot have almost completely disappeared' (Escot was a woollen cloth woven for religious orders): G. Dupeux,

Aspects de l'histoire sociale et politique du Loir-et-Cher, 1848–1914, Paris, 1972, 563; Pinchemel, op. cit., 134; Lequin, op. cit., vol. 1, 191ff.

19 J. Bouvier, in F. Braudel and E. Labrousse (eds), *Histoire économique et sociale de la France*, Paris, 1982, vol. 4, 1736–8.

20 See Faure's article in this collection; J. Gaillard, *Paris, la ville 1852–1870*, Paris, 1977, 430–5.

21 J. Le Yaouanq, 'Aux sources de l'histoire de la petite entreprise parisienne au XIXe siècle (les actes civils publics et les factums d'expropriations)', to be published in a forthcoming collection of essays on the French petite bourgeoisie edited by A. Faure and P. Vigier.

22 J. Scott, 'Men and women in the Parisian garment trades; discussions of family and work in the 1830s and 1840s', in P. Thane, G. Crossick and R. Floud (eds), *The Power of the Past. Essays for Eric Hobsbawm* (forthcoming, Cambridge, 1984); C. H. Johnson 'Patterns of proletarianization: Parisian tailors and Lodève woollen workers', in J. Merriman (ed.), *Consciousness and Class Experience in Nineteenth Century Europe*, New York, 1979, 65–84.

23 Gaillard, op. cit., 525–58; P. Gemahling, 'La concentration commerciale sans grands magasins', *Revue d'économie politique*, 26, 1912, 170–92; P. Moride, *Les Magasins à succursales multiples en France et à l'etranger*, Paris, 1913.

24 Le Yaouanq, op. cit.

25 G. J. Sheridan jr, 'Household and craft in an industrializing economy: the case of the silk weavers of Lyons', in Merriman, op. cit., 102–28; R. Michaud, *J'avais vingt ans. Un jeune ouvrier au debut du siècle*, Paris, 1967.

26 O. Voillard, 'Le travail des brodeuses lorraines au XIXe siècle', *Cahiers d'études comtoises*, 3, 'Actes du colloque sur l'artisanat', Besançon, 1961, 121–31.

27 A. Daumard (ed.), *Les Fortunes françaises au XIXe siècle. Enquête sur la répartition et la composition des capitaux privés à Paris, Lyon, Lille, Bordeaux et Toulouse d'après l'enregistrement des droits de succession*, Paris, 1973, 360ff.

28 See Farcy's article in this collection. On butchers, J. M. Merriman, 'Incident at the statue of the Virgin Mary. The conflict of old and new in nineteenth-century Limoges', in Merriman, op. cit., 138ff.

29 AN C 7468.

30 For the term *bourgeoisie populaire* see A. Daumard, *Les Bourgeois de Paris au XIXe siècle*, Paris, 1970, 250ff.

31 Le Yaouanq, op. cit. In the answers from shopkeeper's organizations, credit seems to have been very important: 26 per cent bought the shop with their own money, 11 per cent bought only with outside money alone, and 28 per cent used both their own and outside money (Enquête Landry, 1913).

32 J. C. Martin, 'Hiérarchie et structure de la société commerçante: les listes d'électeurs au tribunal de commerce de Niort en 1864 et 1874', *Le Mouvement social*, 112, 1980, 57–77; J. C. Martin, 'L'essor de la petite bourgeoisie à Niort au XIXe siècle', paper delivered to the 2nd Round Table on the European Petite Bourgeoisie in the Nineteenth Century at the University of Bremen, 1980.

33 See the answers to the Enquête Landry, 1913.

34 See the works already cited by Moride and Gemahling.

35 A. Cottereau, in Poulot, op. cit., 69ff.

36 M. Lévy-Leboyer, 'Le patronat français a-t-il été malthusien?', *Le Mouvement social*, 88, 1974, 9ff; M. Guilbert and V. Isambert-Jamati, *Travail féminin et travail à domicile*, Paris, 1956, 18; P. Gemahling, *Travailleurs au rabais*, Paris, 1910.

37 AN C 5498, 26 June 1891.

38 See the answers to the Enquête Landry, 1913.

39 Martin, 'L'essor de la petite bourgeoisie'.

40 AN C 7466, E. Normand, President of the *Union des patentés de l'arrondissement de*

Clermont (Oise) commented in 1913 that 'little grocers in the rural areas round here have become the forgotten traders. They sell sugar and petrol more than anything else, both articles allowing no profit.'

41 A. de Tocqueville, *L'Ancien Régime et la révolution*, in *Oeuvres complètes*, II, 1, 148.

42 J. Le Yaouanq, 'La mobilité sociale dans le milieu boutiquier parisien au XIXe siècle (une experience de traitement d'un échantillon généalogique)', *Le Mouvement social*, 108, 1979, 100–2; A. Corbin, 'La mobilité sociale en France au XIXe siècle', in G. A. Ritter and R. Vierhaus, *Aspekte der historischen Forschung in Frankreich und Deutschland*, Göttingen, 1981, 113.

43 A. Daumard, *La Bourgeoisie parisienne de 1815 à 1848*, Paris, 1963, 257–9.

44 J. P. Chaline, 'Les contrats de mariage à Rouen au XIXe siècle. Etude d'après l'enregistrement des actes civils publics', *Revue d'histoire économique et sociale*, 48, 1970, 260–4.

45 J. Le Yaouanq, 'Aux origines du milieu boutiquier parisien au XIXe siècle. La nuptialité et ses aspects sociaux', unpublished paper delivered to the 3rd Round Table on the European Petite Bourgeoisie in the Nineteenth Century, at the University of Paris X, Nanterre, 1981, 16. For Bordeaux, Guillaume, op. cit., 122–30.

46 A. Prost, 'Mariage, jeunesse et société à Orléans en 1911', *Annales ESC*, 36, 1981, 679–83.

47 Speech at the 3e Congrès des Classes Moyennes, Association de défense des classes moyennes, in *Les Etudes fiscales et sociales*, Limoges, 1911, 411.

48 Cf. L. and M. Bonneff, *La Vie tragique de travailleurs. Enquête sur la condition économique et morale des ouvriers et ouvrières d'industrie*, Paris, 1911; F. and M. Pelloutier, *La Vie ouvrière en France*, Paris, 1900; M. Perrot, 'Les classes populaires urbaines', in F. Braudel and E. Labrousse (eds), op. cit., vol. 4, 1; H.-G. Haupt, 'Angestellte in der französischen Gesellschaft vor 1914. Einige einführende Bemerkungen', in J. Kocka (ed.), *Angestellte im europäischen Vergleich. Die Herausbildung angestellter Mittelschichten seit dem späten 19. Jahrhundert*, Göttingen, 1981, 112–41.

49 L. Delpérier, 'Le logement des jeunes employés chez leurs patrons', *La Réforme sociale*, 1911, 392–9; Direction du Travail, *Rapport sur l'application des lois sociales . . . en 1907*, Paris, 1908, CLXIII–CLXV.

50 H.-G. Haupt, 'Les petits commerçants et la politique sociale. Etude sur l'application du repos hebdomadaire en France et en Allemagne avant 1914', to appear in the collection edited by A. Faure and P. Vigier referred to in note 21.

51 M. David, 'L'évolution historique des Conseils de prud'hommes en France', *Droit social*, February 1974, 3–21; T. Zeldin, *France, 1848–1945*, Oxford, 1973, vol. 1, 200–3; in 1910, there were 5212 cases in Paris: 2152 in retailing, 1047 in fabrics, 981 in the metal industry, 692 in the building trades and 340 in the chemical industry. *Annuaire statistique de la ville de Paris*, 1900, 358.

52 See J. M. Gourden, 'Les petits métiers parisiens et leurs fonctions au XIXe siècle. L'exemple des marchands des quatre saisons', Thèse 3e cycle, Université Paris VII, 1983, 202ff.

53 E. Accampo, 'Entre la classe sociale et la cité: identité et intégration chez les ouvriers de Saint-Chamond, 1815–1880', *Le Mouvement social*, 118, 1982, 39–59; G. Jacquemet, 'Belleville ouvrier à la Belle époque', *Le Mouvement social*, 118, 1982, 62–77.

54 AN C 7467, AN F 13 267, but see B. Legendre, 'La vie d'un prolétariat. Les ouvriers de Fougères du début du XXe siècle', *Le Mouvement social*, 98, 1977, 23: 'The shop is, in its origins and clientèle, close to the people, but it goes against this when credit has been reluctantly granted, or at times of long strikes.'

55 J. Rougerie, *Paris libre 1871*, Paris, 1971, 19; Gaillard, op. cit.; *Le Reveil des limonadiers* wrote on 17 August 1899: 'At the drink seller's, workers chat, exchange ideas, criticize established institutions, generate their hopes for social reform', in P. Barral, *Le Département de l'Isère sous la IIIe République, 1870–1940*, Paris, 1962, 190.

56 Y. Lequin, 'Ouvriers dans la ville (XIXe et XXe siècle)', *Le Mouvement social*, 118, 1982, 3–7; Jacquemet, op. cit., 66.
57 Gourden, op. cit., 324–30; Haupt, 'Les petits commerçants et la politique sociale'.
58 Cf. S. Hoffman *et al.*, *In Search of France*, Cambridge, 1963, 1–117. He stresses the disparity between the nationalization of political life and the segmentation of solidarity.
59 Corbin, op. cit., 109; F. Raison-Jourde, *La Colonie auvergnate de Paris au XIXe siècle*, Paris, 1976; A. Corbin, *Archaïsme et modernité du Limousin au XIXe siècle, 1845–1880*, Paris, 1975.
60 See the Enquête Landry; AN C 7463, Chambre de Commerce de Cette, 1913.
61 W. H. Sewell, 'La classe ouvrière de Marseille sous la Seconde Republique: structure sociale et comportement politique', *Le Mouvement social*, 76, 1971, 62–3.
62 Le Yaouanq, 'La mobilité sociale', 100.
63 See the works by Chaline and Prost already cited.
64 See the article here by Farcy; Corbin, *Limousin*.
65 O. Voilliard, *Nancy au XIXe siècle (1815–1871), une bourgeoisie urbaine*, Paris, 1982; C. Charle, 'Le recrutement des hauts fonctionnaires en 1901', *Annales ESC*, 1980, 380–409; A. Prost, *L'enseignement en France 1800–1967*, Paris, 1968, 362–4; J. Lacouture, *Léon Blum*, Paris, 1979, 17.
66 S. Berstein, *Histoire du parti radical*, Paris, 1980, vol. 1, 59–63. On the difficulties of social advancement: F. P. Codaccioni, *Lille 1850–1914. Contribution à une étude des structures sociales*, Lille, 1971, 676; G. Vincent, 'Les professeurs du second degré au début du XXe siècle. Essai sur la mobilité sociale et la mobilité géographique', *Le Mouvement social*, 55, 1966, 47–73.
67 Prost, *Enseignement*; P. J. Harrington, 'Elites, education and mobility in France during the Second Empire', *Proceedings of the IVth Annual Meeting of the Western Society for French History*, 1976/7, 369: 'The educational system of France has been more democratic in theory than in practice'; R. Gildea, 'Education and the *classes moyennes* in the nineteenth century', in D. N. Baker and P. J. Harrigan (eds), *The Making of Frenchmen. Current Directions in the History of Education in France, 1679–1979*, Waterloo, Ontario, 1980; G. Vincent, 'Les professeurs de l'enseignement secondaire dans la société de la Belle Epoque', *Revue d'histoire moderne et contemporaine*, 1966, 49–86; J. Ozouf, *Nous les maitres d'écoles*, Paris, 1967.
68 Daumard, *Les Fortunes françaises*, 150–5, 189–201.
69 G. Désert, 'Structures sociales dans les villes bas-normandes au XIXe siècle', in *Conjuncture économique, structures sociales. Hommage à E. Labrousse*, Paris, 1965, 491–512; P. Léon *et al.*, *Géographie de la fortune et structures sociales à Lyon au XIXe siècle* (1815–1914), Lyons, 1974, 110–11.
70 Daumard, *La Bourgeoisie parisienne*, 428–39.
71 J. Bouvier, *Le Krach de l'union générale 1878–1885*, Paris, 1960, 256–77; J. C. Martin, 'Le commerçant, la faillite et l'historien', *Annales ESC*, 35, 1980, 1251–68; J. Gaillard, 'L'héritage du XIXe siècle. Les classes moyennes traditionnelles (atelier-boutique) dans l'histoire des idées et la vie politique. Leur rôle entre la droite et la gauche de 1880 au début du 20e siècle', unpublished paper for a conference on the French middle classes, Institut d'Etudes Politiques, Paris, 1981.
72 Rapport Landry, op. cit., 18; on Niort see Martin, 'Le commerçant', 1257: 'In this way many workers who had set up on their own, with the help of their wives' dowry, became fair game for bankruptcy.'
73 *Annuaire statistique de la ville de Paris, 1900–1914*. Resultat des ventes des fonds de commerce.
74 Gourden, op. cit., 282–9.
75 Chaline, op. cit., 261.
76 Gaillard, 'L'héritage du XIXe siècle', 1.

77 Cf. P. Nord, 'Commerce and Culture in *fin de siècle* Paris', PhD thesis, Columbia University, 1981, 21–72, 467–558, and his article in this book; J. Bernard, 'Du mouvement d'organisation du petit commerce français', thèse de droit, Paris, 1906, 82–96; and cf. the answer to the Enquête Landry from the Confédération: AN C 7640 (1913).
78 L. Boltanski, 'Taxinomies sociales et luttes de classes. La mobilisation de la classe moyenne et l'invention des "cadres"', *Actes de la recherche en sciences sociales*, 29, 1979, 75–105; I. Kolboom, 'Patronat et cadres: la contribution patronale à la formation du groupe des cadres (1936–1938)', *Le Mouvement social*, 121, 1982, 71–96.
79 P. Nord, op. cit.; J. Gaillard, 'La petite entreprise en France au xixe et au xxe siècles', in Commission internationale d'histoire des mouvements sociaux et des structures sociales, *Petite entreprise et croissance industrielle dans le monde au xixe et xxe siècles*, Paris, 1981, vol. 1, 153–8.
80 Villemin in *Etudes fiscales*, 297.
81 G. Crossick, 'The petite bourgeoisie in nineteenth-century Europe: problems and research', in K. Tenfelde (ed.), *Internationale Forschungen zur Geschichte der Arbeiterschaft und Arbeiterbewegung*, forthcoming, Munich, 1984.
82 AN C 7470; the same argument appears in the reply of the *Credit foncier de France* in Lyons (C 7470) (1913).
83 AN C 7466; see the argument in the reply of the *Union économique des négociants de Lons-le-Saulnier* (C 7473) (1913).
84 AN C 7465, Secrétaire du *Comité du commerce, de l'industrie et de l'agriculture de l'arrondissement de Clamency (Nièvre)* (1913); C 7466, G. Ribou, maire de St F. Avall (Pyrenées Orientales) (1913); C 7468, *Syndicat des épiciers de détail des Vosges* (1913); *Chambre de Commerce d'Amiens* (1913).
85 See the reply from the *Confédération des groupes commerciaux et industriels de France* (1913) (AN C 7640).
86 Raison-Jourde, op. cit., 243–54; P. Sorlin, *Waldeck-Rousseau*, Paris, 1966, 421–3.
87 Haupt, 'Les petits commerçants'.
88 Corbin, *Limousin*, 301–7.
89 See Nord's article in this book; *Annuaire des syndicats professionels*, Paris, 1912.
90 J. Juillard, 'Jaurès et le syndicalisme révolutionnaire', in *Jaurès et la classe ouvrière*, Paris, 1981, 111.
91 AN C 7463 Belloy and Deliquet; Dufourmentelle, 'La défense des classes moyennes', *La Réforme sociale*, 7, 1909, 769; AN C 7460, *Syndicat des commerçants du canton ouest à Montluçon (Allier)* (1913); *Chambre de Commerce d'Annonay (Ardèche)* (1913).
92 J. Expert-Bezançon, *Les Organisations de défense patronale*, Paris, 1911, 256.
93 Gourden, op. cit., 335–8.
94 Haupt, 'Les petits commerçants'.
95 Gaillard, 'L'héritage du xixe siècle', 18–19; *L'Epicerie française*, 2 December 1908 and 12 December 1909; F^{22} 368, Préfet de Police in a letter to the Ministre du Travail, 22 December 1909.
96 M. Perrot, *Les Ouvriers en grève. France 1871–1890*, Paris, 1974, 281–2, 488–9, 535–6.
97 Barral, *Département de l'Isère*, 195; Dupeux, op. cit., 608; T. Judt, *Socialism in Provence 1871–1914. A Study in the Origins of the Modern French Left*, Cambridge, 1979, 224ff.
98 AN C 7468, *Fédération du commerce et de l'industrie de l'arrondissement de Castres (Tarn)* (1913).
99 AN C 7461 *Chambre de commerce de Bourges (Cher)* (1913); C 7460 *Union des commerçants et industriels de Gap* (1913).
100 AN C 7465 (1913).
101 M. Rebérioux, 'Les socialistes français et le petit commerce au tournant du siècle', *Le Mouvement social*, 114, 1981, 57–70; Gaillard, 'La petite entreprise en France', 159–61.

102 Jaurès quoted in J. Gaumont, *Histoire générale de la cooperation en France*, Paris, 1923, vol. 2, 285.

103 H. Portelli, *Le Socialisme tel qu'il est*, Paris, 1980; G. Krumeich, 'Zwischen "republikanischem" und "proletarischem" Block: Die franzosischen Sozialisten vor dem 1. Weltkrieg', *Francia*, 7, 1979, 309–17; M. Rebérioux, *La République radicale? 1898–1914*, Paris, 1975, 42–116.

104 P. Bordieu, *La Distinction. Critique sociale du jugement*, Paris, 1979, 155ff, 283–4.

105 ibid.

5 A forgotten class: the petite bourgeoisie in Belgium, 1850–1914*

G. KURGAN-VAN HENTENRYK

As J. Hannes remarked in an excellent article published some ten years ago, the Belgian petite bourgeoisie has not attracted much attention from historians.[1] As we discovered during the course of our own investigation of small-scale production in Belgium, his plea for a more thorough study of the middle classes has so far evoked little response, and historical research in this area has made but little progress.[2] As it stands today, J. Lewinski's book on the industrial evolution of Belgium during the nineteenth and early twentieth centuries, published in 1911, still remains fundamental.[3] B. Verhaegen's quantitative study, based on census tables, distinguishes between handicraft, small, medium-sized and large enterprises by means of two criteria: the worker/employer ratio, and the utilization of mechanical plant. But the numerical values of these criteria are modified to take into account the evolution of the economy, and the justification for the validity of these modifications is unconvincing.[4] J. Hannes's study of the economic activities of the inhabitants of Brussels was based on the registers for the payment of the professional tax (*patente*) during 1846 and 1847. Following in his footsteps, and using the same source material, we tried in our own research to identify what structural changes had occurred over the fifty-year period, and to examine in greater detail the evolution of small-scale production in Brussels.[5]

Another historian, P. Delfosse, has looked at the ideological and political aspects of the middle classes between 1880 and 1914, the period during which the whole question of the petite bourgeoisie came to the fore.[6] This period, moreover, produced a mass of literature in defence of the petite bourgeoisie, coming from intellectuals, civil servants and politicians belonging to Catholic milieux. These writers were anxious to maintain Catholic influence over the social groups which were alarmed by the advance of capitalism and by the rise of the working class. The most prolific of them were Hector Lambrechts, Victor Brants and Oscar Pyfferoen.[7]

So, starting from only a limited number of serious historical studies, and drawing

* Translated from the French by Paul D. G. Smith.

on our own familiarity with a number of the sources, this essay will attempt to provide a survey of what is understood today about the Belgian petite bourgeoisie: the world, that is to say, of small-scale producers and small traders. It will deal, in succession, with the economic, social, ideological and political aspects of the subject.

What part did small-scale enterprises – artisanal, industrial and commercial – play in the Belgian economy between 1850 and 1914? Even though it is fair to say that the industrial revolution was over by the middle of the nineteenth century, Belgium none the less remained a country of small industrial and handicraft activities. The large enterprises were located, at this time, in the cotton centre of Ghent, and in the industrial basins of the provinces of Hainaut and Liège.[8] Many sectors were marked by intense rivalry between small-scale and large-scale producers, and this was true even of new sectors such as mechanical engineering. For the sale of a steam engine it was possible for a manufacturer with only a few workmen to compete successfully with the large industrial establishments. Particularly in the major cities like Brussels and Ghent, local clients often preferred to buy their engines from such small machine-builders, in order to avoid paying high charges for transport.[9] In spite of the early development of the railway network, a large part of the country still remained untouched by the industrial revolution. Around 1860, for example, production in the Brabantine towns of Louvain and Diest was almost entirely in the hands of artisans and small enterprises. In 1866 only one factory in Diest was steam-powered, and no firm employed more than thirty workers. The traditional industries of these towns – cloth manufacture and distilling – had disappeared. Even the economic life of the capital, Brussels, was still profoundly marked by tradition, and this despite the presence of the financial establishments which were promoting industrialization.[10]

During the second half of the century, Belgium became an industrial power. This was as much due to the development and the diversity of its production as to the unprecedented extension of new energies and new techniques, and the increasing concentration, both of labour forces and of companies, in several industrial sectors. By the end of the century this evolution had brought about the almost total elimination of small-scale production in coalmining, heavy industry, textile manufacturing and glass-making. At the same time, however, small units continued to operate in many other branches of activity. Their perpetuation was encouraged by population growth and by urban development, stimulated in turn by emigration from the countryside and by the relative ease with which it was possible to enter various small industrial and commercial professions.[11]

Although the use of census tables requires considerable caution, the industrial survey of 1896 can none the less provide some helpful data. This census, moreover, was carried out with exceptional care,[12] and during its preparatory stages a significant discussion took place as to the appropriateness of retaining the term 'artisans' to cover independent workers. The Central Statistical Commission opted for their inclusion in the larger category of 'heads of businesses'.[13] The census also made a distinction between domestic industries and small, independent, industrial or handicraft enterprises. This distinction was based on the total separation between their commercial organization and their system of production. In the view of those responsible for preparing the census, the power of commercial organization was such that domestic industries had problems similar to those met by large-scale industry. Domestic outworkers were subject to the same fluctuations in the overall economic situation, whereas, despite the fact that their material conditions were otherwise comparable, small master artisans worked for more reliable markets, even though these were generally narrower.[14] So, excluding the 94,000 firms employing domestic labour, the 1896 census counted a total of 236,000 enterprises. Of these, 165,000 employed no workers at all, and another 54,500 had no more than four. In other words, at this date, 95 per cent of Belgian industrial enterprises could be classed as artisanal or small-scale. They employed 36 per cent of the total population involved in industry, but only 14 per cent of the workers. The 17,000 large-scale concerns occupied 43 per cent of the active industrial population, but 60 per cent of the workers.[15] Observers were struck at the time by the concentration of small units in some twenty-five trades or groups of trades. In most of these, small-scale production predominated.[16]

Nearly half of these enterprises – most of them family businesses – made clothing or boots and shoes. Other branches characterized by small units were building, transport, and the traditional metal-working occupations such as those of blacksmiths, locksmiths and stove-makers, boiler-makers and tinsmiths. Some branches were up against competition from mechanized workshops, for example in bakery, joinery, sawmilling and boot- and shoemaking. Under the pressure of this competition the nature of certain trades was being transformed. For shoemakers, hatters, jewellers and wheelwrights, in particular, repair work was taking the place of actual production. Changeovers from production to commerce were becoming frequent. New inventions, and factory production of new articles, hastened the disappearance of dozens of occupations. Coopers' wares, for example, were eliminated by the competition from enamelled products, whilst carpentry declined with the increasing substitution of iron for wood. 'Spa' articles – decorated wooden objects much in vogue during the eighteenth and early nineteenth centuries – gave way to photographs and chromolithographs.[17]

Nevertheless, during the years of economic expansion preceding the First World War, the number of people employed in crafts grew. This growth was certainly not as rapid as that in large-scale and medium-sized industry, but it closely followed population growth. It was particularly steady in the branches which provided for the needs of urban consumers.

The importance of small-scale industrial and commercial ventures in the employment of the occupied population is confirmed by the study we have carried out on the inhabitants of the city of Brussels who were subject to payment of the professional tax during the nineteenth century.[18] In spite of certain gaps, this fiscal source – the registers of tax-payers – has the advantage of giving quantitative information on activities in the tertiary sector. Such information is not included in the census tables prior to 1910. The registers enable us to detect at least some of the cases where several activities were combined, and to establish hierarchies within the different categories of those obliged to pay the tax in order to exercise their profession: mainly heads of businesses, artisans, manufacturers or tradespeople. A comparison of the data for the years 1847 and 1892 reveals the basic features of the evolution of the middle classes (*classes moyennes*) within the heart of the Brussels area during this time span.

Overall, the number of people paying the professional tax rose faster than the population. Brussels remained a city of artisans and small industries, whilst undergoing the same kind of developments as those seen in Paris during the Second Empire. Thus, while the textile and metal branches went into decline, as a result of the profound changes in conditions of production brought about by the industrial revolution, the trades and industries which directly served the urban population, on the other hand, developed considerably. Alongside the small workshops there appeared larger enterprises, with more concentrated workforces, although these rarely numbered more than a hundred. The predominant type of firm remained the family one, employing only a few workers. The development of Brussels' political, administrative, financial and cultural functions also led to an expansion of luxury and precision trades, and of printing and of the clothing trades. In this last sphere, the demands of a wealthy clientèle stimulated such specialized activities as embroidery, *passementerie* and artificial flower-making, whilst tailors' workshops and dressmaking workshops diversified, both in scale and in terms of the quality of the finished products.

Although industrial activity is undoubtedly underestimated, the principal phenomenon of the evolution seen in these years is the explosion of the tertiary sector. Amongst the lower categories of those who paid the professional tax, the expansion was massive. The numbers within these categories grew more rapidly than those in the higher categories, although there is a general upward tendency towards a higher tax assessment, particularly striking in the case of shopkeepers. In spite of the appearance of new, more integrated, modes of distribution, the predominant unit in Brussels retailing remained the small shop. In 1892, 87 per cent of the 5505 shopkeepers registered were still taxed on turnovers of less than 12,500 francs, compared to 93 per cent of the total of 3484 shopkeepers registered in 1847. Within this stratum of small shopkeepers, however, a significant change had taken place. In absolute terms, the number of shops with turnovers of less than 2000 francs had diminished, whilst businesses with turnovers of between 4000 and 12,500 francs had substantially grown in number. The general expansion of commercial activity in Brussels was accompanied by a spectacular proliferation of all sorts of taverns, cafés, restaurants and hotels, evidence of the city's liveliness.

The growth of the commercial and industrial petite bourgeoisie during the period was also accompanied by modifications in the city's layout. Economic activity, particularly in the tertiary sector, tended to spread out along an axis running from north to south, replacing the old east–west axis. A contrast also emerged between the neighbourhoods to the west and the south-west, and those of the centre, and the north and east of the 'Pentagon' – the heart of the capital. In the former neighbourhoods economic activity grew far more rapidly, servicing the basic needs of the city's inhabitants: food, building and clothing. There was a profusion of workshops, shops and taverns, frequented by the local people. Almost without exception, the owners of these various establishments were rated in the lower categories for the professional tax: a population of artisans, small businessmen, shopkeepers and tavern keepers, many of them situated close to the borderlines separating the petite bourgeoisie from the working classes. The activities of the central neighbourhoods, and of those to the north and east, on the other hand, provided for more than merely local needs. They were directed more towards a wealthy clientèle, and turned this part of the city into a commercial and entertainments centre.

The majority of those who paid the professional tax may be identified with the middle classes. Taking into account certain legislative reforms designed to remove, or at least diminish, the tax burden on several categories of artisans, the relative importance of those who were most heavily taxed had not significantly altered. But the proportion of small tax-payers had notably increased by the end of the century. At the same time, many of these had risen slightly in the tax ratings.

From this date onwards, under the combined influence of technological progress and capitalist concentration, a process began which was to become even more marked during the twentieth century, namely the evolution from a state of competition with large-scale producers towards one of complementarity or dependence. As a result of this, small-scale enterprises still account for approximately half of the jobs in Belgium today.

The study of the social history of the petite bourgeoisie in Belgium has not yet been undertaken. All that can be done here, therefore, is to stress the effects of the abolition of corporations, under the French regime, and to emphasize the importance of the development of liberalism during the nineteenth century. In opening up access to small-scale enterprises, these factors encouraged the growth and the diversity of the middle classes. It was undoubtedly within the intermediate economic and social groups that social mobility, linked to economic development, was the most intensely experienced. For them, rising or falling on the social scale meant something quite tangible. These strata acquired a consciousness of belonging neither to the class above, nor, even less, to those below. The hope of being able to reach the highest levels of the social hierarchy, and the fear of sinking back to a lower level, were the main motives determining the behaviour of members of the middle classes (*classes moyennes*). Their identification under the label 'petite bourgeoisie' is indicative of their aspirations.[19]

Nothing illustrates more clearly this frame of mind, and this concern to respect social hierarchies, than the complaints expressed on the subject of railway travel. Many members of the petite bourgeoisie were faced with the following dilemma: whether to travel third class, inexpensively but in disagreeable company, or whether to buy second-class tickets, often beyond their means. They consequently demanded a reduction in the price of second-class tickets, so that their children would not have to 'rub shoulders with ill-bred workmen'. Rich passengers, in turn, would have to occupy the first-class compartments. Some even went so far as to recommend such discriminatory measures as reserving special carriages for the holders of workers' season-tickets: 'passengers who are obliged to maintain a certain decorum can be greatly inconvenienced by the proximity of those who, on account of their trade, wear dirty clothes'.[20]

It was only towards the end of the nineteenth century, after the shopkeepers of some of the large towns had attempted to create their own, independent means of expression, that the petite bourgeoisie came to be considered as a social class. The following extract from the report of one of the organizers of the oral enquiry of the National Commission for the Petite Bourgeoisie provides a good account of the image the petite bourgeoisie ascribed to itself. Remarking upon the difficulty of conducting this enquiry, the reporter writes:

> During the course of the enquiry on labour,[21] the witness usually spoke of his class interests; he felt himself to be in a position of strength because he had the support of working-class solidarity; his own, individual demands were the same as those of his comrades at work; he was often the spokesman for some group or association. In the present case there was no such attitude. The Commission sought out the testimony of tradesmen and artisans, in a word of this petite bourgeoisie which is wholly impregnated by the practices and ruthlessness of competition, and by a deep-seated spirit of individualism. We expected our witness to talk not of others, but of himself. We wanted him to reveal to us the facts he normally conceals with such jealous care: the resources at his command; where he obtains his raw materials; who his customers are. We asked the petite bourgeoisie to expose the causes of its setbacks, or disclose the secret of its prosperity. . . . In search of such declarations the Commission approached a class which is systematically secretive, and which, in general, has no corporative organizations.[22]

As it indeed transpired, much energy had to be spent in order to gather a sufficient quantity of oral evidence. Considerable effort went into establishing contact with members of the petite bourgeoisie and winning their confidence, and the results were more or less successful, depending on the locality.[23] The analysis of the ensemble of individual testimonies recorded, however, reveals that an explicit identification in terms of a social class – the petite bourgeoisie – was rare. More frequently expressed was the impression of belonging to a narrower social group, such as that of shopkeepers, or to a particular professional category. What emerges overall is that the frontiers defining the petite bourgeoisie are vague, and that the criteria employed to distinguish this class from others do not always correspond with social reality.[24]

If small-scale producers and tradesmen are considered to belong to the petite bourgeoisie, the criterion applied in order to distinguish them from workers is the independence and responsibility they had in the exercise of their professions. This criterion is certainly to be found in the thinking of the nineteenth century, but it does not necessarily tally with the experience of those to whom it was applied. Its ambiguity is clearly revealed in connection with independent artisans, as the following argument, put forward by the liberal minister Frère-Orban in 1848, suggests. Justifying exemption from payment of the professional tax proposed for several categories of artisans, when they worked alone, or with the sole assistance of members of their family, the minister explained:

> Although the tax levied on this category of artisans is very low, it is still unjust in principle; they may work directly for private persons, and not in the employ of a master in their trade, but in reality they are simple workers, with a right to the same exemptions.[25]

The confusion persisted until the end of the nineteenth century. During the industrial census of 1896 it was discovered that some 20,000 artisans were listed as 'workers' in the population registers kept by the communal administrations. When the census-takers enquired, these artisans replied that they had no employer.[26]

How did these artisans perceive themselves, then? The problem is a difficult one to resolve. It was not unusual for the creation of professional friendly societies to be encouraged by the closeness of the social conditions of masters and their workers in traditional industries. Many such societies were founded during the nineteenth century, especially in the Flemish region of the country, where the corporative tradition had not disappeared. These societies had a religious character, and masters and men were placed on an equal footing for relief in the case of being disabled for work.[27]

With the rise of working-class movements, and the appearance, at the end of the century, of early social legislation, the attitude of the petite bourgeoisie became more complex. Even if its members came to demand some of the advantages conceded to the working class – reductions in railway fares, Sunday rest, inexpensive housing – they were not willing to regard them as measures which, by assimilating them with the workers, would entail loss of social standing. The question of railway travel, as we have seen, exemplified this attitude. In a similar fashion, benefiting from the legislation on workers' dwellings did not imply social regression. On the contrary, when a worker became a home-owner he also learned thrift and sobriety, becoming ready 'to enter the class of the petite bourgeoisie'.[28]

Up until the end of the nineteenth century shopkeepers and small businessmen had few organizations for the defence of their professional and economic interests. The earliest such organizations appeared in the large towns, where employers belonging to the same profession began to group together. The oldest association of this type – that of the jewellers, clock and watchmakers and goldsmiths of Antwerp – dates back to 1855. But out of the thirty-odd associations in existence at the end of the century, most were founded during its last twenty-five years.[29] It was this quarter of a century which saw the birth of an awareness of the problem of the petite bourgeoisie. A certain element of the class attempted to constitute an autonomous political movement, but the efforts in this direction were sporadic, and without success. P. Delfosse has studied this autonomous fraction of the petite bourgeoisie which hoped to take advantage of the adoption of universal suffrage in 1893 (universal suffrage which was moderated by plural voting) in order to create its own political party, 'the anti-co-operative' or 'tradesmen's' party. Its members were recruited mainly in the large towns. It launched virulent attacks both against the Catholics, then in power, and against the Belgian Workers' Party, and it called relentlessly for measures against co-operative stores, held responsible for the crisis in shopkeeping. Even though it met with little electoral success, the movement none the less obliged the Catholics in power to take up the question of the petite bourgeoisie.[30]

For them it was an important issue, a question not only of checking the rise of socialism, but also of enlarging their electoral base, necessary after the extension of the suffrage in 1893. The action undertaken by the Catholics took several forms. On the one hand the Catholic press set about sinking the anti-co-operative party, either by harsh criticism of the movement, or by refusing to publish the speeches delivered by its candidates during the election campaign. The stupidity and violence of these speeches was denounced, however. The same press, on the other hand, afforded generous coverage to the national and international congresses of the petite bourgeoisie which had been largely infiltrated by personalities from the Catholic world.[31]

In effect, Catholic intellectuals, journalists, civil servants and politicians came to the defence of the middle classes, by their writings, their participation in the setting up of congresses of the petite bourgeoisie, and by their parliamentary initiatives. Several of them went abroad to seek information, particularly to Germany which was a pioneer in this field. The leading figures of this movement were two university professors, Victor Brants and Oscar Pyfferoen, along with a civil servant at the Ministry of Industry and Labour, Hector Lambrechts. The latter became the outstanding personality of the movement of the middle classes in Belgium.[32] All three, moreover, were influenced by the thought of Le Play and wrote regularly for the review of his disciples, *La Réforme sociale*.[33] In 1901, at the instigation of a deputy for Liège, Gustave Francotte, a parliamentary group for the defence of the interests of the petite bourgeoisie was created. Its members were exclusively Catholic deputies.

In reply to those who held that economic progress would sooner or later bring about the disappearance of master artisans and small tradesmen, the Catholics argued that it was necessary to maintain the middle class as an element of social peace. The suppression of this class would deprive the workers of any chance of advancing socially by self-help, and would engender conditions of potential disorder. As a class which acted as a buffer between the capitalist bourgeoisie and the working class, the petite bourgeoisie, with its attachment to the family, to existing institutions, to the country and to religion, was the best possible bulwark for social order, and one which the ruling classes ought to protect. But the task was rendered delicate by the fact that in order to counteract the growing influence of socialism amongst the workers, and to strengthen their electoral hold in rural areas, the Catholics had developed their own system of co-operatives. They therefore resorted to a position of compromise, which held the petite bourgeoisie itself responsible for the problems it was facing, whilst encouraging it to adapt to modern society by organizing under the state's aegis.[35]

Since the whole machinery of the state was in the hands of the Catholics, they could themselves establish the particular mechanisms designed to take petit-bourgeois interests into account, even whilst respecting the state's role as arbitrator. As early as 1896 the recently formed Ministry of Industry and Labour began to study the possibility of creating a service for the middle classes. It was inaugurated in 1899, under the name of 'The Office for the Middle Classes' (*Bureau des classes moyennes*), the first official institution to which these questions were specifically attributed. The next step followed in 1902 with the setting up of the National Commission for the Petite Bourgeoisie, a fact-finding commission which was to play the same role for the middle classes as that played for the working classes by the Labour Commission, after 1886.[36]

The commission carried out its investigations over several years. An examination of the oral evidence, and of the individual testimonies in particular, reveals the gap between the aspirations which were voiced by members of the petite bourgeoisie, and the kind of response that the state was prepared to make to satisfy them. In its relations with the state the petite bourgeoisie was apparently under the impression of having been neglected or, worse still, unfairly treated, by the existing system. What clearly underlay the numerous grievances and demands was an obsession with competition, on the one hand, and a concern, on the other, about the solvency of the clients of producers and shopkeepers. The petit-bourgeois reaction was simultaneously a defensive one and a repressive one. Basically, state intervention was called for not so much to support the promotion of the middle classes as to curtail or eliminate the activities of those who were to blame for their misfortunes. It is important here to highlight the range of these victims of petit-bourgeois resentment. Contrary to the assertions of P. Delfosse, the most keenly resented competition emanated from traditional forms of commerce: pedlars, markets and fairs. The specific category of pedlars was easily the favourite amongst the targets singled out by the witnesses; next came co-operatives and, more especially, co-operative stores. Although they too were feared, department stores came far behind, and did not provoke such aggressive complaints.

On the necessity of turning to the state for the protection of the petite bourgeoisie, the witnesses were by no means in agreement. State intervention, after all, could present a threat to individual liberty. The contradictory opinions expressed about making Sunday a legal day of rest provide a good example of this disagreement. The need to reconcile a deep-seated individualism with aspirations for security and equality found expression in the denunciation of the advantages enjoyed by other social strata, in the demand that such advantages be extended to the petite bourgeoisie, or, alternatively, in the demand that these advantages be limited, or even taken away from those who benefited from them. However, the measures which the state was asked to implement – whether these were regulations or measures to do with the functioning of justice or of taxation – all coincided with a conception of the state as a policeman, or an arbitrator. The state represents the ultimate arbiter when the conflict between individual interests cannot be resolved; the exercise of the state's authority here is recognized and accepted by all. On the other hand, its direct intervention as a power which can set up institutions and organize new enterprises is very rarely called for. After all, the state's agents already provided the petite bourgeoisie with enough grounds for resentment, on account of their status, and for the manner in which they went about the state's administrative business. On this point it is possible to detect different attitudes in different parts of the country. Thus the Flemish provinces appear more individualistic and to have a stronger notion of the state-as-policeman. This attitude seems less prevalent in the Brabant and Walloon regions. In these there was a petit-bourgeois demand to share the advantages already granted to the working class. This, and the desire to improve material and social conditions, presupposed more active intervention by the state.[37]

The studies by P. Delfosse and L. Gaiardo have shown how the problem of the petite bourgeoisie posed a dilemma for the ruling Catholic bourgeoisie. The ambition of this bourgeoisie being to ensure the integration of all social classes into the Catholic world, it was impossible to satisfy demands emanating from the petite bourgeoisie without exacerbating the conflicts between that class and the working class, on the one hand, and between the petite and large bourgeoisie on the other. The state's policy was consequently to reject all interventionism and any measure designed to protect the petite bourgeoisie. Instead it took indirect action with a view to increasing the petite bourgeoisie's ability to defend itself. In place of the protectionist remedies of a repressive and defensive nature advocated by members of the petite bourgeoisie, the state embarked upon a policy of promoting professional associations and encouraging the development of professional training, intended to enable the middle class to adapt to the circumstances of capitalist concentration. At the same time the importance of the petite bourgeoisie's role as a buffer class between the proletariat and large-scale employers was magnified. Thus the Office for the Middle Classes was an active supporter of the propaganda in favour of the creation of 'bourgeois unions' (*syndicats bourgeois*). These might be professional unions, formed in accordance with the terms of the law of 1898, co-operative societies – such as the small tool-purchasing associations founded in some 15 towns in 1904–5 – or other simple associations which came into existence.[38] The campaign was pursued by the Department of the Middle Classes, created in 1906. In 1908 this department was succeeded by that of Trades and Business, which carried on with the task of improving conditions of apprenticeship and encouraging professional training. According to figures published by the Ministry of Industry and Labour, the number of middle-class associations went up from a little over a hundred in 1906 to 689 in 1913, evidence of the considerable efforts made by these departments.[39] Nevertheless, it was not until the inter-war period that a real programme for the middle classes was formulated, and not until after the Second World War that any real trade unionism appeared in small and medium-sized enterprises.[40]

There remains the question of whether, before 1914, the Catholic Party succeeded in monopolizing the issue of the petite bourgeoisie to its own advantage, and whether, in attending to the grievances of this class, it was successful in enlarging its electorate. The Catholics' natural opponents were the liberals. This party could count on the anti-clerical traditions of certain strata of the middle classes, and on their adherence to the fundamental principles of liberalism. But even though they declared themselves to be attached to the petite bourgeoisie, the liberals were hardly in a position to recommend the active protection of this class by the state. Resolutely hostile to state intervention, the liberals, like the Catholics, were tied to the ruling classes. They consequently took little action in favour of the petite bourgeoisie, leaving their traditional political opponents a clear field. However, the adoption of proportional representation in 1899, along with the growth of the influence of the progressive wing of the Liberal Party, was to enable them to ally with the socialists in combating the Catholic government, and to win the support of the small proportion of the petite bourgeoisie which was active in freethinkers' societies and freemasonry.[41]

As for the socialists, who, after the extension of the suffrage in 1893, represented the main danger for the Catholics in power, their attitude was largely conditioned by the electoral situation. It must be remembered here that in 1894, on the morrow of this extension of the vote, the socialists became the Catholics' principal opponents in Parliament. Their policies, based on working-class demands, did not embrace those of the petite bourgeoisie. But although they may have been convinced that in the long run small-scale production and trading would disappear, they none the less refused to do anything which would hasten this disappearance, and gave their support to the measures presented for the improvement of the petite bourgeoisie's situation. After the electoral reform of 1899 – the introduction of proportional representation, designed to save the Liberal Party and consolidate the anti-socialist front – the position of the socialists with regard to the petite bourgeoisie underwent a change. The first elections under the new system, in 1900, constituted a serious defeat for the socialists, and led them to a finer appreciation of the electoral importance of this class. Thereafter the socialists made overtures towards small-scale producers and tradesmen, arguing that their interests coincided with those of the working class. According to the socialists, 'the only way of helping out the petite bourgeoisie is to save the working class from misery, since the petite bourgeoisie lives mainly off the working class'.[42] In practice this attitude did not win over the petit-bourgeois voters, since the socialists' priority still remained the struggle in favour of the working class.[43]

At the end of this brief survey of the Belgian industrial and commercial petite bourgeoisie prior to 1914, it is necessary to stress once again how little this class has been studied. The principal reason for this would appear to lie in the fact that for a large part of the nineteenth century, and even into the twentieth century, the social question, and, subsequently, the influence of Marxist thought, led to the issue of these social groups being avoided. True, these groups are extremely difficult to define and to comprehend, but it was also believed that they were doomed to decline. At present, historians have at their disposal few reliable statistics on the numbers of the petite bourgeoisie and their patterns of growth, and a critical appraisal of the statistical sources available is hardly encouraging. Similarly, on the social aspects of the subject, the evidence, for most of the nineteenth century, is scarce. This is because the problem did not emerge until late in the century, and the members of the petite bourgeoisie rarely displayed a positive class consciousness. In the end it is on the ideological and political facets of the subject that the sources are most abundant, in particular from the end of the century onwards, when the petite bourgeoisie became a section of the electorate of considerable importance to the political parties struggling for power.

NOTES

1 J. Hannes, 'De kleine producent en de kleinhandelaar in de 19de eeuw', *Archives et Bibliothèques de Belgique*, special issue (No. 10), 1973, 55–65.

2 G. Kurgan-van Hentenryk, 'Belgique. La petite entreprise de la fin de l'Ancien Régime à nos jours', in *Petite entreprise et croissance industrielle dans le monde aux* XIXe *et* XXe *siècles*, Commission internationale d'histoire des mouvements sociaux et des structures sociales, Paris, 1981, vol. 1, 189–223.

3 J. Lewinski, *L'Evolution industrielle de la Belgique*, Brussels and Leipzig, 1911.

4 B. Verhaegen, *Contribution à l'histoire économique des Flandres*, 2 vols, Brussels and Paris, 1961. See also Kurgan-van Hentenryk, op. cit., 193–4.

5 J. Hannes, *De economische bedrijvigheid te Brussel, 1846–1847. Controle en aanvulling van de nijverheidstelling van 15.10.1846*, Brussels and Paris, Centre Interuniversitaire d'Histoire Contemporaine, Cahiers (81), 1975; G. Kurgan-van Hentenryk, 'Les patentables à Bruxelles au XIXe siècle', *Le Mouvement social*, no. 108, 1979, 63–88. G. Kurgan-van Hentenryk and G. Viré, 'Les registres des patentables, source de l'histoire de Bruxelles à la fin du XIXe siècle', *Acta historica Bruxellensia, IV, Histoire et Méthode*, Brussels, 1981, 367–415.

6 P. Delfosse, 'Les classes moyennes face au problème de la croissance (1880–1914). Les positions de la fraction autonomiste des classes moyennes', CREHIDES, No. H.7601, Louvain-la-Neuve, 1976; and 'Positions catholiques et rôle de l'Etat', CREHIDES, No. H.7602, Louvain-la-Neuve, 1976. These two studies have been partially published under the titles 'Die belgischen Mittelklassen und das Problem des Wachstums. Positionen der autonomen Fraktionen der Mittelklassen zwischen 1880 und 1914', in H.-G. Haupt (ed.), *'Bourgeois und Volk zugleich'? Zur Geschichte des Kleinbürgertums in 19. und 20. Jahrhundert*, Frankfurt and New York, 1978, 162–81; and 'La petite bourgeoisie en crise et l'Etat: le cas belge (1890–1914)', *Le Mouvement social*, no. 114, 1981, 85–103.

7 Amongst their publications, we may mention here H. Lambrechts, *Le Problème social de la petite bourgeoisie envisagé au point de vue belge*, Brussels, 1902, and *Trente années au service des classes moyennes*, Brussels, 1935; V. Brants, *La petite industrie contemporaine*,

Paris, 1901; O. Pyfferoen, *La crise de la petite bourgeoisie*, Brussels, 1899. The early organization of small urban producers and tradespeople, and the role of these authors in the growing self-awareness of the middle classes, has been studied by L. Gaiardo: 'L'organisation de la petite bourgeoisie urbaine (1890–1914)', unpublished memoir (*mémoire de licence*), History Department, Free University of Brussels, 1979.

8 On the industrial history of Belgium, see the collective work, *L'Industrie en Belgique. Deux siècles d'évolution 1780–1980*, published for the exhibition organized by the Crédit Communal and the Société Nationale de Crédit à l'Industrie, Brussels, 1981.

9 A. Van Neck, *Les débuts de la machine à vapeur dans l'industrie belge, 1800–1850*, Brussels, 1979, 400.

10 See Kurgan-van Hentenryk, 'Belgique. La petite entreprise', 197–8; M. Theys, *La Population de Diest pendant les deux premiers tiers du XIXe siècle*, Brussels, 1977, 135.

11 According to J. de Belder, retail trading witnessed considerable growth between 1850 and 1864, and between 1880 and 1885; 'Adel en burgerij 1840–1914', in *Algemene Geschiedenis der Nederlanden*, 12, Haarlem, 1977, 87–8.

12 On this question see Kurgan-van Hentenryk 'Belgique. La petite entreprise', 190ff., and 'Les patentables à Bruxelles', 63.

13 *Bulletin de la Commission centrale de statistique*, vol. XVII, 1890–6, session of 11 July 1896, 156–7.

14 A. Julin, 'Le recensement général des industries et métiers au 31 octobre 1896', *La Réforme sociale*, July–December, 1900, 513–14.

15 *Recensement général des industries et des métiers (31 octobre 1896)*, vol. XVIII, 1902. *Exposé général des méthodes et des résultats*, 150ff.

16 E. Waxweiler, 'La Belgique est-elle un pays de grande industrie?', *Bulletin du Comité Central du Travail Industriel*, 1 August 1901, 727–8; Brants, op. cit., 211ff.; J. Lewinski, *L'Evolution industrielle de la Belgique*, 196 and 337.

17 J. Lewinski, op. cit., 206ff.

18 See note 5.

19 J. Hannes, 'De kleine producent', 56–7.

20 Ministère de l'Industrie et du Travail, *Commission nationale de la petite bourgeoisie*, Séances d'enquête orale, vol. 1, 1903, 175 and vol. 5, 1904, 201, 313 and 409. See also G. Kurgan-van Hentenryk, 'La petite bourgeoisie belge et l'Etat au début du XXe siècle', read at the 3rd Round Table on the Petite Bourgeoisie in Western Europe before 1914, Paris-Nanterre, 1981.

21 The reference here is to the enquiry carried out by the Labour Commission, set up after the revolts of 1886.

22 Ministère de l'Industrie et du Travail, *Commission nationale de la petite bourgeoisie*, Rapports et voeux, Ghent, 1908, 33.

23 General report of the commission, 57ff.

24 The oral enquiry was conducted in 89 communes, between 11 August 1902 and 19 April 1904. According to the general report, 1333 witnesses were heard, during 162 sessions. The results of the enquiry were published in seven volumes, between 1903 and 1904. We have begun a more thorough investigation of this enquiry, paying particular attention to the evidence of the 1129 witnesses who came forward to volunteer information. The results of our investigation will be published shortly in the *Revue Belge d'Histoire Contemporaine*.

25 Documents parlementaires, Chambre, 1848–1849, No. 44. Session of 24 November 1848, 40ff.

26 *Recensement général des industries et des métiers (31 octobre 1896)*, vol. XVIII, 68.

27 E. Vandervelde, *Enquête sur les associations professionnelles d'artisans et ouvriers en Belgique*, Brussels, 1891, vol. 1, 18.

28 *Commission nationale de la petite bourgeoisie*, Séances d'enquête orale, vol. 1, 131, 154. See also Kurgan-van Hentenryk, 'La petite bourgeoisie belge et l'Etat'.

29 Ministère de l'Industrie et du Travail, *Rapport sur l'activité de la section des classes moyennes de 1899 à 1906*, Office des classes moyennes, Brussels, 1907, 156ff.
30 See note 6. From 1895 onwards, the independent deputy Gilliaux was the only member of parliament to defend the interests of the autonomist movement. He met with considerable hostility from the Catholic Party (Delfosse, 'La petite bourgeoisie en crise et l'Etat', 91–2).
31 Delfosse, 'Les positions', 6–7. The *Rapport sur l'activité de la section des classes moyennes* (see note 29 above) typically forgets to mention the 'Vrije Burgerbond' of Ghent – active in the anti-co-operative movement – in its list of existing middle-class associations.
32 Gaiardo, op. cit., 150, 173 and 177–8.
33 Delfosse, 'Les positions', 48.
34 Gaiardo, op. cit., 155.
35 Delfosse, 'La petite bourgeoisie en crise et l'Etat', 86.
36 H. Lambrechts, *Trente années au service des classes moyennes*, xivff.
37 See Kurgan-van Hentenryk, 'La petite bourgeoisie belge et l'Etat au début du xxe siècle'.
38 *Rapport sur l'activité de la section des classes moyennes de 1899 à 1906*, 161–2.
39 ibid., 156ff; G. Duplat, *La Classe moyenne. Son rôle, son action politique, sa situation économique*, Brussels, 1914, 319ff.
40 Kurgan-van Hentenryk, 'Belgique. La petite entreprise', 212–14.
41 Gaiardo, op. cit., 160; J. Bartier, 'Partis politiques et classes sociales', in J. Bartier, *Libéralisme et socialisme au xixe siècle*, Brussels, 1981, 280ff.
42 Speech by the socialist deputy Terwagne, Annales parlementaires, Chambre, 1900–1, session of 3 July 1901, 1728.
43 Gaiardo, op. cit., 156ff.

The research focus

6 Masters and manufacturers: social values and the smaller unit of production in Birmingham, 1800–50*

CLIVE BEHAGG

A clear analysis of the changing role of the small unit of production in Britain, in the first half of the nineteenth century, has been hindered by the acknowledged overlap, within this economic sector, between the artisan small master and the 'classic' petit-bourgeois small producer. Both were employers of labour and capital in a small way and both operated in a subordinate capacity to the needs of large-scale capital. But whereas the artisan small master has been seen, generally, as the representative of a traditional form of production based upon the decentralized workshop, the petite bourgeoisie has increasingly been recognized as the comparatively recent creation of accelerating industrialization after 1800.[1] The wealth of material available which emphasizes the role of the artisan in the early radical movement has been complemented, more recently, by work which has highlighted the importance of the commitment of certain petit-bourgeois groups to economic liberalism as part of the process of restabilization following the Chartist challenge.[2]

Nevertheless, the recurrent desire of historians to use the bland occupational data available in census material, pollbooks, and so on, for quantitative surveys, has exacerbated the problem of definition within the small producer sector. The need to explore and explain critical differences in social consciousness *within* occupational groups has been subordinated to the pragmatic need to seek an 'objective economic homogeneity'[3] to suit specific purposes. However close he may have been to the artisan small master in terms of objective economic criteria the distinctive social identity of the petit-bourgeois producer evolved, at least partly, as an explicit rejection of the values of the world of labour to which the artisan related. This essay

* This paper was presented to the Round Table on the Petite Bourgeoisie in Western Europe before 1914, at the University of Bremen, March 1980. It was also subsequently presented to the University of Birmingham, School of History Postgraduate Seminar in November 1981. I should like to thank the members of both seminars for their comments and also Dorothy Thompson who kindly read the original draft.

hopes to clarify to some degree the development of this social identity and to study its internal dimensions, in an area where the small workshop remained the 'typical' unit of production throughout the period. It will be suggested that the emergence of the small producer as an ideological buttress against the continued survival of artisan values in the workplace was largely the result of crucial changes in the economic relationship between capital and the small unit within the total system of production. Through the medium of this changing economic context small-scale production in certain of its forms was actively discouraged. In this sense the transformation of the nature of the small producer was a vital part of the broader process whereby an older artisan-based culture was being supressed and replaced.[4]

THE STRUCTURE OF PRODUCTION

Often those who lived through the experience of rapid industrialization in the first half of the century sought to account for qualitative changes within production by emphasizing the swift decline of the craftsman-retailer.[5] As an explanation this is deceptively simple, as an examination of Birmingham in the late eighteenth century may illustrate. By this time the town had not only established itself as a centre for industry, predominantly small metal-ware, but it was also a centre for trade.[6] The marketing facilities provided by both the inland and overseas outlets of the town's merchant and factoring houses had for some time been essential to the functioning of the matrix of small workshops upon which production was based. At the same time merchant capital underpinned the system's credit structure. The subordinate role of the small producer has a long history, as the work of Franklin Mendels and Hans Medick on the 'proto-industrial' stage of economic development has recently emphasized.[7] Nevertheless, the nature of the market, the high reliance upon hand technology and, in some areas, the existence of a 'dual economy' of agriculture and industry, gave the artisan some degree of independence within this authority structure. The work of Marie Rowlands and David Hey has given some indications of how this might have operated in the small metal-ware trades of the Midlands.[8] Such independence may have been reflected in those work rhythms often anomalously referred to as 'pre-industrial', and also in the artisan's acceptance of the libertarian democratic tradition.[9]

Nevertheless, the pattern of dependency had itself been long established by the start of the nineteenth century. Over the course of the next fifty years the balance of the relationship moved against the artisan although the accelerated pace of industrialization often encouraged the actual development of artisan trades. This is not, then, to argue that the small firm became a marginal feature of production. As Geoffrey Crossick has demonstrated, far from being 'transitional' the small producer was to play a vital and continuing function as industrial capitalism advanced.[10] But this function was changing as the small firm moved from a central role in the productive process to one which was essentially subsidiary to, and supportive of, larger units of production.

Merchant capital continued to play an enabling role within the structure of production in Birmingham throughout the first half of the nineteenth century. An examination of the personal estates of the forty-eight merchants and factors who died in the town between 1820 and 1840 reveals large fortunes, comparable to any made within industry (Table 1). However, the second quarter of the nineteenth century saw a growth in the number of large firms in the town's major industries. Rapid investment in new plant in boom periods like 1824–5 and 1834–6, was balanced by the economies of scale and increased mechanization, to avoid a declining rate of profit during periods of recession. By the 1840s a large number of sizeable firms had emerged aiming at low costs per unit of output and against whom the smaller firm was unable to compete directly.

It would, of course, be quite wrong to present this as a straightforward absorption of the smaller firms by the larger ones. As elsewhere the development of capital-intensive industries in Birmingham often encouraged the multiplication of the smaller units of production. Large brass foundries or wire mills, like that of William Fox employing 258 hands in 1832, supplied hundreds of small firms with the materials they needed to produce the small metal-ware for which the town was renowned. At the same time entrepreneurs, reluctant to shift all their assets to a fixed capital commitment, often retained a large number of outworkers even where they had established a basis in factory production. Outworkers, in the full variety of forms the term implies, were particularly useful in absorbing extra demand at peak periods. This relationship between factory and workshop has been described by David Landes as 'symbiotic' and it is a fairly familiar characteristic of this particular (and, incidentally, unnamed) stage of capitalist development.[11] But although the relationship was a reciprocal one the pattern of dependency was emphatically biased against the smaller unit.

It is crucial at this stage to obtain a clear idea of the different levels of enterprise with which we are dealing. The absence of systematic data for British firms in this period makes such a comparison, within the system of production, very difficult. Here the estimates of personal wealth available in probate documentation may provide an insight when correlated with occupational groupings. An examination of the wills and administration papers made out in the town of Birmingham for the period 1820–40 reveals a fairly distinctive pattern of personal wealth within each trade (Table 1).[12] Each displays a clustering up to the £600 level and the lower part of this section is obviously the area of maximum overlap between the artisan as employer of labour and the petit-bourgeois producer. A second major clustering of personal estates from £1000 and upwards can also be detected and here we are dealing with the various levels of the larger bourgeoisie. This is no less crucial a distinction to make for although the petite bourgeoisie operated in a context ultimately circumscribed by dominant middle-class values we have been well warned against any tendency to divest it of its distinctive social identity as defined, at important points, against the world of the larger bourgeoisie.[13] The clarity of this important distinction for the small producer has often been obscured by the

Table 1 *Estimated personal estates at time of death, Birmingham, 1820–40*

	£s											Thousands of £s									Row totals
	20	*50*	*100*	*200*	*300*	*450*	*500*	*600*	*700*	*800*	*900*	*1*	*1.5*	*2*	*3*	*4*	*5–9*	*10–14*	*15–19*	*20+*	
Cutler and file-maker		1	3	1	2	2						2	1		1	1	1				15
Gilt toy-maker		1	3	3								1	2		1		2				13
Jeweller	4	1	5		3	3		1				2	2		1	1	1	1			25
Steel toy-maker	3	1	5	3		3				1			2	2	1	3	2				26
Wire-worker			8	1	1					1		1	1				1	1		2	17
Brassfounder	5	2	12	13	9	3		6		6			3		2		2	1	1	3	68
Small metal-ware maker*	6	5	28	17	17	12		7		7		6	6	5	6	5	5			1	133
Button-maker	2	2	4	7	3	4		8		4		1	6	3	2	2	3	2	1	2	56
Cooper	1		6	1	2	1															11
Woodturner	1	3	1	1	1	1		1									1	1			11
Tailor	1	1	8	6	1	5		1					1	4		2	1			1	32
Merchant or factor					3	1				1		3	1	4	2	4	12	7	2	8	48
Total number of estates on Table 1																					455

Source: Probate documentation, parishes of Birmingham, Aston and Edgbaston, at Lichfield Record Office (Episcopal Court of Lichfield) and the Public Record Office (Prerogative Court of Canterbury).

* Consists of forty-two different trades from awl-maker to watch chain-maker.

retrospective desire of large manufacturers to represent their origins as lowly. The table also indicates an ambiguous middle ground of estates around the £800 mark, either the most stable of the small firms or the smaller of the large firms.

This kind of clustering is fairly characteristic of almost all trades and for this reason the more traditional trades like tailoring have been included alongside the new and highly mechanical trades. The pattern represents rather more than the spread of opportunity at any one time in a free market economy. Rather there was a very specific set of differentials worked into the structure of each trade. Certainly these differentials were apparent to contemporaries. As early as 1799 Matthew Boulton had explained to a select committee that, 'There are many manufactories at Birmingham that do not employ £100: some about £1,000 and, speaking in general of the higher description of manufactories about 6 or £7,000.' Boulton complicated the picture by also asserting that 'All the great manufacturers I have ever known have begun the world with very little capital.'[14] Thus he had not only drawn attention to the differential operating in production but he had also implied a mobility linkage between its two elements: that the large had at one time been the small. From his second generalization, of course, Boulton would have done well to exclude himself having inherited a thriving business from his father and having married a woman with a dowry of £28,000. In his observations Boulton had moved from economic analysis to justification within a particular class perspective. The historian should not confuse the two.

The organic metaphor was frequently used, in the first half of the century, to describe the relationship between small and large units of production, the implication being that the small could grow into the large given the right conditions. Research into a number of trades in a range of areas suggests that such an analysis has more place in middle-class rhetoric than as a plausible explanation for the growth of the firm in the major industries. In textiles, for example, it is quite clear that the individuals who established factories were, broadly speaking, those who had co-ordinated the related processes during the outwork or domestic stage of development. The metaphor, however, formed an important element in an attempt to reconstitute the unity of the classes at the point of production. The argument ran that the thrifty working man could aspire to become a small producer and from there the economic possibilities were limitless. Apart from its obvious social and economic implications this was a very powerful argument in favour of bourgeois democracy. If the factory was the workshop full grown and the factory owner simply the working man writ large, then it followed that workers' interests could be politically represented by their masters.

Thus contemporary analysis (from outside the working community) stressed the characteristics of mobility, opportunity and independence in the role of the smaller firm. Thomas Osler, a large-scale glass manufacturer, echoed Boulton's words in 1824 when he observed that, 'I do not think there are 20 brassfounders in Birmingham who employ so large a capital as twenty thousand pounds each. But there are hundreds of brassfounders who are at work on a capital of perhaps less than £500.'[15]

Samuel Timmins, a brassfounder who would have fallen into the first of these two categories, asserted in his industrial history of the town published in 1866 (and the basis of every subsequent economic history of Birmingham) that, 'The large number of small manufacturers are practically independent of the numerous factors and merchants they supply.'[16] The optimism of contemporaries has been echoed in the familiar analysis of the town's social and economic history rendered by recent historians.[17] The emphasis on opportunity and independence in examining the small producer has led to an underplaying of the emergence of class consciousness and the importance of conflict both inside and outside the workplace.

In fact, for any firm the twin questions of 'independence' and 'viability' were determined, to a great extent, by the nature of its credit and marketing facilities. The larger the firm the more likely it was to evolve a self-contained marketing structure. Richard Tangye attributed the success of his engineering firm to his ability to avoid the normal outlets: 'Instead of relying upon agents who often "sold" us instead of selling our goods we established our own houses at Newcastle upon Tyne, Manchester and Glasgow . . . selling direct to the users . . . instead of through middlemen whose interests were sometimes in contrast with ours.'[18]

Clearly these larger concerns often usurped the role of the merchant and factor by supplying credit to, and marketing the goods of, the smaller producers.[19] John Turner, who ran a large button manufactory employing 150 hands in the 1830s, explained how this operated in his own trade: 'As a rule a few larger houses supply the material to these smaller masters of whom there are over 100 in the town, and they take all they produce, *thus becoming the real employers*.'[20]

Where large firms were unable to evolve their own outlets they remained tied to the merchant and factor. The relationship was always a delicately balanced one with credit as its fulcrum. Where the enterprise was large enough for the producer to allow credit to the merchant or factor the relationship was more likely to balance in its favour. James Luckock, a manufacturer of cheap jewellery, found himself in this position in the 1820s. With annual sales of £8000 and profits of £2000 per year his was not a giant concern but the credit equation was resolved in his favour:

> Our mode of doing business was this: we had 20 customers among the Birmingham factors, who, on going on their journeys of two or three months would take about £100 worth of our stock (each) returning to us at the end of each journey what remained unsold and taking from six to fifteen months credit on the remainder.[21]

Luckock died in 1836 leaving a personal estate of £3000 and it is obvious that firms like his, although small in comparison with the giant enterprises of the cotton kings, were certainly large enough to escape the pattern of dependency which characterized the small producer proper. In fact V. A. C. Gatrell's recent work on Lancashire in this period has emphasized the importance, even in that area, of firms comparable in size to Luckock's, whilst also demonstrating that they lay beyond the reach of the traditional mechanisms of upward economic and social mobility.[22]

This is a crucial factor since within the small producer sector the emergent differences of social identity between the artisan small master and the petit-bourgeois small manufacturer (and for the sake of convenience and clarity these two distinct terms will be adopted) were most manifest in the response to that pattern of dependency which comprised the context within which all small units of production commonly operated. Cash flow problems constrained these concerns to operate on a weekly rather than a monthly or quarterly basis with their creditors. Dependency began with the initial purchase of raw material. T. C. Salt, a large-scale lamp manufacturer with a capital of £10,000 tied up in his own concern, explained how, by 1833, the decline in prices (which most trades had, by then, experienced) and the unstable nature of the market had reduced the credit margin which the large firms allowed when supplying raw material:

> When I first embarked in business in Birmingham [1815], it had been the practice from time immemorial to make all their purchases the first twelvemonth without paying anything, and if you cleared off the purchases of the first twelvemonth in the next twelvemonth it was considered regular payment; now if I purchase metal I pay for it in the same day, cash, and that practice is general in the purchase of metals.[23]

This was likely to prejudice the whole nature of the small producer's operation, emphasizing his subordination to either the larger firm or to merchant capital. As Salt observed: 'They go to a merchant, he gives them an order for metal somewhere, taking first of all the profit upon it . . . and then they bring their goods in at just what prices he pleases.'[24] At the same time the acknowledged necessity for a weekly 'turnover' exacerbated the small producer's disadvantages in making the sale. Thus he was locked into a viciously inverted political economy whereby he obtained his raw materials in the dearest market and sold his finished goods in the cheapest.

The small-scale nature of these enterprises obviously restricted the advantageous use of both the division of labour and bulk discount. As the market contracted during a recession it was the small firms who felt the effects first. The larger firms often simply reduced the work that was farmed out to them, hoping to offset fixed capital costs by retaining work for their main plant. W. G. Rimmer has noted that in Leeds at such times the outworking firms 'died like flies in the night'.[25] The weekly economic commitment left little margin for error and the small producer swiftly moved to crisis point. A 'Tradesman of Small Capital' explained the difficulty to the Home Secretary in 1826:

> In my conversations with different gentlemen who have been in the habit of turning tens of thousands in the year, they say that things are so bad they do not care how little they do and that if at the year's end they shall find they have not gained one farthing they shall think themselves fortunate providing they can but escape great loss . . . but then to me and such as me to do nothing is certain ruin because we have nothing to depend upon but trade.[26]

In the rarefied competitive atmosphere of the three decades following 1820 many of the factoring establishments, where small producers often made their sales, were dubbed 'slaughterhouses', a reference not so much to the retail meat trade as to the 'slaughter of the Innocents'.

These pressures were felt, with varying degrees of intensity across the entire spectrum of small production, from the artisan, working outside the factory and employing other journeymen and apprentices, up to the small manufacturer employing as many as perhaps thirty or forty hands and attempting to act in a managerial rather than a manual capacity. At one extreme end of this spectrum lay the 'garret-masters'. These were often artisans pushed into independent production by underemployment. They worked in their own homes either by themselves or aided by their families. It was with this group that the credit nexus with the factor was firmest and the reduced status of the outworker most marked. This is also the area where independent production shaded into the, largely unskilled, sweated trades of Victorian Britain with their characteristic emphasis upon female and juvenile labour.[27] Strictly speaking the 'garret-master' was neither small master nor small manufacturer although, of course, there were points at which either might be found co-ordinating the activities of the garret-master.

THE DIFFERING RESPONSES WITHIN THE SMALL PRODUCER SECTOR

The pressures and problems may have been universal, but the way in which the different types of small producer responded within this context is crucial for our purposes. This may be clearer if we examine in detail both the pressures and responses in two specific trades and then return to the general discussion.

First, then, to look at the position of the small producer in one of the 'new' trades dominated by the larger firms. Charles Walters was a screw-maker operating in a small way with an initial capital of £130 and a weekly profit margin (after paying a wage bill of around £30) of about £5. What little evidence there is of his operations dates from the early 1830s, but even at this stage he was in competition with the larger firms and he lamented the passing of the small master:

> Times are not what they were – formerly ignorant men – a sort of upper workman were masters in the trade – Mr James came into it – took a lead to drive such masters out and now is bringing in men of more general knowledge and of rank in life with himself, and consequently more able competitors as to quantity and quality.[28]

By 1842 James James, to whom Walters refers, was employing 360 hands in one of the town's most impressive new factories. Similarly the firms of Hawkins and Ledsams, making the same product, employed 190 hands and 140 hands respectively.[29] A fourth large firm in the trade, that of T. H. Ryland, grew from an initial investment of £2000 produced by family connections (Ryland was a third generation industrialist and made a judicious marriage). By 1850 his plant alone was worth £15,000. Nevertheless Ryland still felt justified in reflecting, in his autobiography 'I began without any capital to speak of'.[30] It is only by examining the scale and problems of a small manufacturer like Walters that such claims can be put into perspective. Ryland's initial enterprise, though small compared to the size of the same firm over the next decade, was large enough for him to escape the pattern of dependency, relating to marketing, credit, economies of scale and so on, in which Walters found himself trapped.

Walters was unable to compete directly. The larger firms attracted the best labour, by paying higher wages, and produced their goods at the lowest prices. He survived only because he was able to fulfil a service function for the larger firms by producing a middle-sized screw which, for technical reasons, they could not produce in bulk. Nevertheless, he was in the grip of the factor who marketed his product, a man by the name of Nettlefold (who subsequently went into production himself in partnership with Joseph Chamberlain). It was vital for the small producer to maintain credibility in the eyes of the factor. If this credibility was dented, then, as Salt observed, 'in consequence of that doubt he [the creditor] allows a less discount and surcharges him'.[31] Nettlefold insisted on a thorough inspection of Walters's books before undertaking to market his goods. Though he 'expressed himself in a gratifying way at the regularity of the people and the aspect of things',[32] Walters lived in fear that he might discover his unsuccessful attempts to supply other factors in the town.

The 'regularity' of the workforce of which Nettlefold so fulsomly approved is a vital element in all of this. Credit was the enabling element within production. In order to appear credit-worthy the small manufacturer had to run his firm in a 'business-like' way. The form that this took was increasingly defined by the work discipline of the larger concerns. In 1842 Robert Grainger, the Factory Commissioner, considered James James's to be the best regulated workforce in the town. For Walters the regulation of a workforce more used to the traditional work patterns of the workshop was a rather more difficult proposition. He was attempting to operate on a workshop scale and yet, at the same time, to reject workshop norms and values. A long holiday break could turn profit into loss whilst the observance of 'Saint Monday' was certainly strongest at this level. As Walters complained:

> Sunday appears to indispose the people and Monday being a sort of Saint holiday among the working classes of this town Thursday generally arrives before all are capable of moving on – one day is a day of exertion Friday and the quantity set is exceeded. . . . I endeavour to move en masse.[33]

Such 'factory discipline' was essential to the economic viability of the concern and was a pre-requisite for expansion. This was a very real area of conflict between Walters and his workforce whom he felt constrained to describe, at one point, as 'riff-raff'.

In the event the development of new machinery around the mid-century rendered such concerns as Walters's redundant. By 1866, when Joseph Chamberlain wrote his analysis of the screw trade for Timmins's volume, there were only the larger firms left in production. Chamberlain declared this to be 'an unmixed good',[34] a viewpoint doubtless influenced by his part ownership of one of the town's largest screw-making firms. The disappearance of the small firm in this part of the trade should not, of course, lead us to see the petit-bourgeois manufacturer as a strictly transitional figure in the same way that the independent artisan was to be. The small manufacturers' role of servicing large-scale industry and filling the gaps in production, was a permanent one.[35] But the servicing required and the gaps to be filled changed through time and this increased the instability of individual firms.

The importance of some of these points may be borne out by a brief examination of gun manufacture, which until the second half of the nineteenth century underwent little in the way of internal, structural change. Here the major part of the work was subcontracted to small masters, and industrial expansion only served to extend the process of decentralized production. Gun barrels, forged and rolled by steam in large factories since the turn of the century increased the demand for the smaller units of production which generally carried out separately the nine processes involved in the completion of the gun. There was a strong craft basis here perhaps reflected best in the continuing insignificance of female and juvenile labour. In 1841 women and girls made up only 3.6 per cent of the total gun-making workforce. By 1851 this had only risen to 4 per cent. The figures for a more mechanized trade like button-making would have been closer to 40 per cent in 1841 and 57 per cent in 1851.[36] The organization of work was along traditional lines with the proliferation of small masters co-ordinated by the merchant capital of the gun-makers and contractors. Even where the various work processes had been gathered under one roof by a contractor each unit continued to work, in a fairly self-contained manner, under a small master. It is perhaps these traditional opportunities of mobility to small master status which are demonstrated by the probate material available for the gun trade (Table 2).

Above all the structure of the gun trade was preserved by the vagaries of the market. Reliant upon international conflict for its continued prosperity it was hit, after 1815, by the longest period of peace for generations. Demand was sporadic and uncertain and in such a situation the circulating capital of decentralized workshop production was a safer investment, for the contractor, than the high fixed capital costs of factory production. In the event of recession it was the small master who bore the burden of fixed costs.

This, however, meant that by the mid-century the gun contractors were locked into a continuing relationship with a mode of production the underlying artisan-based values of which they uniformly rejected. An engineer from the Woolwich Arsenal who examined the Birmingham gun trade in 1854 declared it to be fifty years behind other industries in the town.[37] The nature of the market forced the contractors to accept a system, and an implicit set of values, that was in the process of erosion in most trades. The price, for them was a high one. Traditional rhythms

Table 2 *Estimated personal estates in the Birmingham gun trade, 1820–40*

	£s												*Thousands of £s*							*Row totals*
	5	*20*	*50*	*100*	*200*	*300*	*450*	*500*	*600*	*700*	*800*	*900*	*1*	*1.5*	*2*	*3*	*4*	*5–9*	*10–14*	
Gun-maker				1	3	2	3	1	3		3		4	4		4	2		1	31
Gun barrel-maker		1			1		2											1		5
Gun furniture-forger				2	3		1													6
Gun barrel-ribber					1	1														2
Gun barrel-borer		1				1														2
Gun barrel-fitter				1																1
Gun lock-smith	1	1				1														3
Gun-smith				1																1
Gun-stocker				1	2	1														4
Gun-finisher		1	1	1		1														4
																				—
Total number of estates on Table 2																				59

Source: As Table 1.

of weekly and annual holidays meant that production levels could vary wildly. John Goodman's subcontracting workforce were capable of producing 1755 guns per week when working at full capacity. However, depending upon the traditional holiday calendar, production could fluctuate between this figure and the lowest weekly total of only 93 guns.[38] Trade societies varied in strength but were at their strongest when the contractor had just received a large order. The agreement of prices on these occasions could take up to six weeks.

Here, then, the small master was able to retain artisan values and norms. These could include the familiar enforced collective agreement on price levels, as James Clare discovered in 1840. Having subcontracted to produce forty gunstocks at 10 per cent below society prices he was hauled before the society and asked to explain his actions. When he refused to recant his workshop was lobbied by nearly a hundred members of the society who threatened to prevent him from receiving work of any sort.[39]

We may, then, be able to isolate two very different responses to accelerating industrialization, on the part of the small producer; one individualist and the other collective. It is within the context of this differentiation that the increasingly apparent separation of the petit-bourgeois manufacturer from the artisan small master was taking place.[40] This is also the area of maximum ambiguity and we can make no *a priori* assumptions about the nature of social relations at the point of production within this general sector. The choice of action for the small producer was being presented in a positive fashion after 1820 by both middle-class and artisan agencies. Nevertheless the area for manoeuvre for the small producer was also being narrowed by a systematic attack upon the artisan ideal.

THE ARTISAN ALTERNATIVE UNDER ATTACK

The collective nature of the artisans' response to attempts to erode their position can be seen partly in an increase in trade society activity between 1820 and 1850. These societies appealed to working conditions and prices which were considered customary and used modes of expression understood to be traditional. This was the case even within relatively new trades organizing themselves for the first time. With a strength which varied from trade to trade and in relation to the trade cycle, they attempted to enforce the artisan concept of 'the legitimate pursuit of trade'.[41] This was given a strident emphasis by the development, in the early 1830s, of an early socialist critique which placed the emphasis upon the primacy of labour to production. A labour exchange, opened in the town in 1833, aimed to provide a market place within which the small master could exchange his goods and avoid the marketing channels of the factors and larger manufacturers. The scheme proved popular with the small masters in a wide range of trades. The *Labour Exchange Gazette* noted that, 'Scarcely a meeting on the subject . . . passes over unmarked by the outpourings of the vial of wrath of some sufferer under the slaughtering trade.'[42] Robert Owen, who stood behind the scheme, had hoped that the town's larger manufacturers would support it financially. However, they refused to do this for obvious reasons. The exchange would have guaranteed one corner of the market to the small master. Here he could have existed free from the accepted constraints of the small producer. In withholding financial support, as a result of which the scheme collapsed, the larger manufacturers had made the initial move in a systematic attack upon the artisan alternative for the small producer.

The artisan concept of what constituted the 'legitimate pursuit of trade' had little to do with a free market economy. This was a point made by a group of button manufacturers during a trade society strike in 1825: they refused 'to submit to such specific terms and prices as a self-created Union Club shall choose to dictate – a system hostile to free trade [which] if generally adopted must soon annihilate this country as a manufacturing nation'.[43] Clearly the values embodied in this kind of activity reflected a commitment to an accepted standard of life rather than to acquisition, or expansion in a business sense. This is perhaps best attested to by the resilience of the 'Saint Monday' tradition, within the town, until the middle of the century.[44] Compared to the acknowledged free-for-all of economic liberalism artisan values could be a hard taskmaster for the small producer. They involved accepted restrictions on apprenticeship, labour dilution and certain types of machinery, as well as a rigid adherence to negotiated prices. This might threaten a small firm's viability or place an absolute limit on expansion. Nevertheless it remained the option of the small producer to act with the societies in the traditional manner provided these conditions were accepted. The *Pioneer* called upon members of trade societies, in 1833, to 'Declare to existing masters that you are willing to admit them to your Union if they choose to enter themselves as workmen.'[45]

Because such a choice operated within restricted economic boundaries compared to those of economic liberalism, the artisan as small master had little future as long as the dominant ethos within industrialization remained a highly competitive one. As the economic relationship moved against him the artisan adopted a variety of means by which to salvage small master status. As a result of these attempts, however, he often found himself to be a small master in form rather than substance. The continuance of subcontracting within the factory could, in this sense, be seen as an attempt to retain the viability of the smaller artisan unit of production by the simple device of moving it, *en bloc*, into the manufactory. Here prices would be negotiated and daily, weekly and annual work rhythms operated, as if the component work units were still fragmented in a decentralized workshop pattern. This also involved the disadvantages of payment for rent, bench space and power within the factory, and perhaps also discount on the prices of goods 'sold' to the manufacturer. Douglas Reid's work on the decline of the 'Saint Monday' tradition by the 1860s pinpoints, with some precision, the stage at which the artisan small master recognized the emptiness of his bastardized small master status and began to accept a role as wage labourer within a more formalized work structure.[46]

Nevertheless between 1830 and 1850 trade unionism, Owenism and finally Chartism provided a vigorous critique of what was, at this time, a highly immature capitalist system.[47] For the large manufacturer any attempt to breach craft control of both the content and pace of the labour process necessarily involved undermining the artisan's role as an independent producer. Systematic work discipline involved a rejection, or at least a reformulation, of the artisan values upon which these movements were based. Thus the existence of a substantial sector of the economy which related to such a scale of values, and which lived them out in work routines and relationships outside the factory only served to weaken the impact of labour discipline within the factory itself.

This process of undermining the artisan's alternative of small-scale production, however, involved some niceties of definition. The attack on the artisan small master could not be confused with an attack on the small producer as such, for two reasons. First, because as has been suggested the small firm was actually a vital part of the total process of production and its role was to be a continuing one. Secondly, the small firm was a vital part of the justification for the anomalies of capitalism. It was essential that men like Ryland and Chamberlain could stress the original small-scale nature of their ventures. This went some distance towards justifying the fact that their continued expansion directed the changing context within which the small firm existed. The reality of a limited traditional mobility (often more occupational than economic or social) from journeymen to small master, which had been at the heart of the decentralized workshop structure, was being usurped by a largely mythical social mobility which attested to the possibility of a meteoric rise to large-scale manufacturer status by the exercise of basic human qualities. For the small manufacturer, of course, the acceptance of this line of thought gave limitless horizons to what was actually, as we have seen, a highly circumscribed economic universe.

As a result, whilst certain forms of small-scale production were constantly lauded as examples of entrepreneurial spirit and individual endeavour, others were consistently pilloried. A large-scale button manufacturer told the *Morning Chronicle* investigator in 1850:

> If a man were of irregular and dissipated habits and did not like to conform to the rules of a shop, or if he had any dispute with his employer he would occasionally become 'saucy' and set up for himself . . . one inducement for them to set up for themselves in this way is the liberty it enables them to take of playing at cards in beer shops and of drinking and smoking away Monday and Tuesday which they cannot have in a regular shop.[48]

The artisan free from the constraints of factory discipline was a heretic:[49] as a result of this, by the middle of the century, the small master in his turn had become a scapegoat. He was increasingly equated with the 'garret-master' and the responsibility for declining prices, wages and quality was laid upon his shoulders. As early as 1830 one wire-work manufacturer had complained that 'they plunder the honest manufacturer of a remunerating profit, the industrious artisan of fair wages and they make "workmen" of whom nature never meant to handle a hammer (except to break stones)'.[50] Nevertheless as an observer in the brassfoundry trade candidly observed 'it is difficult to say whether the dishonest competition of men who have capital, or the ruinous trading of men who have none is the active cause'. It was largely against such attacks that the small masters involved in the ill-fated labour exchange scheme defined their interests. James Morrison, editor of the *Labour Exchange Gazette*, and himself referred to helpfully by one middle-class observer as a 'master-man',[51] complained that the rules of the game were being laid down in a way that precluded participation by the small master:

> The competition of the wealthy man, then, who by the weight of his capital can bear all before him, can drive out the smaller master by lowering prices; . . . this competition then is fair and honourable. But let it be opposed by the less important manufacturer . . . and his competition becomes 'unlawful, unnecessary and unfeeling'.[52]

As the nineteenth century progressed the small producer increasingly acted in ways congruent with the norms established by the larger manufacturers. This was not simply a straight mechanical reflection of the new economic environment in which he found himself. It was also at least partly an imposition from above mediated through economic and cultural channels. The need to retain respectability in the eyes of his creditors forced him to run his firm on a 'business-like' footing. In this respect he was adhering to a set of standards essentially set by the larger firms. Before Nettlefold would give Walters an order he had to be sure of the 'regularity' of his workforce. For Walters this involved a re-orientation of the labour process amounting to the rejection of an entire culture. Failure to act in such a way might mean that his business would be categorized as part of that non-respectable sector of small firms whose continued existence was seen to threaten the economic viability of the town.

This may, in itself, throw some light upon the vexed question of the small producer as 'good' or 'bad' employer.[53] Even allowing for the fact that such considerations must have varied from case to case, confusion here results almost entirely from the ambiguous overlap between the petit-bourgeois manufacturer and the artisan small master in this economic sector. The interpretation which claims a workshop closeness between employer and employed appeals ultimately to an ideal embodied in an artisan scale of values. However, the basis of analysis of what made a 'good' or a 'bad' employer was itself changing in this period. As the decentralized workshop pattern was increasingly distorted by the rise of the larger firms both masters and men came to value (for rather different reasons) a more formal workplace relationship. This was reflected in both the role of the unions and also in the paternal role which accrued to the factory owner.[54] With great rapidity agreements on half-holidays, sickness benefits (through thrift schemes) and a changing leisure pattern replaced the more intangible benefits of the less formal relationship which was still being offered in some parts of the artisan sector. As a result the small manufacturer was likely to be seen as a 'bad' employer in the terms established by the mid-century. His survival partly depended upon the rejection of artisan values, whilst his slim profit margin meant that he could not well carry out the obligations of a more formal relationship.

NOTES

1 On the ambiguity of this overlap in cultural and ideological as well as economic terms, see E. P. Thompson, *The Making of the English Working Class*, 2nd edn, Harmondsworth, 1968, 819; R. Gray, *The Labour Aristocracy in Victorian Edinburgh*, London, 1976, 110–11, 131–5; R. S. Neale, *Class and Ideology in the Nineteenth Century*, London, 1972, 34–6; F. Bechhofer and B. Elliott, 'Persistence and change: the petite bourgeoisie in industrial society', *Archives européennes de sociologie*, XVII, 1976, 78; G. Crossick, 'The emergence of the lower middle class in Britain: a discussion', in G. Crossick (ed.), *The Lower Middle Class in Britain*, London, 1977, 35; *An Artisan Elite in Victorian Society*, London, 1978, 47–53, 114–34; 'La petite bourgeoisie britannique au XIXe siècle', *Le Mouvement social*, 108, 1976, 28–9, 33–4, 41, 54 (and his essay on Britain in this book); I. Prothero, *Artisans and Politics in Early Nineteenth-Century London: John Gast and His Times*, Folkestone, 1979.

2 On artisan radicalism, see particularly Thompson, op. cit.; Prothero, op. cit.; D. Thompson, *The Early Chartists*, London, 1971, 1–30; P. Hollis, *The Pauper Press*, London, 1970. On stabilizing role of petite bourgeoisie see Crossick's essay on Britain in this book, and J. Foster, *Class Struggle and the Industrial Revolution*, London, 1974, 175–7.

3 J. Vincent, *Pollbooks: How Victorians Voted*, Cambridge, 1968, 6. For a critique of this position, see Neale, op. cit., 65–7.

4 For a general analysis of this process, see R. Malcolmson, *Popular Recreations in English Society 1700–1850*, Cambridge, 1973; in Birmingham, Samuel Timmins, writing in 1866 reflected 'The habits of the people have changed greatly for the better during the past 30 years. The "bull-baiting" and "cock-fighting" of 60 years ago have died out' (*Birmingham and the Midland Hardware District*, Birmingham, 1866, 223). See also D. Reid 'Interpreting the festival calendar: wakes and fairs as carnivals', in R. D. Storch (ed.), *Popular Culture and Custom in Nineteenth Century England*, London, 1982.

5 W. Hawkes Smith, *Birmingham and Its Vicinity as a Manufacturing and Commercial District*, Birmingham, 1836, 20.

6 M. J. Wise, 'Birmingham and its trade relations in the early eighteenth century', *University of Birmingham Historical Journal*, 1949, 71.

7 F. Mendels, 'Proto-industralisation: the first phase of the industrialisation process', *Journal of Economic History*, 32, 1972, 255–6; H. Medick, 'The proto-industrial family economy: the structural function of household and family during the transition from peasant society to industrial capitalism', *Social History*, 3, October 1976, 296; D. Landes, *The Unbound Prometheus*, Cambridge, 1969, 43.

8 M. B. Rowlands, *Masters and Men in the West Midland Trades Before the Industrial Revolution*, Manchester, 1975, 52; D. Hey, *The Rural Metal-workers of the Sheffield Region: A Study of Rural Industry Before the Industrial Revolution*, Leicester, 1972, 36. For Sheffield, F. K. Donnelly and J. L. Baxter prefer to use Albert Soboul's term 'dependent artisanry' to describe the working population: 'Sheffield and the English revolutionary tradition', in S. Pollard and C. Holmes (eds), *Essays in the Economic and Social History of South Yorkshire*, Sheffield, 1976, 91.

9 On both themes, see E. P. Thompson, 'Time, work discipline and industrial capitalism', *Past and Present*, XXXVIII, 1967, and *The Making of the English Working Class*; Prothero, op. cit.

10 Crossick argues this in his essay on Britain in this book.
11 Landes, op. cit., 118–19; Mendels, op. cit., 246–7; D. Bythell, *The Sweated Trades. Outwork in Victorian England*, London, 1978, 143; C. Lis and H. Soly, *Poverty and Capitalism in Pre-industrial Europe*, Hassocks, 1979, 159–61. For particular areas see W. H. B. Court, 'Industrial organisation and economic progress in the eighteenth century West Midlands', *Transactions of the Royal Historical Society*, 4th series, XXVIII, 1946, 87, 93. W. G. Rimmer, 'The industrial profile of Leeds, 1740–1840', Thoresby Society publications 113, *Miscellany* 14, pt 2, 1967, 147; C. Erickson, *British Industrialists: Steel and Hosiery 1850–1950*, Cambridge, 1959, 187; P. Searby, 'Weavers and freemen in Coventry 1820–1861. Social and political traditionalism in an early Victorian town', PhD thesis, University of Warwick, 1972, 108–9; F. Bédarida, 'Urban growth and social structure in nineteenth century Poplar', *London Journal*, 1 (2), 1975, 177–80.
12 The difficulties of using such material should not be underestimated. The estimate of personal estate or personalty made at the time of death was only a very general calculation. It excluded freehold property and, often, debts.
13 R. Q. Gray, 'Religion, culture and social class in late nineteenth and early twentieth century Edinburgh', in G. Crossick (ed.), *The Lower Middle Class in Britain*, 134; Foster, op. cit., 246–50.
14 Report from the Committee appointed to enquire into the state of the copper mines and copper trade of this kingdom, *Parliamentary Papers*, 1799 (663), X.
15 4th Report from Select Committee on Artisans and Machinery, *Parliamentary Papers*, 1824 (51), V, 319–20.
16 Timmins, op. cit., 223.
17 T. R. Tholfsen, 'The artisan and the culture of early Victorian Birmingham', *University of Birmingham Historical Journal*, IV, 1953–4; A. Briggs, 'The social structure of Birmingham and Lyons', *British Journal of Sociology*, 1, 1950; *Victorian Cities*, Harmondsworth, 1968, 184–8.
18 R. Tangye, *'One and All'. The Autobiography of Richard Tangye of the Cornwall Works*, Birmingham, 1889, 97.
19 Although merchants and factors retained their relative position there were less of them operating as the century progressed. In 1803 the Directories show 175 different concerns; by 1839 this had dropped to 128.
20 J. P. Turner, 'The Birmingham button trade', in Timmins, op. cit., 441 (my italics).
21 J. Luckock, *A Sequel to Memoirs in Humble Life*, Birmingham, 1825, 20.
22 V. A. C. Gatrell, 'Labour, power and the size of firms in Lancashire cotton in the second quarter of the nineteenth century', *Economic History Review*, second series, XXX (1), 1977, 124.
23 Report from Select Committee on Manufacture, Commerce and Shipping in the United Kingdom, *Parliamentary Papers*, 1833 (690), VI, Q. 4628.
24 ibid.
25 Rimmer, op. cit., 151.
26 H. O. 40:20 (Public Record Office).
27 Bythell, op. cit., 145, 163.
28 Walters to Musgrave, 14 February 1832.
29 Children's Employment Commission, Second Report, Part 1: Reports and Evidence from the Sub-Commissioners, *Parliamentary Papers*, 1843 (431), XIV, f. 153–7.
30 T. H. Ryland, *Reminiscences*, Birmingham, 1904.
31 Select Committee on Manufacture, Trade and Commerce, Q. 4628.
32 Walters to Musgrave, 28 March 1832.
33 ibid., 7 February 1832.
34 J. Chamberlain, 'The manufacture of iron wood screws', in Timmins, op. cit., 605.
35 See Crossick's essay on Britain in this book.

36 See Foster, op. cit., 226, for use of such an index to indicate breakdown of the craft basis of trades.
37 Report of Select Committee on the Manufacture of Small Arms, *Parliamentary Papers*, 1854 (12), XVIII, Q. 336.
38 ibid., Q. 3473.
39 *Birmingham Journal*, 8 August 1840, 24 October 1840. For the involvement of small masters in trades societies, see S. Pollard, 'The ethics of the Sheffield outrages', *Transactions of the Hunter Archaeological Society*, VII (3), 1954, 121.
40 For the importance of this differentiation, see R. Q. Gray, 'Religion, culture and social class', 51, and Bechhofer and Elliott, op. cit., 81.
41 For a more extensive development of this theme, see C. Behagg, 'Custom, class and change: the trade societies of Birmingham', *Social History*, IV (3), October 1979, and 'Secrecy, ritual and folk violence: the opacity of the workplace in the first half of the nineteenth century', in Storch, op. cit.
42 *Birmingham Labour Exchange Gazette (BLEG)*, 26 January 1833.
43 *Aris's Gazette*, 8 August 1825.
44 See D. A. Reid, 'The decline of St Monday', *Past and Present*, LXXI, 1976.
45 *Pioneer*, 7 September 1833.
46 Reid, op. cit.
47 G. Stedman Jones, 'Class struggle and the Industrial Revolution', *New Left Review*, 90, 1975, 50, 60, 67. For the continuing reliance of the mid-century economy on hand technology, see R. Samuel, 'Workshop of the world: steam power and hand technology in mid-Victorian Britain', *History Workshop*, 3, Spring 1977.
48 *Morning Chronicle*, 4 November 1851.
49 Foster, op. cit., 229, 'the self imposed work routine of the craft worker served to insulate him from employer control'.
50 *Monthly Argus and Public Censor*, May 1830.
51 Joseph Parkes to J. Abercromby, 12 January 1834. Papers of 2nd Earl Grey, University of Durham, Department of Palaeography and Diplomatic.
52 *BLEG*, 26 January 1833.
53 For a discussion of the problems involved here see Crossick's essay on Britain in this book; see also R. A. Sykes 'Some aspects of working class consciousness in Oldham 1830–1842', *Historical Journal*, XXIII (1), 1980, 170, where the author notes the prevalence of smaller firms among those prosecuted for contravening Factory Acts in the 1830s.
54 For the emergence of 'new model' employers at the mid-century, see R. Harrison, *Before the Socialists*, London, 1956, 5; P. Joyce, *Work, Society and Politics*, Brighton, 1980.

7 The grocery trade in nineteenth-century Paris: a fragmented corporation*

ALAIN FAURE

Shops are unexplored territory. Although shopkeepers may be frequently mentioned in studies on social stratification,[1] or in essays on the history of the relationships of production,[2] and although such analyses are certainly better than the usual observations borrowed from Zola's *Au bonheur des dames*,† the essential questions about shopkeepers none the less remain unanswered. This is because of the scarcity of concrete information, on the one hand, and the absence of any problematic, on the other. Does this mean to say that whatever their professional specialization, and whatever the size of their business, the men and women who lived by the retail trades occupied the same position in society and had common interests and common enemies? And if indeed they did form a social group or class, what period saw the making of this class? What was its stability over the years? What rules governed the renewal of its members? Finally, what exactly is the history of retail distribution itself? The organization of production, the competition between rival systems of distribution, the different modes of consumption practised in society are all determining factors for shopkeepers, with regard both to their economic function and to their social utility.

The difficulties besetting the study of the retail trades are numerous. The documentation is widely dispersed or buried deep in sources that are not easy to exploit. There was no official enquiry in France before 1912. The solution lies in monographs, patiently worked-out analyses, trade by trade, which take into consideration all the economic and social aspects of the history of each one. This approach avoids the cumbersome statistical machinery of quantitative history, and is the only one capable of producing the information needed to work out a problematic, with rigour and without losing touch with reality. The monograph, moreover, was particularly favoured by the social sciences of the nineteenth century, and one of their most

* Translated from the French by Paul D. G. Smith.

† A new English translation of this novel, by April FitzLyon, and entitled *Ladies' Delight*, was published by J. Calder (London) in 1957.

precious methodological contributions: witness the enquiries of the Paris Chamber of Commerce (simply a collection of monographs), the works of Le Play and of his followers, or the earliest enquiries of the Labour Office (*Office du travail*), at the Ministry of Commerce.

Needless to say, a monograph in isolation makes little sense. There is always a risk of its becoming engrossed in the picturesque and peculiar details of a given trade. Only studies conducted in parallel, following similar guidelines and asking the same underlying questions, can provide the grounds for any general reflection about this section of the economy and of society. This article, which deals only with the grocery trade in Paris, is more modest in its intentions. Based primarily on the study of bankruptcies between 1880 and 1895, it does not pursue the history of the trade up to the present day. A simple monographical essay, then, but written with the following conviction in mind: the infrastructural analysis of a trade is indispensable if we wish to understand the image which its members had of themselves, the institutions which they created for the defence of their interests, and, more broadly, their acts and behaviour in society.

A CORPORATION UNDER LOUIS-PHILIPPE (1830–48)

Contemporary clichés, and much retrospective idealizing, have blurred the image of what shops were like in this period, known as the age of the 'notables'. Even the simple fact that the shop was then a relatively new phenomenon is generally overlooked. In grocery, as in other trades with popular clientèles, the itinerant dealer, with his loud street cries, had only gradually been supplanted by the shopkeeper during the course of the eighteenth century. This omission is but a minor oversight, however, when set against the whole nostalgic vision of the trade conjured up by some of its members, at the turn of the century. In their view the grocery trade which their predecessors had known was an activity upon which the gods smiled; an honest occupation with no unfair competitive trading practices and no inequalities within the trade. The sole preoccupation for a grocer in those days was ensuring that the business would be handed down to his son or to his son-in-law. Today, the analysis of the historians who hold that in France, in 1848, 'the petite bourgeoisie meant shopkeepers' is reached, of course, from an entirely different standpoint. But the conclusions drawn are not so very different: the employers behind the till, already fulfilling a market function of distribution alone, represent a distinct social category, marked off from the people by property ownership. In political terms also, they represent a distinct force, on account of the number of them who manage to qualify as electors. The period, then, is portrayed either as that of the historic emergence of the petite bourgeoisie, or as the golden age of the shopkeeper.

These interpretations call for careful scrutiny. A detailed analysis of the milieu of grocers furnishes an excellent case to study, since they were amongst the most numerous of the retail traders of the French capital. Is it true, then, that one grocer's shop was worth much the same as another? An examination of the lists of men who qualified for the vote by the amount of taxes they paid does not support this hypothesis. In 1846, for example,[3] scarcely 290 out of a total of 1649 retail grocers to be found in the general trade directory (*Bottin*) attained the level of taxation needed to qualify as electors. More than eight grocers out of ten did not have the vote. Moreover, the distinction between voters and non-voters was not due primarily to taxes paid on landed property: only a third of the grocers who were enfranchised owed their vote to the taxes they paid on real estate. Even more striking, the higher the professional tax (*patente*) paid by the grocer, the less likely was it that he was a property owner.

But if the grocery trade as a whole remained a realm of small-scale enterprises (a mere handful of grocers paid the kind of taxes required in order to be able to stand for election) there was none the less an unmistakable hierarchy within the trade. Beneath a multitude of small- and medium-sized shops, scattered throughout every neighbourhood of the city, there existed a number of really tiny retailers, still termed 'hucksters' in the assessments for the professional tax. In 1806, 18 per cent of Parisian grocers were hucksters.[4] A whole world separated such little matchbox concerns from the businesses of the grocers who were prosperous enough to have the vote. The shops of the latter flourished in the fashionable residential districts of Paris: Chaussée d'Antin, the area around the Palais-Royal, or in the rue Vivienne. The barons of the trade were to be found in the Saint-Avoie quarter, in the network of little streets around Saint-Merri. Here they were close to the wholesalers and at the heart of one of the areas of the highest grocery sales. Amongst these grocery élites, and here only, there was sometimes family continuity within the trade,[5] or continuity in complex dynasties of several families and generations. So, to summarize, there were a few important families, surrounded by a host of little shopkeepers. Grocerdom was a world of contrasts.

The real aristocracy of the trade, however, was not composed of these few big retailers, but of the group of wholesalers and large dealers. Their warehouses were located in the rue de la Verrerie, a kind of central market – like *les Halles* – for the grocery trade. Here were stored all the wares sold by the grocers of the capital: 'colonial produce' (sugar, coffee and tea), foodstuffs from pasta to jam, as well as diverse cleaning materials for the house and a multitude of products for lighting. Because of their control over supplies, the wholesalers also controlled the shops. In their transactions with the retailers, however, they showed considerable flexibility, concerned as they were to maintain their outlets: discounts and rebates in return for prompt payment, and cautiously granted credit terms for shopkeepers in difficulty. Thus the middleman ruled, but he was a constitutional monarch. A few grocers, those whose wealthy customers meant that they had considerable sales, purchased their wares directly from the producers, but this was exceptional. Doing business with a rich clientèle, which never paid on the nail and sometimes did not pay at all, was not without its risks. As a whole, then, and in spite of the inequalities between its members, the grocery trade formed a unified group behind its suppliers, an authentic commercial corporation.

As for the wholesalers, their power stemmed from a manufacturing sector which was highly fragmented, particularly where foodstuffs were concerned. The producers themselves rarely tried to intervene directly in the market, either with the retailers or with the consumers. The wholesaler's role, therefore, was to collect the various goods together before delivering them to the grocer, in bulk and unprocessed. All the preparation of these wares for sale – weighing out, packaging and labelling – was carried out in the shop itself. Groceries at this time were produced by anonymous manufacturers and bore no brand names. Consequently, for the choice and the handling of his merchandise, the good grocer had to have quite as much know-how as many artisans. The assimilation between producers and retailers was only natural at a time when the vast majority of grocers' shops also comprised processing works. These works were by no means marginal in comparison with the specialized workshops. Thus, in 1848, the 1130 grocers' shops of the capital which also incorporated workshops produced 17 per cent of the jam, 23 per cent of the chocolate and 77 per cent of the roasted coffee. As a small-scale food industry, the grocery trade employed in its premises a whole host of apprentices and assistants, the shops' factotums. Their 'savings', we are told,[6] gave them the prospect of setting up on their own in the trade. At the beginning of the nineteenth century commerce and industry were far from being generally divided into distinct spheres of activity. Indeed the evolution towards this separation was only just commencing.

Just as the work in the shop still had an individual character, so also the relations which evolved between the seller and the customer were of a personal nature. The shop was a place where each measured his or her respective strength, and the very act of buying was conflictual. The grocer who catered to a working-class clientèle had to adapt to the habits and requirements of its custom: long opening hours (6 a.m. to 10 p.m.), and the retail of goods in infinitesimal quantities. 'The people do not buy cheeses in large quantities, nor even a pound of sugar or a pint of oil . . . they buy in small quantities, even a single clove. In the morning they buy only what they need for lunch, and in the evening only for supper.'[7]

Credit, of course, was important, because chalking up sales on a slate made sure that the customer would return regularly. The higher prices which were the consequence of selling in tiny quantities may be considered as the interest which the grocer charged on these inevitable little debts. The absence of fixed and marked prices, and the anonymity of the products, meant that the customer was supposed to know what the market prices were, and to have the possibility of checking on the quality of his or her purchases. The manifest unlikelihood of this placed all shopkeepers under a permanent cloud of suspicion. Finally, buying on tick, with all its possible confusion, and buying in trifling quantities, encouraged the salesman to look out for even the slightest chance of a little extra profit: cheating on the weights sold (rendered all the more easy by the fact that the metric system was extremely slow in gaining acceptance), and, above all, adulteration of the foodstuffs sold. The innumerable dodges of the trade were frequently denounced at the time. Inspectors responsible for the observation of trade regulations deplored the consumers' generally passive attitude, whilst repeatedly calling the attention of the authorities to the people's latent hostility towards shopkeepers. They warned of the serious disturbances that might result from this hostility 'in the case of food shortages or high prices'.[8] If indeed it is property which marks the division between the classes, it is as much for the profits it allows property owners to make as for the manner in which these profits are made.

HOUSEWIVES' DELIGHT

During the second half of the nineteenth century the production and distribution of foodstuffs were fundamentally transformed. Retailing was penetrated by methods and thinking in total opposition to its existing traditions. In grocery, after 1860, capitalism began to undermine the old corporative structure. At the origin of these changes was the extraordinary success of a venture conceived and directed by Félix Potin, one of the founding fathers of mass consumption.

Potin's large food stores followed the same golden commercial rules that some of his illustrious contemporaries were applying in their department stores for drapery and fancy goods. A large turnover – the heart and the principal aim of the whole system – was combined with a calculated scale of profits: entice the customers in with low prices on a few essential articles (loss leaders) in order to get them to buy all the others. But food was not drapery and the methods of supplying the traditional shops were no good for the large new grocery stores. For these everything had to be created, starting with new commercial channels. Potin began his career as a direct buyer on the major import markets and, particularly for sugar, by negotiating supply contracts with the producers themselves. The low prices he thus obtained permitted the sale of his loss leaders. But there was also another bottleneck. By this date food production was no longer entirely domestic or confined to the shops, but it remained none the less widely dispersed in numerous small units. Potin began to manufacture his own products, and this on an ever-expanding scale. By the end of the century his factory at La Villette, and his warehouses in the suburb of Pantin, were turning out enough to feed a whole city. Highly integrated, then, Potin's firm had become an immense selling machine.

However, this diversified capital could have borne no fruit had it not been for a revolution in selling practices. The principles were elementary: to maximize the seller's profits inspire the buyer with total confidence; precise profit margins; marked prices; cash payments. Customers whose purchases were delivered to their homes (a large part of the clientèle) were obliged to pay their bills without delay. Sales in minute quantities, necessitating endless handling, were out; everything was sold in fixed units of weight or volume, or in the larger fractions of these units, and with no extra charges added. The wares arrived at the shops already weighed out, packaged and, above all, labelled with the company's name. For Potin's shops did not sell groceries, they sold Félix Potin products. The end of selling goods loose meant the appearance of brand names, along with their harbinger, advertisements. Potin invented neither brand names nor advertisements, and others, exploiting the new medium on a far grander scale, would follow in his footsteps. But he may be considered as the real innovator for both, and his very success indicated the way to follow in the disciplining of consumers. Even prior to the capital, however, the idea which was the secret of Potin's success was to build up a clientèle loyal to his name and convinced that the cheapness, the full weight, the freshness and the reliable quality of products all came down to the name on the label.

So, what with advertising, the industrialization of production and the elimination of middlemen, distribution had decidedly entered a new age. After Potin, whose company was unique in its integration, the modern grocery trade in Paris grew in two related domains: the factory and the large food store. The decades after 1880 saw the emergence of a large-scale food industry: canneries, chocolate factories, jam factories, distilleries, biscuit factories and so on. Henceforth the manufacturers themselves also emerged from their anonymity and sought to create their own outlets. Advertising imprinted their brand names on everyone's consciousness, whilst the professional retailers became mere subordinates in patterns of consumption beyond their control. The triumph of advertised products not only transformed the retailer into a simple stockist of packets, bringing to an end his intervention in the production processes, it also radically altered the act of selling. Personal exchanges gave way to automatic gestures programmed by the power of signs. Economic imperialism made its debut on the home market. Finally, for the best-known brands, the retailer was forced to accept only the smallest of profits. The heavy demand created for such articles turned them into reference items which the shopkeeper had to be prepared to sacrifice if he wished to keep his clientèle.

Though less spectacular and more irregular, the development of large-scale retail grocery was nevertheless the other important phenomenon of the second half of the century. In 1860 the Chamber of Commerce noted seven large establishments beginning to attract the customers of the 'little grocers'. Already Potin was not alone. Using the same commercial methods as the leader, this large-scale grocery sector was one of the major clients for the producers. Although it showed steady growth, which accelerated after 1900, it none the less failed to attain the gigantic proportions hoped for in some business circles.[9] The vitality of this sector was due to the long-term decline in coffee and sugar prices, brought about by industrialization and customs reforms. Taking advantage of its supply methods, the large-scale grocery trade systematically cut prices on these commodities. This was offset by higher profit margins on fresh foodstuffs which began to appear in grocers' shops at this time: fresh fruit and vegetables, confectionery and, sometimes, meat and poultry. Thus, as it grew, the trade became less specialized, a development which also added to the lure of the big stores. Domination of cut-price brand name articles, price wars on basic items: what was left of traditional grocery in all these storms?

THE NEW YOUNG GROCERS

As a necessary preliminary step towards answering this question we need to know the number of grocer's shops, and how this number varied. In theory this may appear straightforward, but in point of fact the nature of the sources makes the counting of commercial establishments particularly tricky. The nominal rolls for the professional tax would of course constitute the best source, but no such lists exist prior to 1885, and for the period after this date, the utilization of these enormous registers would need a whole team of researchers. Trade directories, where they have survived – as is the case for the grocery trade – remain therefore the most reliable guides (Table 3).

Table 3 *Grocery shops in Paris*

Year	*Number of establishments*	*Index*	*Source*
1860	3370	100.0	Chamber of Commerce
1891	4494	133.3	Annuaire Garnaud
1896	5094	151.1	Annuaire Seigneurie
1910	4179	124.0	Annuaire Seigneurie
1914	4334	128.8	Annuaire Seigneurie

Two phases emerge in this period of just over half a century. From 1860, the year in which the suburbs around Paris were annexed to form today's twenty *arrondissements*, up to the mid-1890s, there was a very significant increase in the number of shops. The apparent boom between 1891 and 1896 is not feasible, and is to be explained by the change of source. The growth was then followed by a profound crisis, which began to ease off towards the end of the period. This overall view is misleading, however, because it conceals contradictory tendencies inside the city of Paris.

Table 4 shows that within the chronological phases identified above, the evolution was quite different for the central zones of Paris and the peripheral ones. The oldest centre of the city – the 1st, 2nd, 3rd and 4th *arrondissements* – was an area of continuous depopulation, and saw grocers steadily thinning on the ground. As for the remaining *arrondissements* of the original, pre-1860 city, the situation in these was more or less the same, whatever the demographic changes. During the first phase, from 1860 to the mid-1890s, in only three of these *arrondissements* did the number of grocers actually increase, and only by a small proportion. After 1891 all these *arrondissements*, with the exception of the 9th, saw numerous departures. Over a period of fifty years, the ten *arrondissements* of central Paris lost a third of their grocer's shops (573 establishments). By 1914 the grocers of the centre of Paris represented only a little over a fifth of the total for the city. In the outer, working-class districts – the 13th, 14th and 15th, the 18th, 19th and 20th, and the 11th and 12th *arrondissements* – the first thirty years following their incorporation into the

Table 4 *Paris grocery shops: analysis by* arrondissements

Arrondissement	*Number of retail grocer's shops*			*Number of inhabitants per shop*			*Evolution of the population (%)*	
	1860	*1891*	*1914*	*1861*	*1891*	*1911*	*1861–1891*	*1891–1911*
1st	131	76	60	683	894	984	−24.1	−13.2
2nd	122	86	54	669	813	1118	−14.3	−13.6
3rd	174	113	92	570	785	944	−10.5	−2.1
4th	183	165	120	593	598	944	−9.1	1.7
5th	202	226	184	533	515	660	8.1	4.2
6th	168	142	78	571	697	1320	3.2	3.9
7th	121	146	90	603	655	1181	31.1	11.0
8th	119	102	54	587	1046	1938	52.9	−2.0
9th	182	105	122	590	1149	981	12.4	−0.9
10th	177	223	152	642	693	995	36.0	−2.2
11th	252	427	378	499	500	641	69.8	13.4
12th	166	287	310	396	394	488	224.8	34.0
13th	127	275	306	447	396	466	98.3	30.6
14th	133	279	370	395	402	442	113.3	45.7
15th	138	332	412	406	354	484	109.6	69.4
16th	86	135	98	427	653	1532	140.1	70.2
17th	174	306	272	432	564	794	129.3	25.1
18th	288	374	434	369	508	633	99.7	29.3
19th	231	304	292	331	418	534	66.3	22.5
20th	196	392	456	357	358	396	100.1	28.9
Paris	3370	4495	4334					

city of Paris saw the number of shops increasing by leaps and bounds: 955 new ones. This increase was proportional to population growth, and, in two of the left bank *arrondissements*, the 13th and the 15th, even overtook it. During the second phase, after the mid-1890s, however, the rate of growth levelled off. The number of inhabitants per shop went up everywhere, and here and there (in the 11th and the 19th) the total number of shops went down. The dynamic growth in the outer *arrondissements* did not in the end compensate for the number of disappearances from the city centre, and this explains the net decrease for the whole period. But the drop was only slight, and the total number of grocer's shops in Paris remained remarkably high.

The massive elimination of grocers from the city centre, this decentralization of the trade, is further evidence of the erosion of traditional grocery. The principal victim of this erosion was the old élite, implanted in the commercial quarters and the established bourgeois residential neighbourhoods of the centre. Was this a result of the destruction wrought by the Prefect Haussmann, and a repercussion of the concomitant demographic decline of these districts? Doubtless, although this explanation does not give the whole picture, and is not valid for the whole of the centre of Paris. It was here, after all, in the historic centre, mainly along Haussmann's broad new thoroughfares, that the new, large-scale grocery stores opened up and prospered. There were not many such stores, but each one drew customers from a vast area, gradually squeezing out the small traditional shops which had survived in the old back streets. According to a retired grocer, writing in 1906, this new grocery trade in the centre 'monopolized food sales'.[10] Around 1900 it comprised a group of seventy to eighty firms, ten of which employed more than fifty shop assistants each, and ten more of which over a hundred. In 1910, forty of these grocery firms had turnovers of more than a million francs a year, and together employed over a third of the total number of shop assistants. With the exception of the giants, such as Potin, with his four main branches in 1905, or Damoy, whose store in the Boulevard de Sébastopol had a staff of 300, the firms were still family concerns, both in terms of who managed them and who put up the capital. Although it is quite possible that there were cases of family links between the old élite and the new, the top of the trade as a whole had been taken over by a new generation. This generation enjoyed economic power far greater than that of the older one, and applied commercial methods which were very different.

In striking contrast with this situation was the commercial proliferation in the former suburbs annexed in 1860. As these working-class districts grew, small retail traders set up shop. Grocers appeared not only along the high streets of what had been, until quite recently, the villages surrounding Paris, but sprang up in the interstices, in the wake of new populations moving in. For many small communities of the working-class city, the grocer's shop, along with the wine merchant (cum-tavern), and perhaps a butcher's and a baker's, were the only shops. The social division of the space of the capital opened up a kind of California for small retailers, an immense and neglected market ripe for colonization.

The shops were in the image of their customers. The large-scale retailing sector made no effort to go into the outlying areas of Paris, and the newfangled modes of consumption did not concern the workers. From which strata of society, then, did the large stores attract their customers? Neither from the lowest nor from the highest. For the comfortable paunches of the latter there was a distinct sector of high-class purveyors. No, the food stores catered essentially to the middling ranks of the middle class and to the upper echelons of wage-earners, non-manual employees and minor civil servants. When, in 1905, Potin ventured to open up a new store in the working-class Saint-Antoine neighbourhood, he located it carefully on the corner of the Avenue Ledru-Rollin, one of the major new bourgeois thoroughfares being driven through the district and contributing to its rapid social transformation. Conversely, wherever relatively important working-class populations continued to live within the city centre, little grocery shops continued to exist alongside the large new food stores, and this without the slightest clash of interests. Thus, in the 3rd *arrondissement*, for example, the rolls for the professional tax indicate that between 1895 and 1905 the total number of grocery businesses declined. But this decline only affected the ordinary shops. Fifty-three of these disappeared. The number of tiny retailers, or hucksters, remained constant, and even rose slightly in the Arts et Métiers *quartier* (neighbourhood) of this *arrondissement*.[11] The workers, and domestic out-workers of the traditional industries of this *quartier* continued to frequent these tiny dealers, ignoring the vast food emporia but a short walk away on the Boulevard de Sébastopol or in the Place de la République. In a word, 'the worker didn't give a damn for Potin'.[12]

Potin, in return, did not care that much about the workers. For the capitalists of the food industry the working class was not yet a market. Its purchasing power was too slight and too intermittent to be worthy of their attention. The advertisements for the leading brands of food products were not aimed at the workers. Even had they been, would these advertisements have had any effect? It is unlikely, since the people clung to their traditional habits of consumption. They had no intention of relinquishing their direct control over the products they were buying. Bills and catalogues were not going to tell them what they needed. They continued to buy on tick, and in the same tiny quantities. 'We had customers coming in every day just for half a pound of sugar and sixty grammes of coffee.' These characteristics explain one of the more surprising aspects of the grocery trade in Paris prior to the First World War, the complete absence of companies with numerous branch stores. Elsewhere in France such chain-stores were developing with remarkable success, and leading to hard times for many traditional grocers. But in Paris the small, independent shops still held their own. Between the small retailers and the large ones what evolved was not so much direct competition as a sharing out of clientèles. The prosperity of the small grocers was a consequence of nothing other than class divisions. Thus emerged a situation in which the grocery trade of the peripheral zones of the capital was a replica of the traditional grocery of the centre, but displaced in time and space. The pioneers setting up shop in the 1860s were the successors to the mass of small grocers of the July Monarchy. Although it had lost its leading lights, the old corporation of that period came to life again.

THE SHOP'S PASSENGERS

Who were the members of this new young generation of small-scale grocers? Amongst all the sources which have survived, the records of bankruptcies give the clearest answer to this question. This is not as paradoxical as it may appear. With a little common sense and some background knowledge of the trade, it is not difficult to discriminate between elements which give evidence of what was normal and those which only reflect the particular features of a commercial downfall. The source none the less remains silent on many points. The official receivers who dealt with the bankruptcy cases did not make lengthy enquiries or prepare defences. All that interested them in the history of the bankrupt business were the facts which might be of use in judging the claims of creditors. Thus the only documents which bear directly on the business, that is to say its inventory and its list of creditors, give a distorted and fixed image of it. All too often, for example, the file gives no clues as to the origins of the initial capital. The prime interest of these bankruptcy documents lies elsewhere, in the biographical details which they contain. In a few words and a few dates the contours of a private destiny are revealed. Vital lacunae in the documentation make it impossible to situate the grocery group precisely in its larger social context, but we can at least explore in some detail the manner in which these small employers reached their position, and analyse the systems of selection through which they had passed.

The bankruptcy records of course concern only a small proportion of businesses in relation to the total number of shops. Thus in no way do they constitute a cross-section of the trade at a given date, such as a record of inheritances might furnish for the study of fortunes. Nor do these documents provide any basis for a serious economic analysis, such as might be possible with figures on the value of the businesses over a long period. The usefulness of these records becomes apparent only after a large number of cases have been studied comparatively. The conclusions here are based on the examination of a total of 983 cases. Going through the files was a time-consuming and complicated process, and partly for that reason was limited to the years 1880 to 1895. This period, it will be recalled, was one of expansion for the grocery trade of the outer *arrondissements*.[13]

Within the total number of cases studied a large proportion obviously concerns the grocers of the working-class districts of Paris. As evidence of this we can look at the cost of the grocery business, which was already amongst the lowest for retailing businesses as a whole (only a few shops, such as greengrocer's or stationer's generally cost less):

Table 5 *Price of grocery businesses, 1880–95*

	%
Less than 5000 francs	21.1
Between 5000 and 10,000 francs	26.8
Between 10,000 and 20,000 francs	28.6
Between 20,000 and 40,000 francs	17.6
More than 40,000 francs	6.3

Table based on 142 cases for which this information is given.

Source: Bankruptcy files (see note 13).

At about this period the authors of a professional handbook for grocers[14] were writing that a capital of at least 10,000–15,000 francs was necessary for setting up a grocery shop, one at least where business would not simply ‘vegetate’. In the cases we have seen in the table above, however, nearly one shop in two had cost less than 10,000 francs. The more expensive ones were located almost exclusively in the city centre. These were big bankruptcies of big concerns, illustrative of the crisis which traditional grocery was going through. ‘Competition from the large firms’, and ‘discounts offered by their competitors’ are the kind of remarks that the official receivers noted to account for these failures. Moreover, regardless of the size of the concern, the number of grocers going bankrupt in the city centre was higher than the average. In 1891 these grocers represented 30.8 per cent of the trade as a whole, but suffered 34.3 per cent of the bankruptcies. The divergence, which is suggestive of the greater fragility of these city centre businesses, was even larger in certain *arrondissements* (the 4th and the 6th) and at certain dates. Thus during the years of commercial crisis, from 1884 to 1887, the percentage of bankruptcies from the ten central *arrondissements* rose to 35.6. The small shops survived the slump better than the larger ones, and the cyclical crisis reinforced the effects of structural changes.

For the majority of bankruptcies, however, it is impossible to ascertain what had happened. For lack of assets 613 cases were dropped. In three cases out of five the remnants of the shopkeeper's fortune were so insignificant that it was pointless bothering the holders of debt claims. The files on these cases are just empty folders. These grocers, condemned to commercial oblivion, were not on the whole in massive debt, scarcely more than 11,000 francs on average. But all their wealth lay within the four walls of their shop; a few bills protested, the loss of value of the business after the bankruptcy, and the concern disappeared without more ado. So it is important to bear in mind that the visible proportion of these bankruptcy cases was made up, so to speak, of the ones who were lucky in their bad luck.

What were the personal antecedents of those who 'survive' in the archives? They are known in 252 cases:

Table 6 *Origins of bankrupt grocers, 1880–95*

Bankruptcy of a first grocery shop		
– grocer's shop assistants		120
– wage-earners		35
– shop owners		8
Bankruptcy after one or several previous grocery businesses		
– grocer's shop assistants		48
– others		41
wage-earners	9	
shop owners	13	
unknown	19	

Source: Bankruptcy files (see note 13).

Apprenticeship emerges as the principal route to owning a business. But alongside this classic itinerary, other channels appear: from shops and from the proletariat. As former greengrocers, florists, corn chandlers or bakers, some of these grocers had already tried their hand at retailing, more often than not with conspicuous lack of success. For them grocery was a last refuge, a final chance of paying off their debts. Because the shops cost so little, the trade tended to collect the leftovers of all the retail trades. The crisis had doubtless increased the number of these transfers over to the grocery trade. A higher proportion of grocers were recruited from the ranks of wage-earners, although these included a certain number of servants or lower employees. It was not infrequent for the grocery shop to be opened after marriage with a grocer's widow, and in these cases the bankruptcy was generally caused by the heavy investments made by the husband, anxious to expand the business. The ambition was generally misplaced. The bankruptcies of shops set up by former wage-earners were usually put down to 'bad management' or 'incompetence' by the official receivers. It was wage-earners who were the most easily beguiled by the seller's promises, and the most easily misled as to the value of the business. The worker was ill at ease in the world of tradesmen: the knowledge required, the contacts and the *savoir-faire* were all foreign to him. Above all, the idea of becoming his own boss by entering a retail trade did not have at all the same meaning for him as setting up as a self-employed worker at home, or as an independent artisan; rather it meant joining the ranks of those who exploited his comrades, and repudiating his class.

Whether they were old hands or newcomers to the trade, three grocers out of five had, at some time or another in their career, worn a shop assistant's apron. Grocering clearly remained a profession. True, the processing work carried out on the premises seems to have been in slight decline, except for the roasting of coffee beans. But otherwise nothing had changed in the retailer's other individual tasks. The shop assistants continued to learn on the job, picking up the numerous technical details and tricks of the trade necessary for the handling of loose goods, and for their arrangement. 'You had a lot of lugging about to do, it wasn't simply a question of serving madame.' Henceforth, only the grocers of the working-class districts demanded any kind of qualification for the job. 'A shop assistant who had worked in small grocery shops knew his wares. One who had worked only for Potin didn't know anything; he recognized the packets, that's all.' By observation and by practice the assistant gradually mastered the empirical science of dealing with the public; adapting stocks and profit margins to the sort of customers he had; deciding just how much honesty was needed to keep them coming back; learning how to cope with complaints[15] and how to converse with each customer, how to reply to their questions about such and such a new product. A grocer worth his salt had to be capable of doing market research.

In reality, internal promotion within the trade was highly selective. At the very least there were 6200 shop assistants working in Parisian grocery shops in 1890. Only a tiny minority of them could hope to find a place in the ranks of the employers. The labour force in no way gives the impression of a younger generation studiously preparing to take over, of apprentices slowly gaining instruction in their chosen career. The image is one rather of a jostling mass of young men, constantly joined by new recruits from the provinces, shifting endlessly from job to job, and mainly attracted to the trade by the prospect of free board and lodging, partial compensation for the meagre earnings. The working conditions were every bit as tough as those in industry. The day passed by without any break, and always under the watchful eye of the boss, on the look out for pilfering. The only time off was on

Sunday afternoons, and this in winter only before 1905. Moreover, being a shop assistant was not a lifetime career. Married shop assistants were slightly suspect, and over the age of thirty it became difficult to find a place. Around 1900 revolutionary syndicalism consistently failed to win recruits in the grocery trade. According to one of the threadbare clichés of social historiography, the reason for this would be that grocers' shop assistants had already acquired the dominant mentality of future employers. Certainly, being a shop assistant was a temporary occupation, but most embarked upon it with little hope of promotion, as a simple interlude before going into a factory or an office.

Since this was the case, what social mechanisms were at work behind selection? It would be very useful here to know more about the backgrounds from which our bankrupt grocers originated. But if the records provide abundant details on their individual antecedents, they remain practically silent on this fundamental point. The only clues they give emerge from the different ways in which the business had been financed.

Table 7 *Sources of capital for Paris grocery businesses*

Antecedents	*Wife's fortune alone*	*Wife's fortune plus loans*	*Inheritance (or wife's dowry at marriage)*	*Personal savings*	*Loans*	*Personal savings plus loans*	*Total*
Wage-earners	3		1	5	1	2	12
Shop assistants	9	3	11	6	16	6	51
Former grocery shop owners	1		1	10	8	4	24
Total	13	3	13	21	25	12	87

Source: Bankruptcy files (see note 13).

The examples, granted, are not very numerous, but they suffice none the less to draw some conclusions about the relationships between personal antecedents and the source of capital for the business: family, savings or loans. Amongst the grocers setting up shop for the first time, it was only for the former wage-earners that personal capital played a decisive part. In these cases marriage usually came first, nine years on average before the shop was opened. In general, at this time, the very notion of savings was out of the question for most workers, who had none. So for these couples, setting enough aside to buy their own business was a long and laborious process. Such social ascent from the working classes was quite exceptional, however, and it is significant here that most of the wage-earners who managed to buy their own businesses with their own savings were Parisians by birth, and came from the labour aristocracy of the traditional Parisian industries, or from machine shops. Otherwise, for a wage-earner, there remained the possibility of marrying the capital, of finding either a widow or an heiress. This was a hotly disputed 'market', but it seems that wage-earners had as much success in it as any. The constant pressure from men explains another unusual feature of the Parisian grocery trade, namely the rarity of grocer's shops run by women on their own (11 per cent of the businesses in 1901, and 6 per cent of the bankruptcies). Elsewhere in France very nearly half of the grocery shops were run by women (45.6 per cent). Is it fair to say that for wage-earners-turned-grocers, the happy few were those who put their aspirations to a higher social status before all else in their lives? One did not rise into the ranks of the petite bourgeoisie without making some sacrifices.

The shop assistant's nest egg, built up during the years of his employment by another grocer, was very rarely sufficient to buy a business. For the shop assistant group, it was the wife's dowry, with or without loans, which served to buy the shop in almost a quarter of the cases. If we include inheritances, this proportion becomes more than 40 per cent. Here, precisely, however, it is important to make a distinction. Out of twenty-three examples, only nine former shop assistants came into their businesses by either marrying a woman who had inherited one, or by directly inheriting one themselves. It is not particularly surprising that relatively few of the businesses were directly inherited from a father (six cases), since the milieu as a whole was largely dominated by provincials (77 per cent of the grocers who went bankrupt). Furthermore, with only one exception, the shops handed down to a son, like those taken over by a son-in-law, were ones located in the city centre, and always amongst the more valuable (over 30,000 francs). Is it possible that because of its attention to failures, the source tends to underestimate the number of grocer's shops which were inherited? We have already seen that it was the grocery trade of the centre of Paris, the only part of the trade where dynasties sometimes existed, which was the hardest hit by commercial transformations. But that is here beside the point, and the source confirms that continuity or family stability inside the grocery trade was restricted to its upper echelons. True, marriage was a frequent means of setting up in business for the smaller grocer, but marriages of this sort were of a financial, rather than dynastic significance. The grocer's shop of the working-class neighbourhoods of Paris did not stay in the same family from one generation to the next. Moreover, taking the shop assistant group as a whole, their marriages, more often than not, were simple working partnerships. This is suggested by the typical profile of their career: after eight years working behind a counter as a shop assistant, they got married and set up shop at the same time, around the age of twenty-eight.[16] Grocery was an occupation for couples, and a certain understanding between the husband and wife was one of the principal conditions for a smooth-running business. Many of the bankruptcy cases prove this point by their evidence of what could happen when this understanding was lacking.

A marriage for money enabled only a lucky minority to set up in business. What of the others? Here the source of capital was quite simply the family, or, more widely, a network of friends and relations. Legacies and loans were really only two forms of the same mode of financing a business, that is to say assistance of all kinds provided by the milieu from which the grocer came. When the shop was paid for with the dowry that the husband received with the wedding presents, or with the product of a mortgage taken out on property left by the parents, then the capital came directly from the family. When there were loans, they came from the place in the provinces where the grocer was born, from the locality to which, in many cases, he returned to celebrate his wedding. It is clear that family connections played a vital role here, but the official receivers' remarks are too cursory to allow us to go into greater detail. Nor do we have a clear idea of the exact nature of the relationships with these 'relations', or what kind of friendship existed with these 'friends', who, in the case of the grocers of Parisian extraction, made funds available. But whatever the precise identity of their financial backers, the former shop assistants who set up on their own, with no contribution from a widow or an heiress, always did so with an inheritance, both broadly and strictly speaking. The bankrupt grocers were born mainly in the Paris basin, and the departments around it. This geographical distribution is evidence of a migratory flow of young men, going up to the city to try their luck. Such migration had always been important, and was a typical pattern for men who became employers.[17] So land, in the end, was the main source of shopkeeping capital. Via the sons, modest peasant fortunes were reinvested in the urban retail trades. This period, after all, was one in which rural crafts, intimately bound up with agriculture, went into decline. This not only made hands available for the factories, it also released capital for the city. It would be most instructive to be able to analyse in greater depth the habitual methods used for financing small-scale businesses, and to examine how these fit into the general evolution of the economy.

The maintenance and reliability of these traditional methods of financing saved many a small shopkeeper from becoming tied to a wholesale wine merchant. This was certainly one of the hazards of the grocery trade, although Martin Saint-Léon overstated its importance.[18] Thus, in the bankruptcy records, only a handful of grocers, and all of them amongst the larger ones, had benefited from credit made available by wine merchants. Such loans, though considerable, were always accompanied by an obligation to purchase supplies from the company belonging to the backer. The grocers dealt almost exclusively with the grocery wholesalers, and hardly at all with the food producers. A careful examination of some of the lists of creditors shows that grocers remained very diffident in their direct buying from the manufacturers, purchasing only jams and pasta in this manner. The dealings with the wholesalers kept the same hallmark of mutual interest that we have already noted for the period of the July Monarchy. For the retailers these relationships offered a convenient way of obtaining the wares, along with easy terms for their payment. For the wholesalers they guaranteed the existence of a large number of outlets, and meant that they could continue to control prices. Thus although they were now excluded from the supply contracts for the large-scale grocery stores, the development of small-scale groceries in the outlying working-class districts meant that the wholesalers had lost none of their former power.

For the third group of grocers in Table 7 – those who went bankrupt after one or several previous commercial ventures – their last business, the one that leaves its trace in the records examined, was usually financed by personal capital. This consisted, of course, of the money raised on the sale of the stocks of the preceding concern. We come here to one of the most striking features of the Parisian grocery trade at this time, its mobility. Before setting up their itinerant grocery stall, the H. couple, for example, had run two greengrocery shops, one in Bagneux, and the other in the rue Mazarine, and then a wine shop in the rue de Clignancourt. An itinerary such as this one, zig-zagging from one shop and one neighbourhood to another, was the typical lot for almost all Parisian grocers. Another example is provided by a grocer who, after starting out as a grocer's shop assistant, opened up his own shop in Belleville, thanks to his wife's dowry, at the age of twenty-five. Three years later he sold this shop, losing 6000 francs. His next little shop in the rue Geoffroy-l'Angevin did better. Four years later he left this one for a larger grocery shop in the Avenue Saint-Ouen. Of course, sometimes, a grocer spent the whole of his life in the same place. In 1873, François F., for example, took out a lease on some land in one of the countless private streets where slums were being built, in this case at La Villette. He built a grocery shop on his plot, adding a wine shop to it soon after. A major step followed in 1882 when he opened up a lodging-house, with twenty beds. This was a classic social climb for a small retailer in an area of poor working-class dwellings. The tiny dealer in groceries gradually became the proprietor of cheap lodgings, what the French call a 'sleep merchant' (*marchand de sommeil*). As such he was a personage of some note in his miserable neighbourhood.

Such stability was rare, however. After 1900 one Parisian grocery business in five changed hands every year.[19] This sort of mobility was in no way peculiar to the grocery trade. The whole of the small retailing sector was marked by a similar instability. Land registers, or personal recollections[20] all bear witness to it. Success in the trade did not come from enlarging the shop, nor result from a well-known name or a good reputation. Rather, it came at the end of an uninterrupted succession of successful shops, each one being sold at a profit. Frequent expenses for refitting or improving the shop did not interfere with such a progress. Of course they made for a difficult moment, the credit being used up before the higher takings began to materialize, but once the charges had been assimilated, the shop had acquired greater value for when it was sold again. Thus a small shop in no way constituted the basis of a patrimony. Only really large shops were passed on from one generation to the next. The small grocers of the outlying working-class neighbourhoods would not have dreamt of coming in to the city centre, there to compete with the Potins, the Coutés or the Luces. Just as the capital put up for the small shop came from elsewhere, so also the money made in the trade was used to help out sons and daughters on their way to other social destinations. Small retail trading was a sound economic sector, rooted in well-established consumer habits. As a social category, however, it was one of passage, precarious and anonymous. At this period the *grande bourgeoisie*, the fairy godmother of the emerging middle classes, was elaborating an ideological discourse which said just the opposite.

Thus, along the way, the study of the Parisian grocery trade of the nineteenth century has brought us up against a number of historical problems. The conclusions, granted, are modest, and it would of course be unwise to generalize from them. The aim of this essay, in any case, was to use the example of the grocery trade in order to try to define a problematic, and to propose an analytical approach for the study of the retail trades in general.

First of all there is the question of the retail trades in relation to social modes of consumption. And here we mean the retail trades in their entirety. To ignore the competition from the large-scale stores is to misunderstand the general evolution of a trade. We have seen that in grocery the large stores and the small ones gradually effected a sharing out, both of geographical space and of clientèles. The losers in this process were the traditional grocers of the city centre. This state of non-competition was reached because of the total contrast between the different clientèles' purchasing powers, between their purchasing habits, and between their attitudes towards the grocer and his merchandise. It is banal today to talk about revolutions in distribution, brought about by authoritarian town planning, and the imposition of new styles of social consumption. But the archaeology of selling itself has yet to be explored.

The next point concerns the formation and the selection of the members of the trade who made it into the ranks of the employers. It is important here not to overlook the facts that shops were places in which salaried work was done, and that the renewal of the managerial ranks was as much a question of selection as of promotion. The parallel with the productive industries is clear, and by no means fortuitous, considering that processing remained for a long time an essential part of the work carried out in the shops themselves. So, how did one become an employer? It is a good question, but a better one would be how did one not become an employer? In other words, in what ways did money dictate the selection of employers? It is not enough here simply to remark upon the non-intervention of capitalist forms of credit. It is necessary to go further and to bring to light all the importance of the traditional and customary modes of financing a business: small or extended family networks, friends, relations, provincial and ethnic communities. If the small employers of the retail trades remained so long an autonomous group – 'archaic' even, some might be tempted to say – this privilege resulted less from the disdain in which banking and trading capital held the small grocers' customers, than from the vitality of parallel credit channels.

Finally – and this theme is linked to the preceding one – what role did the retail trades play in social reproduction? This question raises that of family inheritances, and social mobility within the world of shopkeepers. There are two extreme versions, two contradictory hypotheses, on this point. One version has the trade in the hands of a precise group of dynasties, with direct descent of the businesses, and a controlled policy of matrimonial alliances. The trade is thus a reserved domain, closed off to outsiders. In the other version, the employers of the trade are constantly being replaced, with no family continuity. They are individuals who benefit from pre-existing networks of financial backing, and the trade is thus an open milieu, a free zone. We have seen that both models apply to the Parisian grocers of the last century. A small fringe of large businesses, originally in the hands of a few families, gradually passes out of their control, and, as a result of commercial mutations, falls under that of large-scale joint-stock capital. On the other side there is a plethora of small businesses, run by sons who have come up to the big city, and which draw the savings from beneath innumerable provincial mattresses. But buying a shop was not like buying a plot of land. Succeeding generations of small grocers have always consisted of families on the move, never taking root.

NOTES

N.B. The translation of this article was paid for by the Centre d'histoire de la France contemporaine, at the University of Paris X, Nanterre.

1 See, for example, A. Daumard's contribution, on Paris, in *Les Fortunes françaises au XIXe siècle*, Paris-La Haye, 1973.

2 See the first part of the study by C. Baudelot, R. Establet and J. Malemort, *La Petite Bourgeoisie en France*, Paris, 1974, 10–40.

3 The year 1846 has been chosen on purpose as a year following the new law on the professional tax (*patente*), passed in 1844. The application of this law in Paris tended to increase the amount of taxes paid by the lower categories of taxpayers, amongst which were the grocers.

4 Rapport du directeur des contributions directes (Archives de la Seine, DP^2 (1)).

5 The French Grocers' Association (Syndicat de l'Epicerie française, 32, rue du Renard, Paris) possesses a manuscript entitled 'Letters from a grocer's shop assistant'. This is a collection of the voluminous correspondence which Jean-Alexandre Bauche addressed to his father, a grocer at Lardy (Seine-et-Oise) between 1807 and 1810. The donator of the collection provides the following biographical notes about Jean-Alexandre, who was his grandfather: 'He died in Paris on 19 August 1839, leaving three sons set up in the trade in Paris: (1) Jean-Alexandre, in the rue Saint-Lazare from 1833 to 1855; (2) Emile-Nicolas, established in the rue de Sèvres from 1836 to 1854; (3) Camille-Marie, a grocer in the rue de Bondy between 1847 and 1862. This is a rare example of a line of Parisian grocers which covered nearly the whole century, since I myself had the honour to be a member of the corporation until 1881, and to have been vice-president of the French Grocers' Association.'

6 Chambre de commerce de Paris, *Enquête industrielle de 1847–1848.*

7 S. Mercier, *Tableau de Paris*, vol. XII, Paris, 1789, 78.

8 See, for example, the files at the archives of the Préfecture de Police, 'Police alimentaire' (DB 462, 463 and 465).

9 The Louvre department store had an ambitious project for a vast food bazaar, to be opened in 1889 at the same time as the Terminus Hotel (P. du Maroussem, *La Question ouvrière, IV, Halles centrales de Paris et commerce de l'alimentation*, Paris, 1884, 172–3).

10 L. Arnou, in *L'Epicerie française* of 20 April 1906. This was the organ of the Grocers' Association.

11 This conclusion results from an investigation of the rolls for the *patente* tax in the 3rd *arrondissement*, carried out in 1976 by Mlles J. Federici and C. Vroelant (Archives de la Seine D^2P^9).

12 Extract from a long and fascinating conversation with M. René R., recorded in June 1978.

Monsieur R. was a grocer's assistant in Paris before 1914, working at one stage in a Potin store. After a spell as a travelling salesman, he ran his own grocery shop in Belleville between 1922 and 1960. Other extracts from this same conversation are quoted in the text.

13 The task of extracting the information from the records (Archives de la Seine, D^{11}, U^{3}) was carried out by Mlle J. Federici, and paid for from university credits for research projects. The work was divided into two stages. First the information contained in the records was transcribed onto prepared file cards. The different elements were then collated, year by year. As it turned out, many of the elements could not be fitted into the categories selected, at least not without missing much of the valuable documentary evidence contained in the dossiers. Moreover, only a small number (thirty) of the possible correlations was attempted. Consequently our research by no means exhausts the potential of the source. A meticulous qualitative analysis, and a more elaborate statistical processing, could certainly extract more from it.

14 Demonceaux and Savigny, *Comptabilité des épiciers*, Paris, n.d., 22.

15 'You get fussy customers coming in to bring back a tin of food . . . you can always really insist, and then she'll keep her tin, go home and eat it, thinking all the while that it's not any good, that it won't do. So it's better to say "Yes, Madame, you're perfectly right," and give her another tin. The tin she's brought back, you can always eat it yourself later. You can't send it back to the makers.'

16 Out of 135 cases where these details are given, 93 grocers setting up in business for the first time did so in the year of their marriage.

17 See L. Chevalier, *La Formation de la population parisienne au xixe siècle*, Paris, 1949, 173–85.

18 Etienne Martin Saint-Léon, *Le petit commerce français, sa lutte pour la vie*, Paris, 1911, 43–4.

19 According to the *Annuaire statistique de la ville de Paris* (product of substitution taxes for town dues).

20 Madame A., a butcher's wife at Maison-Blanche, in the 13th *arrondissement*: 'In those days people didn't like to see a shopkeeper staying a long time. Customers got tired of always dealing with the same person. It was well known that it was better to sell a business after five or six years. . . . You never saw a shopkeeper staying in the same shop for forty years' (interview recorded in August 1978).

8 The small shopkeepers' movement and politics in France, 1888–1914*

PHILIP NORD

The small shopkeeper in France is reputed to have shifted political allegiance from the left to the right at the end of the last century.[1] I propose to test this claim by tracing the political and ideological evolution of interest group organizations which purported to represent the modest retailer. These groups, I will argue, did indeed evolve rightward. The shopkeeper movement, at its origins in the 1880s, was linked closely with radical socialism. This association disintegrated in the ensuing decade as *boutiquiers* yielded to the temptations of nationalism. As the nationalist wave receded in the first years of this century, the shopkeeper movement drifted toward the conservative right, toward social Catholics and *Poincaristes*, who welcomed and rewarded shopkeeper support while trying to capitalize on it. This shift to the right should not be understood narrowly. The shopkeeper movement did indeed exchange one set of political friends for another, but in the process it also changed its conception of the shopkeeper's place in social and political life, its posture *vis-à-vis* the state and the various branches of government (legislative and executive), and finally, its actual relations with other pressure group organizations, particularly those representing big businessmen and employees. The complex and thoroughgoing transformations that overtook the shopkeeper movement cannot be summed up by a simple assertion of a move to the right.[2]

Paris in the 1880s was the scene of numerous unsuccessful attempts to launch a shopkeepers' movement. Retailers in the past had been represented as practitioners of a particular *commerce* or as members of the larger business community, but never as retailers. Efforts to organize shopkeepers at last bore fruit in 1888 with the formation of the *Ligue syndicale pour la défense des intérêts du travail, de l'industrie et du commerce*, the first such organization to attract a sizeable following – well over a hundred thousand at its peak[3] – as well as the first to last beyond a few years, surviving up to the outbreak of World War I. The new League's political

* I would like to thank Philippe Vigier, Gerhard Haupt, Robert Paxton and Arno Mayer for their generous assistance and constructive criticism in the preparation of this study.

leanings were distinctly radical socialist. It was founded by militants grouped around two newspapers, the *Crise commerciale* and the *Union démocratique*. The former paper, 'organ of all those who want to combat the monopolistic department store', prided itself on its political neutrality, its willingness in the interests of the shopkeeper to deal with any and all politicians – as long as they were 'true patriots'.[4] The *Union démocratique*'s political connections by contrast were far more explicit. Most of its staff can be identified as radical socialist, with the radical deputies Gustave Mesureur and Maurice Vergoin heading the list.[5] From its first appearance in 1887, the *Union démocratique* regularly published proceedings of the various radical socialist and free-thinking committees which dotted the Parisian political landscape. Co-ordinating the dispersed efforts of Parisian radicals was stated editorial policy.[6]

The first president of the League, Léopold Christophe, a commission agent, rue du Faubourg-Poissonnière, was a freemason and veteran republican who had agitated against the Second Empire.[7] Under his leadership, the League agitated, particularly through pressure on its radical socialist friends, to obtain a revision of the business tax, the *patente*. The League demanded a more stringent taxation of the department store, the shopkeeper's most dangerous competitor, invoking the principle of 'specialization' to justify its claims for punitive legislation. Every man was entitled to earn a decent living through the practice of a trade; but anyone who practised more than one trade threatened the livelihood of others and was guilty of monopolistic practices (*accaparement*).[8] At a minimum, violators (in other words, department stores) ought to be obliged to pay a tax for every specialty they traded in.

An entire vision of the world was contained in the principle of specialization. An article that appeared 31 October 1896 in the League's official newspaper *La Revendication* gives some idea of that vision:

> the money you bring from all over Paris and spend in those commercial agglomerations is absolutely lost to you. . . . If, on the other hand, the hatter did business with her neighbour the shoe merchant, and the shoe merchant reciprocated, then both would make money and be all the more willing to do business with the neighbourhood butcher, *charcutier* and wine-seller.
>
> In helping your neighbours to earn a living, you are making customers for yourself and creating an environment of mutual respect.
>
> If centralization is bad in political matters, it is even more harmful from an economic point of view.[9]

The economy of the *quartier* was conceived as a virtual autarky. All that endangered the economic independence of the local community, all that favoured centralization, there was the enemy. This way of looking at things, of course, had political ramifications. For the League, the 'enemy' included not only department stores, cooperatives, the financial feudality, indeed, all the institutions characteristic of an organized capitalism, but also the modern, bureaucratic state. A. Girard, member of the League's 2nd *arrondissement* committee, ran for office in the parliamentary by-elections of 1887. He demanded a revision of the constitution, suppression of the senate and the office of the presidency, government decentralization, autonomy for the commune of Paris, closer surveillance of the conduct of bureaucrats, and the election of judges.[10] Central to the League's political programme was a determination to arrest the concentration of political power and to preserve or revive local liberties. Direct democracy, it was hoped, would rescue the state from the stranglehold of a monopolistic oligarchy; a government restored to the people, 'the people who made 1789' – *ligueurs* were always ready to invoke the nation's revolutionary heritage[11] – would in turn undertake the reforms essential to preserve *petit commerce* (starting with *patente* revision) and safeguard neighbourhood autonomy.

The League's fierce localism lies at the root of its extreme xenophobia. The League feared the economic power of outsiders; it demanded erection of tariff barriers against manufactures produced abroad as well as punitive legislation against the department store. Shopkeeper distrust of foreign competition was extended to include all persons deemed to be foreign: the English, Americans, Italians, Jews and, above all, the Germans. The League wanted protection; protection against competition but protection as well for a community whose integrity and solidarity were judged to be under assault from outsiders.

League ideology was not in fact individualist. To be sure, *ligueurs* refused to organize purchasing co-operatives or the joint sale of merchandise in the name of retailer independence. They envisaged with horror 'a regime of *syndicats*'; they feared the 'power of associations'.[12] But they detested the economic liberalism of a Paul Leroy-Beaulieu no less than the collectivism of a Jaurès. The League saw itself as a defender of the family and the workplace, conceived not as institutions of free and equal individuals bound by contractual relations, but as little communities organized hierarchically and cemented by ties of sentiment. *La Revendication* is sprinkled with appeals to women and workers, the 'natural allies' of *petit commerce*. It was necessary for all loyal citizens to band together against the bourgeois aristocracy, against the financial feudality. The League claimed to speak not in the name of the individual, but of a beleaguered *peuple* preyed upon by the forces of monopoly and cosmopolitanism. From its over-heated patriotism, its solemn invocations of the Great Revolution, to its defence of *morcellisme* against *accaparement*, of the hard-working citizen against the rapacious monopolist, it was also an ideology that bore striking resemblances to radical socialism.

Just as the extreme elements of the radical socialist movement succumbed to the Boulangist temptation, so with the extreme elements of the *Ligue syndicale*. Several of the League's section chiefs, notably Digard of the 15th *arrondissement*, campaigned for Boulanger.[13] The *Union démocratique* itself became an influential revisionist mouthpiece. Even *La Revendication*, on the eve of the January 1889 by-elections in Paris, toyed with the possibility of supporting *le brav' Général*. 'Perhaps', remarked an article that appeared on 10 January, 'a vote for Boulanger represents a leap into the unknown', but 'frankly, what we have to lose, is it so precious that we must fear the unknown?'[14] It was not without some justification that Girard credited the General's astonishing success in the by-elections to the votes of disgruntled small shopkeepers.[15] Nevertheless, while the League may have been momentarily swayed by the revisionist campaign, it was never persuaded to endorse Boulanger publicly, nor did it sever ties with the radicals of the rue Cadet.

The radicals, alarmed at how close they had come to losing their shopkeeper constituency, were prodded into action. In 1890, Mesureur convinced the Chamber of Deputies to organize a special commission to consider legislative proposals for a revision of the *patente* and managed to get himself appointed chairman. A bill, bearing the signatures of the Chamber's best-known radical deputies,[16] was submitted for consideration, duly reported out and, in modified form, made law in 1893. It contained a provision for taxing department stores on the basis of the number of *commerces* practised.

Counter-currents were at work, however, eroding the League's ties with radical socialism. The political volatility of shopkeepers, so clearly manifested during the crisis of 1889, attracted the attention of anti-semites, ex-Boulangists, and Christian Democrats. This emergent radical right taught itself to speak a rhetoric with a strong appeal to the shopkeeper, a lesson all the more easily learned as many of the new right's militants were shopkeepers themselves. The League responded favourably, sometimes enthusiastically. Edouard Drumont's diatribes against the department store are only too well known.[17] The marquis de Morès made it abundantly clear that his unbounded hatred for 'that *phylloxera* which goes by the name of *kike*', was to be interpreted to include 'the Schneiders of le Creuzot [sic], the Rothschilds of the Bank, and the Ruels of the Bazar de l'Hôtel de Ville'.[18] In a conference before the abbé Garnier's *Union nationale*, Jules Guérin stated the anti-semite's position succinctly:

> The country has fallen prey to a handful of financiers, of speculators and *accapareurs* organized in international syndicates, manipulating the rise and fall of our markets, ruining the small shopkeeper and the petty producer; these are the people who pull the strings that move the political parties which direct the nation's affairs.[19]

Remarks like these, which played on the shopkeeper's patriotism, his fears of the rich and the powerful, and his distrust of politicians, did not fail to strike a sympathetic chord. In 1892, when Drumont was brought to trial for having libelled Auguste Burdeau, a prominent and well-liked deputy, *La Revendication*, without knowing the details of the case, leapt to Drumont's defence. Drumont reciprocated with an endorsement the following year of Christophe's candidature for a senate seat and with an offer of free publicity in *La Libre parole* – an offer the League promptly accepted.[20] In 1890, an editor of the *Crise commerciale* (Louis Bréhant), accompanied by two *ligueurs*, made advances to Morès who reacted positively: 'Your idea is wonderful! Your perseverance magnificent! I will study the question closely; leave me some copies of the *Crise commerciale* and of *La Revendication*, but I assure you in advance of my backing.'[21] And Guérin, on more than one occasion, was invited to expound his anti-semitic message before League audiences.[22] In 1898, Louis Gazon, vice-president of the League, became one of the first to join Guérin's *Ligue antisémite*.[23]

Gazon was also the League's most important contact with the remains of the Boulangist movement. Throughout the 1890s, Gazon – and another *ligueur* Louis Pagèze – were involved in a series of unsuccessful efforts to regroup the scattered Boulangist committees which had survived the debacle of 1889.[24] These ex-Boulangists considered themselves socialists. Their socialism, however, was not collectivist, but national; they sought the salvation of the 'worker', not in the abolition of private property, but rather, in the expulsion of foreign workers or the expropriation of a minority of *accapareurs* or in the extinction of exploiting Jews. Gazon put it this way in an article that appeared in *La Revendication* in 1895:

> Only one [party], still new to many, can profit from an alliance of all the nation's workers . . . to rule. And that's the party called 'socialist'.
>
> Let it then set to work . . . let it expose to the working class the trap laid for it by parliamentary politicians and monopolists in creating consumer co-operatives; let it combat the great commercial agglomerations, and it will recruit to its banner new phalanxes who will swell the ranks of those fighting to defend their livelihoods against a cosmopolitan and hack-ridden plutocracy that favours the few.[25]

In the long run, however, it may have been Christian Democracy which exercised the most lasting influence on the shopkeeper movement. In 1891, Léon Harmel founded *L'Union fraternelle du commerce et de l'industrie*, which dedicated itself to defence of the small shopkeeper, a victim of the anarchy of free market individualism.[26] The *laissez-faire* policies of the modern state, imposed according to the *Union fraternelle* by a cabal of Jews and freemasons, threatened the family, the small shop, and the corporation, natural groupings admirably constructed to organize the life of the individual. The lines of authority in these institutions were clearly drawn; the men in charge knew their subordinates personally and could not shirk their moral obligations, as did politicians, bureaucrats and corporate directors. The man who faced his moral duty, here was the true Christian in the *Union fraternelle*'s scheme of things. And so the Union preached economic and political decentralization as a means of breathing new life into local bodies (*corps locaux*), the breeding grounds of Christian values and cells of a future Christian revival.

This perspective, albeit religious in origin and inspiration, resembled League ideology in several respects. Both League and Union identified the same dangers – the centralized state and the financial feudality – and denounced them for the same reason, because they threatened the autonomy of local life. To be sure, differences remained. The Union, preoccupied with the necessity of restoring economic order, favoured organization of all kinds, the co-operative included, not to mention the corporation. The Union, unlike the League, was reluctant to call on state aid, preferring that *petit commerce* save itself by its own efforts through purchasing societies and similar arrangements. And as for politics, the Union was far more authoritarian. But there was still enough common ground between the two organizations to permit an entente. The League moderated its hostility toward co-operatives; it no longer asked that they be abolished but simply that they pay the *patente* like any other commercial enterprise (co-ops at that time were exempt from the business tax). The Union for its part accepted the principle of specialization.[27] This rapprochement was due in large part to the efforts of A. Trépreau who was both a League and Union official and served as an intermediary in negotiations between the two groups.

Trépreau won a sympathetic hearing for the shopkeeper's case at the *Congrès national catholique* of 1897.[28] The following year, both *La Croix* and the Union published the League's electoral programme.[29] Christophe himself was invited to speak before attentive Catholic audiences, winning over influential Catholic politicians such as Senator Edouard de Lamarzelle in the process.[30] What had begun tentatively as a rapprochement with Christian Democracy was taking on the character of an alliance, uniting the shopkeeper movement with some of the most powerful and established defenders of the Church's place in French society.

The attentiveness of anti-semites, national socialists and the like to shopkeeper complaints accounts only in part for the drift of the shopkeeper movement toward the radical right in the 1890s. The diminishing attractiveness of other political options and also a waning enthusiasm for pressure group tactics narrowed the alternatives available to the movement, which found itself as much pushed as pulled to the right.

From the beginning, the *Ligue syndicale* had eschewed overt political commitments. The interests of the shopkeeper were best served, it was believed, through *patente* reform, which could only be obtained if the League avoided compromising political alliances. The fruit of this tactic was the reform of 1893 – but the reform proved a bitter disappointment. The new law actually lowered the tax assessment for all stores, both in Paris and the provinces, save for a handful of giants – the *Bon Marché*, the *Louvre*, and the *Printemps*.[31] A further revision had been proposed by the ex-royalist Georges Berry but was hopelessly bottled up in the Senate. Pressure group tactics had apparently led to an impasse. The League, which had staked so much on this approach, was bound to suffer. The League's difficulties were compounded by the imminent retirement of Christophe (he was born in 1834). With him would go one of the League's ablest orators as well as an important source of financial support.[32] By the end of the decade, *La Revendication* was no longer appearing regularly.[33] If salvation was not to be found in the League, perhaps a less ambiguous intervention in the political process was called for. But what were the options available to shopkeepers?

The shopkeeper could scarcely turn to collectivism. Proponents of collectivism, joined one might add by many prominent 'bourgeois' economists, confidently predicted that the inexorable progress of commercial and industrial concentration would eventually prove the shopkeeper's undoing. Squeezed between the proletariat and big business, the little man was doomed to extinction.[34] Collectivists who regarded with hostile eyes private property in any form, whether large or small, were not unduly disturbed by this prospect. And as collectivism won converts among socialists, shopkeeper relations with the working-class left became increasingly tense. In the early 1890s, the League had been able to campaign jointly against department store abuses with the Broussist *Chambre syndicale des employés*. By the end of the decade, the entente had collapsed in recriminations, the victim of shopkeeper hostility to co-operatives and increasing socialist militancy.[35]

Social polarization posed particular problems for Parisian radicalism, which straddled both working-class and petit-bourgeois constituencies. In September 1898, construction workers and railwaymen in Paris went out on strike. The government, headed by the Radical Brisson, handled the situation gingerly at first, angering shopkeepers who were exasperated by the work stoppage and inclined to blame the crisis on the ministry.[36] When the government then resorted to a massive show of force, socialists and union men throughout the capital mobilized in opposition. In refusing to choose between the worker and the small shopkeeper, Parisian radicals alienated both.

As for the Opportunists, they remained in the eyes of the small shopkeeper – and rightly so – the party of big business. In the last months of 1897, the most important business organizations in Paris – the *Comité central des chambres syndicales* (Charles Expert-Bezançon), the *Alliance syndicale des chambres syndicales* (Alfred Pinard), the *Syndicat général des chambres syndicales* (Alexis Muzet), the *Comité de l'alimentation* (Alphonse Marguery), and the *Chambre syndicale du bâtiment* (Bertrand) – agreed to pool campaign efforts in the approaching national elections through the formation of a *Comité républicain national du commerce et de l'industrie*. The *Comité*, chaired by Expert-Bezançon, a manufacturer of chemicals, made no secret of its hostility to socialism; indeed, anti-socialism was its *raison d'être*. The *Comité* pledged its full support to the Méline government which warmly returned the favour.[37] Waldeck-Rousseau, Raymond Poincaré, and Paul Deschanel turned their considerable oratorical talents toward promoting the cause of big business. The League reacted with deep suspicion to the *Comité Expert-Bezançon*. The *Syndicat général* was on record against specialization; the *Alliance syndicale* had dismissed the League's programme as 'utopian dreams'; and many of the *Comité*'s constituent groups backed free trade.[38] Moreover, as a *ligueur* explained to *La Croix*, the *Comité* was composed 'above all of big-shot industrialists and merchants', of 'Jews and types we'd label without hesitation *accapareurs*, all of them the enemies of small business'.[39] Fighting socialism and preserving a stable pro-big business government, these were the *Comité*'s main preoccupations. The organization held little appeal for the small shopkeeper. *L'Epicerie Française* remarked of a banquet sponsored by the *Comité* in 1898: 'We observed the presence of many speculators, well-heeled industrialists, of numerous lawyers and doctors, deputies or would-be deputies, but of our own kind, of the modest and the humble, of that great commercial majority, of the Third Estate which still exists whatever people say, not one.'[40]

The Dreyfus affair then erupted at a moment of crisis for the shopkeeper movement. Enthusiasm for pressure group tactics had reached a low ebb. Political options were narrowing. The Parisian shopkeeper was drifting away from Radicalism and displayed a growing sympathy for the rhetoric of the radical right. This sympathy was crystallized into full-fledged support by the affair.

Nationalism scored stunning victories in Paris in the municipal elections of 1900 and the national elections of 1902. Whether in terms of praise or blame, observers from *La Petite République* to *Le Temps*, from the *Comité Mascuraud* to the nationalists themselves, agreed that the small shopkeeper was responsible.[41] The League's reaction to the Dreyfus crisis is difficult to assess for lack of documentation, but other shopkeeper groups went on record as opponents of revision.

In the summer of 1899, Marcel Habert and Paul Déroulède attempted to persuade troops returning from the funeral of President Félix Faure to march on the Elysée. Brought to trial on charges of sedition, they were acquitted, to the delight of *L'Epicerie Française* which applauded 'the audacity of these two brave men'. The chairman of the jury had been a grocer, which moved the grocers' newspaper to exult: 'From now on, people will associate with our profession the epithet: Patriotic like a grocer.'[42] During the electoral campaign of 1902, Marguery (himself a dabbler in Radical politics) made a considerable effort to win *Comité de l'alimentation* backing for pro-Dreyfusard candidates like Brisson, Millerand, and others. The effort provoked a rank and file revolt, Marguery resigned, and *Le Radical* was moved to brand the *Comité* an 'electoral propaganda agency for nationalism'.[43] Another organization of radical tint, the *Chambre syndicale des maîtres tailleurs*, found itself unable to concede the possibility of Dreyfus's innocence even as it gave loyal support to the Combes government (until the *Affaire des fiches*). Nor did Dreyfus's exoneration in 1906 change the *Chambre syndicale*'s mind.[44] Staunch patriotism accounted in large part for this wrong-headed tenacity, but also a festering hostility to socialism. During both the 1900 and 1902 elections, *La Petite République* and *L'Aurore*, infuriated by nationalist successes, published angry articles laying the blame on shopkeepers. To shield workers from the corrupting influence of the retailer, Jaurès called for an extension of the co-operative movement.[45] After the first round of the 1902 elections, Albert Goullé wrote in *L'Aurore*:

> Can you hear them exulting? All the false-weighting merchants, all the adulterators, all the debasers of money, all the pimping hotel-keepers fighting over the patronage of prostitutes, all the milk-dealers who poison new-borns, the whole band of grocers, bakers, butchers, pot-house keepers, *charcutiers*, . . . that whole thieving bunch waiting in ambush to fleece the passer-by is overjoyed.[46]

Nationalist candidates gleefully reproduced such insults and postered them all over the city.[47] The *Comité des étalagistes* – formed in 1899 by members of the *Chambre syndicale des marchands de chaussures en détail* to combat unfavourable changes in shop-display regulations[48] – reacted to the left's broadsides by publicly declaring its support for nationalist candidates. An *étalagiste* poster affirmed:

> For the second time, in 1900 as again today, we believe it our right and duty to renounce passivity, to sound the rallying cry of the army of small commerce. We see on the one side, the collectivists, the adversaries of *petit commerce*. . . . On the other, the anti-collectivists and therefore the defenders of small commerce and small industry.
>
> The collectivists and their allies are partisans of class warfare, trying to drive a wedge between the employer and his workers and employees. We reject such fratricidal struggle.[49]

While in Paris shopkeepers spent their energies in a disorganized outburst of reaction, provincials led by Henri Destréguil of Tours moved to assert a greater control over the shopkeeper movement. An acolyte of Drumont's Catholic socialism, Destréguil approved of shopkeepers intervening forcefully in electoral politics, but favoured a sober, controlled approach. Destréguil had already successfully grouped shopkeeper organizations in the Tours region into a commercial party, the *Ligue du parti commercial des départements du centre*,[50] and was anxious to try out this approach on the national level. Trépreau, who had become vice-president of the *Ligue syndicale*, brought the Parisian organization around to Destréguil's point of view. In 1901, representatives from the major shopkeeper organizations around the nation agreed to the formation of the *Parti Commercial et Industriel Français* (PCI), 'so named in opposition to the *Parti Ouvrier* of M. Guesde'.[51] The provincial character of the new organization can be seen clearly in the composition of its steering committee. Of the party's twenty-one officers, only seven were Parisians and only four belonged to the League.[52]

Trépreau made plain the new organization's determination to serve as a 'dike against collectivism'. And, he added:

> just as in the middle ages, the action of corporate institutions was perhaps not unconnected to the magnificent movement of the communes, so today, the same kind of action, reconstituted under the cover of Leagues and Unions on the one hand, of *syndicats* on the other, can only further a movement of regeneration destined to wrench France from the oligarchy that now is strangling her.[53]

Parliament, the PCI complained, was so obsessed with problems of a 'purely political' character (such as the religious question) that it neglected economic issues of vital importance to France's well-being. The PCI undertook to reverse the nation's political priorities. It failed and, admitting defeat, withdrew into a more apolitical stance, becoming a simple pressure group like any other. The party signalled its new status with a change of name. The *Parti Commercial* gave way to the *Fédération*, later the *Confédération des groupes commerciaux et industriels*. The League did not take part in this new organization and paid dearly for its independence, losing a substantial portion of its membership to the *Confédération*.

The period of the Dreyfus affair marked a watershed in the history of the shopkeeper movement for two major reasons. In Paris, the movement broke down as shopkeepers abandoned pressure group tactics to play a more direct role in political life, specifically through participation in the nationalist surge. Provincial organizations filled the void; the shopkeeper movement, formerly under Parisian hegemony, became a national movement in which provincials enjoyed substantial representation. In the process, the League lost its position of leadership in the shopkeeper movement. The ideology of the *quartier*, it appeared, was in retreat. But what was to take its place?

A Confederation spokesman wrote in 1906: 'insensibly, without being aware of it, by the force of events, we are returning to the *maitrîses* and corporate juries of yesteryear to which every apprentice had to submit a *chef d'oeuvre* before he could be admitted to the status of worker.'[54] For the Confederation, the rise of the *syndicat*, of professional organization, prefigured the emergence of a new corporatism. The *syndicat* had a double role to play. To it, first and foremost, fell the responsibility of finding a solution to the crisis of small business. From the Confederation's point of view, this crisis was not solely the consequence of department store competition. One 'must not condemn large-scale industry, large-scale commerce nor attempt to do them injury'.[55] The duty of the *syndicat* was rather 'to make small and medium-sized businesses stronger' by organizing purchasing co-operatives, by improving credit facilities and professional education.[56] Small shopkeepers themselves were in no small part to blame for their economic predicament; it was incumbent upon them to modernize, to abandon routine and to recognize that their salvation lay in collective action under the auspices of trade associations. Secondly, the *syndicat* was looked on as an instrument to combat the enemies of private property. It was up to the trade association to lead the fight against the bureaucratic state with its pretensions to regulate economic life and impose social reforms like the weekly day-off (*repos hebdomadaire*), workers' pensions, and the income tax. The Confederation conceded the necessity of some legislative change but always insisted that reform measures be applied and administered by the employers' associations themselves. But the most fearful enemy confronting property owners was the workers' movement. It was hoped that *syndicats*, through sponsorship of effective apprenticeship programmes, could train sober-minded workers resistant to the temptations of socialism. But more to the point, the *syndicat* could serve as a rallying point for all the friends of order. Against an emergent working-class bloc, it could mobilize a bloc of the middle classes (*classes moyennes*).[57]

In the years preceding World War I, the corporatist elements in the Confederation's thinking became more accentuated. Demands were made for a commercial and industrial parliament elected by *syndicats*, with the power to legislate on economic questions, questions that the Chamber of Deputies was judged incompetent to handle. At a minimum, the Confederation insisted, the state administration ought to be required by law to consult syndical organizations on all matters of interest to them. The Confederation had some success on this score, establishing regular relations with the Ministry of Commerce in the years before the war.[58] The Confederation's drift toward a more explicitly corporatist position was accompanied by an increasingly emphatic patriotism. German products were denounced; measures against foreign workers were demanded; and the law extending military service to three years was enthusiastically supported. Many ex-nationalists became active in Confederation affairs, Maurice Quentin for example, municipal councillor from the 1st *arrondissement* and former secretary-general of the *Ligue des patriotes*. The increasing conservatism of Confederation policies by no means diminished its influence in the shopkeeper movement. Quite the contrary. In 1911, the remnants of the *Ligue syndicale* affiliated with the Confederation. The *Union fraternelle* had become by the outbreak of the war a regular participant in the Confederation's national congresses.

The ideology of the *quartier* was not entirely forgotten in the Confederation's programme. The principle of specialization was preserved, and although less stress was placed on political reform, it was still believed important to seek out the friendship of deputies. But which ones? Instead of a Mesureur, politicians of a distinctly conservative stamp were cultivated, men such as Georges Berry, the former nationalist Gabriel Failliot and the Progressist Edouard Néron.[59]

The ideology of the shopkeepers' movement, it appears, had undergone a major transformation. The *syndicat* rather than the local community was envisaged as the focal point of the retailer's life. Shopkeeper militants looked less to state protection but were more and more adamant in demands for a consultative role *vis-à-vis* the executive branch. And finally, shopkeepers no longer conceived of themselves as belonging to the people; they were now members of the *classes moyennes*.

Several reasons can be advanced to account for the re-orientation of shopkeeper thought. Catholic influence ought to be mentioned first of all. The *Union fraternelle* was, I believe, the first commercial grouping to preach the virtues of organization, a position that sprang naturally from the Catholic critique of individualism. The Union was also the first commercial organization to envisage a full-scale mobilization of the middle classes. This idea, however, was not entirely its own. It was borrowed, rather, from social Catholicism, from French Catholics such as Pierre du Marroussem, Frantz Funck-Brentano and Etienne Martin Saint-Léon, who in turn borrowed the tactic from its true pioneers, the Belgian Catholics J. Stevens, Hector Lambrechts, and Oscar Pyfferoen.

In 1899 and again in 1901, the Belgians hosted 'International Congresses of the Petite Bourgeoisie', which attracted the attention and participation of French intellectuals, in particular Georges Blondel and Funck-Brentano, both followers of Le Play.[60] Indeed, the world-wide enthusiasm sparked by these congresses generated interest in the formation of a permanent body to study the problems of the petite bourgeoisie. In 1904, the *Institut international pour l'étude du problème des classes moyennes* was founded, with its headquarters in Brussels and Stevens as its director.[61] French social Catholics such as Victor de Clercq, an *Action Libérale* militant and a veteran of the *Union fraternelle*, and Martin Saint-Léon, archivist at the

Musée Social and a lecturer for the *Semaines Sociales*, affiliated to the *Institut* and undertook to propagate the *classes moyennes* point of view at home. Martin Saint-Léon was particularly active in the affairs of the Confederation both as speech-maker and organizer.[62] Catholic influence within the shopkeeper movement reached a peak in 1910 with the appointment of André de Paloméra as president of the Confederation. A businessman from the Charente, de Paloméra headed the Cognac branch of the *Action Libérale Populaire* (ALP) and exercised sufficient influence within the party to have the shopkeeper question raised and dealt with sympathetically at the ALP congress of 1908.[63]

The dislocation of the shopkeeper movement at the turn of the century under the double impact of nationalism and rising provincial power profited not only social Catholics but also advocates of more harmonious relations with the rest of the business community. Throughout the pre-war decade, the secretary-general of the Confederation was one Edmond Bellamy, a Parisian businessman of some means, president of the *Chambre syndicale des papetiers* and secretary of Expert-Bezançon's *Comité central des chambres syndicales*.[64] But big business hegemony over the shopkeeper movement was nowhere exercised with as much open cynicism as in the case of Georges Maus's *Fédération des commerçants-détaillants*.

Maus, director of an important department store *Les Phares de la Bastille*, founded the Federation in 1906 to combat application of the recently passed weekly day-off (*repos hebdomadaire*) law. Busy during the week, workers did much of their shopping on Sundays. If stores were closed on the Sabbath, the retailer stood to lose one of his most lucrative days of trade. The Federation denounced the *repos hebdomadaire* as the work of foreigners determined to ruin business in Paris and encouraged shopkeepers not to co-operate in the law's implementation.[65] The government, faced with the bad faith of employers like Maus, ultimately backed down, conceding widespread exemptions. Rigorous application of the law became impossible. In 1910, agitation by department store employees in Paris for a shorter working day led to violent clashes between employee pickets and police, who were reinforced on more than one occasion by company thugs. Employee unions identified Maus as the *éminence grise* behind employer resistance.[66] No weapon in the employer arsenal was unfamiliar to him. In 1906, he subsidized the formation of the *Fédération nationale des employés*, a yellow union, which, however, never managed to attract a sizeable following, collapsing four years after its birth in a humiliating financial scandal.[67] Union-breaking and subversion of social reform (the Federation also opposed the income tax) seem to have been the principal pre-occupations of Maus's organization.

Not surprisingly, the *Comité des étalagistes*, which had intervened to such great effect in the elections of 1902, was affiliated to the Federation;[68] Gabriel Garreau, one of the organizers of the *Comité*, was for many years Maus's chief lieutenant. But the Federation's political centre of gravity actually lay further to the left. Maus sought out the patronage of high-powered politicians such as Raymond Poincaré and Paul Deschanel, who willingly presided over important Federation functions, annual banquets and national assemblies.[69] Indeed, Poincaré sat briefly on the *comité d'études* of the *Fédération nationale des employés.*[70] But on a day-to-day basis, the Federation's best contacts were the radical deputies Adolphe Maujean (who represented a district in the Paris suburbs) and Louis Puech of the 3rd *arrondissement*. During the Dreyfus affair, Puech had been accused of selling out to the nationalists.[71] And Maujean, who in Maus's words had 'had the courage in a memorable parliamentary session to face down the revolutionaries', enjoyed a reputation as a red baiter.[72] Right Radicals and left Progressists, sharing deep-rooted antisocialist convictions, proved the Federation's best allies.

The Federation, defender of employer prerogative, and the far stronger Confederation, advocate of a creeping corporatism, were not so far apart that a rapprochement was impossible. Nor for that matter was an entente between the shopkeeper movement and the forces of order – big business and establishment politicians – to be ruled out. That these two possibilities were realized owes much to the perseverance and imagination of Maurice Colrat, marquis de Montrozier.

Colrat was particularly well-equipped for the task. He was welcome in Progressist circles and had important connections in the business world. Colrat began his career as a secretary in Poincaré's law office. He later did election work for Poincaré and for Eugène Motte, both Progressists. While campaigning for Motte, scion of a wealthy textile family, during the latter's successful 1902 parliamentary bid against Jules Guesde, Colrat met his future wife, Anne Delaune, daughter of a Roubaix textile magnate and Progressist deputy from the Nord.[73] The *Association de défense des classes moyennes*, founded in 1907, was Colrat's brainchild. Both the Confederation and the Federation belonged – as well as the *Union des syndicats patronaux des industries textiles*.[74] The *Union*, organized in 1902 by the mill-owner R. S. Carmichael, was a spin-off of Jules Méline's *Association de l'industrie et de l'agriculture française*.[75]

Thirty years earlier, textile manufacturers and conservative politicians would not have paid the slightest attention to the sufferings of the shopkeeper. In the 1880s and 1890s, it could still be hoped that expanded production and its by-product, industrial concentration, would solve the material problems of the working class. A dose of paternalism, some conceded, might also be necessary. The more pessimistic demanded protectionist policies that would guarantee the businessman a privileged position in local markets and, by safeguarding the businessman, would safeguard the welfare of his workers. But all agreed that business, whether through the free play of market forces, a show of goodwill or an exercise of regulatory power could, acting alone or with minimal assistance from the state, resolve the social question. The rise of socialism and trade unionism threatened such fond hopes. A good many conservatives providentially discovered the virtues of the little man. His sober and regular habits gave promise of a more stable world. But he was to be valued most for his strategic social location, at the juncture where capital and labour met. The small shopkeeper, by virtue of his middling rank, blurred the lines of social cleavage and tempered the shock of the class struggle. A diminished confidence in the ability of business to solve the social question spawned a militant *Mittelstandspolitik*.[76]

It was necessary to rally all the healthy, independent forces of the nation. This meant, above all, rallying the *patronat*, the entire employing class, around the banner of social defence. As the deputy Failliot explained to the Third Congress of the Association: 'People speak of "big commerce", "little commerce", "big industry", "little industry"; but in my opinion, *messieurs*, this way of classifying things does not imply a division. There are *commerçants* and industrialists, and that's all there is to it as far as I'm concerned.'[77] A unified and organized business community could and would defeat the forces of socialism and revolutionary syndicalism. On the eve of the national elections of 1910, the Association, in conjunction with the Confederation, drew up an 'economic charter' which was circulated among prospective candidates. Endorsed by the nation's most important business associations, from pressure groups representing heavy industry (the *Comité des forges*, the *Comité des houillères*, the *Union des industries métallurgiques et minières*, etc.) to the Paris-based syndical chamber organizations headed by Pinard, Muzet, Marguery and others, the charter made plain the business community's determination to preserve the sanctity of private property, to combat the advance of the state (*étatisme*), and to resist social reform (specifically the income tax and the *repos hebdomadaire*).[78] In the fall of the same year, the *Comité de défense et d'études fiscales*, an offshoot of the Association chaired by Carmichael (a former president of the Confederation served as first vice-president), organized an impressive meeting at the Salle Wagram attended by more than 3500 businessmen. The meeting's keynote speaker was Raymond Poincaré, who, to frenetic applause, summed up the assembly's spirit in these terms:

> Yes, *messieurs*, it pleases me to repeat what the preceding speakers have said: we demand respect for private property, liberty for the private household, the right to secrecy for businessmen; we insist upon the regular operation of public services and the freedom of labour. But in so doing, it is not our intention to advance the cause of reaction, to oppose fiscal and financial reform with a preconceived hostility. But we do say no to the principles of inquisition and tyranny which, under the guise of progress, are being insinuated hypocritically into our laws.[79]

Still, it would be mistaken to view the employers' drive toward unity on the eve of World War I in purely negative terms. It was more than crudely anti-socialist as these words by Colrat suggest:

> It appears to me . . . that in the modern world, the common exercise of the same profession establishes tighter bonds between men than an identity of origin. . . . As for ourselves, we demand self-government for the professional constituency, for professional organizations; we want the same kind of administrative autonomy that our forebears won in by-gone years for the geographic constituency.
>
> We know the name used to dress up acts of sabotage, direct and deliberate attacks on the lives of citizens. This kind of syndicalism gives the word an evil

> reputation. The bourgeoisie must not allow professional organization to be confused with the organization of disorder, the *syndicat* to be confused with revolution.[80]

The Association advocated political decentralization in order to strengthen the *syndicat*. The devolution of state power, moreover, was expected to reinvigorate regional life, another project close to the hearts of middle-class militants. This programme could not be implemented, however, without first destroying the parliamentary oligarchy that smothered the nation's vital energies, and to this end, the Association supported proportional representation.

> By changing administrative structures, by enlarging electoral districts and giving a voice to minorities, proportional representation will little by little lead to the replacement of electoral committees with economic associations in the nomination and control of our elected representatives. We can even hope that such a system will bring us closer to a form of representation based on profession.[81]

Not all business groups, of course, were prepared to go this far, but there were some measures on which agreement was complete. At a second mass meeting of businessmen, held in 1913, the assembly repeated the same anti-socialist sentiments expressed in 1910; but it also proclaimed its staunch support for the three-year military service law. An impressive array of business interests, ranging from groups defending the small shopkeeper to those defending big business, lined up solidly to support the legislative centre piece of Poincaré's *réveil national*.[82]

The shopkeeper movement began in Paris in the 1880s as a defence of the little man against the consequences of large-scale organization; by 1914, it had been transformed into a national movement committed to Poincarist policies and enmeshed in an anti-socialist business coalition that pointed the way toward a new corporatism. The growing influence of conservative, often Catholic provincials who did not share in the radical traditions of the Paris shopkeeping community proved decisive in this transformation. The dislocation of the movement at the time of the Dreyfus affair facilitated the emergence of a new generation of militants. The provincials consolidated their position through an alliance with intellectuals, businessmen and politicians sympathetic to the shopkeepers' cause and anxious to exploit the conservative potential of *petit commerce*. In a complete turnabout, big business became the shopkeeper's surest ally and the employee his most determined opponent. The shopkeeper movement evolved away from the ideology of the *quartier* toward a syndicalist, if not corporatist perspective. Its passion for direct democracy was transmuted into a desire for professional representation. At the end of the century, the shopkeeper had seen society as divided in a struggle pitting the people (an amalgam of wage-earners and shopkeepers) against a centralizing oligarchy; by the eve of the war, the principal conflict dividing society had become the struggle between the middle classes on the one side, and on the other, the workers' movement in alliance with the interventionist state.

Elements of continuity, however, can be discerned amidst all these changes. The shopkeeper remained firm in his patriotism, particularist in his loyalties (whether to the *quartier* or the *syndicat*), and obstinate in his demands for a more direct and active role in government affairs. Throughout, shopkeeper ideology proclaimed the virtues of smallness, independence and family life. However unstable the life of the individual *petit commerçant* the place of the retailer in the social structure was sufficiently fixed to permit the emergence of a distinctive retailer world-view with recognizable constants. And, even though the principal focus of this study has been the metamorphosis of shopkeeper ideology, it would be mistaken to attach the epithet 'protean' or 'opportunist' to the retailer movement as though it were easily manipulated by cynical politicians and unscrupulous demagogues. If the movement evolved in the direction of nationalism at the turn of the century, it was in part because other political options were not available and in part because nationalism presented itself as the defender of values cherished by the shopkeeper and as the determined opponent of his most feared enemies. The same can be said of the shopkeeper movement's participation in the *réveil national*. In both cases, patriotism played an important role in determing the movement's political choices, but I have wanted to stress that other factors were at work as well. The nationalists always praised the courage of the little man in his struggle against a corrupt and oligarchical government. On the eve of the war, conservatives promised shopkeepers political and economic reforms that would increase their influence in the nation's affairs. The right, in other words, moved toward the shopkeeper as much as the shopkeeper moved toward the right.

The shopkeeper movement, in the period 1888–1914, moved from left to right, from Radicalism through nationalism to Poincarism. This political re-orientation, however, was but one aspect of a global transformation that involved profound changes both in the shopkeeper's conception of his place in the social and political life of the nation and in his actual relations with major institutions such as the state, organized business and the workers' movement.

NOTES

1 The rightward evolution of small shopkeepers, the lower middle class, *les classes moyennes* has been argued for by: Raoul Girardet, 'Pour une introduction à l'histoire du nationalisme français', *Revue française de science politique*, 1958, 522; René Rémond, *The Right Wing in France from 1815 to de Gaulle*, 2nd edn, Philadelphia, 1971, 216; Paul Rutkoff, 'Revanche and revision: Paul Déroulède and the Ligue des Patriotes, 1897–1900', PhD thesis, University of Pennsylvania, 1971, 199–200; D. R. Watson, 'The nationalist movement in Paris, 1900–1906', in D. Shapiro (ed.), *The Right in France, 1890–1919*, London, 1962, 80.

2 Save in passing, I do not propose to discuss in this study the economic and social origins of retailer demands nor the reactions of political parties and other pressure groups to the rise of the shopkeeper movement. These themes are treated in more depth in my PhD dissertation, 'Commerce and culture in *fin de siècle* Paris', Columbia University, 1982. They have already been treated in summary fashion or in relation to countries other

than France in: Arno Mayer, 'The lower middle class as historical problem', *Journal of Modern History*, 1975, 409–36; R. Gellately, *The Politics of Economic Despair. Shopkeepers and German Politics, 1890–1914*, London, 1975; Heinrich Winkler, *Mittelstand, Demokratie und Nationalsozialismus, Die Politishe Entickwicklung von Handwerk und Kleinhandel in der Weimarer Republik*, Cologne, 1975; G. Crossick, 'The emergence of the lower middle class in Britain: a discussion', in G. Crossick (ed.), *The Lower Middle Class in Britain*, London, 1977, 11–60; Richard Hofstadter, *The Age of Reform*, New York, 1955.

3 In 1894, the *Ligue syndicale* claimed 148,000 adherents, or 10.5 per cent of the some 1,411,396 retailers who paid the business tax or *patente* (schedule A) in 1890. It has been estimated that the CGT in 1902 had only 100,000 members. Cf. 'Partie officielle', *La Revendication*, 31 January 1894; L. Christophe, 'A Mme Carnot', *La Revendication*, 30 June 1894; Etienne Martin Saint-Léon, *Le Petit Commerce français*, Paris, 1911, 19; E. Dolléans, 'Les temps héroïques du syndicalisme (1892–1902)', *L'Homme réel*, 1937, 21. The figure of 148,000, however, should be taken with a grain of salt. *Chambres syndicales* were allowed to affiliate to the League collectively; their members were thereafter counted as *ligueurs*, whether or not they paid dues to the League or took any part in its activities. As for the League's social composition, several hypotheses can be advanced. On the basis of a preliminary analysis of several fragmentary membership lists, it appears that the League recruited with most success among clothing merchants and retailers of luxury goods, located in Paris's central *arrondissements*. A *ligueur*'s clientèle was thus more likely to be bourgeois than working class, and he himself to live in relative comfort than on the brink of proletarianization.

4 E. Berry, 'Ni politique, ni religion', *La Crise commerciale*, 15 April 1888; 'Les vampires du commerce', *La Crise commerciale*, 15 November 1887.

5 'Séances des comités et groupes', *L'Union démocratique*, 17 January 1887; 'Rédaction', *L'Union démocratique*, 3 January 1887.

6 La Rédaction, 'Notre programme', *L'Union démocratique*, 3 January 1887.

7 Pierre du Marroussem, *La Question ouvrière*, vol. III, *Le Jouet Parisien*, Paris, 1894, 271; 'Christophe', *La Revendication*, 7 March 1889.

8 'Projet de revision de la loi sur les patentes', *La Revendication*, 30 May 1889; 'Elections municipales du 16 avril 1893', *La Revendication*, 16 April 1893.

9 Louis Gazon, 'A votre tour, Mesdames', *La Revendication*, 31 October 1896.

10 A. Girard, 'Election municipale', *L'Union démocratique*, 16 July 1887; Le Comité autonomiste, radical, socialiste et commercial du quartier Bonne-Nouvelle, 'A. Girard', 16 July 1887.

11 La Rédaction, 'Programme de *La Revendication*', *La Revendication*, 5 July 1888; Gustave Fabius, 'Les libertés commerciales au XIXe siècle', *La Revendication*, 24 August 1890.

12 E. Rabasse, 'Le question de l'intermédiaire dans le "*Radical*"', *La Revendication*, 12 January 1890.

13 Archives of the Prefecture of Police, Paris (APP), B/a 1467, 12 February 1890; and list of officers published in *La Revendication*, 31 December 1894.

14 E. Rabasse, 'N'est-ce pas le moment?', *La Revendication*, 10 January 1889.

15 'Le commerce et les élections du 27 janvier', *L'Union démocratique*, 31 January 1889.

16 In an *exposé des motifs* attached to the bill, the slow progress of *patente* reform was blamed on the recent political crisis. The shopkeeper, the *exposé* argued, was essentially a friend of order. Protection of his welfare was the surest guarantee against a recurrence of such disturbances in the future. Archives Nationales (AN C5498).

17 Edouard Drumont, *La Fin d'un monde*, Paris, 1889, 40–1.

18 APP B/a 1193, Clipping from *L'Assaut*, 27 April 1890.

19 APP B/a 1104, 6 April 1897.

20 E. Rabasse, 'M. Drumont', *La Revendication*, 26 June 1892; Edouard Drumont, 'La candidature Floquet', *La Libre Parole*, 29 December 1893; 'Comité de centralisation', *La Revendication*, 24 July 1892.
21 APP B/a 1193, Clipping from *L'assaut*, 27 April 1890.
22 See, for example, APP B/a 1104, 28 November 1895.
23 APP B/a 1092, 2 March 1898.
24 'Comité de centralisation', *La Revendication*, 2 May 1889; APP B/a 1517, 28 April 1894.
25 'Pas de politique', *La Revendication*, 15 May 1895.
26 Pierre Sorlin, *La Croix et les juifs*, Paris, 1967, 64. The account given below of the *Union fraternelle*'s way of thinking is based on information found in the *Bulletin de l'Union fraternelle de l'industrie et du commerce*. Harmel summed up the *Union fraternelle* point of view in a speech reprinted in the July 1897 issue of the *Bulletin*, 2–4.
27 'Réponse à *La Croix*', *Affiches Tourangelles*, 11 November 1897; 'Rapport', *Bulletin de l'Union fraternelle*, October 1897.
28 'Congrès national catholique', *La Croix*, 5–6 December 1897.
29 'Manifeste de la Ligue de défense du petit commerce', *La Croix*, 4 May 1898; 'Manifeste de la Ligue de défense du petit commerce', *Bulletin de l'Union fraternelle*, March 1898.
30 'La conférence de M. Christophe', *Bulletin de l'Union fraternelle*, December 1898.
31 Sénat, *année 1900, session ordinaire, annexe au procès-verbal de la séance du 4 avril 1900*, 'Rapport fait au nom de la commission des patentes . . .', no. 141, Paris, 1900, 98.
32 Christophe apparently risked bankruptcy to keep the League afloat. See 'Pas d'argent, pas de Suisse', *La Défense commerciale et industrielle*, 28 September 1902.
33 'Avis aux présidents des groupes de défense commerciale', *Affiches Tourangelles*, 4 July 1901.
34 See, for example, the article by Jules Guesde, 'Socialisez', *Le Socialiste*, 14 January 1888; and Jean Jaurès, *Oeuvre de Jean Jaurès*, vol. IV, Paris, 1933, 41.
35 APP B/a 153, 7 August 1890; 'Comité de centralisation', *La Revendication*, 31 March 1895; APP B/a 153, 3 February 1894; see also brochure distributed at 10 February 1899 meeting of the *Chambre syndicale des employés*.
36 APP B/a 1032, 11 October 1898.
37 *La République française:* 'Le banquet du commerce et de l'industrie', 16 October 1897; 'République réaliste', 17 October 1897.
38 'Ligue syndicale pour la défense des intérêts du travail, de l'industrie et du commerce', *L'Union nationale du commerce et de l'industrie*, 11 October 1890; 'Syndicat général', *L'Union nationale du commerce et de l'industrie*, 7 January 1893; 'Banquet de dimanche', *La Croix*, 9 October 1897.
39 'Banquet de dimanche', *La Croix*, 9 October 1897.
40 'Commerce et politique', *L'Epicerie Française*, 6 March 1898.
41 Gérault-Richard, 'Le petit commerce', *La Petite République*, 9 May 1900; *Le temps*, 12 May 1902; 'Chronique', *Bulletin mensuel du commerce et de l'industrie*, May 1902; APP B/a 944, 29 October 1901. The nationalists were perfectly aware that 'the class which, without taking an active part in politics, constituted the largest part of their majority', was 'composed of shopkeepers, *boutiquiers* and the like'. They were also aware of how tenuous their grip on this constituency was.
42 Guillaume Vidal, 'Bravo, *L'épicerie*', *L'Epicerie Française*, 4 June 1899.
43 'La démission de M. Marguery', *L'Ami des petits commerçants*, 5 May 1902; 'Pourri par le nationalisme', *Le Radical*, 21 April 1902. Marguery returned, however, to the presidency of the *Comité* later in 1902 after electoral tempers had cooled down.
44 Sylviano, 'Simple Note', *L'Idéal*, 3 June 1906.
45 'Demain', *La Petite République*, 15 May 1900.
46 'Le petit commerce', *L'Aurore*, 29 April 1902.

47 See, for example, the poster 'Commerçants, défendez-vous' in support of the nationalist candidate Daniel Cloutier (4th *arrondissement*). APP B/a 209.

48 'Chambre syndicale des marchands de chaussures en détail du département de la Seine', *L'Union des syndicats de France*, 1 June 1899.

49 APP B/a 209.

50 'Ligue du parti commercial des départements du Centre', *Affiches Tourangelles*, 6 January 1898.

51 Joseph Bernard, 'Du mouvement d'organisation et de défense du petit commerce français', *thèse de droit*, University of Paris, 1906, 86.

52 'Le parti commercial', *Affiches Tourangelles*, 27 June 1901.

53 'Aux commerçants, aux industriels!', *La Défense commerciale et industrielle*, 21 September 1902.

54 'Congrès de la pâtisserie française', *Bulletin officiel de la Fédération des groupes commerciaux et industriels*, March 1906, 24.

55 A.R., 'Les économistes politiques et la classe moyenne', *Bulletin officiel de la Fédération*, December 1905, 12.

56 ibid.; see also, 'Les achats en commun', *Bulletin officiel de la Fédération*, December 1904; A. Robiquet, 'L'enseignement commercial et industriel', *Bulletin officiel de la Fédération*, December 1904; L. Gauss, 'Role de la Banque Populaire', *Bulletin officiel de la Confédération* (the periodical changed its title in January 1907), August–September 1907.

57 The Confederation very early on referred to itself as 'the most important organization of the middle classes': 'Rapport', *Bulletin officiel de la Fédération*, October 1905, 11. In 1908, the Confederation organized a special *Comité d'études pour l'organisation des classes moyennes*: Alfred Aunis, 'Organisation économique des classes moyennes', *Bulletin officiel de la Confédération*, September 1908, 78. For the Confederation's aggressive intentions *vis-à-vis* the labour movement, see A. Trépreau, 'Nécessité et urgence d'un programme général économique', *Bulletin officiel de la Confédération*, April 1907, 12.

58 'Allocution de M. de Paloméra', *Bulletin officiel de la Confédération*, March 1913, 44; 'Compte-rendu du lle Congrès national, discours de M. Guist'hau', *Bulletin officiel de la Confédération*, March–April 1913, 38.

59 'Compte-rendu du Congrès national', *Bulletin officiel de la Confédération*, March–April 1911, 37; 'Séance du conseil confédéral', *Bulletin officiel de la Confédération*, January–February, 1912, 3.

60 *Premier Congrès international de la petite bourgeoisie, compte-rendu sténographique, tenu à Anvers les 17 et 18 septembre 1899*, Brussels, 1900, 69; *Deuxième Congrès international de la petite bourgeoisie, compte-rendu sténographique, tenu à Namur les 15 et 16 septembre 1901*, Namur, 1902, 135.

61 Hector Lambrechts, 'L'internationalisme et les classes moyennes', *Bulletin mensuel de l'Institut international pour l'étude du problème des classes moyennes*, January 1911, 75.

62 See, for example, 'Rapport du président, M. Robiquet', *Bulletin officiel de la Fédération*, October 1906, 15.

63 'M. Jacques Piou à Cognac', *L'Action Libérale Populaire*, 8 June 1905; *Action Libérale Populaire, compte-rendu du cinquième congrès général tenu à Paris les 3, 4, 5, et 6 decembre 1908*, Paris, 1909, 34ff.

64 'Composition de bureaux', *L'Union nationale du commerce et de l'industrie*, 25 March 1905.

65 Maus and a representative of the *Chambre syndicale des employés*, Martinet, exchanged recriminations before a session of the municipal *Commission d'examen des demandes de dérogations*. Martinet accused Maus of distributing a flier '*Le cri d'alarme*' containing the charges and incitements described above. Maus made no attempt at denial but replied

with a counter-accusation that the *employés* were responsible for the inflammatory posters entitled '*A coup de fusil*' and '*Le sang coulera*'. See *Conseil municipal de Paris, Commission d'examen des demandes de dérogations, séance du 20 décembre 1906*. A copy of the document can be found at the archives of the *Confédération des commerçants-détaillants de France et d'outremer*, 10 rue du Château d'Eau, Paris.

66 See, for example, AN F^7 13718, clipping from *L'Humanité*, 15 May 1910.

67 AN F^7 13718, 1 July 1907, clipping from *L'Action ouvrière*, 15 March 1910.

68 See *Mémoire relatif aux concessions sur la voie publique addressé au Conseil municipal de Paris*, Paris, 1907, 3; this document is conserved at the archives of the *Confédération des commerçants-détaillants*.

69 'M. Poincaré chez les commerçants détaillants', *Le Temps*, 6 June 1907; 'Assemblée générale du 29 mars', *Bulletin mensuel de la Fédération des commerçants-détaillants de France*, March 1909.

70 AN F^7 13718, 12 June 1907.

71 'M. Puech', *La Petite République*, 26 May 1900.

72 Frédéric Clément, 'Les commerçants et la politique', *La République française*, 15 January 1910.

73 The information presented in this paragraph was culled from a variety of sources: Louis Guitard's *La Petite Histoire de la IIIe République*, Paris, 1959; letters from Colrat to Poincaré contained in the *Papiers Poincaré*, Bibliothèque Nationale NAF 15997; and an interview (22 November 1977) very graciously accorded me by Maurice Colrat's son, Bernard Colrat.

74 'Conseil', *Les Etudes fiscales et sociales*, November–December 1909, 1.

75 AN 27 AS 1, *Association de l'industrie et de l'agriculture française, Assemblée générale*, 5 March 1902, 93.

76 The *Association de défense* quite consciously imitated the example set by middle-class defence movements in central Europe. Colrat and his colleagues explicitly used the German word '*Mittelstandspolitik*' to describe their own activities. Maurice Colrat, 'Vers l'équilibre social', *Les Etudes fiscales et sociales*, August–September 1909, 6; 'Le problème des classes moyennes', *Les Etudes fiscales et sociales*, July 1909, 27.

77 'Troisième Congrès annuel, 14–17 novembre 1910', *Les Etudes fiscales et sociales*, November–December (?) 1910, 358.

78 'La charte économique', *Bulletin officiel de la Confédération*, January–February 1910, 2–3.

79 'Salle Wagram', *L'Union des syndicats patronaux de l'industrie textile de France*, November–December 1913 (annexe), 265.

80 'Troisième Congrès annuel, 14–17 novembre 1910', *Les Etudes fiscales et sociales*, November–December (?) 1910, 26–7.

81 Maurice Colrat, 'Vers l'équilibre social', *Les Etudes fiscales et sociales*, August–September 1909.

82 'La situation financière de la France', *L'Union des syndicats patronaux de l'industrie textile de France*, November–December 1913 (annexe), 403–4.

9 The artisan family in nineteenth-century Austria: *embourgeoisement* of the petite bourgeoisie?

JOSEF EHMER

Social historians have in recent years become increasingly interested in the role of the family in the formation of the class structure of industrial capitalist society. A central issue in this discussion is the way in which different social groups and classes developed, in the course of the transition to industrial societies, common features of what we think of as the 'modern family', or adopted elements of the bourgeois family ideal.[1] A different approach uses family relations to measure the density of social relations within classes, or for social distance between classes.[2] Both the theoretical and empirical aspects of this research have tended to focus on the working class, with a lesser degree of attention to the bourgeoisie. In contrast there has been hardly any discussion of the lower middle class in general, or of its individual components, such as master artisans.[3] In spite of the growing interest in the study of the lower middle class, social history has not yet applied to that subject the level of theoretical, methodological and empirical discussion which characterizes its analysis of other social classes.[4]

This limited knowledge contrasts with the commonly held and mostly unquestioned assumptions about the history of the artisan family. The traditional view sees the social life of artisans as characterized by a highly developed and dense pattern of family relations which seem to have been based on both the needs of the family as a working unit and on the handing down of profession and enterprise from father to son.[5] These assumptions can also be found in those recent studies of the political development of master artisans at the end of the nineteenth century which seek to explain their tendency to adopt reactionary and even pre-fascist ideologies in response to economic and social change.[6] The assumption that handicrafts declined during industrialization has been subjected to major criticism, and the argument has now shifted ground, emphasizing a decline of traditional culture and life-style, which are seen as rooted in distinctive family relations. Shulamit Volkov, in her study of German master artisans, writes: 'A single master or a childless married one was indeed a rarity. The family unit was a necessary complement to the traditional craft workshop, and the masters attached ideological and cultural values to it.'[7] She argues further on that the greater the pressure on the traditional family-orientated life-style of master artisans at the end of the nineteenth century grew, the more a patriarchal and authoritarian family ideology became a central point of their 'popular anti-modern ideal'.[8]

Certain things have been taken for granted about the traditional family life of artisans and the way it developed which have had considerable influence on the way that the general social and economic development of this group, and even its political behaviour in the late nineteenth century, have been interpreted. A long historical period is thus at issue, stretching at the very least from the eighteenth to the early twentieth centuries. Research on this subject is only in its early stages, which means that we are operating on somewhat uncertain ground. Yet I think current research allows one to stress three points, which fit uneasily with received orthodoxy. Firstly, the traditional master artisans' mode of life was not as family orientated as is usually assumed. Secondly, the industrial revolution led to a variety of family forms, though for most artisans traditional features predominated over modern ones. Thirdly, in developing a modern family structure, master artisans, or at least the leading ones, followed the pattern of the industrial bourgeoisie rather than that of the lower classes. These are the problems with which I am concerned in this essay. My evidence is based on Austrian – mainly Viennese – sources and, as far as possible, quantitative evidence has been used.[9]

TRADITIONAL ARTISANS

One of the most important results of research into historical family forms is the stress on the specific meaning of family in different socio-economic formations. In central Europe the term 'family' itself was not in common use up to the eighteeenth century. The 'house' (*Haus*) was considered the basic social unit, meaning a group of persons living and working together, some – but not all – of whom would be related to the head of the household.[10] Within this general pattern the family forms of traditional artisans showed specific differences from the family forms of other social classes in 'Old Europe'.[11] The handicraft mode of life was strongly shaped by the guild system, which regulated not only economic relations, but also social, legal, religious and other affairs.[12] The individual artisan's family had only limited autonomy within this system of control. All the important stages in the artisan life-cycle – such as apprenticeship, working and tramping as a journeyman, marrying and setting up as an independent master – were a matter not of individual strategies but of collective rules. The labour force of the workshop was provided, limited and controlled by the guild. It was chiefly based on apprentices, journeymen and female servants, with only partial use of the master's wife and children.[13] The freedom to work the trade was given to an individual master for his lifetime, and it expired at his death. The right to practise the craft – which rested on the right to use a specific workshop – was therefore not usually handed down from the master to one of his sons. At an old master's death it returned to the guild which would pass it to a new master while bearing in mind the needs of the old master's widow and daughters. Marrying them might be the only way of getting a trade. Therefore it was frequently transferred via a daughter to a son-in-law, or via a master's widow to her second or third husband. If the master's sons did follow their father's calling they usually served their apprenticeship in the house of another craftsman. Afterwards they were expected to tramp for some years, and if they too managed to set up themselves as masters, it was unlikely to be in their father's house or even town.[14]

All these peculiarities derive from the master artisan's economic status, which was not based on private property in the modern bourgeois sense but on property that was guild bound. Some authors stress the 'traditional collectivity' of this handicraft mode of life, in contrast to 'modern individuality'.[15] This context has to be kept in mind when we deal with the traditional artisan's family. This picture is inevitably an idealized one. A more differentiated view would require attention to change over time, as well as to the differences within and between crafts. Trades which are usually not organized in guilds, like innkeepers, or others with long traditions of wage labour, like the building trades, show divergent social relations. The same happened where bourgeois private property developed within the guild system. The guild system itself was systematically weakened in the course of the eighteenth and early nineteenth centuries by the authorities as well as by the growing market economy, and was finally abolished in Austria in 1859. Yet in this process some of its elements obviously survived, partly because they fitted into new economic and social conditions, partly because of the persistence of cultural traditions.[16]

Quantitative evidence of the strength of, and change within, the traditional master artisan's mode of life can be obtained for only parts of the system rather than the whole, and I have decided to concentrate upon the situation and fate of sons, for this is generally seen as a core element in the traditional artisanal family. Having children of juvenile age at home, and spending a lot of material and emotional energy on them, is a dominating feature of the 'modern family'. The same – though in patriarchal terms and based on the dominance of the male sex – was an important element in the 'bourgeois mode of family life' as it developed structurally and ideologically within the educated and industrial bourgeoisie during the nineteenth century.[17] As a result, information about the position of sons in master artisans' households should give quantitative evidence about the extent of the trend from traditional family forms to the 'modern family', and should also show how far artisans adopted elements of the bourgeois family ideal. This will contribute additionally to any discussion of the social gap between bourgeoisie and petite bourgeoisie, and its growth or diminution.

We can obtain such an indicator if we use listings of inhabitants. If we examine the households of master artisans, the presence of sons older than twelve years (generally the lowest age for starting an apprenticeship) and older than twenty years

Table 8 *Juvenile and adult sons in the households of master artisans*

	1754	*1762*	*1794*	*1827*	*1850*	*1857*	*1880*	*1919*
Percentage of households with sons 12 years and older								
Provincial towns (n)								
Perchtoldsdorf (62/84/69)	16.1					23.8	49.2	
Gmunden (150)		20.7						
Stein (60/69)		28.3				47.7		
Salzburg (302)			22.8					
Freistadt (183)								34.4
Viennese districts (n)								
Gumpendorf (154/728)				35.1		27.2		
Sechshaus (80)					33.8			
Herrengasse (57)						33.9		
Schottenfeld (348)						31.5		
Hernals (191)							24.6	
Percentage of households with sons 20 years and older								
Provincial towns								
Perchtoldsdorf	6.5					16.7	25.4	
Gmunden		7.3						
Stein		5.0				22.1		
Salzburg			9.6					
Freistadt								19.1
Viennese districts								
Gumpendorf				14.3		12.2		
Sechshaus					13.8			
Herrengasse						15.3		
Schottenfeld						10.9		
Hernals							11.5	

Sources: Listings of inhabitants in the collection of the 'Familie im sozialen Wandel' research project at the Institut für Wirtschafts- und Sozialgeschichte, University of Vienna.

(by which age apprenticeships should have finished) will indicate both the working presence of juvenile sons, and the possibilities of succession to their father's trade. Table 8 presents such data for some small provincial towns of the eighteenth and nineteenth centuries and for specific Viennese districts of the nineteenth century.

We can see that in the eighteenth century the numbers are rather low. Only a minority of the master artisans' households include juvenile or even adult sons. This must be partly due to the specific demographic situation of urban artisans. The number of their children was limited by late age of marriage, by large age differences between the spouses (e.g. the widespread re-marriage of widows) and high rates of infant mortality. Nor should we completely exclude the practice of birth control among traditional artisans, which may have been caused by the absence of a need for children either in the household's labour force or as security against illness and old age.[18] Yet, the most important factor is none of these, but the practice of leaving home, which detached male children from their families.

Other data provide the same conclusions on the transfer of a trade. Continuous lists of masters from the eighteenth and early nineteenth centuries have survived in many crafts. As Table 9 shows, it was very rare for a master to have the same surname as his predecessor, thus eliminating the possibility that a son had followed his father. This is virtually absent from some trades while in no others did it reach more than a quarter of all transfers of trade. All the examples presented in Table 9 are taken from the wealthier trades, which were sometimes linked to the ownership of a house. That means that even in cases where substantial capital was involved – a matter of little importance amongst crafts such as tailors and shoemakers – patrilineal inheritance was unusual. Inheritance of the profession is a different matter. The guilds usually offered better opportunities to sons of masters than to others. Although we hardly find a family carrying on with the same workshop, handicraft dynasties are a different matter, and some existed for centuries in different places at different times, but always within the same trade.[19]

Generally, though our evidence remains limited and scattered, we can assume that the life career of a traditional artisan was influenced far more strongly by his attachment to a guild rather than to a family. In the artisan's mode of life collective social relations played a more important role than family relations.

THE ARTISAN FAMILY AND SOCIAL CHANGE

From the eighteenth century a growing capitalist market economy, early forms of industrialization, and attempts by the authorities to encourage a more liberal and efficient commercial system all had an increasing effect on the traditional artisan mode of life. A variety of family forms developed from the traditional pattern, according to the position of different handicrafts within the process of economic and social change.

New forms of family life, in sharp contrast to the traditional form, can be first detected among those master artisans whose trades were developing in a capitalist

Table 9 *Transfer of trades amongst Austrian artisans*

Trade and period	*Number of changes of trade*	*Number of changes between persons of same surname*	*%*
Gingerbread-makers (*Lebzelter*)[1]			
Lower Austria + Vienna 1659–1851	375	92	24.5
(Seventeenth century			14.8)
(Eighteenth century			27.6)
(Nineteenth century			31.3)
Barber-surgeons[2] (*Bg. Bader + Barbiere*)			
Vienna 1740–1790	60	2	3.3
Viennese suburbs 1745–1805	185	8	4.3
Silk-weavers[3] (*Seidenzeugmacher*)			
Vienna 1733–1755	50[a]	12	24.0
Nail-makers[4] (*Nagelschmiede*)			
Country masters, Lower Austria 1762–1785	7[b]	1	14.3
Lace-makers[5] (*Posamentierer*)			
Vienna 1804–1829	133	17[c]	12.8
Bakers[6] (*Bäcker*)			
Vienna 1815–1820	31	7	22.6
1899–1901	46	14	30.4
Carpenters[7] (*Tischler*)			
Vienna 1889–1914	378	28	7.4
	Number of new masters	*Sons of Viennese masters among them*	*%*
Tailors[8] (*Kleidermacher*)			
Vienna 1825	54	4	7.4
1836	102	11	10.8
1845	112	5	4.5
1859	154	5	3.2
	Number of masters	*Surnames at least twice in list*	*%*
Goldsmiths[9] (*Gold- u. Silberschmiede*)			
Vienna 1851	528	56	10.6
1890	545	140	27.7
	Number of boys completing apprenticeship	*Number who had served in father's workshop*	*%*
Gold wire-pullers[10] (*Golddrahtzieher*)			
Vienna 1757–1800	79	12	15.2
1801–1835	119	31	26.0
1836–1849	56	5	8.9
1850–1861	137	7	5.1

continued

Sources:

1 Mitterauer, Familienbetriebliche Struktur, 201 (see note 14 for full details).
2 Ch. Steiner, 'Die Bader und Barbiere (Wundärzte) in Wien zur Zeit Maria Theresias (1740–1780)', PhD thesis, Vienna, 1975.
3 Meisterbuch, WStLA, Innungen-Bücher 50/1.
4 Meisterbuch, Archiv der Wiener Schlosserinnung.
5 Protokoll, WStLA, Innungen-Bücher 41/1.
6 Kalender, Archiv der Wiener Bäckerinnung.
7 Grundbuch der Tischler Genossenschaft 1888–1914, Archiv der Tischlergenossenschaft, fol. 1–500.
8 Einverleibungsbuch, WStLA, Innungen-Bücher 29/16.
9 Verzeichnis, WStLA, Innungen-Akten A88.
10 Freisprechungsprotokolle, WStLA, Innungen-Bücher 21/1 fol. 1–96.

Notes:

a Includes 7 marriages of widows or daughters.
b Includes 5 marriages of widows.
c All are definitely changes from father to son.

direction. This may have been a small minority, of course, but as a group their ideology and social behaviour were influential. Early examples of this transformation from master to entrepreneur can be found among the scythe foundries in the upper Austrian mountains. In the seventeenth and eighteenth centuries some of these foundries had become highly capitalized, often combining production with commerce and employing dozens of workers. The owners of these foundries established a dense family network, to the extent that in 1784 five families owned half the hundred or so foundries. These scythe-making dynasties had also devised successful rules to pass the family property along the male line, from fathers to sons. In fact we can find families where this happened continuously from the sixteenth to the nineteenth centuries.[20]

Silk weaving was the most advanced trade in eighteenth- and early nineteenth-century Vienna. The guild of silk weavers was established under government protection in 1711. As in other absolutist states, the Austrian authorities tried to promote new industries by recruiting from abroad trained artisans along with their families.[21] A large number of early Viennese silk weavers were immigrants from northern Italy.[22] It was not uncommon for brothers to come to Vienna together, and they would be followed by other relatives. Between 1711 and 1745 nine members of the Locatelli family from Bergamo became master weavers in Vienna, with the first Viennese-born Locatelli becoming a member of the guild in 1736. Dense family relations of this kind among early silk weavers derive from their specific recruitment pattern, and it contrasted with the pattern of social reproduction amongst traditional artisans. As time passed, only a small minority of silk weavers were able to maintain their family traditions. In the first half of the eighteenth century not more than 24 per cent of all changes of trade occurred between persons of the same surname (Table 9). It is significant that almost all of these were not only master weavers but also owners of *Fabrikprivilegien*, the freedom to run an enterprise outside guild control. They were also the dominant group within the guild, the richest, generally its leaders (*Zunftmeister*), and the persons whom the authorities made responsible for the quality of production (*Beschaumeister*). If one examines the forty-two wills from members of the silk weaver's guild that have survived for the period 1711 to 1792, one finds no property at all in seventeen cases and only a little in a further seventeen. On the other hand, eight persons left property worth more than 10,000 gulden, and all were members of families with businesses that were handed on for several generations.[23] This was the new form of master artisan family continuity.

In the last decades of the eighteenth and the first decades of the nineteenth centuries silk weaving in Vienna reached its peak. At the turn of the century it involved up to a fifth of the Viennese labour force. The labour organization was complex but dominated by the putting-out system (*Verlag*): large manufacturers or merchants did employ workers in centralized workshops, but they mainly gave out silk to formally independent master weavers and to journeymen. The result was a widening social gap between those master weavers who established themselves as manufacturers and the mass of the others who worked for them, though both groups were independent masters and members of the guild.

The family histories of individual manufacturers give evidence of the importance of the family in stabilizing their social and economic position, and securing its intergenerational continuity. Sons came to be seen as the 'natural' means to transfer wealth, capital and family identity from one generation to the next in these more capitalistic enterprises. Family strategy involved educating them carefully and binding them in the long term to the family enterprise. Paul Mestrozzi was born in 1771, the son of a very poor silk weaver, and started as an outdoor worker for a large manufacturer, but in the 1810s he owned one of the largest silk enterprises of Vienna, employing at times over 600 individuals inside and outside his factory. In his memoirs he described the education of his two sons: they served as ordinarily indentured apprentices, but were in addition trained in painting, technological subjects, commercial law, book-keeping and in the Italian language.[24] Such an extensive training tied sons to their father's house for many years, though it did not preclude temporary absences. Laurenz Kühtreiber, who obtained the freedom of the company in 1827, wrote to the guild that he had been an apprentice in his father's factory for six years, then had worked in Germany and France for four years and had finally been engaged again in his father's workshop for three years, during which time he also studied painting at the academy of arts.[25] The marriage strategy of these rich master weavers involved seeking ties to large capital or alternatively to those social groups with high status or influence such as nobles, state officials and professionals. Josef Adensamer began as a journeyman and became a master weaver in the 1820s. By 1830 he was employing twenty-two journeymen, and in the process of continuous expansion. His eldest son received some technical education, studied Italian and French and for several years lived with business friends of his father's in Germany and Switzerland. In 1855, at the age of twenty-five, he became his father's associate, at the same time as a nephew who had also grown up in Josef Adensamer's household. In 1859 he married the daughter of a professor at the polytechnic institute. The second son attended the Schottengymnasium, one of the most famous élite schools of Vienna, subsequently going to university and becoming a lawyer. The final son graduated from the more practically orientated *Realschule* and obtained his work in his father's factory. He subsequently became director of a silk mill in Riva, bought by his father to supply the Viennese factory, and married there an Italian countess. Of the two daughters of Josef Adensamer one married another silk manufacturer, the other a high civil servant. This pattern continued in the following generations, establishing kinship ties with other capitalists, state officials, university professors and other high status families.[26]

The structure of the household, revealed in census lists, shows the importance of the family for this social group. Amongst master artisans as a whole, it was only those who had left their petit-bourgeois background and become prosperous entrepreneurs, whose households contained three-generation families, with adult and even married sons living together with their spouse and children in the father's household.[27]

At the other extreme stood the poor master weavers who worked for these large manufacturers, for they too reveal a specific family structure that was different from that of the traditional handicrafts pattern. As guild rules were continuously relaxed in the textile trades, journeymen became both legally and economically capable of marrying and founding households of their own. Small master artisans thus lost a traditional method of controlling dependent labour by including it within the household. As silk weaving required auxiliary workers, it became increasingly necessary to use the labour of members of the family. The family work units in this trade were created not by artisan tradition, but by the reverse, the destruction of this tradition by the establishment of the capitalist manufacturing system with the economic and social transformations that went with it. The households of master weavers, when compared with other crafts, show both the lowest numbers of apprentices and journeymen and the highest numbers of juvenile sons staying at home and having the same occupation as their fathers. It is only among the silk weavers that we can find large numbers of married journeymen with households of their own, the structure of which look much like those of master artisans.[28]

The experiences of both the rich and the poor masters in textiles were substantially different from those in the food trades such as baking, where work organization and technology hardly changed in the eighteenth and nineteenth centuries. The trade was closely regulated by the authorities, and the number of masters was kept low. As a result, the masters remained a relatively homogeneous social group, and virtually all of them were able to take advantage of the growing population of Vienna. It was rare to find any of these master bakers in the lower tax groups and most of them had between half-a-dozen and a dozen journeymen and apprentices in their households.

There is an ambiguity about the baker's family. On the one hand, we can see elements of the traditional artisans' mode of life, like apprenticeship outside the home and tramping by journeymen. On the other hand, there was a trend towards the inheritance of the trade through the male line which, if not overwhelming, was certainly more advanced among bakers than among other traditional crafts. The successors of eighteen of the thirty-one Viennese master bakers who died between 1815 and 1820 have been clearly identified. In nine cases the bakery was carried on by the widow, but only one of these remained alone. Four widows married again, and another four ran the bakery for some years, until a son grew up and became a master, at which point he took over the trade. In one extreme case this took twelve years. Widows sometimes remained in their son's households after handing over the trade. Of the other cases, the bakery was transferred to a stranger in six of them, and directly to a son in only three.

Another distinctive feature of the bakers was that they usually did not work until their death but could afford to retire. All but two of the fourteen masters who died between 1815 and 1820 at over sixty years of age were already retired. Some of them had even left Vienna to spend their old age in the countryside, sometimes at corn mills that they owned, sometimes even on small estates. In a similar fashion to the silk weavers, the richest of the bakers would hold official positions such as that of civil flour observer (*k.k. Mehl-Beschauer*) or municipal flour measurers (*magistratischer Mehl-Messer*).[29]

If we turn to the majority of Vienna's traditional crafts we find a pattern of development different from both the complete transformation that characterized the textile trades and the relative stability amongst the bakers. These must be analysed within the context of the specific socio-economic conditions of small-scale production in the metropolis. The economic development of eighteenth-century Vienna was characterized by the rapid growth of domestic production in textiles, mainly silk weaving. From the early decades of the nineteenth century the industrial revolution transformed the economic structure of the city. As the possibilities of mechanization grew, textile manufacturers founded factories in the countryside. By the middle of the nineteenth century the Viennese domestic textile industry was undergoing a rapid and dramatic decline.[30]

The factory industries such as machine building, on the other hand, were at an early stage of development, and they did not become significant until the last decades of the century. It was the expansion of small-scale production that was the characteristic feature of the economic development of Vienna in the middle decades of the nineteenth century. The expanding market for consumer goods combined with a rapid improvement of the transport system to produce a shift to ready-made and standardized mass production in many crafts, mostly in the clothing and garment trades, and in the wood- and metalworking industries. The organization of this expanding small-scale production was complex: if some masters produced directly for consumers, most worked for large retailers, manufacturers or merchants, who opened up the world market for small-scale production. For the master artisans this meant, on the one hand, subordination to the interests of the larger entrepreneurs or, more generally, to the economic laws of the capitalist market. The result was a social and economic instability, a 'sporadic and syncopated rhythm of work' as Bruce Laurie has called it.[31] On the other hand this meant participation in an expanding market and perhaps the opportunity to enlarge the workshop. A result of this duality of both pressure and opportunity was the high degree of differentiation that emerged among the master artisans, between crafts but also within them.

These seem to be common features of this stage of industrialization, when artisan production is drawn into the capitalist market economy by subordination under the *Verlagssystem*. A speciality of Vienna – and perhaps the central European pattern – was the fact that this development took place with the continuing dominance of formally independent master artisans and a general continuation of their traditional labour relations.[32] During this period of expansion master artisans satisfied their needs for dependent labour in the same way that they had done previously, by taking apprentices and journeymen into their households, but they did so now in large and unlimited numbers. Those who benefited from the new economic opportunities sometimes had more than two dozen of them living in. In the Viennese suburb of Gumpendorf in 1857 18 per cent of all carpenters, 20 per cent of all locksmiths and 11 per cent of all shoemakers had more than five male hands in their households. On the other hand about a third of the masters in these trades had no employees at all. Yet even master artisans with many employees experienced the fragility of small business. They could not secure a continuously high level of production. Leaving aside seasonal and cyclical variations the productive capacity of the workshop depended heavily upon the personal efficiency and physical labour of the master. The number of employed hands was high at an early stage of the life-cycle. In old age the number of both hands and children fell back.[33]

Large numbers of workers in the households of master artisans was a characteristic feature of mid-nineteenth-century Vienna. The labour force was a very unstable one, with journeymen usually staying no longer than a few weeks with the same master. There was an ambiguity in the relations between masters and men. Memoirs testify to a collective drive for high output in the peak period from Friday night to Saturday evening, and both master and journeymen would sometimes generate a common solidarity against the putter-out (*Verleger*). Yet the self-same workshops would be dominated by deep social conflicts between masters and men, and by a strong sense of hierarchy. Nevertheless, a degree of close identity within the workshop might be entrenched by common leisure activities, above all visits to pubs, street singers and theatres, often during working days, or in the evenings and on Sundays.[34]

Andreas Scheu, one of the leaders of the early Austrian labour movement, was an apprentice in the 1850s to a gilder, who employed five journeymen and four apprentices and produced ready-made gilded mirror frames for wide distribution. Scheu remembers the atmosphere in the workshop:

> The relations between master and men were quite cheerful (*gemütlich*). If a profitable contract put Mr Penauer [the master] in a good mood or if a certain number of frames had to be prepared for gilding the next morning, he would order beer from the neighbouring innkeeper to refresh and stimulate the journeymen, who

> worked as if there was a competition on. Both the master and his wife sat amongst them using their brushes as eagerly as the others. From the third room, through an open door, one could hear the master's son Karl, playing merry tunes on the zither.[35]

It must be emphasized, however, that such cheerful relations between masters and men did not exist everywhere. In other memoirs, apprentices and journeymen describe their masters as 'veritable tyrants and hangmen'.[36]

It is clear, though, that household and workshop were one for the Viennese master artisans at the climax of the industrial revolution, with production and family life inseparable spheres. Yet it is wrong to talk of a family work unit. The rapidly changing demand for labour meant that continuous work would not be provided for family members, and the normal solution was to have recourse to apprentices and journeymen as demand directed. At one moment work would hardly keep the master alone occupied, at another a large number of hands would be required. Family members seem to have been involved in production only at times of very high, even feverish, activity.

The instability of the putting-out system together with declining productive capacity in a master's old age reduced the chances of inheritance still further. In the first half of the nineteenth century the number of sons who succeeded to their fathers' trade continued to be rather low. For example, amongst the *Posamentierer* who produced haberdashery, lace, ribbons and so on, in only 17 of the 133 changes of trade between 1804 and 1829 was a new master introduced 'at his father's place'.[37] Yet a remarkable trend must be noticed. Both tailors and gold wire-pullers – though at different levels – indicate a peak of masters' sons entering the trade in the 1830s (Table 9). In these years the expansion of the number of masters was prevented by law. It would seem that being a master's son was more important in times of 'closed guilds' and became less important in the decade of the 1850s with its rapid economic growth.

The differing economic development and social traditions of trades are further reflected in the census lists of 1857. Once again I shall focus on the position of master artisans' sons. Table 10 shows the mean number of juvenile and adult sons in master artisans' households, as well as those of a younger age. This additional column could give some indication of differences in fertility, or at least of infant survival. Besides the intrinsic interest of this information, it demonstrates that low or high numbers of resident juvenile or adult sons are not so much a result of differential fertility as of behaviour patterns in leaving home.

The group with the highest numbers of juvenile and adult sons includes building trades (*Baumeister*), carriers (*Fiaker*, *Lohnkutscher*) and innkeepers (*Gastgewerbe*). In the middle of the nineteenth century these trades show the pattern established previously. These trades stood outside the guild system and had long traditions of wage labour. Innkeepers and carriers partly solved their needs for dependent labour by employing their sons. These trades were among the richer ones, which means

Table 10 *Sons in the households of master artisans, Vienna, 1857*

Trade (n) (Head of household a master artisan and married)	*(1) Mean number of sons aged 2–11 years (master's wife aged 20–45 years)*	*(2) Mean number of sons aged 12 years and older (master's wife aged 37 years and older)*	*(3) Mean number of sons aged 20 years and older (master's wife aged 45 years and older)*
Building trades (24)	0.56	1.08	0.80
Innkeepers (59)	0.62	0.88	0.69
Carrying trades (35)	0.46	0.84	0.65
Food trades (42)	0.73	0.80	0.37
Textile trades (235)	0.86	0.77	0.42
Metalworking trades (86)	0.82	0.64	0.29
Woodworking trades (254)	0.75	0.49	0.30
Dressmaking trades (330)	0.59	0.54	0.32
All trades (above and others) (1164)	0.70	0.65	0.40
Standard deviation	0.91 n = 849	0.94 n = 723	0.76 n = 374

Sources: Census lists of various Viennese districts, 1857 in the collection of the 'Familie im sozialen Wandel' research project at the Institut für Wirtschafts- und Sozialgeschichte, University of Vienna.

that thoughts of inheritance might have influenced sons to stay longer at home.[38] What is particularly striking is that this group combines a high continuity in male succession with rather low fertility. It is possible that fertility in these trades was influenced less by the need for family labour than by the wider influences that can be seen amongst other petit-bourgeois groups which used birth control to assist upward mobility.[39]

The food trades also enjoyed good economic conditions. They had been affected only marginally by the expanding capitalist economy, and bakers and butchers were able to maintain their independence while taking advantage of the growing market. These trades were noticeable for maintaining their traditional work organization. The tradition of having employed hands living in the household was preserved, partly because of unusual working hours, such as night work. On the other hand juvenile and, to a lesser extent, adult sons were quite common.

Similar numbers of resident sons can be seen in the textile trades, but due to completely different conditions. Their high fertility is in accordance with the common model of proto-industrial demographic behaviour.[40] The high rates of juvenile and adult resident sons reveal them to have been an important part of the household labour force, for the family did really exist here as a work unit, although we must remember that domestic textile production was in rapid decline in the middle of the nineteenth century.[41]

The last group includes woodworking, metalworking and clothing trades. It was amongst such carpenters, turners, locksmiths, tailors and shoemakers that we can clearly see the expansion of small-scale production in the 1850s. At the same time, we find the continuation of the old pattern of leaving home at about twelve years of age, as the low rates of juvenile and adult sons show. Once again, then, we can see the durability of aspects of the traditional artisan's mode of life, even in times of rapid economic growth.

Differences between types of trades as revealed in the 1857 census can also explain the trend shown in Table 8. Artisans' households containing juvenile and adult sons are in general far more common for the nineteenth than the eighteenth century. This trend continues in provincial towns during the nineteenth century, but not in Vienna. To understand this peculiarity of Vienna we have to consider the distorting effect on the statistics of the decline of domestic production of textiles in Vienna. Masters in the textile trades were almost half of all the masters of the Gumpendorf sample in 1827, a little over a third in Gumpendorf in 1857, and were almost non-existent in Hernals in 1880. As the textile family work unit declined, so the traditional non-family-based trades became more highly weighted in the social structure of small-scale production.

The traditional artisan family was thus characterized by neither family labour nor inheritance of the enterprise by the sons. Where those patterns developed in the nineteenth century, they did so as a response to economic change – whether the growth of an élite of more prosperous masters leading more capitalistic enterprises, or the concomitant expansion of depressed outworking enterprises which closed in on family labour to replace the declining control of the labour force that had once characterized them. Where small master-artisan firms expanded successfully on older lines in the middle of the century, they continued the traditional artisan pattern within which the family was of fundamental importance for neither labour nor inheritance.

ARTISANS IN AN INDUSTRIALIZED SOCIETY

If most handicrafts came under severe economic pressure during the Great Depression,[42] the very end of the century saw better prospects appear.[43] Quantitative evidence for the 1890s suggests that master artisans experienced renewed economic growth and greater social stability in Vienna.[44] The number of masters grew faster than the population as a whole, while the mean number of employed hands in small-scale production stayed relatively stable at 2.8 per master. Yet in comparison with the period of the industrial revolution, master artisans at the end of the century were much less of an economic force, although some half of the Viennese labour force remained in small-scale production. On the other hand, the internal differences amongst the masters had become weaker too. At the turn of the century there were fewer self-employed masters than in the 1850s, but there were also fewer masters employing more than five hands. There were various reasons for this.

Crafts which had faced real factory competition – textiles are the clearest example – had largely disappeared. Others had survived by a combination of production, repairing and retailing. Finally, there were the new trades that had grown up as a result of changing patterns of consumption or technological change.[45] The general picture seems to be that the growth of small-scale production in the middle of the nineteenth century was a precocious one produced by lags in the industrialization process, whereas trades and crafts at the turn of the century could now find opportunities to integrate into the structures of the new industrial society.

Within the process relations between masters and men were radically changed. The most important change is that more and more workers left their master's household. In 1880 about 17 per cent of the whole Viennese population were employees of one kind or another living in their employer's household; in 1910 about 9 per cent.[46] The changing structure of the labour force in small-scale production contributed to this trend. The expansion of the 1850s was based to a considerable extent on the exploitation of apprentices whereas adult workers had become increasingly important by the turn of the century. In 1857 there were forty-one apprentices to every hundred journeymen. By 1910 the figure was only twenty-one.[47] Journeymen now expected to marry and establish households of their own at a comparatively young age.[48] The new prevalence of 'free wage labour' in small-scale production transformed the relations of masters to men into those of small entrepreneurs to members of a working class.[49] Yet, as the ambiguity in the personal relations of masters to men declined, so employment seems to have become more stable.

For master artisans this involved a steady separation of work from family life. Here was the origin of the isolation and introspection of the artisan family. The home and workshop became progressively separated.[50] In all these ways master artisans participated in that process of familialization which characterized most of those in the lower classes towards the end of the nineteenth century. But as master artisans tried to transform their crafts into family enterprises with inter-generational continuity they strengthened social characteristics closer to those of the bourgeoisie than to those of the lower classes.

This trend towards family enterprise and inter-generational continuity among master artisans is indicated in various ways in the sources, but they do not provide as much systematic evidence as one might wish. One can draw a quantitative comparison between the early and late nineteenth century for only two Viennese trades – bakers and goldsmiths – and both belong among the richer trades. They can therefore hardly be taken as typical of the whole of Viennese small-scale production.

Bakers show a clear increase between 1815/20 and 1899/1901 in the rate of handing down the enterprise from father to son (Table 9), and this increase occurred without demographic change. The mean age at which a baker became a master was constant at thirty-one years, while the mean age of death of a master remained likewise constant, at fifty-seven years.[51]

If we turn to goldsmiths, there are complete lists of all Viennese masters in the trade for every year between 1774 and 1890.[52] Some families can be found throughout the whole period under observation, at times without even the workshop's address changing. But, as we have already observed in connection with other trades, these long-running family traditions were only typical for a small group, for those masters prominent in their guilds and trade authorities, serving as *Obervorsteher* (guild master) or *Regierungs-Schätzmeister* (the authority who estimated values). These specific cases apart, it is extremely difficult to extract from the masters' lists quantitative evidence about trends towards family enterprise and inter-generational continuity. The only method available is to search for names that occur twice or more in the list for a single year. The recurrence of a name does not of course necessarily mean that these masters belong to the same family, still less that they are father and son, but it leaves open the possibility that this was the case. If this measure does not give an exact figure, it does indicate the range of possibility. I have compared the lists of 1851 and 1890 to reveal the behaviour of master artisans in the first and second halves of the century. The number of masters changed little during this period – 528 in 1851 and 545 in 1890. The number of surnames occurring at least twice in the listings increased in this period from 56 to 140. In 1851 there were six cases where two masters of the same name lived at the same address, compared with nineteen in 1890. These figures are not unequivocal, but they do suggest a reasonably strong trend towards family enterprise amongst goldsmiths.

Confirmation comes from other less systematic sources. Some goldsmiths in the 1880s revealed family connections in the name of their business: 'Bucher und Sohn' (Bucher and Son), 'Goldschmidt Michaels Söhne' (Goldschmidt's Sons), 'Brüder Hutter' (Hutter Brothers), or 'Ratke und Neffe' (Ratke and Nephew). One can see some organized handing down of workshops in some late nineteenth-century trades. Elderly masters would relinquish their trades, and some days or weeks later their sons appeared in the lists.[53] This growing expectation that a son would work in and inherit his father's trade is similarly revealed in the founding of Societies of Masters' Sons. The bakers were the first, founding their society of Master Bakers' Sons in 1888, and they were followed by plumbers in 1889, butchers in 1891, locksmiths in 1895, innkeepers in 1898, and carpenters in 1903.[54]

All these arguments are based on individual trades. In order to generalize about master artisans as a whole, we must turn to census lists to discover how common it was for sons of masters to stay in their father's household. Unfortunately, we have no list later than 1880, and the evidence thus concerns the period when the putting-out system was still dominant in Vienna, social instability was high, and the economic pressure on small-scale production at its peak. It is therefore not surprising to find in Table 8 that there were rather low numbers of master artisans' households with juvenile and adult sons in the Vienna suburb of Hernals in 1880. The same table also shows a strong contrast between Hernals and Perchtoldsdorf, a small market town some miles south of Vienna. Here the trend is clear, with a comparatively high number of artisan households including resident sons in 1880.

In fact, the economic situation of the artisans of this provincial town differed markedly from those in the capital. In Perchtoldsdorf trades had not been transformed that much by the *Verlag*. In 1880 there were far fewer master artisans than in Vienna (Vienna/Gumpendorf 1827: 39 per cent of all male heads of household were master artisans; Vienna/Hernals 1880: 30 per cent; Perchtoldsdorf 1880: 10 per cent), but they seemed to be economically consolidated. Their occupational structure was balanced according to local needs: of the food, clothing and building trades each represented a quarter of the town's master artisans. The rest were for the most part connected to viticulture. In 1880 the master artisans of Perchtoldsdorf show no signs of shading into proletarianized labour.[55] They all seem to have been independent producers. It was economic and social conditions such as these which made masters' sons in general (as opposed to those in specific trades) stay in their father's household.

An examination of individual households in Perchtoldsdorf reveals some other notable features. In twenty-nine cases sons had a declared occupation. Of these eighteen were the same as that of the father, but with interesting nuances. On some occasions, sons were declared not as journeymen but manager (*Geschäftsführer*), partner, or 'father's associate'. These terms were common amongst the industrial bourgeoisie, but had not previously been used by artisans. Those sons whose job was not the same as that of their fathers are also revealing. Eight out of eleven cases were declared as pupils, mainly of higher commercial and technical schools (*Gewerbeschule, Realschule, Handelsakademie*). This tendency to higher education has two implications. Those who returned to their father's workshop after completing school must have brought with them a degree of managerial competence and thus strengthened the workshop's economic base. Those others who went on to clerical or professional occupations must have entered into the wider social network of the lower middle class, containing well-to-do master artisans, civil servants, professionals and so on.

The same trend can be detected in Vienna for individual cases. In the Hernals sample for 1880[56] one finds many artisan households with adult sons described as 'practicants', 'managers', and so on. Similarly, master artisans' families contained students attending gymnasium or university. If a son of a well-to-do master became an artisan in a trade other than that of his father, it would be more probably another wealthy trade – bakers' sons would become pharmacists, and so on. All these phenomena indicate the similarity in social development amongst the master artisans of a small provincial town and those of the metropolis. We must nevertheless consider the differences revealed in Table 8. What characterized handicrafts in general in the Perchtoldsdorf of 1880 was, in the far more differentiated economic structure of Viennese small-scale production, only true for a rather small group of fairly well-off masters.

Thus we see that as artisanal industries consolidated in the late nineteenth century, so households became more family centred and specialized; thus was created the family-focused cultural life-style which historians have wrongly assumed to be traditional. Now it was that the more bourgeois pattern was established of sons working in the enterprise with a view to inheriting it in due course.

CONCLUSION

Studies of the political and social ideology of master artisans in the late nineteenth century have stressed the importance they attached to family life and family traditions. The patriarchal family was an important element of the artisans' 'popular anti-modern ideal'. This paper has argued that the artisans' traditional mode of life was not in fact as family orientated as is usually assumed. It was, on the contrary, the nineteenth century which saw the emergence of a new concern for the family amongst master artisans. Yet this development was neither a uniform nor a linear one. It developed hardly at all amongst economically depressed and socially isolated sections of the artisanat, but became strong where it was economically consolidated and socially integrated. The bourgeois family ideal did not therefore reflect the past and the present mode of life of all master artisans, simply the developing mode of life of their upper ranks. The pattern of family life and the ideology about the family did not develop in a vacuum for master artisans, but within a broader social atmosphere which was characterized in the late nineteenth century both by ruling-class attempts to 'familialize' the classes beneath them, and by a trend towards new ideological positions on gender divisions.[57]

In this perspective an authoritarian and patriarchal family ideal amongst late nineteenth-century master artisans can hardly be interpreted as an attempt to escape from a threatening present into a happier past, but rather as an attempt to adapt to the structures of a developed industrial capitalism. Indeed this combination of 'modernization' in their actual lives alongside a backward-looking ideology applies to more than the family life of master artisans, but to their whole mode of life in the late nineteenth century.

The bakers, for example, were fully aware of the benefits of new technology and advances in chemistry. They even offered prizes for the technological improvement of ovens. In the relations of masters to men they sought to stabilize the labour force by imitating patterns in factory industry. Journeymen who stayed with the same employer for a couple of years were given awards, and their names published in the bakers' journal.[58] Simultaneously, though, master bakers were investing a great deal of money in glorifying their past and their traditions. They employed an expert to organize the guild archive, issued books on bakers' traditions, and so on.[59] The 'Society of Master Bakers' Sons' might gather to hear speeches on modern technology and commercial practices, but that did not diminish their fondness for participating in festival processions, dressed in traditional costume, and lined up behind the old banners of their guild.[60]

Viennese goldsmiths similarly provide evidence to support the argument that the development of family business was accompanied by the strengthening of a romantic ideology of the handicraft and the guild. In 1887 they changed the name of their

Table 11 *Examples of household structure in nineteenth-century Vienna*

<table>
<tr><td colspan="2">1 Textile manufacturer, Vienna/Gumpendorf 201 (1857)</td></tr>
<tr><td colspan="2">Head, 66 years, widowed, Warenfabrikant (goods manufacturer)</td></tr>
<tr><td colspan="2"> son, 32 years, single, öffentlicher Gesellschafter (partner)</td></tr>
<tr><td colspan="2"> son, 30 years, married, öffentlicher Gesellschafter (partner)</td></tr>
<tr><td colspan="2"> his wife, 22 years</td></tr>
<tr><td>Coachman, 46 years</td><td rowspan="6">all single</td></tr>
<tr><td>Servant, 31 years</td></tr>
<tr><td>Servant, 19 years</td></tr>
<tr><td>Servant, 30 years</td></tr>
<tr><td>Maid, 22 years</td></tr>
<tr><td>Maid, 31 years</td></tr>
<tr><td colspan="2">2 Master locksmith, Vienna/Gumpendorf 159 (1857)</td></tr>
<tr><td colspan="2">Head, 39 years, married, Schlossermeister (master locksmith)</td></tr>
<tr><td colspan="2"> wife, 35 years</td></tr>
<tr><td colspan="2"> son, 7 years</td></tr>
<tr><td colspan="2"> daughter, 14 years</td></tr>
<tr><td colspan="2">Clerk (Buchhalter), 60 years, single</td></tr>
<tr><td colspan="2">Journeyman, carpenter, 32 years, single</td></tr>
<tr><td colspan="2">Servant (Hausknecht), 37 years, single</td></tr>
<tr><td colspan="2">Six journeymen locksmiths, aged 18–38 years, all single</td></tr>
<tr><td colspan="2">Eleven apprentice locksmiths, aged 9–17 years, all single</td></tr>
<tr><td colspan="2">Journeyman locksmith, 34 years, married</td></tr>
<tr><td colspan="2"> wife, 32 years</td></tr>
<tr><td colspan="2"> son, 2 years</td></tr>
<tr><td colspan="2"> son, 5 years</td></tr>
<tr><td colspan="2">Washerwoman, 40 years, widowed</td></tr>
<tr><td colspan="2">3 Master weaver, Vienna/Gumpendorf 218 (1857)</td></tr>
<tr><td colspan="2">Head, 59 years, Webermeister (master weaver)</td></tr>
<tr><td colspan="2"> wife, 42 years</td></tr>
<tr><td colspan="2"> son, 15 years, apprentice weaver</td></tr>
<tr><td colspan="2"> daughter, 24 years</td></tr>
<tr><td colspan="2">4 Master baker, Vienna/Hernals 23 (1880)</td></tr>
<tr><td colspan="2">Head, 45 years, married, Bäckermeister (master baker)</td></tr>
<tr><td colspan="2"> wife, 42 years</td></tr>
<tr><td colspan="2"> son, 18 years, Bäcker-Praktikant (baker practicant)</td></tr>
<tr><td colspan="2"> son, 17 years, Apotheker Praktikant (pharmacist practicant)</td></tr>
<tr><td colspan="2"> son, 14 years, Studiosus (student)</td></tr>
<tr><td colspan="2"> son, 3 years</td></tr>
<tr><td colspan="2"> daughter, 8 years, schoolgirl</td></tr>
<tr><td>Six journeymen bakers, aged 17–29 years</td><td rowspan="5">all single</td></tr>
<tr><td>Two shopgirls (Ladenmädchen), aged 19 and 22 years</td></tr>
<tr><td>Servant, 48 years</td></tr>
<tr><td>Maid, 28 years (Stubenmädchen)</td></tr>
<tr><td>Cook, 28 years</td></tr>
</table>

Sources: Census lists Vienna/Gumpendorf 1857, Vienna/Hernals 1880 in the collection of the 'Familie im sozialen Wandel' research project at the Institut für Wirtschafts- und Sozialgeschichte, University of Vienna.

association from *Gold-Silber-und Juwelenarbeiter*, as it was known throughout the eighteenth and nineteenth centuries, to the more traditional and romantic sounding 'smith' (*Juweliere, Gold- und Silberschmiede*).[61] The same people were usually active both in modernizing business and cultivating traditions. In the 1890s the leading figure among the carpenters was Johann Jedlicka. He was for several years director of the carpenters' association (*Vorsteher der Tischlergenossenschaft*), that is the master artisans' craft association established through the 1883 trade laws. In this well-paid function he was far more representative of the modern 'artisan bureaucrat' than an old guild leader. In fact, Jedlicka was in his politics an active anti-semite and promoter of the Christian social movement. In 1896 he adopted aggressively modern capitalistic methods to break a journeymen's strike. He organized a lock-out that encompassed not just the master carpenters but the furniture factories as well.[62] On the other hand he spent much time organizing the guild's historical archive, and in 1894 he published his *History of the Carpenters' Guild of Vienna*.[63] In public meetings he was known as a proponent of a resurrected guild system, which he believed would enable the masters to 'appear as respected citizens' like 'their forefathers'.[64]

These are no more than limited examples, of course, but I think they raise questions which lead back to the problems with which we started. Firstly, research on the master artisans' politics and ideology should keep in mind the existence of different strata among the master artisans, not only between but also within the trades and crafts. The politics of artisan organizations and the ideas of their leaders should not be analysed in terms of common master artisan or even lower middle-class interests, but with reference to that social differentiation. The social background of those who wrote the leading articles in masters' newspapers and of those who spoke in committees and at meetings should be more carefully explored. Secondly, reactionary aspects of master artisan politics and ideology have too frequently been analysed in terms of decline, pressure and social breakdown. And within this framework, the ideal of a traditional artisan family has been seen as a response to the decline of that family under the pressure of economic change. Yet, as I have suggested in this article, that ideal artisanal family cannot easily be established in the Austrian past; it appears to have been a new creation. I think it is stimulating to try a different approach: to see these elements within the context of the formation of a petite bourgeoisie, as the ideas of master artisans seeking to establish this position within bourgeois society, and searching for an adequate ideological identity.

NOTES

1 The most comprehensive discussion of this problem is H. Rosenbaum, *Formen der Familie. Untersuchungen zum Zusammenhang von Familienverhältnissen, Sozialstruktur und sozialem Wandel in der deutschen Gesellschaft des 19. Jahrhunderts*, Frankfurt/M, 1982.

2 In England this approach has, for example, been used in the discussion of the labour aristocracy, and in America in many recent 'Class-and-Community' studies. Amongst writings in German, see on the working class H. Zwahr, *Zur Konstituierung des Proletariats als Klasse. Strukturuntersuchung über das Leipziger Proletariat während der industriellen Revolution*, Berlin/GDR, 1978, 115–203; on the bourgeoisie see H. Zwahr, 'Zur Klassenkonstituierung der deutschen Bourgeoisie', in his *Proletariat und Bourgeoisie in Deutschland*, Köln, 1980, 86ff; J. Kocka, 'Unternehmer und Kapitalismus. An Beispielen aus der frühen deutschen Industrialisierung', *Zeitschrift für Unternehmensgeschichte* 24, 99–135 (English translation in *German Yearbook on Business History* 1); on the family and social mobility see J. Kocka, K. Ditt, J. Mooser, H. Reif, R. Schüren, *Familie und soziale Plazierung. Studien zum Verhältnis von Familie, sozialer Mobilität und Heiratsverhalten an westfälischen Beispielen im späten 18. und 19. Jahrhundert*, Opladen, 1980.

3 See R. Lee, 'The German family: a critical survey of the current state of historical research', in R. Evans and R. Lee (eds), *The German Family*, London, 1980, 30.

4 For an overview of recent research on the economic and political development of the petite bourgeoisie see, in addition to the early essays in this book, H.-G. Haupt (ed.), *Bourgeois und Volk zugleich? Zur Geschichte des Kleinbürgertums im 19. und 20. Jahrhundert*, Frankfurt/M, 1978.

5 The work of H. Mitgau has been particularly influential especially H. Mitgau, *Berufsvererbung und Berufswechsel im Handwerk. Untersuchungen über das Generationenschicksal im Gesellschaftsaufbau*, Berlin, 1952.

6 See S. Volkov, *The Rise of Popular Antimodernism in Germany. The Urban Master Artisans, 1873–1896*, Princeton, 1978; J. Boyer, *Political Radicalism in Late Imperial Vienna. Origins of the Christian Social Movement 1848–1897*, Chicago, 1981; Ch. Salmayer, 'Das gewerbliche Kleinbürgertum in Wien. Zu seiner wirtschaftlichen und politischen Entwicklung in der 2. Hälfte des 19. Jahrhunderts', PhD thesis, Vienna, 1980.

7 Volkov, op. cit., 29.

8 ibid., 319ff.

9 Quantitative evidence is derived firstly from listings of inhabitants (*libri status animarum*, census lists). A collection of such listings has been formed at the Institute for Economic and Social History, University of Vienna, in connection with the research project 'Familie im sozialen Wandel'. It includes listings from various Austrian villages and towns from the sixteenth to the early twentieth centuries and from Viennese districts from the nineteenth century. Evidence is in addition derived from sources in the Viennese Guild Archives. Most of them are collected in the Wiener Stadt- und Landesarchiv (WStLA) but some craft associations continue to run their own archives, for example, the bakers, carpenters, locksmiths.

10 See M. Mitterauer and R. Sieder, *The European Family*, Oxford, 1982, esp. pp. 5–10. Differences from the history of the family in England are emphasized by P. Laslett in his foreword to that book.

11 Mitterauer and Sieder, op. cit., 103–9, 168–70; Rosenbaum, op. cit., 121–88. There is nevertheless a widespread tendency to underestimate the differences between the family patterns of artisans and farmers. See, for example, M. Anderson, *Approaches to the History of the Western Family 1500–1914*, London, 1980, 75; Mitgau, op. cit., 19.

12 There are a large number of studies dealing with the multi-functional character of guilds. Among the most influential are R. Wissell, *Des alten Handwerks Recht und Gewohnheit*, 2nd edn, Berlin, 1974; W. Fischer, 'Die rechtliche und wirtschaftliche Lage des deutschen Handwerks', in his *Wirtschaft und Gesellschaft im Zeitalter der Industrialisierung*, Göttingen, 1972; J. Bergmann, *Das Berliner Handwerk in den Frühphasen der Industrialisierung*, Berlin, 1973, 5–34; M. Walker, *German Home Towns. Community, State and General Estate 1648–1871*, Ithaca, 1971.

13 One factor limiting the participation of family members in work was a strong sexual division of labour which inhibited the co-operation of men and women. See M. Mitterauer, 'Geschlechts-spezifische Arbeitsteilung in vorindustrieller Zeit', *Beiträge zur historischen Sozialkunde*, 11 (3), 82f.

14 This view, which stands in strong contrast to the traditions of handicrafts historiography, was first developed by M. Mitterauer; see especially M. Mitterauer, 'Zur familienbetrieblichen Struktur im zünftischen Handwerk', in H. Knittler (ed.), *Wirtschafts- und sozialhistorische Beiträge. Festschrift für Alfred Hofmann zum 75. Geburtstag*, Wien, 1979, 190–219.

15 J. Schlumbohm, '"Traditional collectivity" and "modern individuality": some questions and suggestions for the historical study of socialization. The example of the German lower and upper bourgeoisie around 1800', *Social History*, 5, 71ff. E. Schremmer, 'Review of Kriedte/Medick/Schlumbohm, Industrialisierung vor der Industrialisierung', *Geschichte und Gesellschaft*, 6 (3), 444, has proposed the term 'guild-bound property': 'Der Konzeption der Zünfte liegt eine starke soziale Komponente zugrunde, die das Individualprinzip weitgehend ausschloß.'

16 The rather constant form of material in the archives of some trades may be an indication that changes in legal status had only limited influence on the actual organization of the trades. An international comparison also shows that in spite of legal differences there were common features in the artisan mode of life which derived from their economic situation, work rhythm, relation of work to leisure and other factors. Descriptions of the life-style of master artisans in mid-nineteenth-century America, for example, look quite similar to the Viennese situation at the same time; see the special issue 'Studies in working class culture: some nineteenth-century chapters', *Labour History*, 15 (3).

17 Rosenbaum, op. cit., 251–380; K. Hausen, 'Family and role-division: the polarisation of sexual stereotypes in the nineteenth century – an aspect of dissociation of work and family life', in Evans and Lee, op. cit., 51–83.

18 Mitterauer and Sieder, op. cit., 168ff.

19 ibid., 202ff.

20 Mitterauer, 'Familienbetriebliche Struktur', 205ff.

21 For a general overview see K. Hinze, *Die Arbeiterfrage zu Beginn des modernen Kapitalismus 1685–1806*, 2nd edn, Berlin, 1963.

22 Meisterbuch der Seidenzeugmacher 1711–1779, WStLA, Innungen-Bücher 50/1.

23 M. Bucek, 'Geschichte der Seidenfabrikanten Wiens im 18. Jahrhundert (1710–1792)', PhD thesis, Vienna, 1974, 127ff.

24 P. Mestrozzi, 'Die wichtigsten Momente meines Lebens gewidmet seinen Nachkommen zur stäten (!) Erinnerung im Jahre 1839', Handschrift im Museum für angewandte Kunst in Wien, S 13, 298.

25 Bürger- und Meisterdekrete der Seidenzeugmacher 1797–1848, WStLA, Innungen-Akten A23 50/4, fasc. 89.

26 'Geschichte der Familie Adensamer' (according to oral information by Mr Komm. Rat Egbert Adensamer).

27 A detailed analysis based on census lists for nineteenth-century Vienna is provided in J. Ehmer, *Familienstruktur und Arbeitsorganisation im frühindustriellen Wien*, 1980; on bourgeois family forms see esp. 129ff.

28 ibid., 101ff.

29 Kalender für das Gremium der bg. Bäckermeister in der k.k. Haupt- und Residenzstadt Wien, 1815–1820, Archiv der Bäckerinnung Wien.

30 Ehmer, op. cit., 57ff.

31 B. Laurie, 'Life styles of Philadelphia artisans', *Labour History*, 15 (3), 341ff.

32 The growth of handicrafts during the industrial revolution was first observed by G. Schmoller, *Zur Geschichte der deutschen Kleingewerbe im 19. Jahrhundert*, Halle, 1870; and has

been confirmed by some recent studies. See especially, on the development of another metropolis, Bergmann, op. cit., 147. The predominance of living in masters' households is apparent from the census lists of other central European towns, outside Austria, such as Zürich (Switzerland) and Zagreb (Croatia). These listings have also been collected in Vienna but have been only partially interpreted so far (see note 9).

33 Ehmer, op. cit., 79, 126.

34 For the ambiguous relations of masters and men in nineteenth-century Vienna see J. Ehmer, 'Rote Fahnen-Blauer Montag. Soziale Bedingungen von Aktions- und Organisationsformen der frühen Wiener Arbeiterbewegung', in D. Puls, E. P. Thompson u. a., *Wahrnehmungsformen und Protestverhalten. Studien zur Lage der Unterschichten im 18. und 19. Jahrhundert*, Frankfurt/M, 1979, 143–74.

35 A. Scheu, *Umsturzkeime*, Wien, 1902, vol. 1, 76.

36 G. Habermann, *Aus meinem Leben. Erinnerungen aus den Jahren 1876–1877–1884–1896*, Wien, 1919, 48.

37 Protokoll einer gantzen (!) ehrsamen Meisterschaft der bgl. Posamentiererzunft 1717–1859, WStLA, Innungen-Bücher 41/1.

38 Together with the food trades and building trades, carriers and innkeepers are in the group with the smallest number of masters in the lowest tax class: 'Erwerbsteuerkataster im Jahre 1853', in *Tafeln zur Statistik der österreichischen Monarchie*, NF II, Wien, 1859.

39 On motives for the control of family size in the lower middle class see J. A. Banks, *Prosperity and Parenthood*, London, 1956; J. A. and O. Banks, *Feminism and Family Planning*, London, 1964. On the differences between groups of independents, mainly between tradesmen, innkeepers and craftsmen, see R. Spree, 'The German petite bourgeoisie and the decline of fertility: some statistical evidence from the late 19th and early 20th centuries', paper presented to the 3rd Round Table on the Petite Bourgeoisie in Western Europe Before 1914, Paris, 1981.

40 See H. Medick, 'The protoindustrial family economy: the structural function of household and family during the transition from peasant society to industrial capitalism', *Social History*, 3, 291ff.

41 P. Ayçoberry has pointed out that children's staying at home can be interpreted on the one hand as an attempt to use social advantages offered by their own families, but on the other as a lack of any opportunities in impoverished families: P. Ayçoberry, 'Der Strukturwandel im Kölner Mittelstand 1820–1850', *Geschichte und Gesellschaft*, 1 (1), 78ff.

42 A complete stagnation of crafts and even an absolute decrease of small masters occurred in the years 1875–80; see Salmayer, op. cit., 67ff.

43 In addition to ideological bias, assumptions about the handicraft outlook in the late nineteenth century are also influenced by the exact period under observation. Economic decline tends to be emphasized by those authors who deal only with the Great Depression, e.g. Volkov, op. cit.; Boyer, op. cit.; Salmayer, op. cit. Most historians dealing with a longer period assume a recovery of handicrafts about 1895; see W. Fischer, 'Die Rolle des Kleingewerbes im wirtschaftlichen Wachstumsprozeß in Deutschland 1850–1914', in Fischer, op. cit., 141; A. Noll, *Sozioökonomischer Strukturwandel des Handwerks in der 2. Phase der Industrialisierung unter besonderer Berücksichtigung der Regierungsbezirke Arnsberg und Münster*, Göttingen, 1975.

44 More detailed data are presented in J. Ehmer, 'Ökonomischer und sozialer Strukturwandel im Wiener Handwerk – von der industriellen Revolution zur Hochindustrialisierung', in W. Conze and U. Engelhardt (eds), *Handwerkerschaft und Industrialisierung in Deutschland*, Stuttgart, 1984.

45 Such a differentiated view first emerged out of a series of studies carried out by the German 'Verein für Sozialpolitik' in the 1890s. See E. Adler, *Über die Lage des Handwerks in Österreich*, Freiburg, 1898.

46 Ehmer, *Familienstruktur*, 174.
47 Ehmer, 'Ökonomischer und sozialer Strukturwandel'.
48 Ehmer, *Familienstruktur*, 171ff.
49 This process can be observed in organizational development: master artisans' associations started to become a part of the *Mittelstandsbewegung*, the journeymen's organizations were integrated into the social democratic trade union movement.
50 In some listings both the home and the workshop of masters are noted; see Incorporationsprotokoll der Posamentierer 1859–1927, WStLA, Innungen-Bücher 41/28.
51 Kalender, 1815–1819, 1899–1901.
52 Verzeichnis der Herren Mitglieder der Genossenschaft der Juweliere, Gold- und Silberschmiede (under changing titles) 1774–1890, WStLA, Innungen-Akten, A88/89.
53 Incorporationsprotokoll der Posamentierer, 1879–1910.
54 *40 Jahre Vereinigung von Wiener Bäckersöhnen*, Wien, 1928, 53ff.
55 Census Perchtoldsdorf 1880 (see note 9).
56 Census Wien-Hernals 1880 (see note 9).
57 Characteristic of these tendencies in the intellectual life of Vienna is O. Weininger, *Geschlecht und Charakter*. First published in 1903, this book went through twelve editions by 1911!
58 Kalender, 1890–1914.
59 G. A. Ressel, *Das Archiv der Bäckergenossenschaft in Wien*, Wien, 1903.
60 *700 Jahre Wiener Bäcker-Innung 1227–1927*, Wien, 1927, 65, 94ff.
61 Verzeichnis der Herren Mitglieder, 1887.
62 Boyer, op. cit., 102, 112.
63 J. Jedlicka, *Geschichte der Genossenschaft der Tischler in Wien*, Wien, 1894.
64 Boyer, op. cit., 67.

10 Rural artisans in the Beauce during the nineteenth century*

JEAN-CLAUDE FARCY

The artisans and small traders of the countryside undoubtedly constitute the part of the petite bourgeoisie about which we know the least. This ignorance is understandable in so far as it is of greater significance to study the petite bourgeoisie in the context of the rise of industrial and commercial capitalism, and urban areas are the obvious surroundings for such study.

Yet the place of artisans and shopkeepers in rural areas was none the less an important one. The Beauce, in the department of the Eure-et-Loir, to the southwest of Paris, was a purely agricultural region during the last century, with no industrial activity at all. Towards the middle of the century, the economic sector of artisans and shopkeepers accounted for roughly a quarter of its working population. The study of this social stratum is made difficult by its lack of homogeneity. Its diversity is manifest in its relations to the means of production, in the nature of its activities and in the trades it encompasses, as well as in its wealth and rank in society. According to the descriptions left by nineteenth-century civil servants, artisans and tradesmen included everyone in the Beauce who did not work directly on the land, with the exception of a few dozen members of the liberal professions in each canton. This broad 'definition' is the one we adopted in our use of the various archival sources available. The choice of this definition to delimit the social group under examination corresponds closely with reality. To quote Labrousse:

> In pre-industrial societies artisans cover an extremely wide economic front. They are responsible for most of the production and the distribution in the secondary and tertiary sectors. Economically speaking, at their most humble levels, and in their most rudimentary activities, they resemble wage-earners, they are practically a salaried stratum. At their highest economic levels they merge into the commercial petite bourgeoisie, to become practically a bourgeoisie belonging to the world of small-scale production.[1]

* Translated from the French by Paul D. G. Smith.

Following this same author's advice not to separate the study of artisans from that of small tradesmen, it is reasonable to undertake a preliminary analysis in terms of the kinds of activity exercised. This approach at least permits an evaluation of the numerical importance and of the evolution of the social group in question. Of course, an examination of the internal differentiations within the group must also be attempted, seeking to distinguish between its bourgeois and proletarian elements, in accordance with the lines of social demarcation suggested by Labrousse.

It is by paying particular attention to the internal structures of this rural artisan group that we shall best be able to reply to the questions recently raised with regard to the petite bourgeoisie as a 'misunderstood class'.[2] Our main sources are the archives which concern the milieu of artisans in particular, that is to say, the statistics on the professional tax (*patente*). Since the original nominal rolls for the payment of this tax have not been kept by the departmental archives of the Eure-et-Loir,[3] we used the general records of tax returns,[4] which include annual summaries of the number of people subject to this professional tax. Particularly useful were the registers of statistical and administrative information compiled by the direct taxation officers. Once every three years, between 1846 and 1879, they provide a list of the different trades exercised in each commune, classified principally according to the size of the individual commercial or artisanal establishments. These registers are consequently the prime source for investigating the internal hierarchies existing within this petite bourgeoisie of artisans. During the latter half of the nineteenth century, however, the reliability of this source is affected by changes in the legislation concerning the professional tax. It becomes necessary to corroborate the evidence furnished by these tax records with elements to be found elsewhere, for example in lists of conscripts,[5] in the nominal rolls of population censuses,[6] or in the archives of another financial administration, that of the stamp duty.[7] By confronting the evidence contained in these various sources, it is possible to assess the importance and numerical evolution of rural artisans, the structures and internal hierarchies of the group, and its place in rural society.

Towards the middle of the nineteenth century artisanal and commercial professions employed nearly a quarter of the active population of the part of the Beauce which lies within the department of the Eure-et-Loir.[8] In a sample of youths figuring in the conscript lists for the years 1852, 1853 and 1854, 607 out of 2469 (i.e. 24.6 per cent) belonged to these professions. One young man in four in the rural part of the Beauce worked in this sector. Is this a fair representation of local rural society as a whole?

The summary tables, commune by commune, for the population census carried out in 1851, indicate the number of 'employers' amongst the artisans and tradesmen, and the number of workers they employed. They support the impression given by the conscript lists. For the same geographical area, 23.6 per cent of the active male population counted in the census belonged to this social sector.[9] It incorporated 5794 'employers' and 3115 'wage-earners'. The ratio of just over one wage-earner for two employers is evidence of a very low level of economic concentration.

Statistics on the payment of the professional tax provide further confirmation. Still considering the purely rural part of the Beauce within the Eure-et-Loir, the records of tax returns for 1851 indicate that 5717 people paid the professional tax. This figure is to be compared to that of 5794 artisans or tradesmen set up 'on their own' according to our count in the census tables of 1851. Thus in the mid-nineteenth century the list of payers of the professional tax gives an accurate image, and one whereby it is possible to locate the place occupied by the artisan-tradesman group in a global social context. In the Beauce, then, nearly one person in four in the working population belonged to this social group. If the wage-earners are not included, then it accounted for 15–17 per cent of the active population. The importance of this proportion is to be understood in terms of the degree of autonomy which the Beauce then enjoyed in the economic sphere. Because agricultural techniques had undergone relatively little modernization, a host of artisans continued to make and to repair agricultural implements; others, engaged in the processing of agricultural produce, gave rise to an important food sector. The internal analysis of this group of rural artisans will enable us to understand more clearly the reasons for its importance in a rural area.

Throughout the nineteenth century this importance does not appear to change significantly, although it is not easy to measure the evolution of the numbers of artisans and tradesmen. If we examine first the statistics on the payment of the professional tax, contained in the general records of tax returns, the number of people subject to this tax falls from 5717 in 1851 to 4713 in 1911, that is to say, by 17.5 per cent. But as the population also diminished during the same period, the change in the relative density of payers of the professional tax gives a more accurate account. This density stands at 47.6 per 1000 inhabitants at the beginning of the twentieth century, compared to 52.7 in 1851, corresponding to a decline of less than one-tenth (9.7 per cent) in artisanal activities. This slight decline in the proportion of inhabitants paying the professional tax is not uniformly spread over the whole area.[10] It is more marked in the central part of the Beauce than on its edges. Thus, in the three cantons of Auneau, Janville and Voves, situated in the heart of the Beauce, the overall density dropped by 15 per cent. At the same time, however, the density scarcely declined at all in the small market towns which are the chief towns of these cantons. This is shown by Table 12.

Thus, in the large towns of the cantons, the increase in the number of inhabitants subject to the professional tax (23 per cent) is practically on a par with population growth (26 per cent). It is necessary to look beyond these conclusions, however, since the legislation on the professional tax underwent several important modifications during the course of the nineteenth century, and the gradual increase in the number of categories exempted from the tax[11] diminishes the validity of these statistics. They must therefore be compared with other sources. Amongst the conscripts resident in the Beauce, the proportion of artisans and tradesmen fell from 27.2 per cent in 1812–14 to 24.6 per cent towards the middle of the century. It rose again to 25.4 per cent in 1905–7. This suggests that the overall decline in

Table 12 *Evolution of the number of inhabitants subject to payment of the professional tax: cantons of Auneau, Janville and Voves*

	Years	
	1851	*1911*
Three cantons as a whole		
Population	36,507	34,119
Number of inhabitants paying the professional tax	2,021	1,605
Density (per thousand inhabitants)	55.4	47.0
Chief towns of the cantons		
Population	4,269	5,381
Number of inhabitants paying the professional tax	377	464
Density (per thousand inhabitants)	88.3	86.2

artisanal activities was slight, and more marked during the first half of the century than the second. But we are dealing here with a young population, twenty year-olds, amongst whom the number of salaried workers is much higher than the average for the population as a whole. The professional occupation of the recruits' parents would therefore be more telling. Only at two particular moments do the lists give this information: for the period of the First Empire and for the early years of the twentieth century. The comparison of these two periods shows a more marked decline. Taking only the *arrondissement* of Chartres, the proportion of artisans and tradesmen amongst the parents of the conscripts fell from 27.7 per cent to 20.0 per cent.[12]

A final verification can be carried out on the basis of the nominal rolls prepared for the population censuses. We examined these lists for four neighbouring communes situated in the centre of the Beauce: Denonville, Louville-la-Chénard, Ouarville and Santeuil. Between 1851 and 1901 the number of 'employers' amongst the artisans and tradesmen dropped from 140 to 110. Compared to the evolution of the population, the number of artisans and tradesmen per thousand inhabitants went from 60.4 to 56.6. But if we now include the assistants and wage-earners also employed in the same sector, the totals go from 187 to 158, representing an evolution, in terms of density, from 80.6, in 1851, to 81.2 in 1901. Thus, in the final analysis, we can conclude that the decline in the number of artisans and tradesmen followed demographic decline, without departing from it in any significant way: the relative importance of the artisan-tradesman group changed very little during the nineteenth century.[13] The changes which did take place impinged not upon the overall importance of the social stratum, but rather upon its internal diversity.

In order to analyse the structures of this group of artisans and tradesmen, it is first necessary to establish a classification by sectors of activity and by trades. This can be done with the help of the registers of statistical and administrative information of the direct taxation offices. It is not always easy, however, with these documents, to distinguish between those who paid the professional tax for their activity as artisans, and those who were taxed for their commercial activities. In reality, most artisans also sold the products of their labours, or the articles they made. Similarly, many tradesmen – particularly shopkeepers – were also direct producers at the same time. We shall therefore adopt a classification by sectors of activity which is sufficiently detailed to permit various comparisons.

Table 13 *Distribution by sectors of activity, and evolution of the number of inhabitants subject to the professional tax between 1846 and 1879: cantons of Auneau, Chartres-Sud, Janville and Voves*

Sectors of activity	*1846*		*1879*		*Evolution between 1846 and 1879 (%)*
	Number	*%*	*Number*	*%*	
Commercial activities					
Cereals	14	3.0	34	6.4	+142.3
Livestock	89	19.2	87	16.4	–2.2
Agricultural produce	51	11.0	53	10.0	+3.9
Foodstuffs	55	11.8	83	15.7	+50.9
Textiles	108	23.3	73	13.8	–32.4
Miscellaneous	146	31.5	199	37.6	+36.3
Total for commercial activities	463	100.0	529	100.0	+14.3
Artisanal activities					
Wood	321	16.6	125	8.0	–61.0
Textiles	113	5.8	58	3.7	–48.7
Iron	179	9.2	115	7.4	–35.7
Building	284	14.7	268	17.2	–5.6
Food	405	20.9	422	27.0	+4.2
Leather	193	10.0	77	4.9	–60.1
Transport	18	0.9	50	3.2	+177.7
Sociability	421	21.8	444	28.5	+5.5
Total for artisanal activities	1934	100.0	1559	100.0	–19.4
Miscellaneous	56		135		
Total	2453		2223		–9.4

In the four cantons of central Beauce which we considered, commercial activities are of less importance than artisanal ones, both in 1846 (18.9 per cent) and in 1879 (23.8 per cent). Even if the artisans of 'sociability' – tavern keepers and innkeepers – are counted with the commercial sector, the result is the same: commercial occupations are fewer than real artisanal ones; 36.0 per cent in 1846 and 43.8 per cent in 1879. It is striking, too, that the commercial sector as a whole grew between 1846 and 1879 (by 14 per cent), whereas the number of artisans declined by 19 per cent.

If tavern keepers and innkeepers are not counted amongst artisans, the decline of these is even greater: 26.3 per cent. Yet this conclusion cannot be accepted without some caution; the tendencies are not to be over-emphasized, since the changes in the legislation on the professional tax tended to exempt a greater number of artisans than tradesmen.[11] None the less, the other sources – the census returns and the lists of conscripts – show the same kind of evolution.

Taking the commercial activities as a whole, and excluding the miscellaneous category (composed primarily of tradesmen with no speciality, and in particular of itinerant dealers, growing in number from 79 in 1846 to 101 in 1879), trading in agricultural produce, in the broadest sense of the term (cereals, livestock, etc.), is the most important branch, accounting for one-third of the activities. Overall this branch expanded, particularly where dealing in cereals was concerned: the period was one of increasing cereal production in the Beauce. The number of corn chandlers and corn merchants also grew during the period, stimulated by the opening up of new commercial channels. Farmers sold more and more on the strength of samples, whilst the amounts of corn sold in the markets began to drop considerably. The progress of food retailing is to be explained by the undeniable improvement in the standard of living, which is also evinced by the category 'miscellaneous', reflecting a diversification in the quantity and quality of products for sale. On the other hand, the table indicates a significant decline in the commerce of textiles. The repercussions of this same decline are also apparent in the artisan group. This brings us to one of the difficulties in the definition of artisans, since this textile sector was represented in point of fact by a domestic industry. Essentially its employees were women, paid at piece rates by 'merchant-manufacturers' from Orléans or Chartres. The latter furnished the raw material – wool – for the production of various knitted goods. According to a geographical description of the department, published in 1836, in the canton of Voves 'stockings, caps and woollen waistcoats are made: at least 2000 women are engaged in this knitting work (one-sixth of the population, that is to say), except at harvest time'.[14] In the commune of Oisonville (canton of Auneau), three works together employed 40 men and 300 women and children. According to the same source, as many as 3000 women and children were occupied in knitting woollen articles in the canton of Janville. By the middle of the century this activity had declined considerably. In his report on the canton of Auneau, written around 1850, the direct taxation officer observed:

> The inhabitants of four or five communes formerly had great occupation in the making of stockings, socks, caps and woollen gloves. But this branch of industry has fallen away over the last few years, and today only vegetates; the trade in wool and in sheep – which are very abundant in this part of the Beauce – has alone conserved its earlier activity.[15]

This domestic knitting work was therefore disappearing by the middle of the century. Its decay undoubtedly explains the difficulties met by the lower classes during the 1830s, and the concomitant rise in mendicity. Emigration from the countryside, concerning the rural proletariat first, brought a partial solution to these difficulties. As a consequence, the artisanal and commercial activities in the textile sector, linked to this rural 'industry', also diminished.

Amongst the artisanal occupations, which were in general decline according to the statistics on the payment of the professional tax, a few none the less maintained the same levels or even showed progress. These were primarily the activities which also comprised a commercial aspect: food-processing, transport and sociability. All the other occupations, with the exception of building, were becoming less important. But bearing in mind the exemptions introduced by the reform of the legislation on the professional tax, it is possible to question the reality of these tendencies. A close study of the professions noted in the nominal census tables for the four communes of central Beauce already examined shows that, with the exception of the decline in textile occupations, already accounted for, the other trades in fact showed relative stability.

Table 14 *Evolution of the different sectors of artisanal activity, based on the nominal census tables for the communes of Denonville, Louville-la-Chénard, Ouarville and Santeuil*

Sector	*1851*		*1901*	
	Number	*%*	*Number*	*%*
Wood	27	20.7	20	23.3
Textiles	11	8.5	3	3.5
Iron	11	8.5	10	11.6
Building	21	16.1	15	17.4
Foodstuffs	25	19.2	17	19.8
Leather	16	12.3	10	11.6
Transport	1		1	
Sociability	18	13.8	10	11.6
Total	130		86	

To summarize, the Beauce of the second half of the nineteenth century witnessed a fall in the number of artisans and a certain increase in the number of tradespeople. The trades which accounted for the largest numbers were the ones most directly connected with commercial activity: innkeepers, tavern keepers, sellers of foodstuffs and grocers. The number of artisans servicing the farmers – harness-makers, cartwrights, blacksmiths – doubtless varied little throughout the century. This explains why even at the beginning of the twentieth century all the accounts still insist upon the high density of artisans working in even the smallest of villages. For example, in the village of Moutiers-en-Beauce, which numbered scarcely 400 inhabitants in 1911, 'there were three millers, two bakers, four taverns, two cartwrights, two blacksmiths, two joiners, two cobblers, one tailor and one sheep-dealer. The whole lot of them worked. They wouldn't have any work to do today.'[16]

This stability can be explained by the absence of any major transformation in agricultural techniques. A whole series of crafts – harness-makers, blacksmiths and cartwrights – depended upon the use of the horse as the principal force of work. Every large farm kept ten or so horses, and practically all the implements used on the farm could be maintained and repaired in the village. This explains the size of the bills that the farmers paid artisans every year. An enquiry carried out in 1909 in six large farms in the Beauce[17] shows that on average 6 per cent of the yearly expenses of each farm went on paying the cartwright, the blacksmith, the harness-maker and other craftsmen. These trades only disappeared with the spread of the tractor. As for the other trades, the building trade retained the same importance, whilst undergoing some concentration: fewer employers and more employees. Concentration also affected millers, and those who operated windmills in particular. In general, textile-based activities disappeared from the Beauce countryside after the middle of the nineteenth century. The overall impression (keeping in mind the limitations of the various sources) is one of stability in the sectors linked to work on the land, of decline in textiles, and of progress in food trades, resulting from the rising standard of living. The artisans who worked directly for the consumer (the leather, wood and building sectors) continued to have the same importance, whilst also undergoing some concentration.

As well as examining the particular evolution of the different trades, we must also try to understand something of the internal stratification of this artisan-tradesman milieu. Differences existed not only in the nature of the work, but also in the relative significance of actual productive labour and commercial operations. Within a given trade there could be a wide range of levels, 'turnovers' and profits which could differ enormously. This emerges clearly when we glimpse something of the lives of the men and women belonging to this economic sector, who were questioned at the local assizes, either as witnesses or as defendants. If we look, for example, at the trade in sheep, the assize court hearings of 1857 present two situations which are poles apart. At the lowest level we find a trade in reject sheep, akin to the butcher's trade, and exercised by a certain A. Lamé, and his mother, of Bailleau-sous-Gallardon. Here is how the justice of the peace of Auneau described their activity, on 8 January 1857:

> Lamé's father dealt in reject sheep. Since his death, two years ago, his widow has carried on the trade with the son's help. He roams about the countryside and the market-places, buying and killing the animals. He brings them home where his mother cuts the carcasses up, for sale to individuals in the neighbouring villages, and even sometimes at Auneau.

It was by no means a lucrative business, and the widow Lamé acknowledged that her husband 'had lived partly on public charity' and that she herself 'lived from her work as a day labourer'.[18] Apart from the common ovine factor, this can hardly be compared with the kind of business handled by G. Rabourdin, farmer and sheep dealer of Nogent-le-Phaye, at the beginning of the Second Empire. A local farmer described him thus:

> I have had dealings with Monsieur Rabourdin for three or four years now. I have sold him sheep on several occasions, and he has always paid cash. Although I am not sure of this, I believe that he is well-off. He must have considerable funds for his trade, considering that the farmers are always paid cash for their sheep, and that the people he then sells them to in the markets only pay, in general, after a certain delay.

Another farmer added:

> I have known Rabourdin, and done business with him, for ten or twelve years. He runs a large farm, and deals extensively in sheep . . . Rabourdin is the best dealer I know. . . . He has the confidence of the wholesalers and, if he wanted, could have unlimited credit from them.[19]

Two criteria can be applied in order to situate the different levels within the groups of artisans and tradesmen: that of rental value, and that of the fortune at the time of marriage.

The financial administration tried to differentiate between the different levels inside a particular activity by means of a classification of those paying the professional tax, under several broad categories (A, B, C and D). Thus the first three classes in category A cover wholesalers and large dealers, whilst the last five classes (A4 to A8) correspond with retail traders and artisans. The class to which an artisan was assigned depended on his turnover, the size of his business, and its rental value. Thus a mason who was also a building contractor would be in A4, a master mason in A6 and a mason working in clay and straw mortar in A7. It is more or less fair to say that in going down the classes from A1 to A7 or A8, the level of activity and of income goes down accordingly. Thus this classification can serve to give a rough idea of which were the wholesalers and medium-sized dealers (classes A1 to A4), and which the retail traders and artisans.

Table 15 *Administrative classification of payers of the professional tax in category A: cantons of Auneau, Chartres-Sud, Janville and Voves*

Classes	*Total for the four cantons as a whole*				*Communes with more than 1000 inhabitants*			
	1846		*1879*		*1846*		*1879*	
	Number	*%*	*Number*	*%*	*Number*	*%*	*Number*	*%*
A1, A2, A3	145	6.7	122	6.8	69	10.4	64	10.2
A4	319	14.7	345	19.4	120	18.1	161	25.7
A5, A6, A7, A8	1709	78.6	1310	73.7	474	71.4	401	64.1
Total	2173		1777		663		626	

Turning again to the four cantons of the Beauce already examined (Table 15), we find that large-scale dealers – those whose average individual rental value in 1846 was 244.5 francs – constitute a very small minority. They were wholesale merchants of wine, butter, wood, wool and cloth. Between 1846 and 1879 this group did not expand at all: it continued to represent between 6 and 7 per cent of the payers of the professional tax in the A category. In the more densely populated communes, however, it occupied a larger place (10 per cent). Medium-sized tradesmen (A4), with an average rental value of 221 francs in 1846, were not that far removed from the wholesalers. They included innkeepers, butchers, pork butchers, owners of cafés and livestock dealers, along with the more important artisans. This group played a larger role, and one which developed during the second half of the nineteenth century. By far the largest group, however – three-quarters of the total number of individuals paying the professional tax – consisted of artisans and shopkeepers. For the A5 and A6 classes the average rental value in 1846 was 117 francs, a figure which clearly denotes the distance separating them from the higher classes, those with rental values of 220 francs or more. The artisans and smallest tradesmen (A7, A8) did not have to pay the proportional dues of the tax, and consequently we do not know what their rental values were. This group declined notably between 1846 and 1879 (from 20 per cent to 12 per cent of the A category), largely because of the new tax exemptions introduced. As is to be expected, wholesalers were based primarily in the larger communes, the market towns, but there were exceptions to this rule. In 1879, for example, 20 of the 43 wholesale wine merchants lived in communes with fewer than 1000 inhabitants.

This detailed administrative classification only concerns the A category, and consequently omits certain professions such as millers, and itinerant dealers, which figure in the C category. In the absence of the original nominal lists for the payment of the professional tax, we can refer here to the registers of statistical and administrative information, compiled by the direct taxation officers. In each commune, and for each profession, these registers indicate the sum total of rental values. They therefore give some idea of the respective values for each different profession.

Considering only those professions which are sufficiently well-represented numerically, this table seems to suggest that, in general, artisanal activities had higher average rental values than the commercial ones. However, these averages disguise the different levels that existed within each profession, whilst certain occupations included with the artisans (innkeepers, millers) had very high rental values, tending to distort the calculation of the respective averages for the two sectors. A final drawback here lies in the fact that whilst the administration undoubtedly had little difficulty in estimating the rental value of a workshop (a smithy or a mill, for example), it might well have underestimated the values for certain trades – those in livestock or in agricultural produce, for example – which did not necessarily require commercial premises. Since this is the case, it is necessary to treat the following conclusions, based on these criteria, with some prudence. Artisan society was dominated by millers. It is not surprising to find that they frequently qualified as

Table 16 *Evolution of average rental values in francs, 1846–1879: cantons of Auneau, Chartres-Sud, Janville and Voves*

Trades	*1846*	*1879*	*Evolution (%)*
Livestock dealers	127	204	+60.6
Wholesale wine merchants	291	259	−11.0
Cloth merchants	290	285	−1.7
Itinerant dealers	103	149	+44.6
Carpenters	111	151	+36.0
Cartwrights	113	164	+44.2
Joiners	122	132	+8.2
Blacksmiths	132	138	+4.9
Ironmongers	379	493	+30.0
Locksmiths	160	175	+8.7
Masons	83	100	+20.5
Millers	607	621	+2.3
with windmills	416	383	−7.9
with watermills	1284	1556	+21.2
Bakers	169	249	+47.3
Butchers	166	240	+44.6
Harness-makers	118	150	+27.0
Cobblers	131	139	+6.1
Innkeepers	305	324	+6.2
Tavern keepers	117	148	+26.5
General average: artisans	206	242	+17.5
General average: tradesmen	163	201	+23.6

electors, on account of the taxes they paid. The most important millers were those who owned or worked in mills located on the river Eure (canton of Chartres-Sud). But those who ran windmills were also more important than the other trades, even if the decline of this type of milling is visible in the drop in the rental value of their mills. After the millers (and excluding ironmongers, who were not very numerous), came innkeepers, cloth merchants and wholesale wine merchants. Beneath these we find the artisans of foodstuffs (a rapidly expanding sector as the considerable rise in their rental values shows) and livestock dealers. In general, the trades in wood, iron, leather and building are to be found at the bottom of this scale of rental values. The miller at the top, then, and the mason at the bottom? The differences within the world of artisans could be simplified in this manner: below the millers, the trades based on the sale of agricultural produce, the foodstuff trades, then the mass of artisans working for farmers and consumers. However, the lack of clarity as to the notion of rental value leaves the validity of these conclusions in some doubt. The mason, with no workshop, and only a handful of tools, cannot be assessed according to the same criteria which take into account the market and rental value of a windmill or an inn. Such a comparison gives an image of a hierarchy based on nothing other than the importance of the material installation of each trade. None the less, it remains true that this image reflects the amount of capital invested, and in this sense the hierarchy suggested is not entirely without interest.

A useful comparison is provided here by the analysis of the fortunes which the artisans had at the moment of their marriages.

The usual age for getting married was between twenty and thirty, and it is therefore reasonable to consider the estates brought in upon marriage as a valid indication of the amount of capital necessary in order to exercise a trade. We looked at the records of all the marriages celebrated in the canton of Chartres-Sud between 1811 and 1820.[20] We then examined the tables of marriage settlements drawn up by the Chartres office of the stamp duty administration.[21] This enabled us to identify which marriages had been accompanied by settlements. For 300 marriages between artisans, there were 137 with marriage settlements. In other words nearly one artisan in two, at the beginning of the nineteenth century, got married before a notary. In view of the frequency of such settlements, it is possible to consider the estates brought in upon marriage as representative of the artisans' fortune at the initial stages of their careers. In order to have a representative sample we also looked at the estates brought in by artisans in three other cantons in the Beauce (Auneau, Janville and Voves), between 1811 and 1820, as well as at those of farmers and agricultural wage labourers, useful for comparison. For the 528 artisan couples identified, the average fortune at marriage was 1824 francs.

For 87 couples from the tradesman milieu, also discovered, the average fortune was 6565 francs. To compensate for the numerical weakness of this second category, we included in it the artisans-cum-tradesmen of the food sector: butchers, bakers and innkeepers. Thus at the beginning of the nineteenth century tradespeople

Table 17 *Average fortune upon marriage between 1811 and 1820: based on the tables of marriage settlements for Auneau, Janville and Voves, drawn up by the offices of the stamp duty administration*

Social category	*Number of examples*	*Average fortune (in francs)*
Farmers	327	8524.25
Agricultural servants	459	890.65
Day labourers	259	830.83
Vine growers	63	1066.74
Artisans	528	1824.14
Tradesmen	87	6565.73
Breakdown of artisans:		
masons	125	986.39
cartwrights	45	1897.88
blacksmiths	47	2972.17
textile trades	119	1267.42
cobblers	53	1574.71
millers	45	3000.51

were notably better-off than artisans, contrary to the impression given by their respective rental values. This latter was probably representative of the value of the shop as a building, whereas the total fortune upon marriage also included the capital necessary for building up a stock of wares. Amongst the artisans, the millers are still to be found at the top of the scale, but they are closely followed by blacksmiths. Next come cartwrights, cobblers and the textile-based artisans. At the bottom of this scale of fortunes, as on the scale of rental values, we find the masons. The analysis of the size of fortunes also shows that even within the occupations at the top of the scale – millers and blacksmiths – a wide gap could divide the less well-off from those at the very top of the hierarchy. Even identical types of activity were cut across by considerable gulfs. From this point of view, the classification elaborated by the financial administration, with its classes and categories, reveals just how judicious it was. Thus a group of wholesalers and medium-sized dealers really did exist (classes A1 to A4), even though it was not always identifiable by the measure of its rental value. The example of the cereal merchants and livestock dealers springs to mind. In terms of the capital engaged – suggested by their fortunes at marriage – the members of this sector clearly dominated the mass of shopkeepers and artisans, with the exception of millers and some blacksmiths. These last were closer to the wholesalers than to the most humble artisans, the masons. Thus it is possible to schematize the milieu of the workshop and the shop in the Beauce of the mid-nineteenth century: one-fifth tends towards membership of the bourgeoisie – and the importance of this group increased as the century advanced – whilst the other four-fifths are to be associated rather with the lower classes, though not really with the proletariat.

In effect, the analysis of the social relations between the artisans of the Beauce and the other classes of rural society shows that they cannot really be assimilated with the wage-earning class, even if they have many points in common with it.

One of the most immediately striking features of the Beauce artisan is how closely attached to the land he was. We have already seen how farmers constituted one of his principal outlets. Similarly, tradesmen involved in the sale of agricultural produce – wholesalers or medium-sized tradesmen such as the corn merchants or the livestock dealers – made up one-third of the commercial sector. If we also include the artisans working directly for the farmers (cartwrights, harness-makers and iron workers), then nearly one-fifth of the whole milieu under consideration was directly occupied in servicing farmers and agricultural production. Many artisans also owned land at the same time, and work on their land contributed towards their income. In the canton of Voves, for example, in 1836 when the land register was drawn up, 17.7 per cent of the land belonged to members of the shop and workshop group. According to the census of 1851, this same group represented 17.2 per cent of the active male population in the canton. Thus artisans, and, even more, tradesmen – wealthier in this respect – owned a share of the land that was equivalent to their share of the population. Land formed an essential part of their fortune. For the sample of 153 artisans married between 1811 and 1820 in the canton of Chartres-Sud for whom we also managed to find declarations of estate after death, landed property represented 74.8 per cent of their total fortune: 55.8 per cent as land, and 19 per cent in the form of buildings. As a rule, then, the artisans also had an agricultural smallholding. Practically all the artisans had some kind of agricultural building: barns or stables. The wife would look after a cow, or smaller livestock. The humblest artisans might also seek employment as harvest hands, or as day labourers for the large farms, during the intense work of the summer season.

Since he worked mainly for the farmer – more as a consumer than as a producer – and since he was also a peasant himself, albeit on a modest scale, was the artisan of the Beauce really independent? Where exactly did he fit in between the agricultural wage labourers and the farmers?

In terms of their work, certain artisans can be considered as journeymen. Cartwrights, harness-makers, carpenters and joiners were often employed on the farm itself. Sometimes too they had board, like farm servants. In other words their status was little different from that of a salaried employee. Working independently, on specific orders, they were exempted from payment of the professional tax, either in practice or in accordance with the legislation on the tax. Here is a typical case, that of Jean Langlois, a joiner at Santilly, accused in 1857 of stealing from the farmer who employed him.[22] The farmer thus described his activities: 'Langlois has been working for us since he came to Santilly about eight years ago. Until 15 April of last year he did precious little work for us, and I always paid him on a daily rate.' The indictment specified that he 'was frequently employed on the farm, where he dwelt and where he was well-known; he had a bed there'. It added that his salary of two francs a day represented his only means of support. Langlois no longer paid the professional tax: 'the tax-collector himself requested that this remission be granted. He has never been able to collect the taxes owed by Langlois.'

This example indicates the existence of a plebeian artisan group, merging into the day labourer class. Here the artisan was wholly dependent upon his client-turned-employer. Such cases are to be found amongst the trades requiring few tools and limited capital – building, wood trades and leather. They are far less frequent amongst the trades for which a higher capital investment was necessary, on account of the need for a workshop or a shop – a smithy, a mill or an inn. In these cases the artisan could enjoy a certain measure of independence. In other words, the greater the quantity of labour, the smaller, apparently, was the quantity of capital and the closer the artisan was to the working classes. Conversely, when a significant amount of capital was engaged, the artisan, and even more, the tradesman, belonged to the bourgeoisie.

The analysis of fortunes confirms this interpretation. The electoral lists of 1846 for the three Beauce cantons of Auneau, Janville and Voves include the names of eighty payers of the professional tax – 22 per cent of the total number of voters. Another 30 per cent of the voters were farmers. In 1846 these three cantons counted 1924 inhabitants paying the professional tax. Thus only 4 per cent of the artisans and tradesmen were wealthy enough to have the vote. By way of comparison, approximately 60 per cent of the large farmers paid enough taxes (a minimum of 200 francs a year) to qualify as electors. Overall, then, artisans figure a long way beneath the large-scale farmers on the scale of rural fortunes. The few payers of the professional tax who had the vote were mainly wholesalers or medium-sized dealers, with high rental values: wholesale wine merchants, innkeepers and millers. This gulf between the commercial and artisanal sectors is also discernible in the comparison of their respective fortunes upon marriage (Table 17). At the beginning of the nineteenth century, the average fortune of a farmer was above 8000 francs. That of agricultural wage-earners – servants and day labourers – was somewhere between 800 and 900 francs. We have already noted that for an artisan the average fortune was roughly 1800 francs, and, for a tradesman, 6500 francs. Leaving aside the averages, the distribution of fortunes for different types of artisans proves that they were far from attaining the levels of wealth of the farmers. Certain tradesmen, on the other hand, were every bit as well-off as the large-scale farmers. This still does not mean to say that the artisans can be assimilated with wage-earners. As a group their fortunes upon marriage were more than twice as high as those of wage-earners. There is thus a bracket of fortunes which is specific to the artisan group, and one which distinguishes it from the lower classes. This also suggests that as a social stratum it enjoyed a certain autonomy.

When we try to apprehend the homogeneity of the artisan group by the criterion of the choice of spouse, the same impression of autonomy emerges. In our sample of couples married in the canton of Chartres-Sud between 1811 and 1820, we have indications of the profession of the wife's parents for 301 artisan or tradesman marriages. In 35 per cent of them, the wife came from the same social milieu as her husband. Of the wives, 23 per cent were daughters of agricultural labourers, whilst families of farmers or of vine-growers provided 23 per cent and 14 per cent of the artisans' wives respectively. The dowries brought by the farmers' daughters were modest ones: around 1400 francs when her husband was an artisan; more – approximately 3000 francs – when her husband was a tradesman. The average fortunes on marriage do not therefore suggest that marriage was a means of social advancement. Marriages took place according to one's social situation and one's degree of wealth. The artisans are thus to be situated on a par with an important stratum of smallholders and vine-growers (on the slopes of the Eure valley, where this canton of Chartres-Sud is concerned). They thus form a rural petite bourgeoisie, of which the lower ranks were close to wage-earners. Nearly a quarter of the wives came from this wage-earning stratum. We are therefore dealing with an independent and intermediate class, between the rural proletariat and the group of large-scale capitalist farmers. On the whole – and with the exception of a few wholesalers, millers and innkeepers – it was closer to the former than to the latter. The artisans were on the same social level as the smallholders, with whom they had frequent relations. But, in view of the kind of work its members did, and in view of the insignificance of its capital, a lower sector of the artisan group practically merged into the lower classes. It is consequently not surprising to find that if the artisan stratum was partially recruited from the ranks of wage-earners, it only very infrequently served as a stepping-stone towards a higher social level.

Our same sample enables us to analyse social mobility. Out of the 301 marriages of the sample where we are informed of the professional occupation of the husband's father, 48 per cent of the sons exercised the same trade. Nearly 60 per cent were sons of artisans or tradesmen. Internal recruitment thus predominated. A small proportion of the artisans came from the smallholding sector, as is suggested by the modesty of their estate at the time of their marriages. Finally, 20 per cent of the artisans were children of agricultural labourers. Their fortune on marriage was modest too, and in most cases did not merit the signing of a marriage settlement.

Originating mainly from the same petit-bourgeois milieu, did these rural artisans have much chance of growing richer in the pursuit of their trades? We examined the records of the stamp duty administration, in order to discover what fortunes were left by the couples of our 1811–20 sample, representative of the generation born at the end of the eighteenth century[23] and dying during the period of the Second Empire. We found this information for 213 cases. For these it is therefore possible to compare the profession, and the level of fortune at marriage with those at the time of death. A good third stayed in the same profession all their lives. The registers of property transfer by death describe approximately half as rentiers, as landowners, as being without profession, or as former artisans. These are in fact artisans and tradesmen whose activities had enabled them to lay the foundations for a modest retirement. Loss of social position was limited: only twenty-eight artisans (13 per cent of the total) were qualified as day labourers at the time of their death. The examples of artisans rising to become farmers, or even tradesmen, are extremely rare. Loss of social position could also affect tradesmen: out of the thirty tradesmen whose situation at the end of their lives is known, six had become wage-earners. Since the criterion of profession is not very reliable, however, it is more interesting to compare the fortune at marriage with that at death, and to calculate thereby an average annual rate of enrichment . . . or impoverishment. Of the 213 artisans or tradesmen, 33 died destitute: in other words, nearly 15 per cent died without leaving any worldly possessions. Amongst the 180 artisans or tradesmen for whom we know the fortune at death, 107 had drawn up marriage settlements. For a career spanning forty years on average, their average annual rate of enrichment works out at 5.6 per cent.[24] In other words, an artisan who got married in the early years of the nineteenth century could hope to have tripled the fortune he had at the moment of his marriage by the time of his death, during the Second Empire. But this average rate conceals extreme situations, since more than a third died poorer, whilst another quarter grew richer by more than 10 per cent every year. Thus within the artisan milieu there was great inequality where social success was concerned. Similarly, the analysis of the professions of the children who inherited the artisans' fortunes (all too rarely indicated in the registers of property transfer by death) also shows extremely divergent situations. An artisan's son was often a wage-earner, very rarely a tradesman. More than half of the artisans' sons for whom this information is given were artisans themselves. Outside this stable majority, the cases of a fall in social standing are to be found far more frequently than those of social ascent. This again confirms our account of the place of the artisan group within rural society in the Beauce.

Artisanal and commercial activities provided work for a quarter of the active population of the Beauce at the middle of the nineteenth century. At the beginning of the twentieth century the proportion was slightly lower, but the decline was hardly significant. The sector serviced Beauce agriculture, and its members were relatively well-integrated into rural society, not only on account of who their clients were, but also on account of their own work on the land. This helps explain why the number of artisans and shopkeepers remained so high for a rural region throughout the nineteenth century, other factors being the absence of any major transformation of agricultural techniques, and the general broadening of markets due to the improvement in the standard of living.

Yet this integration within the rural world was not synonymous with dependence. The majority of artisans and tradesmen constituted an intermediate class between the rural proletariat and the large-scale farmers who represented agricultural capitalism in the Beauce. By the criteria of ownership of capital, work on the land, levels of fortune and matrimonial exchanges, this class is to be placed on the same level as that of small-scale farmers. It is fair to describe it as a rural petite bourgeoisie.

Its intermediate position, however, also meant that it was a heterogeneous class. In general the commercial elements of the class were a minority, although they progressed during the century. They can be identified with a 'middling' bourgeoisie, as is shown by the importance of their fortunes on marriage and by the fact that certain wholesalers and large dealers paid enough taxes to qualify as voters. This identification is sanctioned by their classification amongst the higher classes of the A category of the financial administration. The condition of the vast majority of artisans and tradesmen, on the other hand, was a more modest one. For a number of trades which could be followed with only a small amount of capital – the building trade, for example – the boundary separating their members from the labouring classes was by no means clearly defined. The artisan sector as a whole, moreover, was closer to the class of agricultural wage-earners. It was from this class that some artisans were recruited, and to which some (the numbers are difficult to ascertain) also returned. The passages between the artisan group and that of the wholesalers, on the other hand, were far less frequent.

The conclusions established during the course of this study allow us to characterize the artisans of the Beauce as a rural petite bourgeoisie close to the working classes. The numerical importance of the group shows how misguided it is to oversimplify the nature of the social structures to be found in regions of large-scale farming, like the Beauce. Between the dominant class of large farmers – a class that was but a tiny minority numerically speaking – and the mass of agricultural labourers, there was a sizeable 'middle class' of artisans, tradesmen and small farmers. The importance of the class attenuated social tensions and goes a long way towards explaining the stability of rural society in the Beauce throughout the nineteenth century.

NOTES

1 E. Labrousse, preface to *VIII° Colloque d'histoire sur l'artisanat et l'apprentissage* (Faculté des Lettres et Sciences Humaines d'Aix-en-Provence), Aix-en-Provence, 1965, 2.

2 H.-G. Haupt, 'La petite bourgeoisie, une classe inconnue', and P. Vigier, 'La petite bourgeoisie en Europe occidentale avant 1914', *Le Mouvement social*, 108, 1979, 3–20.

3 The 'P' series in the departmental archives of the Eure-et-Loir contains few articles. They are not numbered.

4 The general records of tax returns (*Etats des montants des rôles généraux des contributions*) give the number of assessments for the payment of the professional tax each year, and for each commune of the department. The amounts of the principal sum (in fixed duties), and the proportional duties making up this tax are detailed. The legislation on the payment of the professional tax is complicated, and changed frequently. It may be summarized as follows. Each person subject to the tax paid a fixed sum, the size of which depended upon the population of the commune in which the activity was exercised, and the importance of this activity. The administration evaluated this importance by means of a classification which divided professional occupations into several categories:

A Wholesalers, large-scale dealers (wholesale and retail) and retailers
B Banking and financial establishments
C Industry
D Liberal professions

Within the A category, the one with which we are mainly concerned, there were eight classes. A1 covered wholesalers, A2 large-scale dealers (wholesale and retail), and A4 to A8, shopkeepers and artisans. As well as a fixed duty, the tax also incorporated a proportional duty, based on the rental value of the premises occupied, including industrial plant and dwellings.

The registers of statistical and administrative information of the direct taxation office (*Registres de renseignements statistiques et administratifs des contrôles des contributions directes*) present the advantage of providing a classification of artisanal and commercial occupations, along with the rental value pertaining to each occupation, and this for each commune. However, this classification was effected only once every three years, and only during the years 1846–79. The trades of the same nature and in the same administrative class are grouped together. Thus if a particular commune counted three tavern keepers all in the A6 class, the rental value indicated is that of the three establishments together.

5 The conscript lists are in the 'R' series of the departmental archives of the Eure-et-Loir. The articles of this series are not numbered. Depending on the period, the lists give information which permits an analysis of the professions of the recruits themselves, and, sometimes, of their parents. Furthermore, for the periods of the First Empire and the beginning of the twentieth century, the lists also indicate the addresses of the recruits and of their parents, useful for studying the question of migration from the countryside.

6 The departmental archives of the Eure-et-Loir have a very fine collection of nominal census tables (series '6M'). They provide lists of the inhabitants of every commune, once every five years from 1836 onwards, along with the profession exercised. It is therefore possible to identify the artisans, and their trade, even though the definitions of professions are sometimes very vague.

7 The records of the stamp duty administration are conserved in the 'Q' series (not numbered) of the departmental archives of the Eure-et-Loir. They enabled us to work out the rates of enrichment for a sample of artisans, by comparing fortunes at marriage (in the tables of marriage settlements and registers of public civil acts) with those at death (in the alphabetical tables of inheritances and unclaimed estates, and the registers of property transfer by death).

8 The Beauce which lies within the department of the Eure-et-Loir corresponds with the two *arrondissements* of Chartres and Chateaudun, minus the canton of Brou, attached to the Perche. For our investigation of rural artisans we eliminated from our calculations the three cantons with significant urban populations (Chartres-Nord, Chartres-Sud and Chateaudun).

9 The part of the Beauce which is in the department of the Loir-et-Cher showed a practically identical proportion; 23.2 per cent, for example, in the canton of Ouzouer-le-Marché. See G. Dupeux, *Aspects de l'histoire sociale et politique du Loir-et-Cher, 1848–1914*, Paris and La Haye, 1962, 128.

10 The evolution of the number of inhabitants subject to the professional tax is not the same for all the regions of the Eure-et-Loir. In the Perche, to the south-west of the department, the density grew by more than one-fifth between 1851 and 1911.

11 In 1858 a law exempted from payment of the tax those workers who were set up on their own account, working either in their own homes, or in those of other persons, and who did not employ other workmen or apprentices, nor have a firm name or shop premises. Also exempted were day labourers and outworkers. A law of 2 July 1862 extended this exemption to those workers who did have shop or workshop premises, or a firm name, but who otherwise met the same conditions as those laid down in 1858. Throughout France, 120,000 people were exempted by this new law. Thus from 1862 onwards, joiners, cobblers, coopers, pedlars of small wares and harness-makers ceased to appear in the statistics. Between 1862 and 1863, the number of people assessed for the tax in the canton of Janville fell from 607 to 489. In the canton of Voves the reduction was from 663 to 506. On the subject of the changes in the legislation on the professional tax, see J. Tardieu, *Traité théorique et pratique des patentes*, Paris, 1902.

12 This estimate does not take into account the two 'urban' cantons of Chartres-Nord and Chartres-Sud.

13 This conclusion is not contradicted by the fact that the rural exodus affected artisans more than other social groups. At least for the beginning of the twentieth century it is possible to ascertain how many conscripts whose addresses were in towns came from the country, according to their parents' address (conscripts were usually registered at their place of birth). In the rural part of the *arrondissement* of Chartres (excluding the town of Chartres itself and the chief towns of the cantons), between 1900 and 1904, a little over 12 out of every 100 conscripts born in the countryside were living and working in town. For artisans, the trades in foodstuffs, and the other commercial occupations, the percentages are 13, 20 and 14 respectively. In the small market towns which were also the chief towns of the cantons, more than one young man in three (33.5 per cent) was concerned by the rural exodus. For the three categories of artisanal and commercial occupations mentioned above, the figures are 36.8 per cent, 38.8 per cent and 42.8 per cent respectively. Thus the children of artisans and tradesmen were more likely than others to migrate to towns. As a rule artisan families appear to be larger than others, at least according to the census tables of 1851. Workshops or shops required only a limited number of workers and could only be taken over by one of the children. It is consequently understandable that in the Beauce many children were obliged to leave the countryside.

14 J. Doublet de Boisthibault, 'L'Eure-et-Loir', in M. Loriol (ed.), *La France. Description géographique, statistique et topographique*, 147.

15 Departmental archives of the Eure-et-Loir, 'P' series. Register of statistical information for the tax office of Auneau.

16 M. Barbier, miller of Moutiers-en-Beauce, recollections recorded by the Groupe de Recherches sur les Traditions Populaires de Beauce, *Le Vent du Ch'min*, Saint-Denis, 1979, 55–6. This account gives a total of 19 potential payers of the professional tax at the beginning of the twentieth century, for a population of 400 inhabitants. According to the register of statistical information for the canton of Voves, for 1846, there were then 24 payers of the professional tax for a population of 510 inhabitants. This again confirms the overall perpetuation of artisanal and commercial activities during the second half of the nineteenth century.

17 Dr J. Bailhache, 'La grande culture en Beauce', *La Science sociale*, 1912.

18 Departmental archives of the Eure-et-Loir, II U. Records of the assize court for the first session of 1857.

19 ibid., 4th session of 1857. Evidence given in June and September 1852.

20 Departmental archives of the Eure-et-Loir. Registers of births, marriages and deaths for all the communes of the canton of Chartres-Sud.

21 Departmental archives of the Eure-et-Loir, 'Q' series (unnumbered).

22 Departmental archives of the Eure-et-Loir, II U. Records of the assize court for the first session of 1857.

23 This investigation was based upon the alphabetical tables of inheritances and unclaimed estates. These list all the deaths in the canton, with references to the declarations of fortune – when they existed – entered in the registers of property transfer by death. The archives of the stamp duty administration are not easily available. This, and the fact that many of the individuals we were looking for had changed address, explains why it was impossible to discover the declarations of fortune for all the couples married in the canton of Chartres-Sud between 1811 and 1820.

24 For a comparable period, the average annual rate of enrichment for the large-scale farmers of the Beauce was above 7 per cent.

11 Shopkeepers and the state in Britain, 1870–1914

GEOFFREY CROSSICK

> 'We are a nation of shopkeepers, large and small, and I think that it would be completely unjust to use taxation to penalize skill and hard work, in the way that some are demanding in your country.'
>
> *(An English shopkeeper to Edmond Demolins, who had inquired of him how English traders were responding to the pressure of large-scale competition.)*[1]

> 'Sorry, I cannot assist you. My business is carried on by self, wife and children. All we ask is legislative non-interference.'
>
> *(J. Chappell, linen draper of Holloway in North London,* c. *1892. The words were scrawled in thick blue pencil across a form sent out by the social investigator, Charles Booth, seeking information about wages in the retail trade.)*[2]

> The East End Jewish Shopkeepers' Association was formed in June 1912. Mr Maurice Myers explained at the inaugural meeting that many of these traders were from oppressive countries with powerful and intrusive states. They now tasted freedom in Britain, and wanted no part in associations to act in relation to the government. But, he urged them, 'true citizenship did not mean merely avoiding the attentions of a policeman. It involved an active interest in the affairs of the State.' Especially as legislation now threatened their well being.[3]

The words of these three shopkeepers are unusual, in that each reflects in his own way upon the relationship between retailers and the state. Few shopkeepers in Britain did that during this period, and it is instructive that two of these statements were prompted by contact with continental Europe. As this essay explores some of the ways in which British shopkeepers perceived the state and its relations to their problems, so these three themes will insistently surface. The refusal of Demolins's correspondent to accept that the individual shopkeeper had a distinctive identity and distinctive rights which set him apart from the business community as a whole, and allowed him to see any justice in restraining large-scale capital; the instinctive response of the Holloway draper, anxious at the growth of government and wanting simply to be left alone to cope with his own problems; and the Jewish shopkeepers' experience of a quite different kind of state from those of their past, rejoicing in its purely negative freedoms, and taking notice of it only when it noticed them. It was, however, rare for retail traders in Britain to think readily of the state, except when it threatened their independence, and I shall seek to understand that relationship by examining the overall ideological context within which they responded to the more competitive atmosphere that emerged in retailing from the later decades of the nineteenth century. Only within that context can one understand the overall rejection of the state – of any state – as relevant to their very real problems; as well as the limited ways in which some retailers were prepared to turn to the state. The central and most important section of this essay will be devoted to these themes, while the final part will offer some tentative explanations for the distinctive British experience.

I outlined the competitive problems of British retailing in my survey essay earlier in this book, and there is no need to repeat those arguments, save to stress that the emergence of larger-scale retail operations in the last quarter of the nineteenth century – department stores, retail chains, and rapidly growing consumer co-operatives – was but one element within a set of problems, of which the most important was probably internal competition amongst independent shopkeepers themselves. My concern here is with the way in which smaller shopkeepers responded to these new threats, for it is within that overall response that we shall be able to comprehend the character of their relation to the state. Through parliamentary enquiries, the shopkeeper press and journals, and the records of shopkeeper organizations, the broad divisions amongst shopkeepers can be uncovered, and the contours of shopkeeper ideology discerned. They emerge, for example, through arguments over the adulteration laws, civil service stores, closing hours regulation, the struggle against consumer co-operation, and the response to large-scale capital as it penetrated retailing through department stores and then multiples. Shopkeeper organizations in Britain developed partly in response to these issues, to defend shopkeepers or to agitate on their behalf, and partly to serve the limited needs of individual retailers (debt collecting and price agreements were the most common). It is through the activities and above all the statements of these organizations or their members that much of the evidence must come.

Although traders' organizations can be traced from the middle of the century, the real expansion seems to have taken place in the 1890s. It was then, for example, that the bulk of town grocers' associations were founded.[4] Certain preliminary points must be made before briefly outlining the types of shopkeeper organization. Firstly, these organizations were totally independent of the state, with not even the connection afforded by registration. They certainly had no corporate role, or quasi-official status in trade regulation. Secondly, it is important to note the absence of political organizations, or of national shopkeeper bodies concerned with trade defence, except very briefly and on very specific issues. Nor were there serious economic associations of shopkeepers, and this leads to my final point, for it is striking that Hector Lambrechts, ever anxious to find evidence of shopkeeper organizations, erected careful and differentiated typologies for Germany, Belgium and France, distinguishing types, status and purpose of different associations, but he could offer no more than a brief and shapeless listing when he turned to Britain.[5] There was a flat, uni-dimensional character to these organizations, with limited conflict of ideas and aspirations between them. The most significant distinction was between *intra-trade* and *inter-trade* organizations. The associations of members of a single trade came earliest and were most widespread amongst retailers subject in some way to state regulation – licensed victuallers, pawnbrokers, chemists, bakers, and butchers – and it is notable that grocers and milk sellers followed from the 1880s when they too were subjected to new legislative or administrative interference.

National trade federations appeared more hesitantly, the most successful being the Federation of Grocers' Associations, established in 1891 and organizing in 1903 88 of the 128 town grocers' associations then in existence.[6] The most common local inter-trade bodies were the tradesmen's associations which by the turn of the century were almost ubiquitous, above all in the smaller towns where intra-trade organization was hard to maintain. They appear as sober bodies, acting as pressure groups in local affairs, above all in response to issues thrown up by local government, and to which role they would add social and benevolent activities. The chambers of trade that were formed, generally in larger towns, to bring together as affiliates the town's single trade associations had similar functions, and no town seems to have had both a tradesmen's association and a chamber of trade. The concerns were also similar, responding to local government activity, rates, the price of services (railways, water, post, gas), and so on. The impetus to inter-trade organization often seems to be not so much traders' problems as retailers, but as ratepayers.[7] National inter-trade organizations were almost entirely absent. The first, the National Chamber of Trade established in 1871, could hardly justify the name, for it was a southern-based organization with few branches or affiliates[8] and it soon became an élite organization sending deputations and petitions about government legislation. It disappears from view in the early 1880s, and the only serious inter-trade organization of a national character in our period bears the same name. The National Chamber of Trade (NCT) was founded in 1898 and, although it did have individual members, its main strength came from the affiliation of local tradesmen's associations and chambers of trade – there were 208 affiliated organizations by 1912, concentrated geographically in the North and Midlands.[9] The NCT appears from its minutes as a pressure group to amend government legislative proposals, but rarely assuming an agitational role itself. It is to the short-lived or highly specific agitational organizations that we must look for that – above all those formed to fight the co-operative stores, such as the local traders' defence associations in

1902–3, and the sectarian national bodies that followed, like the Traders' Union and the Central Board of Traders' Defence Associations.

Finally, whom did they organize? There is much patchy evidence, but nothing systematic. Local single trade organizations almost certainly drew into themselves a larger range of the trade than did town tradesmen's associations, and these latter would be led by the local retailer élite – above all the prosperous High Street grocers and drapers. The leadership of retailer organizations was generally better established and more prosperous than the membership, and the latter more so than the trade as a whole. It was rare for the more marginal of shopkeepers to be organized, either the unstable small shopkeepers, especially those in the lesser trades or general shops, or the proletarian shopkeepers who combined it with some other source of income. The exception, as we shall see in due course, was the Shopkeepers' and Small Traders' Protection Association, and similar local short-lived associations, that recruited from amongst the very small.

It is from these organizations, their actions and statements, the words of their representatives and their journals, that much of the evidence that lies behind this paper is derived. Through such material some perspective is formed on their relationship to the state. If this poses precisely the problems implicit in working from organizations to obtain information about a social group – that the act of organizing and entering into the public domain carries with it a shift of attention and perception that might not have been shared by the mass of shopkeepers – then the problem must at this stage remain. The implications are, perhaps, more serious for those countries where shopkeeper organizations made more positive demands of the state than did those in Britain.

In the central section of this paper I shall not present a history of the retailers' response to these new pressures, of their organizations and their demands, but concentrate instead on elucidating and analysing the main characteristics of that response. The liberal economic assumptions, and the view of government that in part flowed from them, which were so prevalent amongst British shopkeepers, shaped the dominant and recurrent response, which was to seek to compete better and to persuade customers that the individual shopkeeper was indeed superior to his larger competitors. The problem for small shopkeepers was that they had no peg upon which to hang a distinctive programme to deal with these new competitors, for they seemed largely wedded to the idea that they were part of a single business community that stretched upwards to large-scale capital. They certainly lacked a clear identity as small shopkeepers – the identity as *petit commerce* in France – whether that identity bore a merely business or a broader social and moral meaning. These themes emerge in the way anxious shopkeepers discussed, and at times agitated over, consumer co-operative stores and multiple retailers; above all in the way that they made virtually no appeal to the state for help in that struggle. Indeed, the state figured in their thinking only when it imposed itself upon them, interfered with or regulated them. The one serious exception to that rule was when the larger and better-established individual shopkeepers appealed to the state to restrict shop opening hours by law. The result was to isolate the very small shopkeepers who began to organize in opposition and to present themselves, for almost the only time in this period, as men and women of tiny ambitions and infinitely greater fears. The interest of this division must conceal neither its uniqueness, nor the fact that the layer of individual shopkeepers that it set apart was a small and comparatively marginal one.

The continuing and largely unchallenged commitment to the assumptions of economic liberalism served to turn shopkeepers in upon themselves in an attempt to meet the new forms of competition rather than to seek external, that is to say state, assistance in limiting them. The term 'assumptions' seems preferable to 'principles', because although explicit statements of faith in a version of classical economics are made,[10] what we encounter far more frequently are behaviour and statements that are dependent on low-level and rarely formulated ideological assumptions. From those assumptions the policies that seemed available with which to meet the increasing competitive problems were firmly limited to the search for superior and hence more competitive methods. Shopkeeper organizations and the retailer press emphasized the need to compete with the new operations, and the search for methods by which to do so. An editorial in *The Grocer* during 1904, headed 'Why grocers fail' and pointing at the very outset to 'these days of great companies, and of branch shops innumerable', concentrated its attention almost entirely upon individual shopkeeper failings – credit, over-stocking, and waste.[11] Analysis of that kind is to be found virtually throughout the shopkeeper movement and the press that it generated, and this insistence on finding both diagnosis and remedies inside the world of small retailers contrasts strikingly with the reluctance to admit their own part in creating their problems which Gellately finds amongst German retailers.[12]

Competition was certainly not limited to prices, but they were the most obvious area for contest and, shopkeepers were forced reluctantly to admit, the most important for their customers. When faced with the civil service 'co-operative' stores in the 1870s, London shopkeepers sought methods by which prices could be reduced to match those of the stores. They did, of course, insist that the government restrict the role of its own employees in these stores, but the extra costs of credit trading increasingly moved to the centre of concern as legitimate shopkeepers tried to lower their prices. *The Traders' Times*, which led the campaign against the stores, insisted that giving a discount for cash trade would return the price advantage to the individual trader. 'This is the legitimate, indeed the only way of combating the co-operative stores.'[13] A later editorial in the same paper urged that proprietary goods were the basis of co-operative price cutting, and had to be resisted 'unless all retailing is to become simply a mere matter of distribution'.[14] Once branded goods were established, however, and retail competition more severe, their advantage as the basis for minimum price agreements came to be seen by retailers. Although the older struggle to match low prices continued to be the dominant means of handling price competition, there emerged in the 1890s a movement for minimum prices, directed at bringing together manufacturers, wholesalers and retailers in a voluntary organization to maintain an agreed level of prices for branded goods. The principal figure in the movement, William Glyn-Jones, saw the tactic as but one phase of 'a very keen fight between the individual trader and the big trade monopolists'.[15] This self-help movement to protect market shares and improve profitability met with success only in the chemists' trade: some one-third of all retailing chemists and eighty-six manufacturers were in the Proprietary Articles Trade Association in 1901.[16] Elsewhere, the movement barely got off the ground. Shopkeepers remained committed to price competition.

The problem was that in the matter of prices the individual shopkeeper was all too frequently beaten by the larger-scale operations. Or so it seemed to the customers. The emphasis then shifted, and while prices remained important, increasing attention was given to the level of service, skill, salesmanship and so on that the traditional shopkeeper could offer. Shopkeepers were in a quandary: were co-ops, multiples, department stores successful in their different ways because they genuinely were better, or because their customers were deluded into thinking so? The question was never resolved, and the shopkeeper movement acted as if both were true, urging individual retailers to improve their own methods of running their businesses and attracting their customers, while seeking to persuade the public that large-scale retailing offered only illusory benefits. 'The enlightenment of the cooper is really all that is wanted' argued one leading agitator in the anti-co-op movement.[17] Publicity and education, as we shall see, were directed at a rational public in the central activity of the campaign. The new retail operations were to be met by the improvement and regeneration of traditional shopkeeping – nothing else was needed or available.[18] An excellent illustration is the sad fate of the Glasgow grocer who wrote to the trade press just before the war, complaining that it was useless urging him to advertise, because the trade and profits of the small Glasgow grocer were very low, as 'he must sell his goods at the same price as the multiple grocer'. He received little sympathy, his emphasis on competition from multiples was ignored, and the activists of the shopkeers' organizations castigated him for his own inadequacies as a trader. George Doland of the London and Suburban Traders' Federation attacked 'these pessimistic, can't-be-done, dead beat, rut-trailing tradesmen who consider they are born too late. . . . The world owes a living only to him who earns it.' All the advice that the Glasgow grocer received was *internal* to his business. The implication was that the cause of the problems lay with him, and that nothing else could be interfered with.[19]

If liberal economic assumptions precluded appeals to the state to help solve retailers' problems, so did the absence of any clear sense of identity as small shopkeepers, as *petit commerce*. This diffuse identity appears most generally in the recurrent expressions of belief in a single business community, of which smaller shopkeepers were a part. Except at the most marginal level – of which more later – there was none of that sense that individual shopkeepers were different in ways that meant policies for them would also be different. While distinctive government departments in Belgium, and specific sections of chambers, even special chambers, in Germany were demanded or created to attend to the special concerns of individual shopkeepers, the shopkeeper movement in Britain demanded a Minister of Commerce, or a cabinet position for the president of the Board of Trade 'to ensure a proper recognition of the importance and magnitude of home and foreign trade and manufactures'.[20] Most shopkeepers seem to have identified themselves as businessmen, part of a community that stretched up to the largest enterprises. Large-scale retailing might be regretted, but nothing could be done about it. This generalized consciousness was doubtless helped by the fact that large retail companies did not themselves organize distinctively. The first sign of that was only in 1913, when the Incorporated Association of Retail Distributors, comprising all the main London department stores, was set up to watch over problems arising out of the Shop Hours Act.[21] The business world was a continuum for small shopkeepers, and they reassured themselves that many passed upwards.[22] Small business was the seed-bed of great, much was made of oaks and acorns, and a reassuring commitment was affirmed to a liberal faith in progress by capital accumulation. For John Jones, a West End London watchmaker, that was why the 5 per cent profit made by civil service stores was unacceptable to the private trader, for with 5 per cent 'nobody can climb out of small beginnings. . . . It is the savings of the smaller people who have tried and are trying to be better off that constitutes the wealth of every trade'.[23] The argument that followed, and it recurs from that enquiry right up to the First World War, was that private joint-stock traders were legitimate, however much they might be regretted, and that they could not be interfered with. This was the argument of the retailers who attacked the civil service stores early in the period, but it did not alter as competition built up. Herman Hamborg, a tobacconist, was asked:

> 'Do you mean that associated trading is a monopoly? – No, I am referring more particularly to the servants under the Crown trading in opposition to ratepayers.' He was asked, what if fifty tradesmen put capital and expenses together to open a large store, would you deem that a monopoly? 'It is a monopoly, but I think that it is one that you could hardly interfere with.' Question – 'Is the State justified in handicapping the joint-stock trader against the private trader? – I think not.'[24]

Similarly, a chemist agreed that the Army and Navy Stores would be acceptable if 'capitalists' took it over.[25] Outside observers noted how the processes of concentration were seen. 'Larger and larger capitals are entering into every form of trading . . . the retailers enter no protest; they accept them as inevitable and irreversible,' noted the *Daily Telegraph* in 1902,[26] while a couple of years later *The Times* observed in connection with the proposal to introduce a cash on delivery postal system that 'people who submit patiently to the operation of laws which are not made or controlled by the Legislature are apt to be very indignant when they can trace any part of their misfortunes to an administrative change'.[27] However unhappy they might have been about the competition from large-scale capital, most shopkeepers in Britain saw themselves as businessmen, and their success as dependent upon the economics of the market. Together, these provided little purchase for a distinct identity as individual shopkeepers, trapped and without ambition. The pervasive sense of the breadth of the business world is in striking contrast to the implications of the demands for *patente* reform in France. The proposal at the Fédération des Groupes Commerciaux in 1905 that in towns of under 100,000 population taxes by specialities should come into effect at a mere five employees reflects the paucity of ambition within the world of even organized *petit commerce*, a sense that small is distinct, and that the very different world of large business starts rather low down the scale.[28]

The notion of the legitimate retailer was thus a fluid and imprecise one in Britain, isolating neither economically nor socially any shopkeeping class with distinct interests. Large-scale private enterprise retailing was in no way illegitimate – that term was reserved in part for consumer co-operation and municipal trading, but more commonly for 'illusive trading', the frauds and deceits and the peripheral trading of factory chocolate clubs, churches, or the pension tea salesmen.[29] The implication is of a diffuse sense of trade identity, a weak commitment to notions of the right of a shopkeeper to practise his trade, to craft or corporate ideals of a shopkeeper's specialist trade as a right, and as his property to be defended. Expressions of a belief in trades' rights do appear. One Highgate chemist argued in 1880 that chemists had years of training, and capital sunk into their businesses, and as a result the civil service stores 'had no moral right to enter into opposition to the chemist'.[30] Twenty years later the president of the Leeds Chamber of Trade, attacking consumer co-operation, told his fellow retailers that 'they owed a duty to their trade, present and prospective, to hand that trade forward unimpaired. Every man was to some extent a steward for the trade in which he was engaged.'[31] Statements such as these are striking for their rarity; they never provided the organizing principles for shopkeeper identity or a shopkeeper movement. The related idea of 'specialism', so central to one kind of small shopkeeper identity, is similarly absent in Britain. I have found it only once, as a vague moral preference for the honest world of the specialist trader, in a statement to the civil service stores enquiry of 1879, but even then the witness saw it as overridden by the realities of trade.[32] Over the next thirty years, retailers were urged by their leaders to diversify to survive, instead of retreating into what they knew best. Multi-line trading and good business methods were urged as the solution to the small shopkeepers' problems, and there is no sign that they resisted the idea on ideological grounds.

The state has so far figured little in this essay. My argument is that the absence of a separate identity of small shopkeepers as a group with distinct social and economic interests is central to an understanding of the way that shopkeepers in Britain sought solutions to their problems of competition, and of the way that the state was to play such a limited part in those solutions. This is essentially a negative point that emerges only in the awkward light of comparisons with the faltering, uneven, but real identities of *petit commerce* elsewhere in Europe. It becomes a stronger assertion when set within the ideological framework that I have sketched over the last few pages. If shopkeepers in Britain asserted no 'right to trade', they also claimed no vital social role. As James Debac of the first National Chamber of Trade put it, at the beginning of my period, 'We are quite prepared to admit that the moment we cease to be of use to the public, the moment any organisation can be brought forward which will distribute cheaper and better than we do, our occupation is gone.'[33] From this point on it is rare to find any social or moral claims made for themselves by shopkeepers beyond the purely instrumental – that they sit on juries, fill municipal and parochial office, and so on. The posture of all levels of the shopkeeper movement is blandly commercial: their right to survival exists purely for as long as they serve an economic function. Above all, they did not try to isolate themselves as a group with a specific social and moral role of the kind increasingly attached to the defence of the *classes moyennes*. The world that these shopkeepers saw themselves as standing for was not significantly different from that of the developing business world as a whole. The image of the department store in the propaganda of the French *Ligue syndicale* depicted it as a symbol of an increasingly intensive, capitalist and immoral society.[34] That imagery has no parallels in Britain, as if the economic universe had been successfully amoralized. That is precisely what classical economics was about, and in the responses of British shopkeepers we see one of its most lasting, and in Europe terms most striking, ideological successes – the amoralization of the question of the survival of *petit commerce*.

That is a vital component in understanding the failure to present a distinct identity or generate a distinct programme which lay behind the relations of British shopkeepers to the state. One catches occasional glimpses of small shopkeepers seeing themselves as on the way out, destroyed by the forces of large-scale commerce. An excellent and early example of a once reasonably placed tobacconist now in decline, and without any perspective through which to interpret his own situation or generate remedies, can be found in the unclear and at times contradictory evidence of Herman Hamborg to the civil service stores enquiry.[35] At the other end of the period, a letter from a small Newcastle shopkeeper is far more explicit:

> I ask only to be left alone to die a natural death. . . . I am being superseded by gigantic trading companies, whose yearly takings count in millions, whose working expenses count only a few coppers to the pound. I once saw a troop of elephants coming along a country road. Their slow but sure approach was thrilling. They came nearer. I stood aside in the hedge. The great animals came along in perfect silence. It was their silence and their inevitable coming that was awful. Great civil service stores and great limited liability companies are coming just as surely and so silently as those elephants came along that country road. The smaller shopkeeper must stand aside.[36]

That vision of despair was not commonly expressed, and it is indeed a despairing one. There is little or no counter-perspective offered, other than the need to fight back as individual businessmen. Fatalism was a precise other side of the coin to the absence of any ideological or social purchase for a genuine and programmatic opposition to the forces of concentration.

If we seek a campaigning response by individual shopkeepers, we will find it only in the reactions to consumer co-operation, for in that alone did they depart from a broad, albeit reluctant, ideological acceptance of mounting competition. Co-operative societies were disliked, feared, denounced – but even here the campaign against them was essentially a self-help one, barely directed at the state. The noisy but brief movement against the civil service stores (most of which called themselves co-operatives) in the 1870s certainly sought state action to prevent civil servants engaging in trade, to impose a turnover tax on them, and similar demands.[37] The fact that they were run by state employees made state-oriented demands almost inevitable, but they were always of a very *ad hoc* kind, and we have already seen how retailers turned towards meeting the competition in business terms. The larger anti-co-operative movement – aimed more specifically at the predominantly working-class consumer co-operatives so strong in the industrial districts – is noticeable for the uncertainty of its tactics, and the general absence of proposals for government action to restrict co-operatives.

Opposition to co-operatives surfaced frequently during this period, but it tended to take the form of local conflicts in which shopkeepers sought to deter working men and women from using what were known as 'the stores', by a variety of threats.[38] The one sustained campaign was launched by the grocers of St Helens in July 1902. The issue took fire, and the shopkeeper press, traders' associations, and even the national press covered it extensively. By early the next year the movement had lost its impetus and was in decline, but its short and vigorous life is illuminating. The St Helens Co-operative Society was in a period of rapid expansion, and had recently opened new and impressive central premises. The local grocers provided the initiative for the formation of a St Helens and District Traders' Defence Association (TDA), pledged to a policy of boycott. Local traders would neither employ nor buy from members of the co-op, craftsmen and tradesmen who worked for it, or bankers, doctors or churchmen who supported it. Above all, traders' employees must not shop there.[39] The totality of that boycott was soon eased, and it insisted more cautiously on refusing to employ anyone connected with the stores, and on establishing 'reciprocal trade relations among all trades and professions'.[40] The movement was essentially and explicitly defensive,[41] but the boycott tactic seemed aggressive in appearance, if weak in practice. The movement built real momentum in St Helens, with support flowing in from other towns, in the late summer and autumn of 1902. One-third of the town's retailers are judged to have joined the TDA, although the smaller traders were thought to have remained absent.[42] Grocers were at the heart of the campaign wherever it took off – hardly surprising, for some 80 per cent of co-op turnover in 1914 was in food of some kind[43] – but the St Helens TDA committees covered a very full range of the town's retail trades.[44]

The spread of the agitation from St Helens was uneven, and most organized retailers received its inception with kind thoughts but a great deal of caution. Only nearby Wigan launched a large-scale response, through the Wigan and District Traders' Defence League, but even they firmly rejected the boycott tactic and concentrated on propaganda.[45] TDAs or their equivalents were created in some fourteen English towns;[46] the Scottish TDA continued from the 1890s; and many other towns' traders' associations gave verbal support. But the movement had no real unity of policy, tactics, or leadership. A variety of national umbrella organizations with few adherents sought to lead the movement[47] but tactical disagreements and a reluctance to embark on a large-scale struggle precluded a sustained and organized agitation. The problem was that there was little to demand, for even the restrained St Helens approach, built around a self-organized and limited boycott, was too much for most TDAs, let alone those towns whose retailers did not form one. The one demand made of the state concerned income tax, for the co-operatives' 'profits' were distributed to members, most of whom earned below the income tax threshold of £160 *per annum*. Many traders' organizations wanted these surpluses taxed at source – but the St Helens leader, John Green, admitted at the outset that they could not expect any success on this issue.[48] Many organizations were in any case unconvinced by the income tax argument,[49] though it remained a recurrent demand. For the rest, it is striking that as one reads reports of meetings round the country, but above all in the key centres of St Helens and Wigan, reads the words of those who address meetings and the questions from the floor, just about nothing is said about government action. And even the self-organized boycott was largely rejected. The education and enlightenment of customers was to be the weapon of the legitimate trade. The Bradford Grocers' Association decided to 'work quietly upon safe lines' and a similar commitment to propaganda alone was the norm.[50] Even James Kendall of the Traders' Union told Blackburn TDA that 'there was not a third-rate grocer who need be afraid of competing in the matter of value with the co-operative societies'. Only the cloak of religion and philanthropy misled people.[51] Enlightenment and comparative price-lists would suffice: the co-operatives' advantages were an illusion. The campaign died away in inactivity. There was nothing to do, no demands for action, certainly no demands for the state to aid retailers.

The ideological centre of the campaign rested less on a defence of the small trader, more on a passionate commitment to private enterprise, individualism and initiative. J. T. Gee of Wigan stressed that it was the initiative of individuals not of groups that was the basis of all advance, and the Wigan and District Traders' Defence League that he led sought 'to establish united action amongst traders to promote their rightful interests, to foster and encourage individual effort as the best remedy for increasing the trade and wealth of the country by supporting private enterprise'.[52] Abuse of the co-operatives came to the fore, above all as the movement lost impetus, with leaders like Robert Walker repeatedly portraying co-ops as business rackets run by a handful of unscrupulous men.[53] Such abuse brought the campaign's chief mouthpiece, *The Tradesman and Shopkeeper*, crashing to the ground in a lost libel action. I return to the limited resources on which shopkeepers could draw to resist, constraints which for me underpin their reluctance to appeal to the state. They built their case not on a firm core of belief in the rights of legitimate trade, but only on a generalized belief in individualism and private enterprise. A later campaign by *The Retailer*, organ of the London and Suburban Traders' Federation, exemplified precisely this, and quite explicitly rejected the legitimacy of legislative restraints on large-scale retail enterprises.[54]

The movement of opposition to consumer co-operation is thus instructive, above all because of the virtual absence of any sense that the state ought to support shopkeepers, regulate co-operation, restrict its scope of operations, and so on. Only over income tax do they direct any demands at the state, and then more in outrage than with any great expectation of change. There was clearly marked variation in the demands and the achievements of shopkeeper movements in other European countries with respect to legislative or administrative support for retailers against co-operatives. Charles Gide gave a detailed survey of how government action was demanded and often obtained on taxation, liability to company law, prohibition from selling to the public (or, in Hungary, having windows on the street!), scale of operation, and so on.[55] There was great unevenness here, but Théodor's unintentionally illuminating account of how he and others had to teach the petit-bourgeois movement in Belgium that you could not simply suppress co-operation, and the conseqential shift of demands towards regulations, limits to fields of action and to customers, new tax laws, and more, all reveals how even one of the more liberal and free trade oriented shopkeeper movements in continental Europe saw the solutions to co-operative competition as to a large degree the responsibility of the state.[56]

A Doncaster tradesman wrote to the *St Helens Newspaper* at the height of the anti-co-operative campaign to ask 'How is it there is all this bitterness against the Stores and nothing is said about Lipton's and all these big companies?'[57] Others clearly asked the same question, for John Green, the leader of the St Helens movement, insisted that 'they could fight Lipton's or any other company so long as they were fighting on lines they themselves were fighting on, that was, without the divi and if they did that they had no fear. (Applause)'.[58] The multiples posed a real threat, even in the heart of the anti-co-operative movement. There were at least fourteen branches of national multiple chains in St Helens in 1901 and seventeen in Wigan, with eleven butchers' shops, ten grocers, and five shoe retailers between them.[59] Indeed, as early as 1894 *The Grocer* argued that the main threat was no longer the co-operatives but 'the large branch shops, which disseminate broadcast peculiar advertisements tending to inflame the public mind, and designed to lead to the belief that, as opposed to their gigantic organisations, unlimited capital, and modern methods of buying, the local trader has a poor choice'.[60] At around the same time, the secretary of the Metropolitan Grocers' Federation told Charles Booth's interviewer that traders with many branches were pushing out smaller men on a substantial scale.[61] Such anxieties grew, and after the turn of the century multiple traders were regarded by individual shopkeepers with increasing fear and concern, while the retailer press carried articles on the subject, and traders' associations debated whether or not multiple shop managers should be admitted to membership. Neither the London and Suburban Traders' Federation nor the National Chamber of Trade was able to give any consistent advice on the matter, and that indecision reflects precisely the ambiguity that characterized retailer responses to multiples.[62]

The problem was the absence of any agreed method of dealing with multiples that might go beyond normal competitive methods, increasingly unsatisfactory though these seemed. Proposals for special taxes on multiples do surface from about 1909, arguing that there was a superfluity of shops, and that local patriotism was offended by the way companies took profits out of the towns in which they were made. The next couple of years saw a flurry of newspaper correspondence, and the very occasional resolution from a traders' association, calling for new taxes on multiples.[63] The anxiety is clear, but nowhere did these ideas become serious demands, and no national, or to my knowledge local, retailer association campaigned for them or formulated concrete proposals. Smethwick Chamber of Trade went further, and uniquely proposed that 'a limit should be put to the number of shops promoted by any one firm'. The National Chamber of Trade pushed the issue to one side, and the Smethwick proposal died.[64] When a member of Hounslow Chamber of Commerce demanded 'a crusade against this commercial hooliganism', the chairman asked him 'if he could suggest some practical remedy for the present state of affairs'.[65] There was none. State action surfaced only briefly as a proposed remedy, and was quickly sunk again. Retailers could turn only to their regular solutions – the regeneration of the individual trader, better service, more businesslike methods, and customer enlightenment to the poor deal the multiples really offered. 'The training of the future generation was the basis which they must go upon', according to one Birmingham grocer,[66] and improved methods linked to the inculcation of a 'spirit of local patriotism among your customers'[67] became the only solution that most shopkeepers could devise. The traders of Bexley Heath took the matter up in a fashion doubtless repeated all over the country, but above all in such small towns that daily sent business commuters to work in the large cities and were now appalled at the flow of retailing capital in the opposite direction. Local patriotism and the retention in the town of profits made there were the idealistic slogans. But customer enlightenment was all that Bexley Heath traders could propose.[68] Not surprisingly, *The Grocer* could offer no way in which the state might protect the ordinary shopkeeper, though its discussion of 'superfluous shops' in 1909 began with multiples, quite explicitly rejected legislative interference, and then turned to the excess of small shops, calling upon local authorities 'to impose greater restrictions upon the conversion of small dwelling houses into shops'.[69] This suggestion that larger individual traders might use the state against the very small is a theme to which we shall return when examining the shop hours campaign. As far as multiple shops were concerned, there were no ideological grounds for resistance that went beyond ordinary competition. As the Kidderminster Traders' Association was told in connection with multiple shops, 'they did not want to check enterprise', but must be on the defensive.[70] Large-scale retail capital, like it or not, represented 'enterprise'. That was the ideological hook that shopkeepers were impaled upon.

After the turn of the century, there was an increasing awareness that they handled these matters differently elsewhere, with publicity for the Danish law on multiples,[71] German legislation on unfair competition,[72] German demands for progressive sales taxes,[73] and so on. There is little evidence, however, that shopkeepers in Britain were tempted. When they did take account of the state, it was almost always because of state-initiated policy that impinged upon them, rather than because of their own initiatives. Such issues are the food adulteration laws and anxieties about how they were enforced;[74] the Liberal social insurance legislation after 1906; and the government's proposal to introduce a cash on delivery parcel service. This may have been relatively trivial, but it united shopkeepers to an uncommon degree, brought together the national traders' associations,[75] and produced a rare shopkeeper agitational success. In terms of issues at least partially set by the state, however, the most interesting, the most important for shopkeepers, and the one in which their own instigating role was greatest, was that of potential interference with the hours of opening of shops, or with the working hours of employees within them. The context is that of no regulation at all of shop opening hours or shop labour, except for an ancient and feebly enforced Sunday closing law; and the interest lies in the way in which, from the later 1880s, the shopkeeping community fractures over the issue, with an increasing proportion of the medium and large individual shopkeepers coming to support state intervention.

A movement for voluntary early closing of shops had begun as early as the 1840s, and had repeatedly sought local agreements amongst shopkeepers to fix closing hours and a half day holiday. These Early Closing Associations (ECAs) had been dominated by the larger individual retailers, with drapers particularly prominent. Local agreements could barely survive for weeks let alone months, for the smaller shopkeepers rarely joined, newcomers refused to accept the agreement, or original members simply broke ranks for competitive reasons. In 1886 and the few years that followed, the national ECA split. The majority of retailer members, led by the more substantial, came to accept that the successful regulation of shop hours was possible only through legislation.[76] A minority, based on the South London ECA, remained committed to voluntary effort, and by the end of 1892 had formed the Voluntary ECA. The majority view of the ECA – and of an increasing majority of retailer associations – was that legislation of some kind was needed to provide for the imposition of specified early closing days, and specified hours of closing on the other evenings; and that these should be imposed by a form of local option, by which a required proportion of local shopkeepers would have to support the measure proposed. If we are to understand the increasing willingness of medium and larger individual shopkeepers to seek a degree of state interference hitherto unheard of in the retail trade, then it is in part to the increasingly competitive atmosphere of later nineteenth- and early twentieth-century retailing that we must turn. Not all competition was over prices, for they represented just one aspect of a wider framework of competition that bedevilled the world of the individual trader. As I argued at the outset, it was not just new retail forms that were responsible, but also intense internal competition, much of it stimulated by an easier entry into shopkeeping with the spread of standardized and branded goods. The movement for shop hours regulation contained people with many motives, but prominent amongst the shopkeepers involved was a desire to control internal competition, initially by means of voluntary agreements over hours that would include both small and large businesses. In a sector of the economy rooted in small-scale individual enterprise, low capitalization and ease of entry, many independent traders turned reluctantly to the state for assistance in limiting competition and restraining costs. Their protection was to lie in the strong element of *local* option that was embedded in most proposals and legislative achievement.

The representatives of these trade associations and ECAs flocked to the parliamentary enquiries established by politicians anxious to avoid decisions on awkward policy problems. Witnesses were overwhelmingly medium and large private traders, businessmen of some substance speaking for themselves and for the medium-sized town shops, but rarely for the really small shopkeeper. A vehement opponent of legislation told the select committee of 1886 that 'most of the witnesses who have been examined belong to the better class of shopkeepers', they represented those shopkeepers who already closed early or would like to have done, and who wanted the smaller, back street shops to do so, for fear of losing business to them.[77] Opponents and supporters alike agreed that it was the lesser shops which would be most affected by the proposed legislation, though they obviously differed on the consequences. 'Those at the bottom of the social scale, I believe, would be ruined,' was the judgement of one opponent, an Old Kent Road draper,[78] but the organizations had by and large come to support state action in this area and their evidence dominated. The motives of the larger traders were clear: they wanted to close, but competition from the small retailers prevented them from doing so. H. A. Kettle, a large oil and colour merchant with several shops, told Booth's interviewer in about 1894 that he wanted compulsory closing. 'Messrs Marsham and Kettle have lost much trade through Thursday closing which they can never hope to regain unless their small neighbours are forced to close too.'[79] James Stacey, of the ECA, presented the case clearly when answering questions from a select committee in 1895:

> 'You may take it that in these days of keen competition, the shopkeepers finding the customers are indifferent to them, and that they will go where things are cheapest, naturally themselves begin to consider how they can get a larger share of custom by selling things cheaper, and to sell their things cheaper they must begin and find out every possible point in the economy of conducting business.' Early closing will make a great saving, and shopkeepers 'are thereby enabled to compete with the man across the way.'
>
> Q. 'From that point of view, the traders come to Parliament to save themselves money? – Yes, and . . .'

> Q. 'And to make them to put, in fact, money in their pockets? – Yes, for one consideration; and as humane men they wish to save their assistants.'[80]

John Cooney of the Scottish Shopkeepers and Assistants Union (which spoke for the larger individual trader) agreed. When it was put to him that 'therefore, you would compel the smaller shopkeeper because of the needs of the larger establishments; that is what it comes to?', he readily assented.[81] The question came down to how small was small? At what point could the really minor traders be excluded? Political necessity meant that those beneath a certain level had to be excluded from the legislation, but very few witnesses were willing to exclude shops run with family labour alone. Competition from them was often serious.[82] However, if a two-thirds vote was required by local option, then the greater the number of small shops included in the legislation, the greater would be the chance of being defeated in the votes for local regulation. The implication was clear, and when Nelson Tradesmen's Association lost by 263 votes to 377 a vote for the introduction of local hours regulation under the 1904 Act, they immediately concluded that a *compulsory* Act of Parliament was required.[83]

In this way the medium and large individual shopkeepers turned reluctantly to the state for help in a closely specified area. In so doing, they aroused two types of opposition. The first was the ideological opposition from individual larger retailers explicitly rejecting any role for the state in economic life. Thomas Layman of the London pawnbrokers, Henry Cushen of the metropolitan grocers, and J. B. Maple, of the large furniture store, opposed all interference, and did so with highly explicit ideological statements.[84] The second form of opposition came from the smaller shopkeepers themselves, for the drift towards legislation amongst the organized retailers left that lower section even more isolated. They were faced with acts in 1904 and 1911 which gave local authorities the permissive powers to introduce closing orders that set maximum closing times if two-thirds of shopkeepers in the trades to be covered approved of it; the 1911 act also made compulsory one half day closing a week. They simultaneously faced increasing pressure, again coming partly from other shopkeepers, for the enforcement of Sunday closing laws.

The very small shopkeepers – not all *petit commerce* by any means, but its lowest levels – found a voice, found an ability to organize, found a sense of identity, all of which were fragile and short-lived. None the less, after the turn of the century, we can see them expressing their hostility to both the state and the larger individual shopkeepers. John Sanders, a small Manchester confectioner, struggled towards a definition:

> I contend that the larger shopkeepers, as an organised body, are envious of the bit of trade that the small shops do, feeling that they could show if they were closed, larger profits and dividends. I distinguish clearly between those who live in their shops, work them themselves, and whose motives are merely to obtain a living, and those who live away from their business, are compelled to employ assistants, and whose motives over and above a living are for increasing profits and dividends.[85]

Explicit defences of the very small amongst individual shopkeepers remain rare, but proposals to regulate shop hours do stir them. Above all they responded to the Sunday closing debate, which seems to have agitated the very smallest of independent retailers, the least substantial of trades: tobacconists, newsagents, confectioners, greengrocers, and fishmongers, as well as the smallest shops in the other trades.

The most prominent of these organizations, the Shopkeepers' and Small Traders' Protection Association, was set up in July 1905 precisely to oppose legislation on Sunday trading, but it came to agitate against local early closing orders as well. These were the lesser shopkeepers in the kind of trades listed above, people dependent on long hours to accumulate sufficient business to make a living, and on the advantages they offered by being open when others were shut. By 1906 the Association had some 8000 members, with confectioners, tobacconists and newsagents dominant.[86] Its organ, *The Shopkeeper*, carried at the head of each issue the statement, 'Object. To oppose all attempts on the part of Parliament or Municipal authorities to unduly interfere with the business of shopkeepers and small traders.' Branches came and went; in June 1909 there were twelve in all, in different parts of the country,[87] but there were many other short-lived and completely local organizations of this kind of which little trace remains, such as the Bradford and District Sunday Traders' Defence League, formed in 1904. Its 200 members succeeded in persuading the town council to reject attempts to enforce Sunday closing.[88] Through one branch of the Shopkeepers' and Small Traders' Protection Association we can glimpse the very small character of its activists. The Leicester branch, with 300 members in 1915,[89] was the most lively and persistent. Its committees for 1908 and 1915 contained 38 different individuals, of whom 32 have been traced. They emerge as the classic small shopkeepers (11 confectioners, 10 'shopkeepers', 4 greengrocers, 2 grocers), but theirs were not the most ephemeral of enterprises. A check of directories at five-yearly intervals shows that only 9 of the 32 appeared in just one directory; 16 in two; 5 in three; and one each in four and five. Their shops were heavily concentrated in a rapidly developing working-class industrial suburb, Belgrave.[90] Shopkeepers such as these organized their fellow small traders against *both* the state, and the organized larger individual shopkeepers. It was these latter whom they were most frequently confronting. The Tradesmen's Association and the Butchers' Association in Wolverhampton tried in 1912 to obtain the enforcement of Sunday closing, but the small shopkeepers of the town organized a successful opposition.[91] No wonder, then, that *The Shopkeeper* denounced all closing bills as 'backed frequently by the big traders' associations'.[92] A similar paper in Wolverhampton always referred to the local traders' association as 'The Big Traders' Association' in its columns.[93] Thus it was that a new alliance seemed to be destroying the small man, a coming together of big company traders (denunciations of multiples were fierce), co-operatives, and the associations and federations of larger retailers. Here we see a distinctive voice not of the petite bourgeoisie as a whole, but of a lower section of it. 'Hands off the Little Man!', proclaimed one of its journals, and the masthead carried an emblem of a naked man with, coiled around him, a serpent marked 'Trusts, Legislation, Combines'. He grips it round the neck, and forces its head away.[94] Its publications, above all *The Small Trader and Shopkeeper*, press a distinctive position. It is one vehemently opposed to all state intervention with shopkeepers, even when it might help them.[95] It denounces reformers and large capitalist traders as allying to destroy the small man. 'We shall draw attention', promised the paper, 'to the frequent attempts made by faddists to obtain legislative sanction for their fads, and the attempts made by large capitalist concerns to use Parliament to enable them to crush their small rivals.'[96] Finally, the origins of such legislation lie with the larger individual traders and the capitalist concerns. The solution lay in a total withdrawal of the state from these areas. The free market alone must suffice as the salvation of small traders.[97]

Here, at last, a section of shopkeepers is forced to reflect upon the role of the state and, however negatively, to give it definition. Shop hours and labour regulation were deemed to be 'entirely outside the legitimate province of Parliament'. *The Small Trader and Shopkeeper* went on:

> Parliament has been allowed to drift into a position it was never intended to occupy – that of a regulator and controller of the personal and business affairs of private citizens. Representative Government exists for the purpose of maintaining, not destroying, private rights; for safe-guarding, not restricting, the freedom of trade. This principle has been lost sight of . . . during recent years.

State action was implicitly interfering and meddling. In a rare moment of wit, the paper proposed essential new legislation. 'That the law of the land shall be, one shop one inspector'; 'That bananas, if sold without their skins, shall be stamped by the County Council as "home peeled"'; and, best of all, 'that pennyworths of treacle should be sold only on skewers duly registered and stamped'.[98] The division within the shopkeepers' world was thus emphasized, with the very small increasingly isolated as the medium and larger individual shopkeepers turned, on this issue and in a very controlled way, to the state for help. It was help against the very small rather than to deal with the new retail forms, and in this respect the difference is striking between the British experience and that of shopkeeper movements elsewhere in Europe. This limited and precise appeal to the state provoked, in its turn, a real if transitory degree of articulate statement and organization by these very small traders. The issue, moreover, was unusual in its effects. Overall, no section of shopkeepers saw the state as relevant to the solution of its problems. Which leads to the question, why?

The understanding of such a response is no simple matter, and these concluding pages can do no more than raise various ideas that might help explain the limited, indeed the largely absent, concern on the part of British shopkeepers for the state and its possible assistance to them, as well as explain the character of the general shopkeeper ideology examined above. This is not the place to explore the relationship of other European shopkeeper movements to the state, but I do not want to underestimate the place of self-help institutions in the response of shopkeepers all over Europe. It would be a gross distortion were I to present the state as the dominant element in analyses and solutions in these other countries. Yet nowhere was state assistance at some level – ranging from encouragement to self-help and pump-priming operations in Belgium, to legislative restrictions on large-scale or illegitimate commerce in Germany – so irrelevant to the debates about the problems of small-scale retailing, and nowhere were governments and politicians so unconcerned with these problems. In other words, most other countries saw the state appear as a recurrent issue on the agenda of *petit commerce*; and *petit commerce* appear as a recurrent issue on the agenda of the state. Much of the outpouring of writings on small shopkeepers in the decades before the First World War sought to dissuade them from what were seen as the excesses of this appeal to the state. Saint-Léon opened his critical discussion of the subject by noting that 'the appeal to the state appears to a great number of medium and small shopkeepers as their only, or at least their principal hope in defending their threatened interests'.[99] Joseph Bernard agreed. 'Everyone complains, and demands government protection.'[100] In Germany the appeal to the state seems to take longer to build up, with a period of retailer organization devoted primarily to self-help approaches. But the 972 petitions from shopkeeper organizations that flowed into the *Reichstag* in February 1891 demanding action against large-scale and illegitimate competition were but an early manifestation of a growing search for state support.[101] The subtleties of these developments, the different specific features of each situation, need elaboration; but the essential contrast with Britain seems to me striking and in need of exploration.

The starting point for that explanation is the success of liberal ideology in Victorian Britain. At the background of so much of the shopkeeper ideology discussed in this paper are the central assumptions of economic and social liberalism. What made that liberal success so emphatic was, in part, that the ideology was not a bourgeois imposition on the petite bourgeoisie, but the outgrowth of a movement and a body of ideas that the petite bourgeoisie was itself involved in constructing. Crucial to bourgeois domination in Victorian Britain was the ability of the liberal bourgeoisie to integrate such people into the political and ideological framework of liberal society. That achievement was less troubled and more successful than in any of the other European countries referred to here, and is the basis for the almost unchallenged domination of economic and social liberalism within the shopkeeper movement. In arguing the role of the petite bourgeoisie in constructing the liberalism of Victorian Britain, one must look at the radical roots of liberal ideology, one strand of which leads to the shopkeeper radicalism of the later eighteenth and early nineteenth centuries. Indeed, when one detects a broader political focus in the later shopkeeper movement, it seems to connect with a radical shopkeeper ideology of distant origins. It surfaces but occasionally, and too much ought not to be made of it. Yet there are intriguing observations made. David Clears of the St Pancras Shopkeepers' Association wrote in 1886 of the right of assistants in smaller shops to work long hours if they so wanted. 'No one', he proclaimed in terms that reach back to the eighteenth-century radical tradition and beyond, 'is justified in denying them their rights as free-born Englishmen.'[102] The radicalism had lost coherence now, but traces survive to show its previous shape. One sees the regular attacks on landowners and landlords, whether in occasional comments or the organized agitations of the Town Tenants' League;[103] on the wealth of the old City companies – the National Chamber of Trade proposed that it be used for scientific trade research and other useful purposes;[104] on the excessive profits of the old professions of lawyers and doctors;[105] and on an idle, rich upper class, attacks that are seen most clearly over the customers of civil service stores[106] but also in attempts to tax the idle more heavily than the productive.[107] All of these forces were seen as now set against the business community. It was for businessmen to direct government policy, in the interests of all business, and that position made sense, perhaps, in a Britain where the aristocracy and old professions retained a political and social prominence. The old critique could retain some relevance.

Such origins help us to understand the way shopkeeper ideology developed; above all, perhaps, given the concerns of this paper, its development through two distinct but historically related traditions, both of which set shopkeepers against the state as a potentially beneficent force. The first tradition was that of the shopkeeper radicalism that I have just referred to. That radicalism, as it developed through to the 1840s, conceived of the state in essentially negative terms, as an oppressive force, the arm of aristocratic oligarchy and of corrupt and oppressive government. The second, and more recent, tradition was that of liberal economic ideas which embodied, above all in their popularized form, the vision of a non-interventionist state. Again, an essentially negative conception. When we examine shopkeeper responses between 1870 and 1914, we find them shaped by both these traditions, in part directly but also as they were mediated through mid-Victorian liberalism. Ideological formulations can persist, but very specific and local experiences served to reinforce them, experiences such as inspection by local government officials under the adulteration acts. Even where shopkeepers wanted regulation, as over shop hours, inspection was often rejected as 'an un-English practice'.[108] And when the smaller retailers opposed shop hours legislation and Sunday closing, they drew on precisely these traditions for their arguments, on the populist heritage of shopkeeper radicalism. *The Small Trader and Shopkeeper* identified it with an age-old struggle for freedom. They must free the country from 'a terror under which it has groaned for the past half-century, losing year by year, little by little, that freedom from restraint for which our forefathers fought and struggled so bravely and so long'.[109] It was much more pervasive than that. When the Town Tenants' League sought legislation to protect shopkeeper tenants against their landlords, general support was tempered by anxieties of the kind voiced by one member of Fulham Tradesmen's Association. 'Living in a country where they claimed freedom and where the Government had recently passed so much legislation to interfere with their business, he was sorry to find a body of traders appealing to the Government to pass more legislation.'[110]

This suggestion, that the image of the state that shaped shopkeeper responses in Britain was a distinctive one that drew on older traditions, indicates the importance of asking just how far turning to the state would imply turning to a modern interventionist state of the kind that large manufacturing capital was increasingly prepared to envisage in Edwardian Britain.[111] The way that the state exists as an ideological construct within the social and political assumptions of the petite bourgeoisie is thus an important factor which differs between different countries. What the shopkeepers turn to is an image of what the state could or should be, perhaps once was; its potential as an economic, social and moral force. It is the image that was crucial in this respect, initially at least. Philip Nord's work on the *Ligue syndicale* in France is helpful here, for he shows its ambivalent view of the state which would save *petit commerce*, but not by modern bureaucratic intervention. Rather, in the service of a republican ideal of local democratic independence, it would prevent the growth of forces destroying the core of republican virtue, and it would do so by restoring 'autarky'. The state to which the *Ligue syndicale* turned was thus an image of a different sort of state, one curiously mediated through myths, political traditions, older trade assumptions, to produce a state that would protect them and their distinctive economic and social vision. Thus, their demands of the state were essentially limited and preventative, seeking the reconstruction of the context where concentration of capital did not subvert the democratic world of the *quartier*, where the bureaucratic and interventionist state that underpinned a modern, organized and highly capitalized economy, could be resisted.[112] The specific traditions that I referred to in Britain were quite different from these, but in a similar fashion they built distinctive images of the state within shopkeeper ideology, and did so in such a manner as decisively to shape the way in which the state was seen to relate to their problems. Directly related to this, of course, was the actual character of the British state as it had developed since the early eighteenth century: a non-authoritarian, non-bureaucratic, and in formal structures rather 'weak' state. The combination of this with a strong ruling class is the paradox that lies at the centre of recent re-interpretations of the eighteenth-century British state,[113] and those characteristics persisted in important material and ideological ways. This essentially decentralized state lacked either corporate or authoritarian traditions, and gave an uncommon degree of autonomy to local administration which was on the whole non-legislative, but within the reach of shopkeepers, and to a degree used by them. If it was breaking down in the late nineteenth century, shopkeeper conceptions of the state derived from the older perspective.

The specific character of the British state thus helped shape shopkeeper awareness and conceptualization of it. At a more general comparative level, institutional, legal and fiscal structures that were connected to the state could direct the manner in which shopkeeper problems were experienced, and the kinds of solutions that seemed available. In this respect I would point briefly to corporate structures and institutions in the first place, and then to fiscal structures. Both were of varying and often unclear importance on the continent, but not at all in Britain. Even where formal guild and corporate structures were long dead elsewhere in Europe, corporate assumptions and institutions seem important to the construction of shopkeeper ideology and demands. In part it might be the actual memories of corporate structures that were at issue, perhaps in Germany and Austria, where they actually saw some revival. Of broader relevance, however, were the semi-autonomous organizations of commercial life that in part linked local business communities to the state, but also existed as institutions that might generate or encourage a distinct small retailer identity. For if one asks which forces regulated trade in Britain, the answer for British retailers would have been essentially the market. There existed no formal institutions, whether of a corporate or non-corporate nature, that regulated trade or trade practices; institutions such as the *Tribunaux de commerce*, or even the *Chambres de commerce*, in France, or the chambers and retailer chambers in Germany. There were not even the quasi-official organizations that developed at the partial instigation of the state to provide services and organizations for retailers, as were set up in Belgium.[114] The relationship between these various institutions and either corporate assumptions and expectations on the one hand, or the state on the other, is complex and differed greatly over time and place. Their persistence as ideological forces, and their ability to shape perception and experience, must relate to the continuance of small-scale communities in many parts of Europe, to the slow pattern of urbanization until the later nineteenth century, which might permit the survival of some of the atmosphere of corporate assumptions even where the form had retreated or been abolished. In varying degrees in different countries – and probably between regions within those countries – the memories of corporate trade structures, their impact on ideological traditions, and their limited re-creation through institutions with a real relationship to the state, are in striking contrast to the British experience.[115] There are two clear consequences. The first is that the state is presented as relevant to shopkeeper concerns. The second is that once such regulating institutions exist, whether old or new, then it is in the interests of the élite of the commercial community to control them.[116] The conflict that such control could provoke itself helped generate a specific sense of identity amongst smaller shopkeepers, and examples of that abound over *Chambres de commerce* in France, or the campaign for distinct *Detaillistenkammern* in Germany.[117] Gellately notes, for example, that in Hamburg retailer protest meetings over department stores or co-operatives generally concluded with a resolution demanding the establishment of a *Detaillistenkammer*.[118]

The influence of fiscal structures is initially more obvious when viewed from Britain. Commentators on France, especially, have shown the importance of the *patente* (trade licence or professional tax) as a weapon of *petit commerce*.[119] The way in which the very existence of the *patente* presented an appeal to the state as an obvious and central plank in the strategy of the shopkeepers' movement is perhaps unduly taken for granted. For the *patente*, its development and revision, openly raised direct questions about state imposition on different sectors and different levels of business, the relationship between state policy and economic development, and the social implications of different *patente* strategies.[120] The influences of this on shopkeeper consciousness and demands were various, but two stand out. The first is the provision, as it were, of a natural turning to the state, through the presence of a fiscal structure which had no equivalent in Britain. From its very inception the *patente* was available as a potential mode of control or attack on new and larger-scale commerce. It increasingly became so in the second half of the nineteenth century, as alterations in the form or graduation of its imposition seemed an excellent way to hinder or even destroy large-scale retail competition. In the words of Terrier, *rapporteur* of the 1893 law, the *patente* was from that point on 'an economic regulator, setting obstacles to monopoly'.[121] The other influence of the *patente* that I want to single out is less precise, and that is its ideological impact in helping to shape the specialization idea, that each retailer should be restricted to his own trade, an idea that carried implications of moral values and not just of trade rights. I have already noted the absence of that notion in Britain, where it was in fact the small shopkeeper who was particularly resistant to it. 'Today is the day of the mixed shop,' proclaimed *The Small Trader and Shopkeeper*.[122] This relates necessarily to the lack of a clear notion amongst British shopkeepers of what constituted a legitimate retailer.

Specialization, in the ideological form with which it developed inside sections of the French shopkeeper movement, was in many ways a corporate idea. More exactly, perhaps, it might be described as the footprint in the sand where a corporate idea once stood. The *patente*, both by its fiscal organization (speciality was an essential aspect of this) and the demands which it inspired, encouraged the ideology of *specialisme*. As such, and in spite of its origins, it acted as a carrier of a mutant form of the corporate sense of 'the trade'. Maybe it was not just in spite of its origins, but in part because of them. The corporate structure had been directly linked to the new *patente* in the Constituent Assembly – 'We suppress these rights, and replace them with a relatively light tax.'[123] Saint-Léon certainly over-simplified the connection, but saw Christophe's 'one man, one trade' as an essentially corporatist slogan.[124] The belief that the state was obliged to protect the citizens' right to work at their trade – a right that became linked to the notion of specialization – was one basis for the demand that the state support *petit* against *grand commerce*. The complex ways in which the ideology of small shopkeepers in Britain differed from conceptions such as these, and the explanations for these differences, are thus very relevant to the theme of this essay. A sense of legitimacy as 'the trade' is important in explaining a willingness to seek the legal support of the state to defend its integrity.

The character of the evolving political structure in Britain carries this argument a further step forward, for it seemed to deny the space into which organizations of small shopkeepers might insert themselves or into which they might be drawn. It was not simply the problems and inherited ideology of shopkeepers in France, Belgium and Germany that made them more important, but the wider political and social conjuncture within which they organized themselves. Throughout continental Europe, it seems, the question of the petite bourgeoisie became important in political and electoral terms, and the attention that its organizations received from the social Catholics in Belgium, the emergence of a *Mittelstandspolitik* in Germany, the increasing political attention given to *petit commerce* in France, all testify to this. If we now know not to see these as simply manipulation from the higher reaches of the political stratosphere, to recognize the indigenous agitations that mobilized these constituencies, nevertheless the wider political attention that they received was of great importance.[125] In all these countries, shopkeepers came to matter to politicians, and politicians came to matter to shopkeepers. Real concessions and interventions from the state followed, however limited their actual consequences often turned out to be. The evidence abounds, and there is no space to rehearse it here. At times the support for shopkeepers would be precise, as when the German Centre Party tailored its economic policy and legislative proposals to the needs of small retailers and artisans.[126] Elsewhere what was sought by centrist politicians was state intervention to aid the petite bourgeoisie without actively controlling the forces that made that aid necessary. In other words, to stimulate self-help activity.[127] As Théodor put it, 'isn't it possible for the state, without replacing individual initiative, to intervene with encouragement and with subsidies?'[128] Everywhere the 'crisis' of the petite bourgeoisie, of the *classes moyennes* became a subject for political concern, a matter of social debate within bourgeois circles. Government commissions of enquiry, ministries and offices, parliamentary investigations proliferated, those very institutions that provided so much of the evidence for historians to draw upon, and whose absence leaves British historians groping for material. They testify not just to a level of crisis, but to a degree of political attention to the world of *petit commerce* that might actually have exaggerated the degree of crisis. A whole new social importance was ascribed to the petite bourgeoisie, in which it came to be characterized as a class embodying the ideals of moral and social independence, the prospects for upward social mobility for aspirant workers, and a buffer class, *une classe tampon*, when those workers aspired to more than mobility. The petit-bourgeois attachment to the institutions and values that mattered for bourgeois social stability came to be of great significance.[129] There was a powerful debate amongst those seeking to support the *classes moyennes* as to just what the legitimate role of the state was in giving aid. That debate was a particularly lively one at the 1910 Congress of the *Association des défense des classes moyennes*, as it became necessary to define precisely where the limits of intervention came; necessary for those involved in the movement and, especially, for those seeking to keep it within acceptable channels.[130] What on earth did the English delegate make of the proceedings, L. P. Sidney of the Middle Class Defence Organization, a highly ideological offshoot of the right-wing and *laissez-faire* Liberty and Property Defence League? The essential point is that bourgeois politicians and parties in these countries were seeking to achieve something long accomplished in Britain: to integrate a potentially disruptive petite bourgeoisie into the existing social order, and to commit it to the defence of that order.[131] It could be a delicate operation, and had often to avoid interference with liberal principles or the processes of capitalist concentration. The activities could backfire, and the gap between solicitous attention and what was actually on offer could itself encourage angry political action by shopkeepers.

The absence of that space to insert themselves into, the absence of that attention from bourgeois politicians, are further elements necessary to an understanding of the lack of any specific shopkeeper politics in Britain during the period covered by this paper. I would not suggest for a moment that shopkeepers were not political, for at the constituency level they lay at the very centre of the membership and organizations of both the Liberal and Conservative parties. 'The *menu peuple*', writes Patrick Joyce of northern industrial boroughs, 'were the indispensable drones of popular politics.'[132] But there was no distinctive political voice, or voices, for shopkeepers in Britain. They identified with the business community as a whole, and the interests that flowed from it. A rare case of distinctive shopkeeper intervention in politics as an interest came when the Trades' Defence Association sought pledges from candidates in the 1880 parliamentary elections that they would do something to check civil service co-operatives. The lobbying had very little effect, and barely went beyond occasional questions at election meetings.[133] As a whole, shopkeepers might present their trade's views to central and local government, but they rarely adopted specific political positions or campaigned for them. Indeed, they often devised careful means to avoid that. When Bradford Chamber of Trade put up six trader candidates for the local board of guardians elections in 1904, they deliberately chose men with different political positions and allegiances.[134] As John Green told his St Helens anti-co-operative movement from the outset, 'they as a body of traders had no politics at all'.[135] Shopkeeper organizations thus quite explicitly sought to keep themselves outside politics. The lack of any distinctive political mobilization was noticed within the shopkeeper movement, and became an object of concern and fear as the rise of a labour and a socialist politics was seen. That sense of their own political powerlessness was fuelled by fears of an increasingly socialist working-class radicalism, fear for property rights, fear of subsidized idleness on the rates, all of which fears found a temporary outlet in the anti-co-operative movement. To F. M. Bussey, the co-operatives were an 'avowedly socialistic and anarchical movement'.[136] A Beswick shopkeeper was more specific about the political connections, arguing that 'the bulk of the officials [i.e. of the co-operative society] belong to different dissenting chapels about here, where such things as Pro-Boerism, Socialism, &c., are taught and applied in Jesuitical fashion in place of fear God and honour the King and love thy neighbour as thyself'.[137] The fear of labour was perhaps at its strongest in London where the unusually high rate incidence upon the lower middle class intensified that interlocking group of fears that I referred to above. Frank Bullen moved into a small picture framing and fancy goods business around the turn of the century, and rapidly came to identify with his fellow tradesmen in a London inner suburb:

> most of whom, like myself, had a severe struggle to live. It makes me positively ill to hear the blatant cant that is talked about the working man, meaning journeymen

> and labourers only. The small London shopkeeper toils far harder than any of them, is preyed upon by them to an extent which must be incredible to those who don't know, is continually being propounded for their benefit by their representatives on the Borough Councils, and is quoted to radical newspapers as the bitter enemy of the working classes.[138]

Yet this resentment generated no identifiable shopkeeper politics. Indeed the only political attempt to organize the 'middle class' in defence of the existing order, the Middle Class Defence Organization founded in 1906 to wage an anti-socialist battle in London local government, gives no specific attention at all to shopkeeper interests. It certainly defined retailers within its constituency, consciously appealed to the middling tax- and rate-paying classes, and talked of their position between Labour and Capital.[139] Neither their propaganda nor their newspaper, *The Elector*, seems to have engaged with any specific economic or political demands of shopkeepers as such. Given its origins and perspective, given its contacts with continental shopkeeper movements, that gap is striking. In the context of the argument in this paper, I hope that it is at least partially explicable. For all their trade organizations, there is very little sign amongst British shopkeepers of a wider politics, an identity as shopkeepers, a specific relationship to the state as relevant to their problems and to the solution of them.

I have sought in this essay to sketch the ideological framework within which British shopkeepers responded to, and sought to understand, the growing competitive pressures from the later nineteenth century; to distinguish it very roughly and where relevant from tendencies outside Britain; and to use that analysis as the basis for establishing and explaining the orientation of British shopkeepers with regard to the state. In spite of my attempts at caution, I have doubtless exaggerated some of those contrasts. The comparative questions abound. Just how distinctive is the ideological and political character of British shopkeepers as I have analysed it here? In their relation to the state, above all their conceptualization of the relevance of the state, I am sure that it is distinctive. But just how important are the developing and inherited state (and state-supported) structures to the character of shopkeeper movements, their demands of, and reactions to, the state? And how important are these inherited structures to the development of a distinctive identity as *petit commerce* which, I have argued, is at least one essential determinant of shopkeeper responses? It is in sorting out such analytical priorities that the real problems seem to lie. A primary value of comparative perspectives must lie in their ability to aid the development of such analytical questions and categories of explanation.

NOTES

The following abbrevations are used in these notes: NCT – National Chamber of Trade; PP – Parliamentary Papers. The place of publication of books, unless otherwise indicated, is London.

1 Edmond Demolins, 'La question des grands magasins', *La Science sociale*, 9, 1890, 317.
2 Booth Collection A20 f 32, at British Library of Political and Economic Science.
3 *Retail Trader*, June 1912.
4 The founding dates of associations are given in *Grocery Trade Year-Book and Diary for 1903*.
5 Hector Lambrechts in Association de défense des classes moyennes, *Les Etudes fiscales et sociales. Troisième çongrès annuel (Novembre 1910)*, Limoges, 1911, 29–61.
6 *Grocery Trade Year-Book*.
7 See, for example, National Chamber of Trade, *Souvenir of the Fourteenth Annual Conference, 1912*, Hull, 1912.
8 There were twenty-one branches and affiliated associations, *National Chamber of Trade Circular*, 1 December 1873.
9 National Chamber of Trade (henceforth NCT), Membership Register.
10 A good example is the evidence of Thomas Layman to the Select Committee on Shop Hours Regulation Bill, *Parliamentary Papers* (henceforth PP), 1886, XII, Q. 771ff.
11 *The Grocer*, 28 May 1904.
12 Robert Gellately, *The Politics of Economic Despair. Shopkeepers and German Politics 1890–1914*, 1974, 37.
13 *The Traders' Times and Weekly Representative*, 19 and 26 June 1880.
14 ibid., 6 November 1880.
15 Quoted in B. S. Yamey, *The Economics of Retail Price Maintenance*, 1954, 140.
16 Henry W. Macrosty, *Trusts and the State. A Sketch of Competition*, 1901, 196–7.
17 F. M. Bussey, editor of *Tradesman and Shopkeeper*, 20 September 1902.
18 See James Kendall of the Traders' Union on co-operation. 'They could challenge it on any point – on its methods, on its prices, on its capacity for helping the people, and giving value. If they only had faith in their trade and trading methods, they could enter upon a new era of prosperity.' Reported in *St Helens Newspaper and Advertiser*, 21 November 1902.
19 *Retailer and Associated Trader*, December 1913, January and March 1914.
20 *Tradesman and Shopkeeper*, 5 March 1904; NCT, Executive Council Minutes, 5 October 1908, in NCT Minute Book, 130.
21 *Retail Trader*, January and April 1913. They presumably felt no need for an organization such as the French 'le Comité de défense des sociétés à succursales multiples', Pierre Moride, *Les Maisons à succursales multiples en France et à l'étranger*, Paris, 1913, 83.
22 *Retailer and Associated Trader*, the organ of the London and Suburban Traders' Federation, poured out self-help articles of a highly romanticized kind, about how the average assistant could climb to be a small and then a large shopkeeper, with a prosperous and substantial business. The rest of the retailer press carried similar material.
23 Select Committee on Co-operative Stores, PP, 1878–9, IX, Q. 3.
24 ibid., Q. 1489–93.
25 H. N. B. Spink's evidence, ibid., Q. 1864.
26 Quoted in *Tradesman and Shopkeeper*, 23 August 1902.
27 Quoted in ibid., 5 November 1904.
28 Joseph Bernard, 'Du mouvement d'organisation et de défense du petit commerce français', thèse de droit, Université de Paris, 1906, 142–3. The proposal was amended to ten employees, but that hardly alters my present point.
29 Some examples only. For attacks on 'illusive trading' of a largely peripheral kind see NCT, Emergency Committee Minutes, 26 September 1907, in NCT Minute Book, 75; on pension tea, *Tradesman and Shopkeeper*, 30 July 1904; on clothing clubs, ibid., 18 July 1903; on genuine frauds as the real threat to retailers, ibid., 6 January 1906; and

generally the triviality of the issues listed by *Retail Trader* under the title 'Tradesmen's grievances', *Retail Trader*, October 1912.

30 *The Traders' Times*, 8 May 1880.
31 *Tradesman and Shopkeeper*, 6 December 1902.
32 Select Committee on Co-operative Stores, Q. 148–9.
33 ibid., Q. 527.
34 Philip Nord, 'Commerce and Culture in *fin de siècle* Paris', Columbia University thesis, 1982. See also Etienne Martin Saint-Léon, *Le Petit Commerce français. Sa lutte pour la vie*, Paris, 1911, 97–9, and Bernard, op. cit., 51–2.
35 Select Committee on Co-operative Stores, Q. 1358–609.
36 *Retail Trader*, July 1912.
37 *National Chamber of Trade Circular*, June 1873; *The Traders' Times*, 15 May 1880.
38 Examples are local and very specific episodes of shopkeeper pressure on workers as employees or tenants. There are good illustrations in R. Jones, 'Consumers' co-operation in Victorian Edinburgh: the evolution of a location pattern', *Transactions of the Institute of British Geographers*, new series 4, 1979, 304; and the evidence of the lifelong co-operative advocate, G. J. Holyoake, to the Select Committee on Co-operative Stores, Q. 5241.
39 For the boycott proposals, *St Helens Newspaper and Advertiser*, 25 July 1902.
40 ibid., 29 July 1902.
41 See for example John Green, president, in ibid., 29 July 1902.
42 ibid., 31 October 1902, 5 December 1902, 13 February 1903.
43 James B. Jefferys, *Retail Trading in Britain 1850–1950*, Cambridge, 1954, 17.
44 *Tradesman and Shopkeeper*, 16 August 1902.
45 *St Helens Newspaper and Advertiser*, 5 September 1902.
46 Ashton, Birkenhead, Blackburn, Coventry, Hartlepool, Hull, Leigh, Plymouth, Preston, Sheffield (United Traders' Association), St Helens, Stockton-on-Tees, Wigan and York.
47 The Traders' Defence Association of England and Wales, based in Hull; the Traders' Union established in November 1902 by the Northern Council of Grocers' Associations; and the Central Board of Traders' Defence Associations.
48 *St Helens Newspaper and Advertiser*, 5 September 1902.
49 J. T. Gee of Wigan could not get a resolution on the subject passed by the Annual Conference of the Trades Protection Association in 1904. *Tradesman and Shopkeeper*, 14 May 1904.
50 *Tradesman and Shopkeeper*, 14 March 1903. Other examples are Tynemouth Grocers' Association, ibid., 6 September 1902; Coventry TDA, ibid., 4 October 1902, who later disown St Helens, ibid., 7 February 1903; Leeds Chamber of Trade, ibid., 6 December 1902.
51 *St Helens Newspaper and Advertiser*, 14 November 1902.
52 ibid., 16 September 1902, 12 September 1902.
53 ibid., 10 October 1902.
54 *Retailer and Associated Trader*, May–July 1914.
55 Charles Gide, *Consumers' Co-operative Societies*, Manchester, 1921 (translation of third French edn, 1917), 141–6. See also his 'Les sociétés cooperatives de consommation et les commerçants', *La Réforme sociale*, 60, 1910, 433–42.
56 M. Théodor, 'Les classes moyennes en Belgique', in Association de Défense des Classes Moyennes, *Les Etudes fiscales et sociales*, 120–2; for Belgium see also Pascale Delfosse, 'La petite bourgeoisie en crise et l'Etat: le cas belge', *Le Mouvement social*, no. 114, 1981, 92–3; for France there is a brief summary in Henry Vouters, *Des mesures législatives destinées à enrayer la concentration du commerce du détail*, Paris, 1910, 154–5.
57 *St Helens Newspaper and Advertiser*, 1 August 1902.
58 ibid., 5 December 1902.

59 *Kelly's Directory of Lancashire*, 1901.
60 *The Grocer*, 7 April 1894, 816.
61 Booth Collection B133 f 35.
62 *Retailer and Associated Trader*, June and August 1914; NCT Parliamentary Committee Minutes, 28 July 1911, in NCT Minute Book, 310.
63 The correspondence columns of *The Grocer* carried a number of letters on the matter. See issues for 13 March 1909, and 1, 8, 15 and 22 January 1910. For resolutions to the National Chamber of Trade on the taxation of multiples, see Parliamentary Committee Minutes, 29 June 1911, in NCT Minute Book, 306; NCT Parliamentary Committee Minutes, 18 September 1911, in NCT Minute Book, 314; Parliamentary Committee Minutes, 9 October 1911, in NCT Minute Book, 317.
64 NCT Executive Council Minutes, 22 April 1912, in NCT Minute Book, 353.
65 *Retailer and Associated Trader*, March 1914.
66 *Tradesman and Shopkeeper*, 13 September 1902.
67 *Retail Trader*, January 1913.
68 *Bexley Heath and Bexley Observer*, 18 August–20 October 1911.
69 *The Grocer*, 6 March 1909.
70 *Retail Trader*, May 1913.
71 *The Grocer*, 22 January 1910.
72 *Retail Trader*, February 1913. The London and Suburban Traders' Federation Council discussed it, *Retailer and Associated Trader*, November 1913.
73 *The Grocer*, 29 January 1910. A Bexley Heath grocer even knew of this, *Bexley Heath and Bexley Observer*, 29 September 1911.
74 For retailer concern about the adulteration laws see the evidence to the Select Committee on the Adulteration of Food Act (1872), PP, 1874, VI; and the Select Committee on Food Products Adulteration, PP, 1895, X; 1896, IX.
75 For the composition of the deputation to the Postmaster General, see the report in *Tradesman and Shopkeeper*, 5 November 1904.
76 For some discussion of this shift in 1886, see the evidence to the Select Committee on the Shop Hours Regulation Bill, PP, 1886, XII: by James Pearse of the East London ECA, Q. 1134ff; John Barr, a South London draper, Q. 1197ff; William Jones of the Holloway and Finsbury Park ECA, Q. 1254ff; Francis Capon of the Stalybridge ECA, Q. 2136ff; and William Sutton, a Newcastle outfitter and hosier, Q. 2392ff.
77 ibid., Q. 2716–39.
78 ibid., Q. 5175.
79 Booth Collection B133 f 23.
80 Select Committee on Shops (Early Closing) Bill, PP, 1895, XII, Q. 287–9.
81 ibid., Q. 876.
82 Examples of such arguments abound. See Sutherst's evidence to the Select Committee on the Shop Hours Regulation Bill, Q. 254, 429; also that of Dixon, Q. 267. Witnesses in 1895 were more forthcoming on this. See Select Committee on Shops (Early Closing) Bill: evidence by Flint, Q. 1054–7; a Bolton witness, Q. 1548–9; Manchester witnesses, Q. 3970–4005; Hartley Wilson of the Liverpool grocers, Q. 4145–53.
83 NCT Executive Council Minutes, 6 October 1905, in NCT Minute Book, 30.
84 Select Committee on the Shop Hours Regulation Bill, Q. 792, 803, 807–17 (all Layman), 3301 (Cushen), 5418 (Maple); Select Committee on Shops (Early Closing) Bill, Q. 4751 (Cushen).
85 Joint Select Committee on Sunday Trading, PP, 1906, XIII, Q. 2377.
86 ibid., Q. 1752–1843.
87 Barrow-in-Furness, Bristol, Cardiff, Greenock, Hammersmith, Kensington, Kilburn, Leicester, central London, Mountain Ash, Penarth, Worcester. *The Shopkeeper*, September 1908–January 1909.

88 Joint Select Committee on Sunday Trading, Q. 3360–85.
89 *Small Trader and Shopkeeper*, January 1915.
90 *The Shopkeeper*, September 1908; *Small Trader and Shopkeeper*, March 1915; various directories of Leicester and Leicestershire for 1894, 1900, 1904, 1909, 1914.
91 *Wolverhampton Chronicle*, 19 June 1912, 10 and 21 July 1912, 7 August 1912.
92 *The Shopkeeper*, September 1908.
93 *Wolverhampton Free Journal*, November 1914.
94 Masthead of the *Small Trader and Shopkeeper*.
95 See James Stewart on the need for limitations on the number of shops in a district. This must be voluntary, he argued. *Small Trader and Shopkeeper*, June 1915.
96 ibid., January 1915.
97 If trade is to flourish, 'all the harrassing measures that now so injuriously affect it must be repealed': *Small Trader and Shopkeeper*, February 1915.
98 ibid., January 1915.
99 Saint-Léon, op. cit., 118. See the much earlier attack on *petit commerce* for seeking state aid in Demolins, op. cit., esp. 303: 'We have reached the point in France where the state is seen as a Providential power to be called upon in all difficulties; unsuccessful shopkeepers turn to it and willingly cry, "Give us this day our daily bread!".'
100 Bernard, op. cit., 41.
101 Gellately, op. cit., esp. 112–47.
102 Select Committee on the Shop Hours Regulation Bill, papers 279. For some of the roots of this radicalism see my comments in the essay on Britain elsewhere in this book, and the references there.
103 See as an example the *Retail Trader* articles on 'an unjust land system', October 1912.
104 NCT Trades Conference Minutes, 22 April 1912, in NCT Minute Book, 359.
105 On lawyers' profits, see *National Chamber of Trade Circular*, 1 June 1873; on the profits of both them and doctors, NCT, *Souvenir*, xviii.
106 Select Committee on Co-operative Stores, Q. 3, 1655, 2258–61; and in Jonathan Hawes, *Class Against Class*, quoted in *The Traders' Times*, 5 June 1880.
107 See the resolution from the North Staffordshire Traders' Association, *Tradesman and Shopkeeper*, 11 April 1903; also NCT Parliamentary and Emergency Committee Minutes, 21 June 1906, in NCT Minute Book, 53.
108 Select Committee on the Shop Hours Bill, PP, 1892, xvii, Q. 3214.
109 *Small Trader and Shopkeeper*, February 1915.
110 *Retailer and Associated Trader*, November 1913.
111 See for example Roy Hay, 'Employers and social policy in Britain: the evolution of welfare legislation 1905–1914', *Social History*, 4, 1977, 435–55.
112 On the last point see Philip Nord's essay in this book. By the end of the decade this 'ideology of the *quartier*' was on the retreat. On the more general vision of the *Ligue syndicale*, Nord's thesis is very illuminating.
113 The central works here are by E. P. Thompson, above all his 'Eighteenth-century English society: class struggle without class?', *Social History*, 3, 1978, 133–65.
114 See for example Bernard, op. cit., esp. 73–7; Gellately, op. cit., 97ff; Delfosse, op. cit., 95ff.
115 See the way in which corporatist elements re-emerge in the *Confédération des groupes commerciaux et industriels*, as discussed by Nord in this book. For the early demise of corporate control in London retailing, see J. R. Kellett, 'The breakdown of gild and corporation control over the handicraft and retail trade in London', *Economic History Review*, second series, 10, 1957–8, 381–94.
116 See for example J.-C. Martin, 'Hiérarchie et structure de la société commerçante: les listes d'électeurs au tribunal de commerce de Niort en 1864 et 1874', *Le Mouvement social*, no. 112, 1980, 57–77.

117 Saint-Léon, op. cit., 163ff; Bernard, op. cit., 181–2; Gellately, op. cit., 97–108.
118 Gellately, op. cit., 103.
119 Saint-Léon, op. cit., ch. 5; M. Hubert-Valleroux, 'Les charges fiscales du petit commerce et de la petite industrie', *La Réforme sociale*, 60, 1910; Bernard, op. cit., 133–63.
120 The debates on the 1844 law illustrate this clearly. See Robert L. Koepke, 'The *Loi des patentes* of 1844', *French Historical Studies*, 11, 1980, 398–430.
121 Quoted by Bernard, op. cit., 136.
122 *Small Trader and Shopkeeper*, January 1915.
123 Hubert-Valleroux, op. cit., 371.
124 Saint-Léon, op. cit., 128.
125 On the tension between attempts to organize the petite bourgeoisie from above, and its own pressures and agitations see important work on Germany, such as Gellately, op. cit., but especially David Blackbourn, *Class, Religion and Local Politics in Wilhelmine Germany. The Centre Party in Württemberg Before 1914*, New Haven, 1980, and his article 'The *Mittelstand* in German society and politics, 1871–1914', *Social History*, 4, 1977, 409–33.
126 Blackbourn, *Class, Religion*, 55–7, 150–2.
127 For Belgium see Delfosse, op. cit.; for the Netherlands, J.-S. Meuwren, 'L'organisation des classes moyennes dans les Pays-Bas', in Association de défense des classes moyennes, *Les Etudes fiscales*, 137–42.
128 Théodor, op. cit., 184.
129 On the social importance of the petite bourgeoisie, see Saint-Léon, op. cit., 93–8; Bernard, op. cit., 197–8; Delfosse, op. cit.; Vouters, op. cit., 25.
130 Association de défense des classes moyennes, *Les Etudes fiscales, passim*, but esp. 174–202.
131 For an excellent description of that process of dissuasion, see Théodor's speech in ibid., 120ff; and for a sharp riposte see de Paloméra's 'Une classe moyenne interessante. Les commerçants de Province', ibid., 346ff.
132 Patrick Joyce, *Work, Society and Politics. The Culture of the Factory in Later Victorian England*, Brighton, 1980, 268–9.
133 For example, *Surrey Comet*, 27 March 1880, 3 April 1880. On the election, see Trevor Lloyd, *The General Election of 1880*, Oxford, 1968, 115–16.
134 *Tradesman and Shopkeeper*, 19 March 1904.
135 *St Helens Newspaper and Advertiser*, 5 September 1902.
136 *Tradesman and Shopkeeper*, 27 September 1902.
137 ibid., 30 August 1902.
138 Frank W. Bullen, *Confessions of a Tradesman*, 1908, 158. For an important recent analysis of the rates crisis and its impact on the London lower middle class, see Avner Offer, *Property and Politics 1870–1914. Landownership, Law, Ideology and Urban Development in England*, Cambridge, 1981, 288–9, 297–313.
139 See the interview with L. P. Sidney in *Tradesman and Shopkeeper*, 24 March 1906; G. R. Sims in *The Referee*, 4 March 1906.

Index

Index

Accampo, Elinor, 19
Action Libérale Populaire, 186
Administrative Reform Association, 75
adulteration, 18, 84, 240, 252, 267
Agrarian League, 50
agricultural produce traders, 223, 224, 228, 229, 231
Agulhon, Maurice, 19
anti-semitism, 9, 52, 60, 111, 178–9, 180, 214
Anti-Socialist Union, 77
Antwerp, 126
Arnsberg, 38
Association de defénse des classes moyennes, 95, 108, 187, 194, 262
Auneau, 221–32 *passim*
Austria, 24, 195–217, 260

Baden, 13
bakers, 8, 39, 41, 53, 89, 98, 99, 100, 103, 122, 163, 166, 182, 200, 203–4, 209, 210, 211, 213, 225, 229, 230, 241
bankruptcy, 13, 20, 42, 69, 102, 107; *see also* grocers
barber-surgeons, 200
bars, cafés, pubs (and owners), 19, 23, 42, 53, 61, 82, 85–6, 87, 98, 116, 123, 124, 197, 206–7, 210, 217, 223, 224, 225, 228, 230, 233, 241
basket-makers, 37
Bath, 73, 74
Bavaria, 42, 53
Bayonne, 106, 109
Beauce, the, 219–38
Beaujolais, 98
Bechhofer, F., 9, 83
Belgian Workers' Party, 127
Belgium, *see* petite bourgeoisie, in Belgium
Bellamy, Edward, 186
Berlin, 23
Bernard, Joseph, 257
Berry, Georges, 180, 185
Bexley Heath, 251
bicycles, 71, 81
Birmingham, 11, 18, 22, 25, 62, 66, 67, 68, 70, 73, 76, 78, 80, 82, 84, 85, 137–54, 251
Blondel, Georges, 185
Blum, Léon, 106
Bochum, 45, 48
book-binders, 46
booksellers, 89
Booth, Charles, 239, 250, 253
Bordeaux, 97
Boulanger, Georges, and Boulangisme, 109, 177–9
Boulton, Matthew, 141
Bourdieu, Pierre, 17, 112
bourgeoisie:
  attempts to control petite bourgeoisie, 16, 74–5, 187–9, 257; *see also* politics, petit-bourgeois
  relations with petite bourgeoisie, 4, 45–6, 54, 82, 103
Bradford and District Sunday Traders' Defence League, 255
Bradford Grocers' Association, 249
Brants, Victor, 120, 127
Bremen, 9, 12, 42, 53
brewers, 50, 70

Bridgwater, 82
Brighton, 87
Bristol, 62, 84
Britain, *see* petite bourgeoisie, in Britain
Brown, Joseph, 70, 71, 78, 84
Brussels, 121, 122, 123, 185
building trades, 12, 38, 39, 40, 54, 61, 66, 85, 99, 100, 105, 122, 197, 200, 205, 206–7, 210, 211, 213, 214, 217, 223, 225, 226, 227, 229, 230, 231, 232
Bullen, Frank, 75, 80, 84, 263–4
Bund der Kaufleute, 53
butchers, 8, 39, 45, 46, 51, 89, 98, 99, 100, 103, 163, 174, 176, 182, 207, 210, 226–7, 228, 229, 230, 241, 250, 255
button makers, 140, 142, 146, 149, 150

cabinet-makers, *see* furniture and cabinet-makers
cafés, *see* bars, cafés, pubs
Cambridge, 65
capital, 9, 10, 141, 144–5, 232
  amounts required in small enterprise, 99–100, 165
  sources of, 101, 115, 117, 168–71, 172
Cardiff, 77, 78, 79
carriers, 206–7, 217
Catholic Party (Belgian), 5, 25, 127, 130, 133
Catholics, social Catholics, 3, 16, 108, 120, 127–30, 175, 179–80, 183, 185–6, 189, 262; *see also* Catholic Party
Centre Party (German), 5, 50, 61, 262
Chaline, Jean-Pierre, 108
Chamberlain, Joseph, 145, 146, 150
Chambers of Commerce, 16
  in Britain:
    Hounslow, 251
  in France, 260
    Bayonne, 109
    Le Havre, 104
    Paris, 156, 160
  in Germany, 25, 245, 260
    Cologne, 45
Chambers of Trade, 241
  Bradford, 263
  Leeds, 246
  Smethwick, 251
Chambre syndicale des employés, 181, 193
Chambre syndicale des maîtres tailleurs, 182
Chambre syndicale des papetiers, 186
charcutiers, 176, 182
Chartism, 73, 74, 87, 137, 149
Chartres, 222–37 *passim*
Chateauroux, 110
chemists, pharmacists, 43, 211, 213, 241, 244, 246
Christophe, Léopold, 24, 176, 178, 179
cigar-makers, 61
classes moyennes, 5, 77, 95, 99, 112, 123, 124, 184, 186, 262
  ideological significance of term, 95–6, 105, 109, 185, 247
Clerck, Victor de, 185
clock and watchmakers, 126, 245
coachbuilders, 40
Cobbett, William, 72
Cologne, 11, 13, 14, 41, 44, 46
Colrat, Maurice, 103, 187–9, 194
Comité central des chambres syndicales, 186
Comité de l'alimentation, 111, 182
Comité des étalagistes, 182, 186
Comité républicain du commerce, de l'industrie, et de l'agriculture, 111, 181
Commission Mesureur, 101
competition, unfair, 43, 51, 53, 102, 246, 265–6
confectioners, 254, 255
Confédération des groupes commerciaux et industriels, 108, 183, 184–8, 193, 246, 268
Congrès national catholique, 180
Conservative Party (British), 75, 263
Conservative Party (German), 52
co-operatives:
  civil service, 240, 243, 245, 246, 247, 258, 263
  consumer, 13, 41, 43, 47–8, 51, 53, 60, 64, 128, 182, 240, 244, 246
    petite bourgeoisie members of, 48, 54

co-operatives: consumer—*continued*
shopkeeper campaigns against, 47, 102, 127, 128, 133, 176, 180, 181, 241–2, 243–4, 248–50, 255, 263, 265, 266
credit, 42
producer, 39, 54
purchasing, 42, 129, 177, 184
coopers, 40, 140, 237
Corbin, Alain, 23, 110
Corke, Helen, 79, 81, 87
corporatism, 15, 22, 24–5, 35, 36, 109, 111, 179, 184–5, 187, 189, 246, 259–60, 261, 268
Cottereau, Alain, 11, 101
credit, 7, 11, 72, 78, 101, 107, 184
landlord, 83
master artisans, 68, 85, 142, 143, 144, 145, 151
shopkeepers, 12, 18, 42–3, 48, 84, 86–7, 157, 158, 243
shopkeepers campaign against, 53, 84, 243
women obtain, 87
Crise Commerciale, La, 176, 178
crisis, economic, 7
1890s, 10, 11–13, 70, 108
impact upon small enterprise, 11–14, 38, 70, 85, 100, 107. 143, 166
Croix, La, 180, 181
Cushen, Henry, 254
cutlery trades, 66, 67, 69, 70, 90, 140

Daumard, Adeline, 21, 23, 101
Debac, James, 247
Delfosse, Pascale, 120, 127, 128, 129
Demolins, Edmond, 239
Denmark, 5, 252
Denonville, 222, 225
department stores, 13, 41, 43, 50, 51, 52, 53, 64, 99, 101, 102, 109, 111, 173, 176, 178, 181, 184, 240, 244, 247
Derby, 83
Deschanel, Paul, 181, 186
Destréguil, Henri, 183
Detaillist, Der, 53
Diest, 121
drapers, 42, 65, 82, 99, 103, 106, 159, 239, 242, 252, 253
Dreyfus affair, 182, 184, 187
Drumont, Edouard, 178, 183
Dupeux, Georges, 98, 111
dyers, 39, 45, 89

Early Closing Association, 252–3
East End Jewish Shopkeepers' Association, 239
Edinburgh, 62
education, 9, 17, 21, 44, 79–80, 106, 202, 211
Education Act (1902), 80
Elector, The, 264
Elliott, B., 9, 83
engineering, 121
Englander, David, 77
Epicerie française, L', 181, 182
Expert-Bezançon, Charles, 181, 186

Failliot, Gabriel, 185, 188
family, 4, 18, 19–21, 49, 51, 113
bourgeois form of, 196, 202–3, 209, 211–12
inheritance and continuity within, 20, 78–9, 106, 156, 157, 169, 172, 195, 197–200, 201, 202, 203, 206, 209–11
introspection of petit-bourgeois, 9, 19–20, 79, 209–12
labour in small enterprise, 9, 12, 20, 39, 48, 100, 169, 205–6, 207, 209, 216, 254
master artisan, 17, 20, 195–217
petit-bourgeois idealization of, 21, 51, 177, 179, 190, 195–6, 212, 214
size, 21, 206–7, 217
as source of capital, 168
farriers, 37, 226
Fédération des commerçants-détaillants, 186–7
Federation of Grocers' Associations, 241
Fédération nationale des Batîments et des Travaux publics, 109
Fédération nationale des employés, 186, 187
Fischer, Wolfram, 39

fishmongers, 255
florists, 166
food trades, 23, 38, 64, 66, 100, 160, 207, 211, 217, 223, 224, 225, 226; *see also individual trades*
Fougères, 97
France, *see* petite bourgeoisie, in France
Francotte, Gustave, 127
freemasonry, 176, 179
Freistadt, 199
Frère-Orban, Hubert, 126
Funck-Brentano, Frantz, 185
furniture and cabinet-makers, 11, 38, 40, 61, 67, 86, 204, 207–8, 223

Gaiardo, L., 129
Gaillard, Jeanne, 11, 23, 111
Gambetta, Léon, 95, 112
garret-masters, 144, 150
Gatrell, V. A. C., 142
Gazon, Louis, 179
Gee, J. T., 249, 266
Gellately, Robert, 243, 260
Germany, *see* petite bourgeoisie, in Germany
Ghent, 121
Gide, Charles, 250
gingerbread-makers, 200
Glasgow, 142, 244
glove-makers, 102
Glyn-Jones, William, 244
Gmunden, 199
goldsmiths, 45, 126, 200, 209–10, 212–14
gold wire-pullers, 200, 206
Great Britain, *see* petite bourgeoisie, in Britain
Great Depression, 12, 13, 20, 36, 38, 39, 49, 70, 208, 217; *see also* crisis
Great Yarmouth, 74
Green, John, 249, 250, 263
Green, T. H., 80
greengrocers, 41, 42, 45, 100, 107, 166, 171, 255
Grocer, The, 243, 250, 251
grocers, 19, 42, 53, 65, 82, 86, 89, 98, 100, 101, 103, 107, 110, 182, 225, 241, 242, 244, 248, 251, 254, 255
in Paris, 20, 111, 156–74
bankruptcies, 107, 156, 164–6
condition before 1848, 156–9
distribution in city, 161–2
geographical origins, 170
move from shop to shop, 171, 174
previous occupations, 166–8, 172
price of businesses, 165
proliferation of small, 163–4
rise of large-scale, 159–60, 163–4, 172–3
shop assistants, 158, 166, 167, 173
sources of capital, 23, 158, 168–71, 172
turnover rate, 107, 171
Guérin, Jules, 178–9
Guesde, Jules, 111, 183, 187
guilds, 35, 36, 37, 38, 41, 43, 50, 51, 53, 61, 67, 109, 124, 196–7, 199, 201–2, 203, 206, 210, 212–14; *see also* corporatism
gun manufacture, 146–8

haberdashers, 42
Hainaut, 121
hairdressers, 38
Halifax, 73
Hamborg, Herman, 245, 247
Hamburg, 41, 53, 260
Hampden Clubs, 73
Hannes, J., 120
Harmel, Léon, 179
hatters, 98, 122, 176
Haussmann, Baron G. E., 162–3
Hennock, E. P., 82
Hey, David, 138
High Wycombe, 86
Honfleur, 106
hosiery trades, 66, 69, 97
house owners:
associations, 77
petite bourgeoisie as, 63, 79, 82–4, 199
petite bourgeoisie as lodging-house owners, 171
relations with tenants, 48, 83–4
Hull, 82

independence, 7, 45, 47, 126, 262
economic, 8, 10–12, 23, 40, 101, 108, 113, 138, 142, 232
ideology of, 9, 43, 177, 190
as radical ideal, 12, 72, 73
industrialization, *see* small enterprise, and industrialization
inheritance, *see* family; wealth left at death
Institut international pour l'étude du problème des classes moyennes, 185
ironmongers, 42, 66, 90
Italy, 201, 203
itinerant traders, 41, 42, 53, 104, 108, 128, 156, 224, 228, 237

Jalla, Daniel, 19
Janville, 221–37 *passim*
Jaurès, Jean, 111, 177, 182
Jedlicka, Johann, 214
jewellers, 42, 69, 122, 126, 140, 142
Joyce, Patrick, 66, 75, 263

Kartel der Schaffenden Hande, 16
Kitson, James, 87
Kocka, Jürgen, 8
Kropotkin, P., 69

Labour Exchange Gazette, 148, 151
Labrousse, Ernest, 219, 220
Lamarzelle, Senator Edouard de, 180
Lambrechts, Hector, 120, 127, 185, 241
Landes, David, 139
Landry Inquiry, 109
Laurie, Bruce, 204
Layman, Thomas, 254
Le Play, Frédéric, and Le Playists, 3, 95, 113, 127, 156, 185
Le Yaouanq, Jean, 21, 23, 103, 106
leather trades, 66, 223, 225, 226, 232
Leeds, 62, 66, 69, 73, 74, 87, 143, 246
Leicester, 255
Lequin, Yves, 104
Leroy-Beaulieu, Paul, 177
Lewinski, J., 120
liberalism, 16, 22, 25, 26, 36, 50, 53, 72, 74–5, 77, 81, 82, 124, 130, 137, 149, 243, 244, 257, 258
Liberty and Property Defence League, 77, 262
Libre Parole, La, 178
Liège, 127
Ligue antisémite, 179
Ligue du parti commercial des départements du centre, 183
Ligue Syndicale pour la défense des intérêts du travail, de l'industrie et du commerce, 5, 24, 110, 175–80, 181, 182, 183, 185, 191, 192, 247, 259, 268
Lille, 106
Limousin, 23, 105, 110
Liverpool, 64
local government, *see* municipal government
Lodève, 16
Loir-et-Cher, 98, 111
Loire, 98
London, 18, 23, 62, 64, 65, 66, 67, 73, 85, 87, 239, 243, 246, 263, 264, 269
London and Suburban Traders' Federation, 244, 250, 251, 265, 267
London Municipal Society, 75
Lorcin, Jean, 18
Louvain, 121
Louville-la Chénard, 222, 225
Luckock, James, 142
Lyons, 5, 13, 20, 100, 106, 107

mail order retailing, 13, 41, 64, 102, 252
Mainz, 46
Manchester, 65, 142
Maple, J. B., 254
Margadant, Ted W., 23
markets and fairs, 41, 128
Marroussem, Pierre du, 185
Mascuraud, Alfred, 111
Master and Servant Acts, 85
master artisans and small producers:
in Austria, 195–217
become shopkeepers, 8, 9, 42, 122, 209
in Belgium, 120–33 *passim*
in Britain, 11, 24, 62–94 *passim*, 137–54
dependence on merchants and large capital, 11, 39, 67–71, 97, 99, 101–2, 138–48, 204–5

master artisans and small producers—*continued*
  enter factory, 67, 70, 149
  factory as stimulus, 69–70, 139
  in France, 11, 25, 95–119 *passim*, 123
  in Germany, 24, 35–61 *passim*
  heterogeneity, 39–40, 66–7, 100, 108, 204–8, 214, 226–31
  household structure, 196, 197–9, 205, 213
  individualism and collectivism, 148, 196–9
  and industrialization, 8, 37–40, 65–70, 96–102, 121–3, 138–44, 195, 199–208, 209, 211
  living-in workers, 47, 103, 196, 209, 217
  marginalization, 40, 66, 126, 232
  organizations, 71, 126–7, 210, 212, 214, 218
  relations with workforce, 15, 18, 24–5, 47–8, 53, 84–5, 94, 103–4, 145, 151–2, 204–6, 209
  responsiveness, 23, 38, 68–71
  rural, 11, 23, 39, 98, 170, 219–38
  shift to 'petit-bourgeois producers', 39, 67, 68, 75, 85, 137–8, 143, 148, 151–2
  situation of sons, 196–9, 206–11, 213
  size of enterprise, 13, 40, 68–70, 97, 139–41, 142
  and trade unionism, 47, 54, 86, 148, 149–50, 218
  and traditional artisan values, 24–5, 67, 69, 71, 85, 86, 137–8, 146, 148–52, 212
  transfers of trade, 197, 200–2
  see also individual trades by name; corporatism; credit; crisis; family; guilds; petite bourgeoisie; politics; small enterprise
Maujean, Adolphe, 187
Maus, George, 186–7, 193
Medick, Hans, 138
Mendels, Franklin, 138
Merthyr Tydfil, 66
Mesureur, Gustave, 176, 178
metal trades, 37, 38, 67, 69, 70, 71, 78, 82, 97, 98, 122, 123, 137–54 *passim*, 204, 205, 207–8, 210, 223, 225, 226, 229, 230
Metropolitan Grocers' Federation, 250, 254
Middle Class Defence Organization, 77, 262, 264
Middlesbrough, 66
milk-sellers, 41, 89, 241
millers, 225, 226, 228–9, 230, 231, 233, 238
Minden, 44
mittelstand, 5, 6, 8, 36–55 *passim*, 76, 78, 109
mittelstandspolitik, 25, 36–7, 52, 54, 55, 187, 218, 262
Morès, marquis de, 178
Morris, R. J., 74, 87
Morrison, James, 151
Motte, Eugène, 187
multiple retailing, 13, 41, 64, 89, 101, 102, 159–60, 163–4, 240, 242, 244, 250–2, 255
Munich, 61
Municipal Corporation Act (1835), 72
municipal government, 72–3, 74, 246
  petit-bourgeois role in, 81–2, 247, 259
  ratepayers' organizations, 75, 76–7
  shopkeepers respond to, 241, 263–4
Münster, 38

nail-makers, 11, 85, 200
Nancy, 106, 111
National Chamber of Trade (1871), 241, 247
National Chamber of Trade (1898), 241, 251, 258
National Commission for the Petite Bourgeoisie (Belgian), 125, 128
National Liberal Party (German), 50
nationalism, 16, 26, 77, 109, 111, 175, 178, 182–7 *passim*, 190, 192
Navy League (British), 77
Neale, R. S., 73
neighbourhood, *quartier*, 22, 48, 79, 124
  ideology of, 24, 176, 184, 185, 189–90, 259, 268

neighbourhood—*continued*
 petit-bourgeois role within, 18–19, 104, 108
Néron, Edouard, 185
Nettlefold, Mr, 145, 151
Newcastle-under-Lyme, 62, 76, 81
Newcastle-upon-Tyne, 62, 142
newsagents, 255
Nièvre, 97
Niort, 22, 101
Noll, Alfred, 38
Northampton, 62, 68, 85
Nottingham, 69, 73, 83

Offer, Avner, 76
Office for the Middle Classes (Belgian), 128, 129
Orléans, 103, 106, 224
Osler, Thomas, 141
Ouarville, 222, 225
Owen, Robert, 148, 149

Paine, Thomas, 72, 73
Paloméra, André de, 186
Paris, 5, 11, 14, 18, 20, 21, 22, 23, 97–111 *passim*, 123, 155–73, 175–91 *passim*, 219
Parti commercial et industriel français, 108, 183
patente, professional tax, 126, 157, 191, 232
 analysis of in Brussels, 120, 122–4
 as evidence of French small enterprise, 97–8, 161, 163–4, 173, 220, 221–30, 232–3, 236, 237, 238
 French reform campaign, 102, 176, 177, 180, 191, 246, 260–1
 French reform (1893), 178, 180, 261
 influence on shopkeeper ideology, 260–1
pawnbrokers, 82, 87, 241, 254
peasantry, 23, 24, 36, 42, 46, 48, 52, 60, 62, 78, 105
penny capitalism, 66
Perchtoldsdorf, 199, 210–11
petite bourgeoisie:
 in Austria, 195–217
 in Belgium, 5, 15, 16, 17, 24, 25, 78, 120–33, 185, 241, 245, 250, 257, 260, 261, 262
 in Britain, 3–4, 5, 11, 15–26 *passim*, 62–94, 137–54, 215, 239–69
 as bulwark for conservatism, 5–6, 16–17, 36, 78, 127–8, 184, 187, 262
 culture, 80–1
 definition and identity, 6–10, 17, 26–7, 95–6, 112–13, 120, 125–6, 231
 differences between shopkeepers and master artisans, 6–7, 8, 37, 43, 54, 95–6, 97, 102, 223–31
 and fascism, 5, 35, 55
 in France, 3, 5, 11–25 *passim*, 64, 78, 79, 95–119, 123, 155–74, 175–94, 202, 219–38, 241, 242, 259, 260, 261, 262, 268
 in Germany, 5, 8, 11–25 *passim*, 35–61, 76, 78, 127, 185, 196, 202, 215, 241, 243, 245, 252, 257, 260, 261, 262
 ideological importance, 4, *see also classes moyennes*; *mittelstand*
 individualism, 74, 76, 78, 81, 125, 128–9, 177, 250
 instability, 81, 107, 110, 171, 234–5
 international congresses, 3, 95, 185
 introspection, 9, 49, 78–81, 125, 209–12
 localism, 22, 23, 63, 78, 80, 104–5, 177, 179
 marriage patterns, 103, 233–4
 as middlemen in outwork, 85–6
 movement in and out of working class, 4, 43, 66
 organizations, 5, 15, 50–1, 53, 73, 99, 102, 108–10, 126–7, 129–30, 132, 133
 relations with working class, 4, 18, 19, 43, 47–9, 53–4, 59, 83–8, 103–5, 107–8, 124–5, 231, 235
 rural, 6, 48, 62, 105, 219–38
  changing structures, 222–6
  distinctive social group, 233–4, 235–6
  landownership amongst, 231–2
  marriage patterns, 233–4
  migration to towns, 237
  origins and mobility, 106, 234–5

petit bourgeois: rural—*continued*
as proportion of population, 220–2
rental values, 227–30
stratification, 226–31, 232–3
wealth at marriage, 230–1
rural origins, 23
sense of own identity, 19, 25, 131, 143
social life and associations, 16, 19, 46, 104
social origins, 105, 166–8, 172
and social policy, 17, 47, 109, 126, 184, 186, 188, 252
see also bourgeoisie; crisis; house owners; inheritance; master artisans; municipal government; neighbourhood; politics; shopkeepers; small enterprise; social mobility
Picardy, 97
Plymouth, 82
Poincaré, Raymond, and Poincarisme, 16, 109, 110, 175, 181, 186–7, 188, 189, 190
politics, petit-bourgeois, 4–6, 14–17
in Belgium, 5, 15–16, 127–31
in Britain, 5, 15–16, 22, 24, 25, 71–8, 257–9, 261–4
in France, 5, 15–16, 22, 24, 108–12, 156, 175–94
in Germany, 5, 15–16, 22, 35–6, 49–55
others seek to organize, 5–6, 10, 15–16, 25–6, 50–2, 127–8, 129–30, 178–90 *passim*, 261–2, 269
radicalism, 4, 5, 15, 19, 72–4, 90, 137, 138, 175–8, 189, 257–8
and religion, 72, 73, 74, 82, 130
and right-wing parties, 25–6, 50–2, 77, 178
shift to right, 5, 14, 15–16, 75, 175, 180, 182–90, 212–14
surviving radical traditions, 15, 51, 75–6, 111, 177, 257–8
and working-class politics, 5, 14, 53–4, 73–4, 75, 126, 181
see also liberalism; *mittelstandspolitik*; nationalism; republicanism; socialism
Potin, Félix, 159–60, 163, 164, 167, 171
potter, 19, 37
Poujadisme, 96
printers, 61, 66, 123
Procacci, G., 19
Proprietary Articles Trade Association, 244
Proudhon, P. J., 12
publicans, innkeepers, *see* bars, cafés, pubs
Puech, Louis, 187
Pyfferoen, Oscar, 120, 127, 185

quartier, *see* neighbourhood
Quentin, Maurice, 185

Radical Party (French), 5, 25, 181
radical socialism (French), 175–6, 177
radicalism, *see* politics, petit-bourgeois
Rebérioux, Madeleine, 19
Reforme Sociale, La, 95, 127
Reid, Douglas, 149
repos hebdomadaire, *see* shop hours
Republican Party (French), 108
republicanism, 5, 6, 22, 24, 108, 109, 111, 176
restaurateurs, 45, 89, 123
retail trade:
in Belgium, 123–4, 132
in Britain, 63–5, 240
concentration within, 13, 64–5, 99, 102, 240, 250
in France, 23, 97–102, 107, 155–73 *passim*
in Germany, 40–3
and industrialization, 41, 160
see also individual trades by name; co-operatives; department stores; multiple retailing
Retailer, The, 250
Revendication, La, 176–80 *passim*
revolutions:
(1789), 5, 111, 177
(1848), 5, 12, 14–15, 25, 36, 47, 49, 51, 55
Rheims, 101
ribbon weavers, 18, 206
Richter, Eugen, 46
Rimmer, W. G., 143
Roberts, Robert, 19, 86, 87
Rosenberg, Hans, 26

Roubaix, 97
Rouen, 103, 106
Rousiers, Paul de, 71, 78
Rowlands, Marie, 138

saddlers, harness-makers, 98, 228, 229, 231, 232, 237
St Etienne, 18, 22
St Helens, 248–9, 250, 263
Saint-Léon, Etienne Martin, 170, 185, 186, 257, 261
Saint Lô, 106
Saint Monday, 145, 149
St Pancras Shopkeepers' Association, 257–8
Salford, 19, 73, 76, 82, 86
Salt, T. C., 143
Salzburg, 199
sans-culottes, 5, 12, 111
Santeuil, 222, 225
Scheu, Andreas, 205
Schleswig-Holstein, 44
schoolteachers, 73, 106
Scottish Shopkeepers and Assistants Union, 254
Sens, 100
Sheffield, 62, 66–70 *passim*, 83, 85
shoe retailers, 89, 176, 250
shoemakers, 39, 40, 42, 54, 61, 66, 68, 90, 97, 99, 122, 199, 205, 225, 229, 230, 231, 237
shop assistants, 158, 166, 167–8, 173, 186, 248, 254, 265
shop hours, 128
  British movements concerning, 245, 252–6, 258
  French regulation of, 184, 186
Shopkeeper, The, 255
shopkeepers:
  in Belgium, 120–33 *passim*
  in Britain, 20, 62–94 *passim*, 239–69
  craftsmen-retailers, 8, 63, 98–9, 138, 158, 223
  dependence on wholesalers, 11, 43, 65, 101, 157
  distribution and expansion, 40–1, 63, 123–4, 159–64
  female, 12, 20, 42, 100
  in France, 95–119 *passim*, 155–74, 175–94
  in Germany, 35–61 *passim*
  heterogeneity, 41–2, 43, 86, 100, 108, 123
  ideal of specialization, 24, 109, 176, 180, 181, 185, 246, 261
  Jewish, 239–40
  marriage patterns, 20–1, 48, 103
  opening hours, 48, 158
  organizations, 53, 76, 99, 110, 126–7, 240–2, 243, 263
  previous occupations, 23, 42, 105, 166–8
  relations with employees, 18, 47
  relations with working class, 4, 18–19, 83–4, 86–8, 158, 189
  response to large-scale competition, 109, 128, 175–94 *passim*, 242–56
  rights of traders, 43, 246, 247, 261
  sense of identity, 190, 239–40, 242–3, 244–6, 254–6
  skill declines, 64–5
  targets of riots, 87
  see also individual trades by name; petite bourgeoisie; politics; retail trade; shop hours; small enterprise; state
Shopkeepers' and Small Traders' Protection Association, 242, 255–6
Sidney, L. P., 262
silk weavers, 20, 100, 200, 201–3, 204, 213
small enterprise:
  economic importance, 40, 88, 96
  expands in depression, 13, 66
  heterogeneity, 7, 97, 100, 106, 108, 226–31
  and industrialization, 3, 8, 10–14, 22–3, 54, 96–102, 121–4
  and large enterprise, 11, 101, 124
  numbers of employees, 13, 38, 39–40, 42, 53, 100, 122, 202–3, 205, 208, 220–1, 222
  as origins of large, 44, 141, 142, 150
  turnover rate, 12, 71, 81, 90, 107, 171, 174
  see also crisis; master artisans; *patente*; retail trade; shopkeepers

small producers, *see* master artisans and small producers
Small Tenements Recovery Act (1838), 83
Small Trader and Shopkeeper, The, 256, 258
Smiles, Samuel, 74
smiths, 23
soap-makers, 39
Social Democratic Party (German), 36, 50, 52–5 *passim*, 61
social legislation, *see* petite bourgeoisie, and social policy; shop hours
social mobility, 4, 18, 95, 108, 141, 150, 262
  and petite bourgeoisie, 7, 8–9, 44–5, 47, 48–9, 54, 105–6, 124, 146, 172–3
  and rural petite bourgeoisie, 234–5
  social meaning of, 49, 86, 105, 167
  see also education; petite bourgeoisie, social origins; white-collar workers
socialism, socialists, 15, 36, 75, 77, 109, 127, 130, 148, 179, 181, 182, 184, 187, 188, 263
  amongst petite bourgeoisie, 53–4, 55, 61, 111–12, 130
  seek petit-bourgeois support, 61, 111–12
Socialist Party (French), 111
Southsea, 76
Spree, Reinhard, 21
Stacey, James, 253–4
state:
  aid to petite bourgeoisie, 17, 25–6, 50–1, 109, 128, 129–30, 245, 250, 256–7, 262
  in British radical tradition, 257–9
  petit-bourgeois appeals to, 17, 51, 60, 128–9, 240, 250, 251, 254, 257, 260–1, 268
  petit-bourgeois attitudes towards, 22
    Belgium, 128–9
    Britain, 72, 239–69
    France, 109, 176–7, 179, 184, 185, 189, 259, 260–1, 268
    Germany, 51–2, 260
Stevens, J., 185
Stockport, 81
strikes, 181
  shopkeeper support for, 18, 48, 104
  in small enterprise, 18, 85, 103–4, 214
Sunday closing, *see* shop hours
Switzerland, 202, 217

tailors, clothing trades, 11, 12, 18, 20, 38, 39, 40, 42, 54, 66, 67, 85, 89, 90, 99, 101, 111, 122, 123, 140, 141, 199, 200, 204, 206, 207–8, 211, 225, 226
Tangye, Richard, 142
tanners, 39
taxation, 17, 47–8, 50, 51, 73, 82, 157, 251, 258, 260–1
  income tax and co-operatives, 249, 250
  see also patente
Tebbutt, Melanie, 87
textile trades, 66, 85, 97, 98, 100, 102, 105, 114, 121, 123, 141, 200, 203, 207, 208, 209, 213, 223, 224–5, 229, 230, 231
Thelwall, John, 72
Thompson, E. P., 8, 72
Tichborne movement, 76
Timmins, Samuel, 142, 146
tobacconists, 89, 245, 255
Tocqueville, Alexis de, 103
Tonypandy, 87
Tours, 183
Town Tenants' League, 258
trade unions, *see* master artisans and small producers
Traders' Defence Associations, 241–2, 249, 266
  Blackburn, 249
  Central Board of, 242, 266
  St Helens, 248–9
  Scottish, 249
Traders' Times, The, 243
Traders' Union, 242, 249, 265, 266
Trades' Defence Association, 263
Tradesman and Shopkeeper, The, 249
Tradesmens' Associations, 241, 242, 254
  Fulham, 258
  Nelson, 254
  Kidderminster, 251
  Wolverhampton, 255

trawling, 80
Trépreau, A., 180, 183
Tribunaux de Commerce, 25
Troyes, 102
Turin, 19

Union Commerciale de Laon, 109
Union démocratique, L', 176, 177
Union fraternelle du commerce et de l'industrie, 179–80

Verein für Sozialpolitik, 27
Vergoin, Maurice, 176
Verhaegen, B., 120
Vienna, 196–214 *passim*
Volkov, Shulamit, 195
Voluntary Early Closing Association, 252
Vorsteher der Tischlergenossenschaft, 214
Voves, 221–32 *passim*, 237, 238
Vron, 98

Waldeck-Rousseau, René, 181
Wales, 73, 84, 87
Walker, Robert, 249
Walters, Charles, 144–6, 151
wealth left at death, 106–7, 139–40, 147, 202, 232, 233, 234–5
weavers, 11
Wells, H. G., 80
wheelwrights, cartwrights, 23, 40, 98, 122, 226, 229, 230, 231, 232
white-collar workers, 36, 64, 103
  petit-bourgeois children become, 9, 21, 44–5, 79–80, 106, 211
  and politics, 75, 78, 108
Wigan, 248–9, 250, 266
Wigan and District Traders' Defence League, 249
Wilkes, John, 73
wine-merchants, 89, 100, 111, 163, 170, 176, 228, 229, 233
Wolverhampton, 255
women:
  effects of workplace–home separation upon, 81
  organization of, 110
  rare as Paris grocers, 169
  in small enterprise, 100, 196–7, 204, 213, 216, 232
  see also credit; family; shopkeepers, female
Württemberg, 13

Zola, Emile, 155